Aboriginal Policy Research

Moving Forward, Making a Difference

Volume IV

Aboriginal Policy Research

Moving Forward, Making a Difference
Volume IV

Edited by

Jerry P. White, Susan Wingert, Dan Beavon, and Paul Maxim

THOMPSON EDUCATIONAL PUBLISHING, INC.
Toronto, Ontario

Information on how to obtain copies of this book is available at:
Website: http://www.thompsonbooks.com
E-mail: publisher@thompsonbooks.com
Telephone: (416) 766–2763
Fax: (416) 766–0398

Library and Archives Canada Cataloguing in Publication

Aboriginal Policy Research Conference (2nd : 2006 : Ottawa, Ont.)
Aboriginal policy research : moving forward, making a difference /
edited by Jerry P. White ... [et al.].

Papers presented at the 2nd Aboriginal Policy Research Conference, held in Ottawa, Mar. 20-23, 2006.
"Volume III", "volume IV".
ISBN 978-1-55077-162-6 (v. III).--ISBN 978-1-55077-164-0 (v. IV)

1. Native peoples--Canada--Social conditions--Congresses.
2. Native peoples--Canada--Government relations--Congresses.
3. Native peoples--Canada--Congresses. I. White, Jerry Patrick, 1951- II. Title.

E78.C2A1495 2006   305.897′071   C2006-906523-3

Managing Editor:	Jennie Worden
Copy Editor:	Kristen Chew
Cover/Interior Design:	Tibor Choleva
Production Editor:	Katy Harrison
Proofreader:	Faith Gildenhuys
Cover Illustration:	Daphne Odjig, *Arriving at the Powwow*, 1982 acrylic on canvas 26″ × 24″ Reproduced by permission of Daphne Odjig. Courtesy of Gallery Gevik, Inc. (Toronto).

Every reasonable effort has been made to acquire permission for copyrighted materials used in this book and to acknowledge such permissions accurately. Any errors or omissions called to the publisher's attention will be corrected in future printings.

Statistics Canada information is used with the permission of Statistics Canada. Users are forbidden to copy the data and redisseminate them, in an original or modified form, for commercial purposes, without permission from Statistics Canada. Information on the availability of the wide range of data from Statistics Canada can be obtained from Statistics Canada's Regional Offices, its World Wide Web site at www. statcan.ca, and its toll-free access number 1-800-263-1136.

We acknowledge the support of the Government of Canada through the Book Publishing Industry Development Program for our publishing activities.

Printed in Canada. 1 2 3 4 5 6 09 08 07 06

Table of Contents

Part Three: Housing And Homelessness

Acknowledgements

We would like to thank some of the many people who poured so much energy into this conference and helped make it a great success. First, we want to acknowledge the tireless efforts put forward by the coordinator, Sylvain Ouelette. This could not have been done without his amazing energy and commitment. At the National Association of Friendship Centres, Executive Director Peter Dinsdale, co-chair of the conference, was a central leader as was Alfred Gay. Many others contributed, but we wanted to specially note the work of Sandra Commanda. At Indian and Northern Affairs Canada in Strategic Research and Analysis, we would like to thank Éric Guimond, Erik Anderson, Patricia Millar, Bob Kingsbury, Norma Lewis, and Norma Chamberlain. At the University of Western Ontario we want to thank President Paul Davenport, Vice President (Research and International Relations) Ted Hewitt, and all the people in accounting and purchasing who played a role. From the Aboriginal Policy Research Consortium at Western, we want to acknowledge Susan Wingert and Nicholas Spence.

For those we have not named directly, we know how much you too have given. For our families, thanks for giving us the chance to do this project, we know you have picked up the extra. Thank you.

Jerry P. White
Dan Beavon
Susan Wingert

Introduction

Jerry White, Dan Beavon, and Susan Wingert

Introduction

In March, 2006, the second triennial Aboriginal Policy Research Conference (APRC) was held in Ottawa, Canada. This conference brought together over 1,200 researchers and policy makers from across Canada and around the world. Aboriginal and non-Aboriginal delegates (representing government, Aboriginal organizations, universities, non-governmental organizations, and think tanks) came together to disseminate, assess, learn, and push forward evidence-based research in order to advance policy and program development. The conference was a continuation of the work begun at the first APRC held in November of 2002. The 2002 conference was co-hosted by Indian and Northern Affairs Canada (INAC) and the University of Western Ontario (UWO),[1] with the participation of nearly 20 federal departments and agencies, and four national, non-political Aboriginal organizations. By promoting interaction between researchers, policy makers, and Aboriginal people, the conference was intended to expand our knowledge of the social, economic, and demographic determinants of Aboriginal well-being; identify and facilitate the means by which this knowledge may be translated into effective policies; and allow outstanding policy needs to shape the research agenda within government, academia, and Aboriginal communities.

The 2002 Aboriginal Policy Research Conference was the largest of its kind ever held in Canada, with about 700 policy makers, researchers, scientists, academics, and Aboriginal community leaders coming together to examine and discuss cutting-edge research on Aboriginal issues. The main portion of the conference spanned several days and included over fifty workshops. In addition to and separate from the conference itself, several federal departments and agencies independently organized pre- and post-conference meetings and events related to Aboriginal research in order to capitalize on the confluence of participants. Most notably, the Social Sciences and Humanities Research Council (SSHRC) held its first major consultation on Aboriginal research the day after the conference ended. These consultations led to the creation of SSHRC's Aboriginal Research Grant Program which supports university-based researchers and Aboriginal community organizations in conducting research on issues of concern to Aboriginal peoples.[2]

The Impetus for the First Aboriginal Policy Research Conference

The idea for holding a national conference dedicated to Aboriginal issues grew from simple frustration. While there are many large conferences held in Canada every year, Aboriginal issues are often at best only an afterthought or sub-theme. More frequently, Aboriginal issues are as marginalized as the people themselves and are either omitted from the planning agenda or are begrudgingly given the odd token workshop at other national fora. While Aboriginal peoples account for only about 3% of the Canadian population, issues pertaining to them occupy a disproportionate amount of public discourse. In fact, in any given year, the Aboriginal policy agenda accounts for anywhere from 10 to 30% of Parliament's time, and litigation cases pertaining to Aboriginal issues have no rival in terms of the hundreds of billions of dollars in contingent liability that are at risk to the Crown. Given these and other policy needs, such as those posed by the dire socio-economic conditions in which many Aboriginal people live, it seems almost bizarre that there are so few opportunities to promote evidence-based decision making and timely, high-quality research on Aboriginal issues. Hence, the 2002 Aboriginal Policy Research Conference was born.

In order to address the shortcomings of other conferences, the APRC was designed and dedicated first to crosscutting Aboriginal policy research covering issues of interest to all Aboriginal peoples regardless of status, membership, or place of residence. Second, the conference was designed to be national in scope, bringing together stakeholders from across Canada, in order to provide a forum for discussing a variety of issues related to Aboriginal policy research. Finally, in designing the conference, we specifically sought to promote structured dialogue among researchers, policy makers and Aboriginal community representatives.

The first conference was seen, worldwide, as an important and successful event.[3] The feedback that we received from participants indicated that the conference provided excellent value and should be held at regular intervals. It was decided, given the wide scope and effort needed to organize a conference of this magnitude, that it should be held every three years. In March, 2006, the second APRC was held.

Aboriginal Policy Research Conference 2006

The 2006 APRC was jointly organized by Indian and Northern Affairs Canada, the University of Western Ontario, and the National Association of Friendship Centres (NAFC).[4] The 2006 APRC was intended to 1) expand our knowledge of Aboriginal issues; 2) provide an important forum where these ideas and beliefs could be openly discussed and debated; 3) integrate research from diverse themes; 4) highlight research on Aboriginal women's issues; 5) highlight research on urban Aboriginal issues; and 6) allow outstanding policy needs to shape the future research agenda.

Although the 2002 APRC was quite successful, we wanted to raise the bar for the 2006 event. During and after the 2002 conference, we elicited feedback, both formally and informally, from delegates, researchers, sponsors, and participating organizations. We acted on three suggestions from these groups for improving the 2006 conference.

First, we made a concerted effort to ensure that Aboriginal youth participated in the 2006 conference, because today's youth will be tomorrow's leaders. The NAFC organized a special selection process that allowed us to sponsor and bring over 30 Aboriginal youth delegates from across Canada to the conference. The NAFC solicited the participation of Aboriginal youth with a focus on university students or recent university graduates. A call letter was sent to more than 100 of the NAFC centres across Canada. Potential youth delegates were required to fill out an application form and write a letter outlining why they should be selected. The NAFC set up an adjudication body that ensured the best candidates were selected and that these youth represented all the regions of Canada. The travel and accommodation expenses of these Aboriginal youth delegates were covered by the conference.

A parallel track was also put in place in order to encourage young research-ers to participate at the conference. A graduate-student research competition was organized and advertised across Canada. Aboriginal and non-Aboriginal graduate students were invited to submit an abstract of their research. Nearly 40 submis-sions were received, and a blue-ribbon panel selected 12 graduate students to present their research at the conference. The travel and accommodation costs of these graduate students were also covered by the conference. The research papers of the 12 graduate students were judged by a blue-ribbon panel and the top five students were awarded financial scholarships of $1,000 to help with their studies.

Second, at the 2002 conference, research sessions and workshops were organized by the sponsors. The sponsors (government departments and Aborigi-nal organizations) showcased their own research, or research that they found interesting or important. At the 2002 conference, there was no venue for accepting research that was not sponsored. For the 2006 conference, we wanted to attract a broader range of research, so a call for papers was organized and advertised across Canada. Over 70 submissions were received from academics and community-based researchers. About half of these submissions were selected for inclusion in the conference program.

Third, the 2002 conference focused solely on Canadian research on Aborigi-nal issues. For the 2006 conference, we accepted research on international Indigenous issues, and many foreign scholars participated. In fact, the UN Permanent Forum on Indigenous Issues held one of its five world consultations at the conference. This consultation brought experts on well-being from around the globe and greatly enhanced the depth of international involvement at the 2006 APRC.

The APRC is a vehicle for knowledge dissemination. Its primary goal is to showcase the wide body of high-quality research that has recently been conducted on Aboriginal issues in order to promote evidence-based policy making. This conference is dedicated solely to Aboriginal policy research in order to promote interaction between researchers, policy makers, and Aboriginal peoples. It is hoped that this interaction will continue to facilitate the means by which research or knowledge can be translated into effective policies.

Of course, many different groups have vested interests in conducting research and in the production of knowledge and its dissemination. Some battle lines have already been drawn over a wide variety of controversial issues pertaining to Aboriginal research. For example, can the research enterprise coexist with the principles of "ownership, control, access, and possession (OCAP)"? Are different ethical standards required for doing research on Aboriginal issues? Does Indigenous traditional knowledge (ITK) compete with, or complement Western-based scientific approaches? Does one size fit all, or do we need separate research, policies, and programs for First Nations, Métis, and Inuit? Many of these issues are both emotionally and politically charged. These issues, and the passion that they evoke, render Aboriginal research a fascinating and exciting field of endeavour. The APRC provides an important forum in which these ideas and beliefs can be openly discussed and debated, while respecting the diversity of opinions which exists.

The APRC was designed to examine themes horizontally. Rather than looking at research themes (e.g., justice, social welfare, economics, health, governance, demographics) in isolation from one another, an attempt was made to integrate these themes together in the more holistic fashion that figures so prominently in Aboriginal cultures. By bringing together diverse research themes, we hoped that more informed policies would be developed that better represent the realities faced by Aboriginal peoples.

This conference was also designed to ensure that gender-based issues were prominent. In addition to integrating gender-based issues with the many topics of the conference, specific sessions were designated to address issues of particular importance to policies affecting Aboriginal women. This included, for instance, a one-day pre-conference workshop on gender issues related to defining identity and Indian status (often referred to as Bill C-31). This pre-conference workshop will have its own book that will be published as a third volume of the 2006 proceedings and the fifth volume in the *Aboriginal Policy Research* series.

The conference also gave considerable attention to the geographic divide that exists between rural and urban environments. Nearly half of the Aboriginal population lives in urban environments, yet little research or policy attention is devoted to this fact. Specific sessions were designated to address research that has been undertaken with respect to Aboriginal urban issues.

The conference engaged policy makers and Aboriginal people as active participants, rather than as passive spectators. By engaging these two groups, research gaps can be more easily identified, and researchers can be more easily apprised of how to make their work more relevant to policy makers. In addition, the conference promoted the establishment of networks among the various stakeholders in Aboriginal research. These relationships will provide continuous feedback, ensuring that policy needs continue to direct research agendas long after the conference has ended.

In the end, 1,200 delegates participated at the conference from Canada and numerous countries in Europe, Asia, Latin America, North America, and the South Pacific. The conference planning included 20 federal government departments and organizations,[5] seven Aboriginal organizations,[6] four private corporations,[7] and the University of Western Ontario. Feedback from participants and sponsors indicates that the 2006 conference was even more successful than the previous one. This was not too surprising, given that there were over 90 research workshops, in addition to the plenary sessions, in which delegates met to hear presentations and discuss research and policy issues.[8]

Breaking New Ground

While the APRC brought people from many nationalities and ethnicities together, it also provided a forum for showcasing Inuit, Métis and First Nations performing arts. The conference delegates were exposed to a wide variety of cultural presentations and entertainment. Métis fiddling sensation Sierra Nobel energized delegates with her youthful passion and the virtuosity of her music. Different First Nations drum groups invigorated the audience. Juno and Academy Award–winner Buffy Sainte-Marie entertained and mesmerized everyone. We saw demonstrations of Métis fancy dancing, and the skill and artistic splendour of two-time world champion hoop dancer, Lisa Odjig. We heard the rhythmic and haunting sounds of Inuit throat singers, Karin and Kathy Kettler (sisters and members of the Nukariik First Nation), and we laughed uproariously at the humour of Drew Haydon Taylor (the ongoing adventures of the blue-eyed Ojibway). The conference was indeed a place where diverse Aboriginal cultures met, and the artistic talents of the aforementioned performers were shared with delegates from across Canada and around the world.

Research, Policy, and Evidence-based Decisions

It was Lewis Carroll who said, "If you don't know where you are going, any road will get you there."[9] Knowing where you are going requires a plan, and that can only be based on understanding the current and past conditions. The first APRC, and the 2006 conference, was centred on promoting evidence-based policy making. We stated previously that, in part, our conference was designed to deal with the communication challenges that face social scientists, both inside and outside of government, policy makers, and the Aboriginal community. Could we bring these different communities of interest together to develop a better understanding of the problems and processes that create the poor socio-economic conditions facing Aboriginal people in Canada? And equally, can we find the basis that has created the many successes in the Aboriginal community? Could we develop the co-operative relations that would foster evidence-based policy making and thereby make improvements in those conditions? And equally, can we develop those relations in order to promote the "best practices" in terms of the successes? We are acutely aware that policy makers and researchers, both those in and out of government, too often live and work in isolation from each other. This means that the prerequisite linkages between research and policy are not always present. This linkage is something we referred to in earlier volumes as the research–policy nexus.[10]

Our aim has been to strengthen that research-policy nexus. The APRC is first and foremost a vehicle for knowledge dissemination and, with a "captive" audience of many senior federal policy makers,[11] the conference was able to enhance dialogue between researchers and decision makers and, ultimately, promote evidence-based decision making. More broadly, both the 2002 and 2006 conferences succeeded in helping to raise the profile of Aboriginal policy research issues, including identifying research gaps, promoting horizontality, and enhancing dialogue with Aboriginal peoples.

Moreover, in order to produce superior quality research, there is much to be gained when researchers, both in and out of government, work in co-operation on problems and issues together. Beyond just disseminating the results of research, the APRC was also about the discussion and sharing of research agendas, facilitating data access, and assisting in analysis through mutual critique and review.

We feel strongly that the highest quality research must be produced, and in turn that research must be communicated to policy makers for consideration in formulating agendas for the future. If you wish to make policy on more than ideological and subjective grounds, then you need to help produce and use high calibre research understandings. It is simply not enough to delve superficially into issues or be driven by political agendas that have little grounding in the current situation. The APRC is designed to challenge ideologically driven thinking and push people past prejudice, superficiality, and subjectivity.

Policy that affects Aboriginal people is made by Aboriginal organizations, Aboriginal governments, and Aboriginal communities. It is also made by national and provincial governments and the civil service and civil society that attaches to those systems. We encourage all these peoples and bodies to embrace the realities they face with the best understandings of the world that evidence can give them.

Volume Four—The Contents of the Proceedings

Section one of this book deals with health related issues. Richmond, Ross, and Bernier (Chapter 1) have heeded the call for health research that moves beyond using the medical model to make comparisons between the Aboriginal and non-Aboriginal populations. Using data from the 2001 Aboriginal Peoples Survey (APS), they employ Indigenous health concepts to explore the patterning of health dimensions within the Métis and Inuit populations. Three key findings emerged:

- Social support is one of the most important dimensions of health across cultural, geographic, and social groups.
- Indigenous conceptualizations of health are multidimensional.
- Aspects of physical, mental, social, and community well-being are encompassed within indigenous health dimensions.

The authors argue that health policy needs to move beyond individual-level interventions. This research supports the contention that culturally appropriate, holistic, community-level initiatives may be particularly effective in addressing health disparities.

Improving health care services is another avenue through which to reduce disparities in health. The involvement of Aboriginal peoples in all stages of health planning increases the effectiveness of the resulting services. Geeta Cheema (Chapter 2) uses qualitative case study methods to explore meaningful participation in Aboriginal health planning. She finds that not all forms of participation are considered to be meaningful; representation and reconciliation are key determinants of meaningfulness. Meaningful participation can be fostered through mutual engagement, building trusting relationships, establishing an Aboriginal advisory committee, and employing Aboriginal population health approaches.

The relatively high rates of suicide among Aboriginal peoples have drawn considerable attention in recent years. In the third paper Hicks, Bjerregaard, and Berman (Chapter 3) examine the transition from the historical Inuit suicide pattern, in which there were relatively low rates, to the present pattern using regional data. They demonstrate that this transition did not occur simultaneously across these regions—Alaska was the first region to experience a sharp increase in suicide rates, followed by Greenland, and Canada's Eastern Arctic. Within these regions, there was a significantly higher number of suicides among young men. How can these patterns be explained? The authors trace these patterns to "active colonialism at the community level," which gave rise to traumas that have been transmitted intergenerationally. They hope that new historical and geographic frameworks will contribute to better suicide prevention strategies.

The papers in this section affirm the importance of research as the basis for health planning, service delivery, and policy. However, in the next chapter Maar, McGregor, and McGregor (Chapter 4) point out that Aboriginal Peoples have experienced few tangible benefits as a result of past research because of serious shortcomings. They note that collaboration and community focus have become ethical issues in Aboriginal health research. This paper describes:

- The development of a community-based Aboriginal research ethics committee on Manitoulin Island
- The work of this committee
- The support mechanism required to sustain such a committee

The authors argue that research guidelines should embody the traditional values and teachings of the First Nation involved in the study.

The chapter by Castellano and Archibald (Chapter 5) synthesizes six papers that were presented in two sessions sponsored by the Aboriginal Healing Foundation (AHF), which was mandated to document the residential school experience and its consequences and to gather knowledge about community healing. The authors propose a new healing paradigm that accounts for the waves of historical trauma experienced by Aboriginal communities, draws upon cultural and western healing traditions, and mobilizes the resiliency of individuals. They present compelling evidence from AHF-funded projects of how community-directed healing can be most effectively pursued.

The final paper in this section (Chapter 6) reports on an ongoing research project examining how sport and recreation can be used to improve the health, well-being, and leadership skills of Aboriginal youth. Forsyth, Heine, and Halas point out that research often atheoretically identifies barriers to participation using short-term and unsustainable programs. In this project, the researchers collaborated with existing sport, recreation, and educational groups in order to apply theoretically driven models to engage Aboriginal youth in culturally relevant ways. They advocate the use of multiple information-gathering methods in order to capture the social context, which shapes sports and recreation participation. The authors also discuss special considerations when undertaking community-based participatory action research.

Section two of this book deal with governance issues. The first paper in this section (Chapter 7) focuses on two themes that have received less attention in the literature on the Inuit and Nunavut: the construction of the geopolitical boundaries in Nunavut and Inuit identity. Légaré argues that these two issues are of critical importance in understanding how Nunavut was constructed and the impact it had on the collective identity of the Inuit. His analysis suggests a growth of regional civic identity and decline of culture-based identity.

Morin (Chapter 8) looks at how the disparate perceptions of treaty implementation between treaty signatories evolved into growing conflict. He selects two treaty regions, Treaties 4 and 6, which cover what is now southern and central Saskatchewan and central Alberta, for a case study to illustrate his argument. He points out that the gap between the perceptions of the Crown and Treaty First Nations continue to be central issues in the negotiation and renegotiation of modern-day treaties, self-government, and land claims.

Issues of gender and political representation are at the forefront of the paper by Cancel (Chapter 9). Her paper examines the contradictions between the gender inclusive rhetoric in the political arena and Inuit women's actual experiences. The events surrounding the 1997 referendum on gender parity in Nunavut provided a rich source of data that were collected through extensive fieldwork. Her analysis suggests that Inuit women's equality in politics is dependent upon stability within the household, which has been undermined by colonialism. The intersection of the public and private spheres of women's lives is a central theme in Cancel's work.

Cornell (Chapter 10) undertakes a different type of comparative analysis. He explores the policy and research issues associated with the organization of indigenous governance in Canada, Australia, and the United States. He argues that, despite the differences between these nations, there are important commonalities related to political and legal heritage, historical displacement, and the contemporary pursuit of self-determination. Based on his preliminary analyses, Cornell offers lessons learned in the process of Indigenous self-governance in these countries. He proposes a research agenda that would assist Indigenous and non-Indigenous policy makers in addressing these issues.

Finally, Jennifer Brennan's paper (Chapter 11) presents the First Nation policy development model, which the Assembly of First Nations (AFN) has created based on the interaction between Indigenous peoples and governments in Canada and around the world. She contends that the failure of most policy and legislative initiatives can be traced to the initial process design. This model is designed to guide the process design in order to establish relationships between First Nations and governments that will produce real social change.

Section three of this book looks at the issues of housing and homelessness. The first paper (Chapter 12), entitled "Urban Hidden Homelessness and Reserve Housing," was developed by Evelyn Peters of the University of Saskatchewan and Vince Robillard of the Prince Albert Grand Council Urban Services group. This research project was a joint effort of academic and community researchers that explores the relationship of availability and conditions of reserve housing to hidden homeless among urban First Nation band members. Peters and Robillard explain the current housing situation that faces First Nations on reserves and then, through survey and interviews with reserve members, most of whom declared themselves as having no home of their own, describe participants' access to housing on reserves. The participants also discuss their perspectives on their ability to obtain housing on reserves and whether they would move to the reserve if they had access to housing there. The authors report that increasing the housing stock would have a significant effect on whether people chose to return to their communities.

The second paper in this section (Chapter 13), prepared by Stewart Clatworthy and Mary Jane Norris, is "Aboriginal Mobility and Migration: Trends, Recent Patterns, and Implications: 1971–2001." Using the recently released data from the 2001 Census of Canada, they examine several dimensions of the migration patterns of four Aboriginal sub-groups: Registered Indians, non-registered Indians, Métis, and Inuit during the 1996–2001 time period. The authors compare migration patterns for this time period to long-term migration trends for the 1981–1996 period. Clatworthy and Norris also look at the 2000–2001 patterns of residential mobility for Canada's Aboriginal populations living in major urban areas. They look at a series of key questions, such as the extent to which migration has contributed to the rapid increase in the Aboriginal population living off-reserve, especially that living in large urban areas; and to what extent residential moves among the Aboriginal population result in unacceptable housing situations. The authors also explore the policy implications surrounding mobility and migration patterns of Aboriginal populations in Canada.

The third chapter in this section (Chapter 14) is presented by Steve Pomeroy on behalf of the National Aboriginal Housing Association. This research paper looks at the need for a national non-reserve housing strategy. After outlining why it is needed and what a strategy would have to include, he examines in detail issues related to affordability and the assessment of need and outlines some of the key issues which need to be dealt with. This exploration of housing needs ends with a clear set of recommendations that have direct bearing on policy development.

In their chapter "A New Open Model Approach to Projecting Aboriginal Populations" (Chapter 15) Stewart Clatworthy, Mary Jane Norris, and Éric Guimond look at what factors underlie population projections and the implications for the development of Aboriginal population projections. Specifically they provide a brief discussion of the traditional or "closed" population projection model, its implied assumptions and its limitations within the context of projecting Aboriginal populations and the structure and components of an alternative projection model which incorporates the main features of an "open" population, illustrating how this type of model can be applied to projecting the registered Indian populations. The authors also discuss some of the existing gaps in demographic research which need to be addressed in order to advance the development of more appropriate Aboriginal population projection methodologies.

Balakrishnan and Jurdi set out in the final chapter, "Spatial residential patterns of Aboriginals and their socio-economic integration in selected Canadian cities," (Chapter 16) to examine the Aboriginal population's residential patterns within metropolitan areas at the small area level. Starting from the premise that Aboriginal Peoples in Canada not only have their distinctive culture and language but also have been disadvantaged in their socio-economic development, they wanted to see if living patterns are similar to other groups that had similar characteristics such as new immigrant Canadians and visible minorities. New immigrants and visible minorities often choose to live in neighbourhoods near others of the same culture and language. Our authors ask whether this is the same for Aboriginal peoples in the cities. The objectives of their study was to examine the spatial residential patterns of Aboriginal peoples in the 23 metropolitan areas of Canada in 2001 to see if the level of segregation increased with the size of the metropolitan area as well as the size of the Aboriginal population. They set out to determine if the patterns for Aboriginal people are similar or different than the charter groups of British and French and various visible minority groups such as the Chinese, South Asian and black communities as well as from other European groups. Finally they wanted to determine if Aboriginals are concentrated in the poorer areas of the cities.

Endnotes

1   More specifically, the conference was organized by the Strategic Research and Analysis Director-ate, INAC and the First Nations Cohesion Project, the Department of Sociology at UWO. Dan Beavon and Jerry White acted as conference co-chairs from their respective organizations.

2   One of the other funding bodies for academic research, the Canadian Institute of Health Research, also has a program (the Institute of Aboriginal Peoples' Health) that supports research to address the special health needs of Canada's Aboriginal peoples.

3   The Canadian government commented on the importance of the APRC in a speech to the United Nations in Geneva on July 22, 2003. More specifically, see the statement by the observer delega-tion of Canada to the United Nations Working Group on Indigenous Populations, Twenty-First Session, July 21–25, 2003.

4   Consequently, there were three conference co-chairs: Dan Beavon, Director of the Strategic Research and Analysis Directorate, INAC; Jerry White, Professor of Sociology and Senior Advisor to the Vice President at the University of Western Ontario; and, Peter Dinsdale, Executive Director of the National Association of Friendship Centres.

5   The federal departments and organizations provided funding support at three different levels. Gold: Indian and Northern Affairs Canada, Human Resources and Skills Development Canada, Department of Justice Canada, Status of Women Canada, Health Canada, Veterans Affairs Canada, Fisheries and Oceans Canada, Canada Housing and Mortgage Corporation, Correc-tional Service Canada, Atlantic Canada Opportunities Agency, Canadian Council on Learning, Canadian International Development Agency, Public Safety and Emergency Preparedness, Social Sciences and Humanities Research Council of Canada, Canadian Institutes of Health Research. Silver: Canada Economic Development, Policy Research Initiative, Canadian Heritage. Bronze: Natural Resources Canada, Statistics Canada.

6   National Association of Friendship Centres, Aboriginal Healing Foundation, First Nations Statistical Institute, National Aboriginal Housing Association, Indian Taxation Advisory Board, National Aboriginal Forestry Association, National Aboriginal Health Organization.

7   Public History, Canadian North, VIA Rail Canada, and Canada Post.

8   There were also four all-day pre-conference workshops organized, which attracted nearly 300 delegates. These four pre-conference workshops included Harvard University's research model on Aboriginal governance; Aboriginal demographics and well-being; Bill C-31 and First Nation membership; and records management for First Nations.

9   This famous quote is actually a paraphrase of what the Cheshire cat said to Alice in Carroll's book, *Alice's Adventures in Wonderland*, chapter 6, "Pig and Pepper," 1865.

10 The research-policy nexus is built on the foundation of dialogue and discourse between those making policy and those discovering and interpreting the evidence that should underscore it. When superior quality research is produced and used in making policy, this completes the structure.

11 While there are many Canadian cities with larger Aboriginal populations, in terms of both propor-tions and absolute numbers, Ottawa was selected as the most logical conference site because it would have otherwise been difficult to engage the participation of such a large number of senior federal policy makers. In many ways, the conference was about educating and exposing this group to the vast array of research that has been done on Aboriginal issues.

Part One:
Health

1

Exploring Indigenous Concepts of Health: The Dimensions of Métis and Inuit Health

Chantelle A.M. Richmond, Nancy A. Ross, and Julie Bernier

Introduction

A wealth of research illustrates the inequitable burden of health and social disparities borne by Indigenous (1) Canadians as compared to non-Indigenous Canadians (2–6). Current patterns of health and social suffering reflect the combined effects of colonial oppression, systemic racism, and discrimination, as well as unequal access to human, social, and environmental resources (7–13). Because such sizable disparities exist between Indigenous and non-Indigenous populations, health conditions for the Indigenous population have generally been described in relation to those of the non-Indigenous population. It is arguable that these kinds of comparisons are irrelevant because Indigenous and non-Indigenous concepts of health are shaped by distinct world views and cultures of experience, which are undeniably different between the two populations. Rarely has attention been paid to the diversity of health concepts *within* the Indigenous population itself. Recently, there has been a call for research to explore health concepts from within Indigenous cultures (9, 13–14) while drawing upon health frameworks that integrate Indigenous perspectives that may be useful for Aboriginal health policy development (15–18). In response, we draw upon Canada's 2001 Aboriginal Peoples Survey (APS) to address the following objectives: 1) to explore dimensions of health for Canada's Inuit and Métis populations; and 2) to examine the stability of these dimensions across and within cultural and geographical contexts.

Indigenous Concepts of Health

In constructing the framework for our research on Indigenous health concepts, we recognized that health is shaped by larger social structures, including family, community, nature, and the Creator (19–22). Health is achieved by maintaining a balance of physical, mental, emotional, and spiritual elements (19). A major paradigm within the cultures of Indigenous Canadians is the medicine wheel, which encompasses a wide conceptual understanding of life and the interrelatedness of all its functions: "life, time, seasons, cosmology, birth, womb, and earth are intrinsically located in the symbology of the circle" (20). Although the medicine wheel originates from Plains Indian philosophy, Little Bear (21) argues there is enough similarity among Indigenous philosophies to apply these concepts generally; still, differences in concepts and emphases may be held by certain Indigenous nations. Typically, the understanding is that each person has a physical part (the body and its physical functioning) and a spiritual part (a connection to the spirit world), both of which are mediated by the emotional and mental capacities of the individual (19). Among the Inuit, these concepts are captured within inuuqatigiittiarniq, a holistic world view of Inuit health (21). Beyond the social dynamics of a community, inuuqatigiittiarniq also depends on the balance and harmony of economic, cultural, environmental, and biological factors (22). A careful balance of these factors is called inummarik, and manifests itself materially in a most genuine person, in a process of continuous, lifelong interaction with people and animals, community and the environment. (22). Our theoretical approach is informed by these ideologies and recognizes that Indigenous concepts of health reflect individual level attributes (e.g., chronic disease, physical activity limitations) *and* broader societal factors (e.g., social supports, community wellness).

Around the globe, concepts of health among Indigenous societies place an emphasis on the larger social system within which the individual lives (23–26) and incorporate three familiar concepts: holism, balance, and interconnectedness. In New Zealand, the Maori Public Health Action Plan summarizes three Maori models of health: Te Pae Mahutonga (Southern Cross constellation), Whare Tapa Whā (health as a house), and Te Wheke (the octopus) (23). Of these three models, Whare Tapa Whā provides a multi-dimensional concept of Maori health and well-being that extends beyond physical health to recognize the dependence of health on a balance of four main dimensions: taha wairua (the spiritual side); taha hinengaro (thoughts and feelings); taha tinana (the physical side); and taha whanau (family) (24). Represented by the four walls of a house, the fundamental crux of this metaphor for health is that if one of these walls should fall, the house will collapse. From Australia, the National Aboriginal Health Strategy Working Party defines health as not just the physical well-being of the individual but the social, emotional, and cultural well-being of the whole community (25). This definition incorporates a *whole-life* view, including the cyclical concept of life-death-life.

The concept of holism is central to ideas of health and wellness among native Hawaiians, as are dimensions of spirituality and culture (26). Traditional native Hawaiian concepts of health encompass cultural values of lokahi (balance), pono (doing the right thing), and kokua (working without expecting reward). These values aim to strengthen and protect the family (extended family), or ohara, and larger community, thereby conceptualizing health not as a personal burden but one that is shared by the whole community (26).

Table 1.1: Health-related Variables from Arctic and Métis Supplemental Surveys

	Métis supplement variables		Arctic supplement variables
1.	*functional difficulty**	1.	*functional difficulty*
2.	*disability*	2.	*disability*
3.	*chronic condition*	3.	*chronic condition*
4.	*positive social interaction*	4.	*positive social interaction*
5.	*emotional support*	5.	*emotional support*
6.	*tangible support*	6.	*tangible support*
7.	*affection and intimacy*	7.	*affection and intimacy*
8.	*perceived social problems*	8.	*perceived social problems*
9.	**self-assessed depression**	9.	**feelings of nervousness**
10.	**self-assessed spirituality**	10.	**feelings of calm**
11.	**number of leisure activities**	11.	**"blue" feelings**
12.	**maximum leisure expenditure**	12.	**feelings of happiness**
		13.	**"down" feelings**
		14.	**community participation**

* Variables in bold are those drawn from the Core Survey

Data and Methods

Our analyses use the 2001 Aboriginal Peoples Survey (APS), which is a rich source of data on the demographic characteristics and living conditions of Indigenous Canadians. The APS was first conducted in the fall of 1991, and its principal purpose was to identify the needs of Indigenous people by focusing on issues of health, language, employment, income, schooling, housing, and mobility. Following the release of the report of the Royal Commission on Aboriginal Peoples (27), which drew heavily on the 1991 data, Statistics Canada was mandated to coordinate a second cycle of the APS in conjunction with numerous national Aboriginal organizations and federal departments representing Aboriginal interests (28). For the 2001 APS, four surveys were developed to capture the cross-cultural variation that exists among the greater Aboriginal population, including:

1. *Core Survey* (all Aboriginal adults 15+ years of age)
2. *Children's Survey* (all children <15 years of age)
3. *Métis Supplement* (Aboriginal adults identifying Métis status)
4. *Artic Supplement* (Aboriginal adults residing in Arctic communities) (28)

Table 1.2: Sample Sizes

Unit of analysis	n	Unit of analysis	n
Métis full sample	**14,127**	Inuit full sample	**3,979**
Métis by gender	**7,035**	Inuit by gender	**1,976**
Males	**7,092**	Males	**1,991**
Females		Females	
Métis by age	**5,256**	Inuit by age	**1,796***
15-29	**7,927**	15-29	**1,932**
30-59		30-59	
60+	**944**	60+	**236**
Métis by geographic region	**877**	Inuit by geographic region	**315**
Atlantic (Maritime provinces)	**1,919**	Nunatsiavut	**957**
Central (Quebec and Ontario)	**10,867**	Nunavik	
Western (Provinces west of Ontario)	**410**	Nunavut	**1,993**
Northern (North of 60° latitude)		Inuvialuit	**385**
Geographic Region 2	**6,786**	N/A	
Urban	**7,178**		
Rural			

*Not all sub-analyses add up to the total sample sizes; these reflect cases or partial non-response.

The 2001 APS was translated into 17 Aboriginal languages and achieved a response rate of 84.1% across 219 communities (28).

Principal Components Analyses (PCA) methods (29–31) were used to explore the dimensions of Métis and Inuit health. Similar methods have been used to explore health dimensions in other populations (32, 33). In the context of our study, these methods were used to explore correlations between a number of health-related variables from the Métis and Inuit supplements of the 2001 APS, thereby allowing us to examine the broader dimensions of Métis and Inuit health. The variables selected for our analyses included those recognized by Indigenous health concepts (19–22) and relate to health function and disability, social function, social relationships, mental health, community participation and wellness, leisure activity, and spirituality (**Table 1.1** – page 5). Our analyses drew heavily from the Métis and Arctic supplements and also incorporated variables from the Core Survey.

Results

Our analyses resulted in 11 and nine PCAs respectively on the Métis and Inuit samples (**Table 1.2**). These results are presented in two general sections. Section

Table 1.3: Inuit Dimensions of Health (n=3,979).

	Social Support (24.6%, 3.35)*	Personal Wellness (14.4%, 2.01)	Physical Function (12.9%, 1.81)	Community Wellness (7.8%, 1.09)
Emotional support	0.86	0.01	0.01	0.06
Positive social interaction	0.84	-0.07	-0.06	-0.04
Affection and intimacy	0.82	-0.01	-0.01	-0.03
Tangible support	0.77	0.06	0.05	0.00
Feeling blue	0.06	0.72	0.04	0.10
Feeling nervous	0.10	0.70	-0.02	0.02
Feeling down	-0.02	0.65	0.05	-0.02
Feeling calm	0.07	-0.67	0.07	0.04
Feeling happy	0.11	-0.67	0.02	0.05
Disability	0.00	0.00	0.89	-0.07
Functional difficulty	-0.01	0.00	0.86	-0.07
>1 Health condition	0.00	0.02	0.67	0.20
Community participation	-0.03	-0.14	0.00	0.78
Perceived social problems	0.01	0.17	0.02	0.69

* The first number represents the percentage of total variance explained by this component. The second number refers to the component's eigenvalue, which represents the amount of variance captured by the component. In a PCA, the first component extracted can be expected to account for a fairly large amount of total variance, and each succeeding component will account for progressively smaller amounts of variance [29].

one describes the dimensions of health for the full Inuit and Métis samples and section two describes results of the sub-analyses, which considered the effects of age, gender, and geographic location on Métis and Inuit health dimensions.

Full Inuit Sample

Four health dimensions emerged from the full Inuit sample (n=3,979), explaining 59% of the total variance: (1) social support, (2) personal wellness, (3) physical function, and (4) community wellness (**Table 1.3**). Social support, the primary dimension, explained 24.6% of the total variance in the observed variables and contained four variables measuring four types of social support: social interaction, emotional support, tangible support, and affection and intimacy. The second dimension, personal wellness, explained 14.4% of the total variance and was formed by five variables designed to measure mental health (i.e., how often in the past month respondent felt down, blue, nervous, calm, and happy). The third dimension, physical function, explained 12.9% of the total variance and included disability, functional difficulty, and chronic condition. The fourth dimension, community wellness, explained 7.8% of the total variance and drew upon the community social problem index and the community participation index. The community wellness dimension represents perceptions about community social

Table 1.4: Métis Dimensions of Health (n = 14,127)

	Social Support (26.7%, 3.21)*	Physical Function (16.3%, 1.96)	Physical Fitness (12.1%, 1.46)	Psychosocial Wellness (9.2%, 1.10)
Positive social interaction	0.86	-0.02	0.02	-0.04
Emotional support	0.86	-0.01	0.02	0.02
Affection and intimacy	0.83	0.01	-0.01	0.04
Tangible support	0.78	0.03	0.01	-0.02
Disability	-0.02	0.90	0.06	-0.01
Functional difficulty	0.01	0.90	0.02	-0.08
Chronic condition	0.03	0.57	-0.14	0.17
Number physical activities	0.05	0.07	0.92	0.02
Maximum expenditure	-0.02	-0.09	0.89	0.00
Perceived social problems	-0.01	-0.12	0.05	0.72
Self-assessed spirituality	0.11	0.06	-0.09	0.60
Self-assessed depression	-0.15	0.16	0.08	0.53

* The first number represents the percentage of total variance explained by this component. The second number refers to the component's eigenvalue, which represents the amount of variance captured by the component. In a PCA, the first component extracted can be expected to account for a fairly large amount of total variance, and each succeeding component will account for progressively smaller amounts of variance [29].

well-being and the extent to which individuals participate in community life as a result.

Full Métis Sample

Four dimensions emerged from the full Métis sample (n=14,127), explaining 64.4% of the total variance in the observed variables: (1) social support, (2) physical function, (3) physical fitness, and (4) psychosocial wellness (**Table 1.4**). As in the Inuit pattern, social support was the primary dimension, explaining 26.7% of the total variance, and was characterized by four variables: positive social interaction, emotional support, tangible support, and affection and intimacy. The second dimension, physical function, explained 16.3% of the total variance, and consisted of three variables: disability, functional difficulty, and incidence of chronic condition. The third dimension, physical fitness, explained 12.1% of the total variance in the observed variables and reflected a strong correlation between two variables that provide a proxy for one's level of energy expenditure: number of physical activities and maximum expenditure spent on physical activities. The fourth and final dimension of Métis health was psychosocial wellness, which consisted of spirituality, depression, and perceived social problems in the community. It explained 9.2% of the variance.

Table 1.5: Dimensions of Health for Inuit 60+ Years (n=236)

	Social Support (12.9%, 3.02)*	Personal Wellness (26.2%, 2.2)	Social Limitations Due to Physical Function (11.7%, 1.63)
Emotional support	0.86	-0.01	-0.08
Affection and intimacy	0.83	0.00	0.07
Positive social interaction	0.78	-0.04	-0.13
Tangible support	0.69	-0.04	0.10
Feeling blue	-0.07	0.67	0.08
Feeling nervous	0.12	0.63	-0.04
Feeling down	-0.14	0.39	0.02
Perceived social problems	0.25	0.36	-0.03
Feeling happy	0.11	-0.61	-0.01
Feeling calm	0.10	-0.68	0.11
Disability	0.02	0.02	0.91
Functional difficulty	0.03	0.04	0.85
> 1 chronic condition	0.24	0.31	0.32
Community participation	0.16	0.17	-0.56

*The first number represents the percentage of total variance explained by this component. The second number refers to the component's eigenvalue, which represents the amount of variance captured by the component. In a PCA, the first component extracted can be expected to account for a fairly large amount of total variance, and each succeeding component will account for progressively smaller amounts of variance [29].

Sub-analyses by Age, Gender, and Geographic Region

Numerous sub-analyses tested the reliability of these full sample patterns against the effects of age, gender, and geographic region. With the exception of elderly Inuit and Nunatsiavut Inuit, the four-dimensional patterns observed in the full sample analyses were stable. The effects of age and geographic region were observed in only two of the 18 sub-analyses, and the influence of gender was not significant.

The patterning of health dimensions among Nunatsiavut Inuit (n=315) was the only pattern for which social support was not the primary dimension (Table 1.5). In its place was the dimension of personal wellness, explaining 26.2% of the variance in the observed variables. The second dimension was social support, explaining 12.9% of the variance. The remaining dimensions, physical function and community wellness, loaded in a fashion similar to that of other Inuit component solutions, explaining 11% and 7.9% of the variance in the observed variables respectively.

Three dimensions of health emerged from the Inuit 60+ (n=236) sample: (1) social support, (2) personal wellness, and (3) social limitations due to physical

Table 1.6: Dimensions of Health for Inuit in Nunatsiavut (n=315)

	Personal Wellness (26.2%, 3.67)[*]	Social Support (12.9%, 1.81)	Physical Function (11%, 1.53)	Community Wellness (7.9%, 1.11)
Feeling nervous	0.81	0.17	0.01	0.10
Feeling blue	0.75	-0.04	0.09	0.03
Feeling down	0.72	0.08	0.07	-0.31
Feeling calm	-0.52	0.31	0.08	-0.19
Feeling happy	-0.60	0.27	0.18	-0.10
Positive interaction	0.05	0.88	-0.03	-0.13
Affection and intimacy	-0.04	0.78	0.00	-0.03
Emotional support	-0.02	0.78	-0.07	0.22
Tangible support	0.01	0.48	-0.04	0.41
Disability	0.11	0.02	0.84	-0.01
Functional difficulty	0.05	-0.04	0.82	0.00
>1 chronic condition	-0.17	-0.05	0.69	0.16
Community participation	-0.02	0.04	0.07	0.69
Perceived social problems	0.11	0.00	0.08	0.58

[*] The first number represents the percentage of total variance explained by this component. The second number refers to the component's eigenvalue, which represents the amount of variance captured by the component. In a PCA, the first component extracted can be expected to account for a fairly large amount of total variance, and each succeeding component will account for progressively smaller amounts of variance [29].

function (**Table 1.6**). This matrix compressed 14 variables into three dimensions instead of four (as was the case among the full Inuit sample), which altered the conceptual meaning of the resulting health dimensions. While the first two dimensions mirrored those found in the full Inuit sample, the third dimension, social limitations due to physical function, demonstrates that aging places limitations on the ability of this population to be active in their community. There is a negative association between physical function and community participation.

Discussion

Guided by Indigenous perspectives on health (17, 19–22), our analyses describe health dimension patterns among Métis and Inuit populations, and reveal important similarities and differences in these patterns across the considerations of age, gender, and geographic location. To begin, we focus on the dimension of social support, which has a profound and unifying role in shaping concepts of health among Métis and Inuit. Conceptualized by four types of social support (positive social interaction, emotional support, tangible support, and affection and intimacy), this dimension reliably explained a substantial amount of variance among observed variables, even when taking into consideration age, gender, and geographic location. Social support is a well-recognized dimension of health in

Western (34–40) and other Indigenous (24, 26, 41–44) societies, but few studies have captured empirically how this relationship is expressed among Canadian Indigenous peoples (8, 45–48).

Our results also indicate important differences in health dimension patterns for Métis and Inuit populations. For instance, physical fitness and psycho-social well-being formed dimensions unique to the Métis, while dimensions of personal wellness and community wellness were exclusive to the Inuit. Part of this difference may be accounted for by the measures available in the survey tool. In comparison to the pointed nature of the Arctic supplement variables, which probed known Inuit-related topics (e.g., relationships with the physical environment), variables in the 1991 and 2001 Métis supplements were exploratory. In comparison with First Nations and the Inuit, there is a scarcity of data on Métis demographics and conditions (i.e., health, education, employment, etc.) (3, 4). In terms of our analyses, the substantive difference across survey supplements meant that only a small number of health variables from the Core Survey were available for comparative analyses. While this was undoubtedly influential on the emergent pattern of health dimensions, careful thought went into selecting variables that were consistent with our conceptual framework.

While most intra-status analyses indicated a fairly homogeneous patterning of health dimensions (i.e., within Inuit *or* within Métis cultures), the ordering of the health dimensions for Nunatsiavut Inuit was different; personal wellness loaded as the primary dimension of health. This difference reflected the significance of mental health among Nunatsiavut Inuit as opposed to social support, which formed the principal dimension among all other Inuit analyses. While our analyses do not permit an explanation of the meaning behind the ordering of the dimensions of health among the Nunatsiavut and why Inuit patterns differ across geographic region, that there is difference across Inuit regions serves to highlight the geographic and cultural heterogeneity across Inuit peoples. That is, despite having a common Inuit status, the populations of each Arctic region (i.e., Nunavik, Nunavut, Nunatsiavut, and Inuvialuit) are independent political bodies covering vast geographic spaces, and each has a unique physical, cultural, and social environment.

While the most profound finding of our results points to the universal importance of social support, our analyses also affirm that conceptualizations of health within these two populations are multidimensional (49). Métis and Inuit conceptualizations of health and healing are shaped by an individual's physical characteristics (e.g., a chronic condition, disability, physical fitness, mental health), and also by characteristics of their families and communities (e.g., social support, social problems in community, community wellness). The blurring of the line between individual and societal characteristics was demonstrated in the third dimension of elderly Inuit health, "social limitations due to physical function," which suggests that their failing physical bodies constrain them from being active members of the community. Such fluidity of health constructs was also demonstrated in the Métis dimension of psychosocial wellness, which encompassed spirituality, depression, and community social problems.

In the context of Indigenous health policy, there is a great need for official efforts to promote health that encourage the interaction of these multiple dimensions (49), particularly those which connect individuals to their communities (16–18). Canadian health policy has failed to encourage the development of programs that promote health via social supports or community connections. As Bartlett (15) illuminates, the majority of Indigenous health policies stem from an "illness-based health care system" that attempts to treat individuals rather than populations. Such policies strive to modify individual behaviours and actions, rather than aiming at community or population-level behaviours. This approach fails to recognize that it is within the larger community context that health behaviours are learned and normalized (50). Much work remains in making health policy and research that is grounded in the societal contexts of Indigenous communities (16–18).

Conclusion

Indigenous health research has tended to examine the Indigenous population of Canada as if it were a relatively homogeneous one, with little recognition of its broad cultural and geographic variation. Because of sizable disparities between Indigenous and non-Indigenous populations, and also because of limited data on Inuit and Métis populations, researchers have been more or less validated in this practice. Our paper moves beyond this paradigm by exploring the dimensions of health within Canada's Inuit and Métis populations and considers the stability of these dimensions across and within cultural and geographical contexts.

Informed by cultural frameworks of health (16, 18–24) and based on data from the 2001 APS, our analyses support four dimensions of Métis health (social support, physical function, physical fitness, and psychosocial wellness) and four dimensions of Inuit health (social support, personal wellness, physical function, and community wellness). Perhaps the greatest contribution of this work points to the significance of the dimension of social support, which has emerged consistently as the principal health dimension among numerous analyses of Métis and Inuit attitudes towards health. While no difference emerged as a result of gender, key differences emerged in analyses of testing age (i.e., elderly Inuit) and geographic location (i.e., Nunatsiavut Inuit).

Given the exploratory nature of these analyses, further research is needed to estimate the predictive capacity of social support on Indigenous health. Our conceptually based analyses provide a solid base of variables which may better inform subsequent analyses of health determinants. Qualitative research may also enhance our understanding of the relationship between Indigenous health and social support, particularly in exploring Indigenous-specific sources and meanings of social support and examining the mechanisms that structure this relationship.

In terms of their health and social conditions, Canada's Indigenous peoples continue to fare among the worst in Canada (2–5). Improving quality of life among Canada's Indigenous population requires health policy and programs that are inclusive (17, 18), community-based, and informed by holistic models that recognize the multiple, interacting dimensions of Indigenous people's health (16, 19–24). A piecemeal health policy that enables individuals, rather than communities, is just not sufficient (15), and our analyses provide some evidence to substantiate this conclusion. In all but one pattern of health dimensions, social support was the main dimension of health. Amid the extreme social dysfunction we witness in many Indigenous communities across Canada today, it is meaningful that our analyses have resulted in this finding. Despite a legacy of colonialism, it is remarkably *hopeful* that concepts and ideals central to Indigenous world views remain so strong today. Now is the time to put action behind words. Improving quality of life among Canadian Indigenous peoples requires more than the identification of health problems and risk factors. By working *with* and respecting the world views of Indigenous peoples, public policy can play a vital role in mobilizing Indigenous communities to move from suffering to equality and health.

Acknowledgements

Chantelle A.M. Richmond would like to acknowledge the support of a doctoral scholarship from the University of Toronto/McMaster University Indigenous Health Research Development Program of the Canadian Institutes for Health Research, Institute for Aboriginal Peoples Health. The authors also acknowledge the support of the Strategic Research and Analysis Directorate, Indian and Northern Affairs Canada.

Endnotes

1 The federal government of Canada legally recognizes Indigenous Peoples of Canada through the Constitution Act (1982) as "Aboriginal," a population encompassing "First Nations, Métis and Inuit." In referring to Aboriginal Peoples, we choose to use the term "Indigenous," the exception being in cases wherein we refer explicitly to federal terms and references (as in the federal survey, the Aboriginal Peoples Survey, from which the data of this manuscript originate).

2 Shah, P. 2004. The health of Aboriginal Peoples. In *Social determinants of health: Canadian perspectives,* ed. D. Raphael, 276–280. Toronto: Canadian Scholars' Press.

3 Adelson, N. 2005. The Embodiment of inequality: Health Disparities in Aboriginal Canada *Canadian Journal of Public Health,* 96 (S2): S45-S61.

4 Young, T.K. 2003. Review of research on Aboriginal populations in Canada: relevance to their health needs. *BMJ* 327: 419–22.

5 Tjepkema, M. 2002. The health of the off-reserve Aboriginal population. *Health Rep;* 13: 73–88.

6 MacMillan, H.L., et al. 1996. Aboriginal health. *Can Med Assoc J* 155: 1569–78.

7 Frohlich, K., N.A. Ross, and C. Richmond. Forthcoming. Health disparities in Canada today: Evidence and pathways. *Health Policy* 79 (2–3): 132-43.

8 Iwasaki, Y., J. Bartlett, and J. O'Neil. (2005). Coping with stress among Aboriginal women and men with diabetes in Winnipeg, Canada. *Soc Sci Med* 60: 977–88.

9 Bartlett, J.G. 2003. Involuntary cultural change, stress phenomenon and Aboriginal health status. *Can J Public Health* 94: 165–67.

10 Waldram, J.B., D.A Herring, and T.K. Young. 1995. *Aboriginal health in Canada: Historical, cultural and epidemiological perspectives.* Toronto: Univ. of Toronto Press.

11 Richmond, C., et al. 2005. The political ecology of health: Perceptions of environment, economy, health and well-being among 'Namgis First Nation. *Health Place* 11: 349–65.

12 Thouez, J.P., A. Rannou, and P. Foggin. 1989. The other face of development: Native population, health status and indicators of malnutrition—The case of the Cree and Inuit of Northern Quebec. *Soc Sci Med* 29: 965–74.

13 Wilson, K., and M. Rosenberg. 2003. Exploring the determinants of health for First Nations peoples in Canada: Can existing frameworks accommodate traditional activities? *Soc Sci Med* 55: 2017–31.

14 Kirmayer, L.J., G. M. Brass, and C.L. Tait. 2000. The mental health of Aboriginal peoples: Transformations of identity and community. *Can J Psychiatry* 45: 607–16.

15 Bartlett, J.G. 2005. Health and well-being for Métis women in Manitoba. *Can J Public Health* 96: S22–27.

16 Kenny, C. 2004. *A holistic framework for Aboriginal policy research.* <**www.swc-cfc.gc.ca/ pubs/pubspr/0662379594/200410_0662379594_e.pdf**>.

17 Castellano, M.B. 2002. Ethics of Aboriginal research. *Journal of Aboriginal Health* (Jan): 98–114.

18 Dei, G.S., B. Hall, and D. Rosenberg. 2002 *Indigenous knowledges in global contexts.* Toronto: Univ. of Toronto Press.

19 Svenson, K.A., and C. Lafontaine, 1999. The search for wellness. In *First nations and Inuit regional health survey, national report,* ed. G. McDonald, 181-216. Ottawa: First Nations and Inuit Regional Health Survey National Steering Committee, 1999.

20 Bird, G. 1993. The first circle—Native women's voice. In *Writing the circles: Native women of Western Canada,* ed. P. Perreault and S. Vance, vii-x. Norman and London: Univ. of Oklahoma Press.

21 Little Bear, L. (2000). Jagged worldviews colliding. In *Reclaiming Indigenous voice and vision,* ed, Marie Battiste, 77–85. Vancouver: UBC Press.

22 Boyd & Associates. Forthcoming. *Inuksiutiin health information framework.* Ottawa: Healthlinx.

23 New Zealand. 2003. *Maori public health action plan 2003–2004*. Wellington: Ministry of Health.

24 Durie, M. 1994. *Whaiora: Maori health development*. Auckland: Oxford Univ. Press.

25 Australia. 2004. *A national Aboriginal health strategy*. Canberra: National Aboriginal Health Strategy Working Party.

26 Casken, J. 2001. Improved health status for Native Hawaiians: Not just what the doctor ordered. *Wicazo Sa Review* 16: 75–89.

27 Canada. *Royal commission on Aboriginal People*. 1996. <**www.ainc-rcap.gc.ca/ch/rcap**>.

28 Canada. *Aboriginal Peoples survey 2001: Concepts and methods guide*. 2001. <**www.statcan. ca/english/freepub/89-591-XIE/89-591-XIE2003001.pdf**>.

29 Farbrigar, L.R., et al. 1999. Evaluating the use of exploratory factor analysis in psychological research. *Psychol Methods* 4: 272–99.

30 Hatcher, L.A. 1994. *Step-by-step approach to using the SAS system for factor analysis and structural equation modeling*. 1st ed. Cary, NC: SAS Publishing.

31 Shadbolt, B., J. McCallum, and H. Singh. 1997. Health outcomes by self-report: validity of the SF-36 among Australian hospital patients. *Quality of Life Res* 6(4): 343–52.

32 Bernier, J., et al . 2004. *Exploring the dimensions of health: A study using the Canadian National Population Health Survey (NPHS)*. Ottawa: Statistics Canada.

33 Scott, K.M., et al. 2000. A challenge to the cross-cultural validity of the SF-36 Health Survey: Factor structure in Maori, Pacific and New Zealand European ethnic groups. *Soc Sci Med* 51:1655–64.

34 Berkman, L.F., and F.L. Syme. 1979. Social networks, host resistance and mortality: A nine-year follow-up of Alameda County residents. *Am J Epidemiol* 109: 186–204.

35 Cohen, S., and S.L. Syme. 1985. *Social support and health*. San Francisco: Academic Press.

36 Wills, T.A. 1985. Supportive function of interpersonal relationships. In *Social support and health*, ed. S. Cohen and S.L. Syme, 61-82. San Francisco: Academic Press.

37 Lin, N., A. Dean, and M.W. Ensel. 1986. *Social support, life events, and depression*. New York: Academic Press.

38 Berkman, L.F. 1995. The role of social relations in health promotion. *Psychosom Med* 57: 245–54

39 Kawachi, I., et al. 1996. A prospective study of social networks in relation to total mortality and cardiovascular disease in men in the USA. *J Epidemiol Community Health* 50: 245–51.

40 Berkman, L.F., et al. 2000. From social integration to health: Durkheim in the new millennium. *Soc Sci Med* 51: 843–57.

41 Hofboll, S.E., et al. 2002. The impact of perceived child physical and sexual abuse history on Native American women's psychological well-being and AIDS risk. *J Consult Clin Psychol* 70: 252–57.

42 Cummins, J.R., et al. 1999. Correlates of physical and emotional health among Native American adolescents. *J Adolesc Health* 24: 338–44.

43 Mohatt, G.V., et al. 2004. Tied together like a woven hat: Protective pathways to Alaska Native sobriety. *Harm Reduct J* 1: 1–12.

44 Hofboll, S., et al. 2002. The impact of communal-mastery versus self-mastery on emotional outcomes during stressful conditions: A prospective study of Native American women. *Am J Community Psychol* 30: 853–71.

45 Daniel, M., et al. 2004. Cigarette smoking, mental health, and social support: Data from a Northwestern First Nation. *Can J Public Health* 95: 45–49.

46 Mignone, J. 2003. Social capital in First Nations communities: Conceptual development and instrument validation. PhD diss., Univ. of Manitoba.

47 Mignone, J., and J. O'Neil. 2005. Social capital and youth suicide risk factors in First Nations communities. *Can J Public Health* 96: S51–54.

48 Richmond, C., N.A. Ross, and G.M. Egeland. In press. Societal resources and thriving health: A new approach for understanding the health of Indigenous Canadians. *American Journal of Public Health*.

49 Rootman, I., and J. Raeburn. 1994. The concept of health. In *Health promotion in Canada: Provincial, national and international perspectives*, ed. A. Pederson et al., 56–71. Toronto: W.B. Saunders.

50 Coleman, J.S. 1990. *Foundations of social theory*. Chicago: University of Chicago Press, 1990.

2

Aboriginal Participation in Health Planning: Representation, Reconciliation, and Relationship-Building with an Aboriginal Advisory Committee

Geeta Cheema

Introduction

Both within British Columbia and Canada-wide, Aboriginal peoples consistently suffer poorer health than their non-Aboriginal counterparts (Canadian Institute for Health Information 2004; Commission on the Future of Health Care in Canada 2002; Foster et al. 1995; Ministry of Health Planning 2002; Royal Commission on Aboriginal Peoples 1996b). The gap in health status between Aboriginal and non-Aboriginal populations is an enduring legacy of colonialism, sustained by the continuing political, social, and economic marginalization of Aboriginal peoples (Hackett 2005; Kelm 1998; Kirmayer Simpson, and Cargo 2003). Given these broad and deeply rooted determinants of Aboriginal health, the health-care system is only one avenue to Aboriginal health improvement, but it remains a crucial one.

Both the federal and British Columbian governments have acknowledged that Aboriginal participation in health-care decision making contributes to overall Aboriginal health improvement. Federally, the goal of the 1979 Indian Health Policy is to "achieve an increasing level of health in Indian communities, generated and maintained by the Indian communities themselves" (Health Canada 2001a). In their guidelines for Aboriginal health planning in regional health authorities, the BC Ministry of Health states: "Involving Aboriginal people at all levels of the [health] planning and development process is integral to successfully being able to create and implement service options that are required to meet Aboriginal community health needs" (Ministry of Health Planning 2001, 2).

Despite the fact that it is endorsed in government policy, there is a dearth of research and literature on Aboriginal participation in health planning, and little guidance for regional health authorities on how to engage Aboriginal peoples in this process. An examination of the extensive literature on citizen participation in health planning reveals that Aboriginal people have not generally been considered in this field. Studies that refer to Aboriginal participation in health planning are mostly limited to Aboriginal participation in health programming (e.g., Griffin et al. 2000), and participatory research (e.g., Dickson 2000; Dickson and Green 2001; Kaufert et al. 1999; Kaufert and Kaufert 1998). Even the application of the term "citizen" has different connotations for Aboriginal peoples than it does for other Canadians in the existing literature on citizen participation (Wood 2003).

This article explores meaningful participation in Aboriginal health planning using the findings of case study research on the Aboriginal Health and Wellness Advisory Committee (AHAWAC) of the Interior Health Authority. Interviews, direct observations, and document review methods were used to gather data that provide rich accounts of the challenges that committee members face in establishing meaningful working relationships between Interior Health officials and local Aboriginal communities. Recommendations based on the analysis of these data are provided.

Aboriginal Health Within the Interior Health Authority

Interior Health was established in 2001 as one of five newly consolidated regional health authorities in British Columbia. Geographically, the Interior Health Service Area includes over 200,000 square kilometers in the southern interior of the province. Interior Health serves approximately 700,000 residents with an annual budget of $1.2 billion.

The service area contains the traditional territory of many culturally distinct First Nations: Shuswap; Okanagan; Ktunaxa; T'silhoqot'in; Nlaka'pamux; St'Wixt; Carrier; and Slt'atl'imx (Interior Health Authority 2003). The Interior Health region is also home to many Aboriginal people originating from other parts of the province, country, and continent. In 2001, there were 36,700 Aboriginal people residing in the Interior Health service area, comprising 5.7% of the overall population of the region, Aboriginal peoples comprise 4.4% of BC's population overall (BC Stats 2004b). There are 54 reserves within Interior Health's service boundaries, yet, only half of the Aboriginal population in the area lives on reserve (BC Stats 2004a). There is a great deal of diversity among the Aboriginal population in this area, and Aboriginal residents do not necessarily share the same culture, history, or health issues.

Despite this diversity, the Aboriginal population commonly experiences health inequities relative to the experiences of non-Aboriginal residents. For instance, the age-standardized mortality rate for status Indians in the Interior Health region ranges from 84.6 to 163.7 per 10,000 (spread across Interior Health's Health Service Areas), while the rate for other residents ranges from 56.2 to 68.9 per 10,000 (1991–99 data. Interior Health Authority 2003). The infant mortality rate, another indicator of population health, reveals a similar trend: The upper range of the infant mortality rate is 10.6/1000 births for status Indians, and 5.6/1000 for other residents (Interior Health Authority 2003).

Mapping the Territory: Guidance from the Literature

This study is informed by the literature and administrative trends in three conceptual areas: citizen engagement in health planning, regionalization and participation, and Aboriginal participation in health-care decision making.

Citizen Engagement in Health Planning

The term "participation" may be used to describe a wide variety of types of public involvement. As demonstrated in Arnstein's (1969) well-known paper "A Ladder of Citizen Participation," participation can range in practice from forms of "non-participation" (at the lowest rungs of the ladder), to degrees of "citizen power" and "citizen control" (at the top of the ladder). Understanding the situation-specific meaning of participation is clearly important.

The term "citizen engagement" implies a particular type of public participation. Its central tenets include "greater emphasis on information and power sharing, and mutual respect and reciprocity between citizens and ... governors" (Abelson and Gauvin 2004, 2). Citizen engagement is a key aspect of the "new public management" that has been widely adopted by governments of Western industrialized countries in the last twenty years and is characterized by decentralization, devolution of responsibilities to other government jurisdictions or third parties, and restructured accountability relationships. This redesign of governance systems is intended to permit more active communication between government and stakeholders and a direct connection between citizens and the policy process, as well as (perhaps paradoxically) a greater market orientation (Pal 2001).

While citizen engagement has become a buzzword in public administration, the popularization of public participation in health care may largely be attributed to the World Health Organization (WHO), which, in the 1978 Alma-Ata declaration, forwarded community participation as a cornerstone of the strategy to achieve the goals stated in the policy statement, "Health For All by the Year 2000" (Zakus and Lysack 1998). Public participation is also consistent with the approaches to health promotion and population health espoused by health researchers and Canadian health care organizations. According to Health Canada, the population health approach "ensures appropriate opportunities for Canadians to have meaningful input into the development of health priorities, strategies, and the review of outcomes" (Health Canada 2001a). Still, even with apparent government endorsement, "the use of citizen engagement mechanisms in the Canadian health system is in its infancy" (Abelson and Gauvin 2004, 3).

The principle of affected interests states that everyone who is affected by the decision of a government should have a right to participate in that government (Wharf and McKenzie 2004). Beyond this basic political right, one of the main stated goals of public participation is to include the concerns and desires of those who utilize the system in the decision-making process, thereby improving decisions and empowering individuals and communities (Perlstadt et al. 1998). Citizen participation in health planning is also purported to increase the accountability of health service providers, improve networking between those providers and community members, to make more efficient use of scarce resources, and to encourage creative problem solving (Pivik 2002). However, several commentators have noted that there is little empirical evidence to support these professed benefits (Blue et al. 1999; Zakus and Lysack 1998). Public participation "in health system planning and decision making remains a largely untested concept" (MacKean and Thurston 2000, 19). Evidence gathering in this area may be plagued by a lack of critical research analysis as well as conceptual ambiguity (Zakus and Lysack 1998).

While citizen participation in health planning is intuitively appropriate, the strategies for and evaluation of participation are decidedly complex. Labonte and Laverack's (2001) caution is useful when appraising citizen participation: "Whenever the term 'participation' is encountered, it should always be followed by the specifications, 'by whom,' 'in what,' 'why' and 'for whose benefits' " (Labonte and Laverack 2001, 127).

Regionalization and Public Participation

The regionalization of health services "generally means an organizational arrangement involving the creation of an intermediary administrative and governance structure to carry out functions or exercise authority previously assigned to either central or local structures" (Church and Barker 1998, 467). Regional health authorities embody the tension inherent in new public management between local participation and accountability, and concerns with economies of scale in service delivery. However, regional health authorities are uniquely positioned with respect to public participation. It is generally surmised that the "decentralization of the [health care] system [has] opened up more opportunities for public input because decision making ... occurs closer to the community" (Maloff, Bilan, and Thurston 2000, 68). Indeed, "more meaningful public participation" is cited as one of the objectives of the transition to the regional model (Kouri 2002, 20), but the extent to which public participation appears a priority for regional health authorities varies (Flood and Archibald 2005).

Regional health authorities have significant responsibilities in Aboriginal health. In British Columbia, they have been given the task of providing acute care, continuing care, prevention services, and some environmental health services to Aboriginal residents in the province, regardless of their legal status or place of residence. However, some of these public services may be offered on reserve by Health Canada or by Aboriginal service organizations, which begets jurisdictional confusion. Aboriginal board members of regional authorities have stated, "The regionalized approach to health appears to many Aboriginal British Columbians to be no more effective in meeting their needs than the previous ministry-centred system" (Aboriginal Governors Working Group 1999, 1). The implications of regionalization for Aboriginal health care have not been significantly addressed in the literature.

Aboriginal Participation in Health-care Decision Making

Prior to European contact, Aboriginal communities in what is now British Columbia had regionally specific, locally controlled, and often sophisticated systems of health care (Kelm 1998). Through the process of colonization, these systems were displaced, de-legitimated, and challenged by new diseases. The history of Aboriginal participation in Western health care has been marked largely by exclusion and paternalism on the side of past governments (Kelm 1998) and the contemporary notion of participation cannot be divorced from this legacy (O'Neil, Reading, and Leader 1998).

In order to understand the contemporary participation of Aboriginal peoples in health-care decision making, it is important first to grasp the basic elements of Aboriginal health care. This involves tracing the complex system of funding relationships and multiple accountabilities (Abele 2004) as they have evolved into the current scheme, in which the government of Canada has responsibility for ensuring the provision of health-care services to status Indians and the Inuit, which are then provided to Aboriginal peoples through a combination of federal, provincial, and Aboriginal-run services. What is given here is a greatly abbreviated version of history that may, at the very least, point to the political influences, competing assumptions, and fragmented service delivery that characterize Aboriginal health care (Commission on the Future of Health Care in Canada 2002). This context profoundly shapes the ability of Aboriginal peoples to participate in health-care decision making.

When British Columbia joined Confederation in 1871, jurisdiction for Aboriginal peoples' health and welfare passed from the local to the federal level. In 1874, the Canadian government passed the Indian Act, effectively cementing federal trusteeship over Aboriginal peoples. Several treaties were signed between First Nations and the Canadian government, but only one (Treaty no. 6, signed in 1876 with the Cree of central Alberta and Saskatchewan) contained any explicit provisions for health care. This treaty contains the infamous "medicine chest" clause that has been subject to differing interpretations regarding the health-care obligations of the Canadian state to Aboriginal peoples. Notwithstanding this, the Canadian government has been formally involved in health service delivery to Aboriginal people since establishing the first nursing stations on reserves in the early 1900s. Rather than viewing this service provision as an Aboriginal right, the federal department of health considers such involvement "a matter of custom and moral duty" (Elliot and Foster 1995, 114).

In the early to mid-1900s, Aboriginal health policy was shaped by colonial notions of racial superiority, the concept of the "white man's burden," and fears of infectious diseases localized in Aboriginal communities (e.g., tuberculosis due to the poor living conditions on reserves) (Kelm 1998). Within this agenda,

Aboriginal peoples "participated" insofar as they were the recipients of this system of care, or were involved in resistance to colonial systems of medicine.

In 1969, Prime Minister Trudeau's White Paper called for the repeal of the Indian Act in order to encourage the greater assimilation of Aboriginal peoples into mainstream Canadian society (Indian and Northern Affairs Canada 2004). Aboriginal peoples resoundingly rejected this plan as an attack on their sovereignty. The plan was withdrawn, but these events marked the beginning of a new phase in Aboriginal/non-Aboriginal relations, and opened the door to discussions of Aboriginal self-government.

In 1979, the federal government adopted the Indian Health Policy. The stated goal of the policy was "to achieve an increasing level of health in Indian communities, generated and maintained by the Indian communities themselves" (Health Canada 2001a). Following the intention of this policy, in 1986, the federal government announced the opportunity for eligible Aboriginal communities south of the 60th parallel to assume administrative control of federal on-reserve health services. The federal cabinet approved the Indian Health Transfer Policy in order to fulfill this commitment. Many Aboriginal communities are currently involved in Health Transfer. In the Pacific Region (British Columbia), as of June 2004, 41 transfer agreements have been signed, affecting 55% of on-reserve First Nations communities in the province (Health Canada 2004).

While Health Transfer has significantly increased Aboriginal participation in health-care decision making, the policy does not encompass all types of health services, and does not apply to all Aboriginal peoples; only those who are status, First Nations, on-reserve communities qualify. Moreover, Health Transfer is not a panacea for Aboriginal self-determination in health. Some Aboriginal communities view Health Transfer as a withdrawal of the federal government's historical duty to protect Aboriginal peoples' health, and thus refuse to participate in it (Culhane Speck 1989). Other communities do not have the capacity to participate (Sommerfield and Payne 2001). All of these factors mean that Aboriginal peoples and communities, both with Health Transfer arrangements and without, still rely to a great extent on services delivered by regional health authorities.

Each province has chosen its own policies and practices in Aboriginal health care with varying forms of Aboriginal participation. In British Columbia in 1991, the government formed six Aboriginal Health Councils across the province. The Health Councils were comprised of Aboriginal representatives from the community and included ex officio government representatives. The Health Councils engaged in strategic planning and setting priorities for funding provided by the provincial government. When the province of British Columbia regionalized its health services in 1997, it was mandated that all regional health boards and community health councils include one Aboriginal governor. However, when the province restructured regionalization in 2001, the requirement for Aboriginal participation in health authority governance was eliminated, along with the entire Aboriginal Health Council structure. Interior Health and the four other newly formed regional health authorities assumed the responsibilities for Aboriginal health planning and resource allocation.

Aboriginal health plans are a ministry-mandated requirement of each BC regional health authority. According to the Provincial Health Officer, Aboriginal health plans must demonstrate "increased Aboriginal involvement in decision making and planning for their population, and ... show establishment of a meaningful working relationship with the Aboriginal community" (Ministry of Health Planning 2002, 87). While the Ministry provides final approval of all regional health authority Aboriginal health plans, to date there has been no formal assessment of the extent to which Aboriginal people are meaningful participants in health planning.

Methods

Participants and Setting

The Aboriginal Health and Wellness Advisory Committee (AHAWAC) was formed on May 6, 2002, when Aboriginal community members and Interior Health staff met to discuss the province's transfer of Aboriginal health responsibilities to the regional health authority. The AHAWAC is comprised of 14 Aboriginal community members, seven Interior Health staff (ex officio) and two Interior Health Board members (ex officio). With two exceptions, all members of the AHAWAC are Aboriginal.

Data Collection

The research relied on interviews, direct observations, and document review. Interview participants were purposefully selected from a list of the 23 members of the AHAWAC, using quota selection to provide geographic coverage and balance between urban and reserve-based research participants. Eleven in-person interviews were conducted in geographically dispersed locations within the southern interior of British Columbia; two interviews were conducted by telephone. Interviews were semi-structured and interview transcripts were central to data analysis.

Additional data collection occurred through direct observations of two types of meetings. Four community consultation meetings offered a significant look at the relationship between Interior Health and Aboriginal communities. At an AHWAC meeting, interview respondents voiced many of the same views and anecdotal stories that they shared with the researcher during personal interviews. This apparent "duplication" served the purpose of data triangulation. Data collected from each of the meetings included descriptive notes (reconstruction of some dialogue and particular events) as well as reflective notes (personal impressions and interpretations). Descriptive notes were subject to the same coding scheme as interview transcripts.

The documents reviewed included the Interior Health Aboriginal Health Plan, Committee meeting minutes, organizational charts, and other relevant organizational documents. Documents were used to understand the activities, goals, and mandate of the Aboriginal Health division in Interior Health. By contributing this additional vantage point, document review complemented personal observations and interviews.

Data Analysis

Data analysis relied both on direct interpretation and categorical aggregation. Various techniques were used for data analysis, including text searches for recurring words, identifying internal inconsistencies, and colour-coding of "issues." In order to define and distinguish themes from the data, the researcher used recorded audiotape to "talk out" the analysis, and played back the tapes to define a logical interpretive path. These recordings document some of the iterative coding procedure in action. Through the analysis, overarching themes of the findings emerged—representation and reconciliation—which identify the tensions that radiate throughout this investigation of Aboriginal participation in health planning.

Emergent Themes

Representation and reconciliation both underscore the challenges that committee members face in establishing meaningful working relationships between Interior Health—a bureaucratic organization accustomed to Western medicine—and local Aboriginal communities that are enduring the effects of historic disenfranchisement, continuing marginalization, and poor health status. In this context, representation is a multifaceted concept. It points to the representational role that committee members each play with respect to "the community" and/or governmental health authority. Representation implies the power to survey, define, and categorize the represented. The committee itself is also a representation—it is not just a working body, but also a symbol of the relationship between Aboriginal peoples and "the government." Representation offers dilemmas that committee members must resolve in carrying out their work. Reconciliation implies the rebuilding of damaged relationships. Integral to the concept of reconciliation is the redefining of a balance of power between parties. Reconciliation is also the process of creating correspondences between competing agendas and conflicting world views.

Findings: Common Aim, Divergent Perspectives

Some of the findings of this investigation are illustrated here by quotes from Advisory Committee members.

Lost in Translation: Defining the Purpose of the Committee

According to the Committee's terms of reference, the committee's purpose is to "provid[e] advice to Interior Health on matters pertinent to the improvement of health and health services for Aboriginal People" (Interior Health Authority 2004, 1). However, this advisory role was not uniformly envisioned by committee members, who variously construe the purpose of the committee. Some of the factors implicated in this role confusion are:

- Division of power

There's that element of "this is an Interior Health committee, and Interior Health has the last say," that this is "an advisory to." So there's still a bit of that power struggle, still that tension.

- Various interpretations of the relationship between advice and implementation

I think that because they are asking for our advice as an Advisory Committee, they should take our advice.

It's not as if we can come and say "we want this and we want that, so give us that."

Similarly, committee members provided a spectrum of views on one of the major roles of the committee: allocating funds that are provided to the health authority by the Ministry of Health through the Aboriginal Health Initiatives Program (AHIP). These funds offer a vital source of revenue to Aboriginal community programs that promote health improvement. A subcommittee of AHAWAC judges community proposals and decides on funding allocation. Funding allocation is unsatisfactory to many committee members, however, because:

- There is real or perceived bias in the subcommittee's funding allocation;

I hear locally, "As long as such and such sits on the [sub] committee, we'll never get any money." So I know it's a sore point.

- Resource scarcity begets conflict;

There's only so many dollars and they've got us all fighting over them. It's typical.

In addition to allocating funds, committee members note that a great deal of the work of the committee is focused on an umbrella of activities that could be termed "education." Committee members depict this educating role in a variety of ways:

- Educating Interior Health about Aboriginal people

[The] number one [role of the committee] was to assist in the education of Interior Health as a new entity with very little history with respect to working with Aboriginal people.

- Information gathering and Aboriginal community capacity building

[A positive experience I've had with the committee] has been having the opportunity to be at a table where I'm able to collect information that's going to help us as [an Aboriginal community] organization run better.

Widening the Circle: The Challenge of Community Representation

According to the committee's terms of reference accountability statement, "AHAWAC is the link between IH [Interior Health] and Aboriginal communities. Committee members are accountable to the communities they represent and should ensure the provision of communication to Aboriginal people. IH acknowledges the committee as representing the Aboriginal People within the First Nations territories served by IH" (Interior Health Authority 2004b, 1).

While the Advisory Committee is intended to be a representational body, community representation is not a linear extrapolation from Aboriginal communities to the Advisory Committee table. Community representation is complicated by the following factors:

- Interior Health Aboriginal Liaisons describe dual representation and dual accountability (to Interior Health and Aboriginal communities);

I'm being pulled in a lot of directions, I guess ... It's hard to meet in the middle and be that one person for everybody.

- Constituent-based representation must be reconciled with regional Aboriginal representation.

We have to represent the interests that we come to the table with, and that's very important because we have such diverse interests ... But at the end of the day, when a decision is being made, the interests are for all Aboriginal people and the well-being of Aboriginal people as a collective.

In addition, despite the fact that many committee members initially equated community representation with committee composition, it is clear that membership itself is not indicative of adequate representation. Community representation also requires:

- Listening to community members

To be truly representing, you have to hear what people are saying if you're going to be at the table speaking on people's behalf.

- Communicating back to community members

So, have we got the representation? Yes. Do we have all of the issues on the table? No. I don't believe that all of the committee members are as diligent in performing their functions of representing and reporting back to their constituencies.

- Formal consultation

I really think that representatives like this on the committee, if they're serious about their position and their role and making plans, they would make it a priority to set up consultations within their areas.

Some members express concern about the committee's ability to represent all Aboriginal peoples for Aboriginal health planning. They identify specific representation that should be included in committee membership or wider Aboriginal health planning:

- "Under-represented" demographics

[On] the committee, I would include people from the communities, some young people from the communities, at least a couple of elders from the communities.

- Aboriginal clients

Engagement of the population that's going to be a recipient of the service—I think that's an indicator of success in planning in Aboriginal communities.

But committee members also identify barriers to wider participation:

- Community lack of interest

Even though we put the questions out there, or we give them the information, you don't get a lot of feedback back. The basic kind of feeling I get from the people is "just take care of it." That kind of apathy thing.

- Complexity of Aboriginal health-care system creates confusion about the health authority's role

You hear the complaint [from Aboriginal community members], "Well, we don't get services from the province" … They're so confused, they don't know who's paying for what or who should be giving them what. It's too complicated.

- Difficulty of reaching marginalized people

To get information out from here to the average person, it takes more than posting it at the Band Office, at the Friendship Centre, emailing folks, whatever … Most of our people live at or below the poverty line, so going online somewhere is not a priority ... It's that group of people that we need to reach ... And who has time to do that? Who's willing to do that?

Consultation poses additional challenges to the Advisory Committee in terms of timely decision making and progress.

People, I don't think, are comfortable making decisions because they have to go back to the community. But you know what? The community put you there, so they're saying make the decision, move us forward.

Square Peg, Round Hole? Reconciling Aboriginal Health and Health Care

Committee members identify various determinants of Aboriginal health, including:

- Colonization

How did we get this way? It didn't happen overnight. [We are] still feeling the impact of two hundred-some years of colonization.

- Social and economic determinants of health

Health is interconnected and linked with socio-economic status, education, general well-being.

Some committee members believe that the committee is employing an "Aboriginal approach" to health planning through the following means:

- Education of mainstream health-care providers and administrators
- Funding allocation

I think the characteristic of [an Aboriginal approach to health planning] ... is just looking at some of the [AHIP] projects that have been supported and the reason why.

But not all committee members are convinced that the committee is employing an Aboriginal approach, or developing a holistic health system. Barriers to this approach are:

- Conceptual opposition of the medical model

When we're doing health planning, we're looking at the absence of disease, that's the medical model. That does not meet with an Aboriginal perspective.

- Ministry "silos" that isolate the various determinants of health

If we're going to be effective ... [health planning] has to become more holistic and integrated. That won't happen because Interior Health has that mandate, MCFD [Ministry of Child and Family Development] has that mandate.

Despite the uneasy relationship between holistic Aboriginal determinants of health and Western notions of health care, most committee members define successful Aboriginal health planning with reference to improved health statistics:

[Success in Aboriginal health planning is] when statistics show that we're meeting the goal [of improved health]. And it is going to be statistic-driven in order to prove that.

But Committee members commonly communicated a sense of frustration relative to the progress of the committee in affecting Aboriginal health:

I've been very frustrated mostly for two years because I just felt like we weren't doing anything, that nothing was changing.

Elements identified as slowing the progress of the committee include:

- Turnover of Interior Health's staff members
- Lack of implementation
- Lack of resources for implementation
- Racism towards non-Aboriginal people at the Advisory committee

There's been some pretty heated discussions, some pretty nasty things said. A lot of racial slurs made. The people on our committee, some of them have some strong feelings about non-Native people and White people and they'll say things, and it's gotten ugly at a couple of meetings.

- Racism of the health authority towards Aboriginal people (associated with inadequate funds)

Interior Health said, "Oh my god, a million and a half dollars over three years? Oh my god! That's far too much money for those Indians, so cut it back." So to me it's like trinkets again: "Give those Indians a few trinkets and they'll be quiet and happy for a while and fight amongst themselves and we're okay, we can carry on with business as usual."

Despite the challenges to progress, committee members consistently stressed the positive aspects of the committee. Commonly, it is the very existence of the committee as a vehicle for Aboriginal health planning that engenders this conviction. A committee member sums up the importance of the committee in this way, and provides a reminder of the recent establishment of this working relationship:

Can [the committee] really affect change? I think so, and I think that is more evident in some areas as opposed to others, but we have to remind ourselves that just because the process is flawed at times, the outcome is worth the challenges, and that Aboriginal voice speaks, maybe too loud at times, maybe not loud enough at others, maybe in the wrong context or the wrong venue ... but speaks nonetheless, and somebody is listening and for a long, long time nobody heard us at all. So both sides will learn.

Meaningful Participation: Accountability, Power, and Validation

Meaningful representation and meaningful reconciliation (the suggested basis of meaningful participation) can be explored through this discussion of accountability, power, and validation of Aboriginal health approaches.

Multi-directional Accountability

Given the committee's position as an intermediary body between Aboriginal communities and Interior Health, meaningful representation implies multi-directional accountability relationships. This includes accountability between Interior Health and Aboriginal communities (vertical accountability), and between the community-based committee members and Aboriginal peoples in the region (horizontal accountability). Intersecting accountability describes converging responsibility for meaningful participation, and conflicting accountability refers to the tension inherent in multidirectional accountability relationships. Mutual engagement describes a relationship that promises to support meaningful participation.

Vertical accountability. Accountability between Interior Health and the committee is founded upon the provision of sufficient support for meaningful Aboriginal health planning and implementation. In this context, meaningful representation requires clear articulation and expectations about the link between the Committee's advice and the health authority's actions; that is, *answerability* (Abelson and Gauvin 2004).

Abelson and Gauvin contend that regional health authorities can sidestep answerability if the participatory process is not based on trusting relationships. They explain:

> RHA [regional health authority] decision making can find superficial, non-binding ways to demonstrate through their business plans that they have responded to community health committee advice. Without the key elements of relationship-building that include a trusting, open exchange between the RHA and community health advisory committee, the answerability criterion may be easily undermined. (26)

Horizontal accountability. It is not merely the link to constituency organizations that determines appropriate accountability; rather, accountability refers to the quality of the interactions between representatives, constituent organizations, and the Aboriginal population. Viewed in this way, meaningful representation implies that community members are aware that they are being represented, and that the representation is credible and responsive (Frankish et al. 2002; Maloff, Bilan, and Thurston 2000; Perlstadt et al. 1998).

Intersecting accountability. For nearly all committee members, relying solely on the Advisory Committee for Aboriginal health planning is not adequate representation. The meaningful representation of communities implies health planning that is informed by knowledge and appreciation of the unique character, needs, and abilities of individual Aboriginal communities and is supported by channels of communication and accountability to and from the committee setting. According to the findings, both community-based members and the health authority have responsibility for gathering knowledge and cultivating relationships with communities.

Conflicting accountability. Conflicting accountability challenges meaningful participation. For community-based committee members, the structure of representation requires them to be accountable to their constituents by supporting the community's interests at the committee table. They must also balance the wishes of their constituents with an overall agenda for Aboriginal health that may or may not meet with their community's vision. Liaisons are similarly challenged in their dual allegiance to Aboriginal communities and Interior Health.

Mutual engagement. Citizen engagement typically refers to processes in which governments take the initiative to involve citizens in policy development; a broader view of engagement includes "mutual engagement." Abelson and Gauvin (2004) contend that mutual engagement is the most robust form of participation, as it implies both strong accountability relationships and community empowerment. All actors in public participation have important parts to play in mutual engagement, but not identical roles.

As Interior Health receives funds for Aboriginal health planning and holds the final place of authority in the advisory relationship, the organization is responsible for providing support (resources, staff, supportive environment) for meaningful participation within the committee. Interior Health must also willingly share decision-making power, as "participation without redistribution of power is an empty and frustrating process for the powerless" (Arnstein 1969, 216).

Meaningful participation extends beyond the Advisory Committee, however. Interior Health plays an important role in Aboriginal community engagement through episodic and ongoing engagement efforts. Initiating these relationships is clearly challenging for the organization, as this work goes well beyond the boundaries of service provision, yet it is not Interior Health alone that determines meaningful participation. Mutual engagement supports Aboriginal self-determination by acknowledging the critical role of proactive community leadership. Community-based committee members are far from passive in shaping the relationship between Interior Health and Aboriginal communities. Through their bridging role as community representatives, community-based committee members can encourage and facilitate or, alternatively, inhibit engagement.

In identifying elements of meaningful participation, the preceding discussion suggests that meaningful participation may be supported and developed. Still, surmounting some barriers to meaningful participation will be more difficult than clearing others, such as low community capacity, lack of implementation, and inadequate resources. A problem that seems even more immutable than these is that of reconciling the conflict between Aboriginal conceptions of health and the biomedical foundation of the health-care organization. The research findings and the literature have suggested a place to achieve some resolution of this latter tension and thereby to facilitate more meaningful participation.

A Meeting Place: Population Health and Aboriginal Health Planning

The population health approach. Population health is "an approach to health that aims to improve the health of the entire population and to reduce health inequities among population groups" (Health Canada 2001b), by focusing on the importance of broad social, environmental, and biological determinants of health on health status. The population health approach is espoused by population health divisions at the federal, provincial, and regional health authority levels, but the necessity of such "special" departments point to the difficulty in reorienting the entire health care system towards the population health approach.

Applying a population health perspective to health planning involves the following five planning principles: holistic view of health, evidence-based decision making, focus on equity, use of partnerships, and empowerment and public participation (Canadian Institute for Health Information 2005). Acting as an educator, resource broker, community developer, partnership developer, and advocate, the health authority can support community empowerment, participation, and inter-sectoral approaches towards addressing the determinants of health (Labonte 2002).

Figure 2.1: Conceptual Intersection for Aboriginal Population Health Approaches

Despite the uncontroversial nature of these principles, population health has not been implemented extensively. Even when supportive research and information is available, "health officials ... seem unable to apply recent developments in social epidemiological theory and population health research findings" (Raphael 2004, slide 99). This inability stems from the difficulty of implementing policies that require inter-sectoral action and a longer time frame to assess effectiveness, as well as political ideologies and medical culture that favour individual, biomedical approaches to health. Thus, despite the implications of a sea change in health policy, population health has, as of yet, been limited to a marginal movement within health care (Evans and Stoddart 1994; Lindbladh, Lyttkens, Hanson, and Ostergren 1998; Raphael 2003; Raphael 2000).

Aboriginal approaches to population health. Aboriginal peoples "do not see themselves as a pan-Aboriginal population because they come from diverse nations, heterogeneous cultures, linguistic groups, and geographies where there is no 'one perspective'" (National Aboriginal Health Organization 2001, 7). There are, however, some shared philosophies regarding health across Aboriginal cultures that could be termed "Aboriginal approaches" (Kinnon 2002).

As expressed by many committee members, the causes and impacts of health and disease extend beyond individuals and reverberate throughout families and communities. Accordingly, "individual behaviours are [recognized as] important, but they are related to a much broader community health approach" (Armstrong 2005, 5). This community-based approach to well-being has led some commentators to characterize Aboriginal health improvement as an aspect of overall community healing (Warry 1998). Community healing implies a quality of community engagement consistent with the higher rungs of Arnstein's (1969) ladder of citizen participation, where the community itself identifies and is engaged in strategies to improve its own well-being. Community healing implies that a health authority takes on supportive (rather than leadership) roles that are consistent with the population health approach.

Commentators on Aboriginal health have suggested that "population health, health promotion, disease prevention, and health protection are principles and approaches that are compatible with an Aboriginal world view" (Kinnon 2002, 4). In fact, Ball (2005) refers to "Aboriginal ways" as "the original population health conceptual framework," stating, "it would seem that Aboriginal ideas about how to support the survival, healthy growth, and optimal development of their own peoples have long embodied the assumptions, aims, and approaches that society is now calling population health" (Ball 2005, 37).

While there are clear commonalities between these two health frameworks, the population health approach best known in mainstream health care must be adapted for its application to Aboriginal health. Scott (2005) discusses both the commonalities and the divergence in the two perspectives, but emphasizes the relevance of population health to Aboriginal health:

> Both Aboriginal views and population health frameworks recognize that well-being is the result of a complex interplay between environment and person ... However, there are key areas where subtle differences between western notions of human need and Aboriginal ideas ... exist ... Soulful dimensions are only ever incidentally recognized within ... the health determinants discussion. Secondly ... culture is important in the restoration of balance and harmony from a contemporary Aboriginal perspective ... Nonetheless, with its focus on the reduction of social inequities, environmental integrity, and self-determination, the population health approach has particular relevance for Aboriginal people in Canada. (Scott 2005, 2)

Despite the affinity between population health and Aboriginal health, there are challenges to the acceptance of Aboriginal population health approaches within health care. Prominent among these is "evidence-based decision making," in which where evidence is restricted to "scientific" peer-reviewed studies that comply with Euro-Western notions of research and knowledge. Since the acceptable knowledge base in this area is nearly non-existent (particularly with respect to "best practice" interventions), there is little impetus for health authorities to alter their approach to Aboriginal health.

The application of Aboriginal population health approaches will require validation within the health authority, especially through leadership support; this, in turn, will determine access to resources. The health authority will also need to build skills and the capacity to employ Aboriginal population health approaches.

Table 2.1: Benefits of Relationship-building Between the Health Authority and Aboriginal Communities

Build awareness, understanding, trust, interpersonal relationships	Establish basis for vertical accountability
Improve clients' access to services by improving awareness and referrals	Gain community input for evidence-based decision making
Improve suitability of services for Aboriginal client group	Develop partnerships for addressing social/political/environmental determinants of health
Establish channels for information flow between the community and health authority	Build capacity of Aboriginal health policy community
Increase knowledge of local communities' health issues and of Aboriginal health approaches	Support community-based efforts for community healing

Source: 2001 Census of Canada

Applying such a framework to health planning is an important point from which to build the shared understandings necessary for trust and true engagement.

The preceding discussion has merely indicated the potential to modify the population health approach for Aboriginal health planning; a fully articulated Aboriginal population health framework is beyond the scope of this research. However, based on the interconnections between participation, population health, and Aboriginal community-based healing (**Figure 2.1** – page 32), an Aboriginal population health framework would be grounded in the elements of meaningful participation elucidated in this research.

Conclusions

The findings presented here illustrate not only the divergent perspectives on Aboriginal health planning held by Advisory Committee members, but also the value placed on the Advisory Committee as a vehicle for meaningful Aboriginal participation. Strengthening accountability relationships and employing Aboriginal population health approaches are two suggested means by which to resolve some of the tensions that inhibit meaningful participation in health planning. This study emphasizes the importance of genuine relationship-building between the Health Authority and Aboriginal communities for achieving gains in Aboriginal health.

It also reveals an intricate understanding of participation featuring representation and reconciliation as key themes, but this understanding of participation is not just a highly localized construct; representation and reconciliation have some parallels in the mainstream participation literature through concepts such as accountability, power sharing, and trusting relationships.

Similarly, the mainstream population health framework offers promising concepts applicable to Aboriginal health, such as participation and social determinants of health. The research suggests that the mainstream population health approach, while valuable in many respects, should be elaborated upon, stretched, and challenged by Aboriginal population health approaches. Such approaches are a means through which to build the relationships integral to meaningful participation in Aboriginal health planning.

This research emphasizes that not all participation is necessarily meaningful, and meaningful participation is not the entire responsibility of any one party. Mutual engagement indicates the combined responsibilities of the health authority, the AHAWAC, and Aboriginal communities in engaging in effective relationships for Aboriginal health improvement. As relevant today as ten years ago, the Royal Commission on Aboriginal Peoples (1996a) reinforces the need for a comprehensive approach to Aboriginal health that involves mutual engagement:

> [Aboriginal people] need to work with non-Aboriginal health and social services agencies to transform relations with them. Mainstream services and agencies need to become more welcoming and more sensitive to cultural difference. And they need to start seeing Aboriginal people as partners in the design, development and delivery of services. (Royal Commission on Aboriginal Peoples 1996a)

Clearly, relationship building through special projects, as well as ongoing, formal, and informal connections, offers benefits to Interior Health and Aboriginal community organizations—some benefits for the health authority are summarized in **Table 2.1**.

True commitment to Aboriginal health will require stretching the boundaries of comfort for the organization. The Royal Commission similarly underscores the need to work beyond the traditional boundaries of the Euro-Western health-care system to improve Aboriginal health. The commission's report states:

> The pattern of causality for a specific illness includes factors outside the boundaries of ordinary medicine—social, emotional and economic conditions that in turn lead back to the complex, destabilizing and demoralizing legacy of colonialism. Obviously, then, more of the same—more illness care services—will not turn the tide. What is needed is a new strategy for Aboriginal health and healing. (Royal Commission on Aboriginal Peoples, 1996a)

According to the Royal Commission, this new strategy involves Aboriginal self-determination in an integrated system of health and social services. But, the Commission acknowledges the critical importance of supportive mainstream organizations in facilitating the progression towards Aboriginal control. Regional health authorities can contribute to this vision by supporting meaningful participation in Aboriginal health planning.

References

Abele, F. 2004. *Urgent need, serious opportunity: Towards a new social model for Canada's Aboriginal Peoples*. Ottawa: Canadian Policy Research Networks, Inc.

Abelson, J., and F. Gauvin. 2004. *Engaging citizens: One route to health care accountability* (no. 2). Canadian Policy Research Networks, Inc.

Aboriginal Governors Working Group. 1999. *Achieving a balance of wellness for all British Columbians: Aboriginal People and regionalization*. Vancouver: Aboriginal Governors Forum.

Armstrong, K. 2005. Lobbying for First Nations specific stream in health living strategy. *First Nations Health Bulletin*, Assembly of First Nations Health and Social Secretariat, Winter/Spring.

Arnstein, S. R. 1969. A ladder of citizen participation. *American Institute of Planners Journal* 35:216–24.

Ball, J. 2005. Early childhood care and development programs as hook and hub for inter-sectoral service delivery in First Nations communities. *Journal of Aboriginal Health* 2(1): 36–50.

BC Stats. 2004a. 2001 census fast facts: BC Aboriginal identity population—band membership, status, on/off reserve. <**www.bcstats.gov.bc.ca/data/cen01/facts/cff0109.pdf**>

BC Stats. 2004b. Statistical profile: Health authority 1—Interior. Province of British Columbia, Ministry of Management Services.

Blue, A., E. Keyserlingk, P. Rodney, and R. Starzomski. 1999. A critical view of North American health policy. In *A cross-cultural dialogue on health care ethics*, ed. H. G. Coward and P. Ratanakul, 215–23. Waterloo, ON: Wilfrid Laurier Univ. Press.

Canadian Institute for Health Information. 2005. Applying a population health perspective to health planning and decision making. Conference presentation slides. Canadian Centre for Analysis of Regionalization and Health, Montreal, May 2005.

Canadian Institute for Health Information. 2004. Aboriginal peoples' health. In *Improving the health of Canadians*, 73–102. Ottawa: Canadian Institute for Health Information.

Church, J., and P. Barker. 1998. Regionalization of health services in Canada: A critical perspective. *International Journal of Health Services* 28(3): 467–86.

Commission on the Future of Health Care in Canada. 2002. A new approach to Aboriginal health. In *Building on values: The future of health care in Canada*, 211–32. Ottawa: National Library of Canada.

Culhane Speck, D. 1989. The Indian Health Transfer Policy: A step in the right direction, or revenge of the hidden agenda? *Native Studies Review* 5(1): 187–213.

Dickson, G. 2000. Aboriginal grandmothers' experience with health promotion and participatory action research. *Qualitative Health Research* 10(2): 188–213.

Dickson, G., and K.L. Green 2001. Participatory action research: Lessons learned with Aboriginal grandmothers. *Health Care for Women International* 22:471–82.

Elliot, S. J., and L.T. Foster. 1995. Mind-body-place: A geography of Aboriginal health in British Columbia. In *A persistent spirit: Towards understanding Aboriginal health in British Columbia*, ed. P.H. Stephenson et al., 95–127. Victoria: Univ. of Victoria, Western Geographical Press.

Evans, R. G., and G.L. Stoddart. 1994. Producing health, consuming health care. In *Why are some people healthy and others not?*, ed. R.G. Evans, M.L. Barer, and F.R. Marmot, 27–64. New York: Aldine de Gruyter.

Flood, C. M., and T. Archibald,. 2005. Hamstrung and hogtied: Cascading constraints on citizen governors in Medicare. Health care accountability papers no. 6. Ottawa: Canadian Policy Research Networks.

Foster, L. T., J. Macdonald, T.A. Tuk, S.H. Uh, and D. Talbot. 1995. Native health in British Columbia: A vital statistics perspective. In *A persistent spirit: Towards understanding Aboriginal health in British Columbia,* ed. P. H. Stephenson et al., 43–93. Victoria: Univ. of Victoria, Western Geographical Press.

Frankish, C. J., B. Kwan, P.A. Ratner, J.W. Higgins, and C. Larsen. 2002. Challenges of citizen participation in regional health authorities. *Social Science and Medicine* 54(10): 1471–80.

Griffin, J. A., S.S. Gilliland, G. Perez, D. Upson, and J.S. Carter. 2000. Challenges to participating in a lifestyle intervention program: The Native American diabetes project. *The Diabetes Educator* 26(4): 681–89.

Hackett, P. 2005. From past to present: Understanding First Nations health patterns in a historical context. *Canadian Journal of Public Health* 96 (Supplement Jan/Feb): S17–21.

Health Canada. 2004. Transfer status as of June 2004. First Nations and Inuit Health Branch. <**www. hc-sc.gc.ca/fnihbdgspni/fnihb/bpm/hfa/transfer_status/signed_agreements.htm**>

Health Canada. 2001a. Indian health policy 1979. First Nations and Inuit Health Branch. <**www.hc-sc.gc.ca/fnihb-dgspni/fnihb/bpm/hfa/transfer_publications/indian_health_policy.htm**>

Health Canada. 2001b. The population health template: Key elements and actions that define a population health approach. Health Canada: Strategic Policy Directorate.

Indian and Northern Affairs Canada. 2004. Negotiation and renewal. <**www.ainc-inac.gc.ca/ch/rcap/sg/sg18_e.html**>

Interior Health Authority. 2004. AHAWAC terms of reference. Interior Health: Aboriginal Health and Wellness Advisory Committee.

Interior Health Authority. 2003. Aboriginal health and wellness plan, 2002/3—2005/6, revised. Interior Health: Aboriginal Health and Wellness Advisory Committee.

Kaufert, J., L. Commanda, B. Elias, R. Grey, T. Kue Young, and B. Masuzumi. 1999. Evolving participation of Aboriginal communities in health research ethics review: The impact of the Inuvik workshop. *International Journal of Circumpolar Health* 58(2): 134–44.

Kaufert, J. M., and P.L. Kaufert. 1998. Ethical issues in community health research: Implications for First Nations and circumpolar Indigenous peoples. *International Journal of Circumpolar Health* 57, suppl 1: 33–37.

Kelm, M. 1998. *Colonizing bodies: Aboriginal health and healing in British Columbia 1900–50.* Vancouver: UBC Press.

Kinnon, D. 2002. *Improving population health, health promotion, disease prevention and health protection services and programs for Aboriginal people.* Ottawa: National Aboriginal Health Organization.

Kirmayer, L., C. Simpson, and M. Cargo. 2003. Healing traditions: Culture, community and mental health promotion with Canadian Aboriginal peoples. *Australasian Psychiatry* 11, suppl.: 15–23.

Kouri, D. 2002. Is regionalization working? *Canadian Health Care Manager* 9(6): 20–24.

Labonte, R. 2002. A population health implementation approach for health authorities. Commissioned by Interior Health Authority.

Labonte, R., and G. Laverack. 2001. Capacity building in health promotion, part 1: For whom: And for what purpose? *Critical Public Health* 11(2): 111–27.

Lindbladh, E., C.H. Lyttkens, B.S. Hanson, and P.O. Ostergren. 1998. Equity is out of fashion? An essay on autonomy and health policy in the individualized society. *Social Science and Medicine* 46(8): 1017–25.

MacKean, G., and W. Thurston. 2000. The impact of public input: Defining participation in health system decisions. *Health Policy Forum* (Spring): 16–19.

Maloff, B., Bilan, D., and W. Thurston. 2000. Enhancing public input into decision making: Development of the Calgary regional health authority public participation framework. *Family and Community Health* 23(1): 66 78.

Ministry of Health Planning. 2002. Provincial Health Officer's annual report 2001. The health and well being of Aboriginal people in British Columbia. Victoria: Office of the Provincial Health Officer.

Ministry of Health Planning. 2001. *Aboriginal health planning: Policy, requirements and guidelines, 2001/2–2003/4.* Victoria: Province of British Columbia.

National Aboriginal Health Organization. 2001. *Strategic Directions for an Evidence-based Decision Making Framework at NAHO.* Ottawa: National Aboriginal Health Organization.

O'Neil, J. D., J.R. Reading, and A. Leader. 1998. Changing the relations of surveillance: The development of a discourse of resistance in Aboriginal epidemiology. *Human Organization* 57(2): 230–37.

Pal, L. A. 2001. *Beyond policy analysis: Public issue management in turbulent times.* 2nd ed. Scarborough: Nelson Thomson Learning.

Perlstadt, H., C. Jackson-Elmoore, P.P. Freddolino, and C. Reed. 1998. An overview of citizen participation in health planning: Lessons learned from the literature. *National Civic Review* 87(4): 347–367.

Pivik, J. R. 2002. Practical strategies for facilitating meaningful citizen involvement in health planning. Discussion Paper no. 23. Commission on the Future of Health Care in Canada.

Raphael, D. 2004. Reducing chronic disease in Canada. Interior Health chronic disease prevention and tobacco reduction think tank. Presentation slides. Kelowna, November 2004.

Raphael, D. 2003. Addressing the social determinants of health in Canada: Bridging the gap between research findings and public policy. *Policy Options* (March): 35–40.

Raphael, D. 2000. Health inequalities in Canada: Current discourses and implications for public health action. *Critical Public Health* 10(2): 193–216.

Royal Commission on Aboriginal Peoples. 1996a. *Gathering strength*. Vol. 3 of *Highlights of the Royal Commission on Aboriginal Peoples*. <**www.ainc-inac.gc.ca/ch/rcap/rpt/gs_e.html**>

Royal Commission on Aboriginal Peoples. 1996b. *Gathering strength*. Vol. 3 of *Report of the Royal Commission on Aboriginal Peoples*. Ottawa: Canada Communication Group.

Scott, K. 2005. Population health: Risk and resistance. *Journal of Aboriginal Health* 2(14): 2–3.

Sommerfield, M., and H. Payne. 2001. *Small independent First Nations: Evolving issues and opportunities in the administrative reform of community health programs*. Nanaimo: Inter Tribal Health Authority.

Warry, W. 1998. *Unfinished Dreams: Community Healing and the Reality of Aboriginal Self-Government*. Toronto: Univ. of Toronto Press.

Wharf, B., and B. McKenzie. 2004. *Connecting policy to practice in the human services*. 2nd ed. Toronto: Oxford Univ. Press.

Wood, P. K. 2003. Aboriginal/Indigenous citizenship: An introduction. *Citizenship Studies* 7(4): 371–78.

Zakus, J., L. David, and C.L. Lysack. 1998. Revisiting community participation. *Health Policy and Planning* 13(1): 1–12. School of Public Administration, University of Victoria, Victoria, BC.

3

The Transition from the Historical Inuit Suicide Pattern to the Present Inuit Suicide Pattern

Jack Hicks, Peter Bjerregaard, and Matt Berman

Introduction: The Historic Inuit Suicide Profile

Historically, suicide was not unknown in Inuit culture. Such a statement might seem obvious. Has there ever been a society where no one ever deliberately took his/her own life? The following quote from the CBC website seems to contradict that idea: "The concept of suicide was unknown to the Inuit before they made contact with colonizers." (CBC Archives 1991)

Franz Boas (1888), however, famously wrote that:

> suicide is not of rare occurrence, as according to the religious ideas of the Eskimo the souls of those who die by violence go to Qudlivun, the happy land. For the same reason it is considered lawful for a man to kill his aged parents. In suicide death is generally brought about by hanging.

John Steckley (2003) has questioned the evidence supporting what he terms the simulacrum of Inuit abandoning their elders to perish when the survival of the entire family group was in peril. He also questions the fictional accounts of Inuit elder suicide that appear in sociology texts:

> Shantu and Wishta fondly kissed their children and grandchildren farewell. Then sadly, but with resignation at the sacrifice they knew they had to make for their family, they slowly climbed onto the ice floe. The goodbyes were painfully made as the large slab of ice inched into the ocean currents. Shantu and Wishta would now starve. But they were old, and their death was necessary, for it reduced the demand on the small group's scarce food supply. As the younger relatives watched Shantu and Wishta recede into the distance, each knew that their turn to make this sacrifice would come. Each hoped that they would face it as courageously. (Steckley)

In Greenland, Alfred Berthelsen (1935) calculated an annual rate of death by suicide of 0.3 per 100,000 population for the period 1900 to 1930. He concluded that the few suicides occurring in Greenland at that time were all the result of serious mental illness. In Alaska, Robert Krauss and Patricia Buffler (1979) calculated that, in the 1950s, American Indians/Alaska Natives had a rate of death by suicide that was considerably *lower* than that of the non-native residents of the state. And, as recently as 1971, the rate of death by suicide by Inuit in Canada was close to that of the non-Aboriginal population of the country. Today, however,

Figure 3.1: Rates of Death by Suicide by Inuit Region, 1999-2003

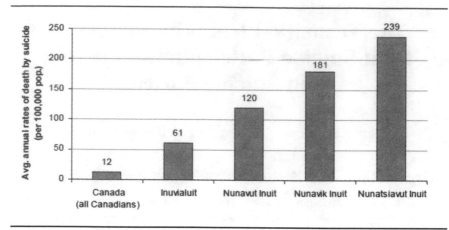

Source: Ellen Bobet Confluence Research 2004

Figure 3.2: Rates of Death by Suicide by Alaska Natives, 1960-2000

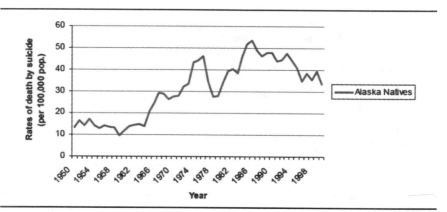

Note:3 year moving averages

Inuit in Canada have rates of death by suicide that far exceed those of other Canadians. The quality of data available on the four Inuit regions in Canada varies considerably, but Inuit in the different regions have quite different rates of death by suicide (**Figure 3.1**).

The Modern Inuit Suicide Profile

Data from Alaska

It is not possible to "unpack" the aggregation "Alaska Natives" to obtain data specific to the various Aboriginal Peoples in the state. Annual deaths are taken

Figure 3.3: Rates of Death by Suicide by Alaska Natives by Sex 1950-2000

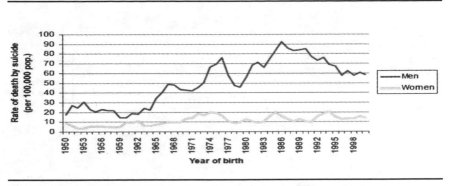

Note: 3-year moving averages

Figure 3.4: Decrease in the Rate of Death by Suicide by Alaska Natives, Males Less than 25 Years of Age, 1986-90 to 1996-2000

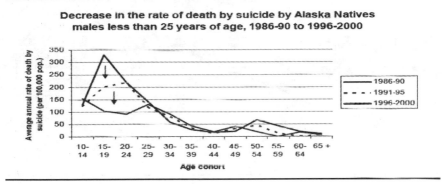

from the Alaska Division of Vital Statistics, unpublished data, and were compiled from individual death records. Because death records were lost for 1953, 1954, 1955, and 1969—estimates for these years are interpolated. Alaska Native population was estimated from US Census data, decennial population counts. The rate of death by suicide by Alaska Natives rose sharply from the mid-1960s to the mid-1970s, decreased somewhat in the late 1970s, rose again in the early 1980s, peaked in 1986, and has fallen steadily since then (**Figure 3.2**). For 2000, the last year for which data is available, the rate was 33 per 100,000.

The increase and decrease in the rate of death by suicide among Alaska Natives has largely been the result of changes in the rate of death by suicide among Alaska Native males—the suicide rate for Alaska Native females has remained relatively low and stable (**Figure 3.3**). Much of the increase in the overall rate of death by suicide among Alaska Natives from 1960 to 1985 was a result of an increase in

Figure 3.5: Average Annual Number of Deaths by Suicide by Men Born in Greenland by Age, 1980-84 to 2000-02

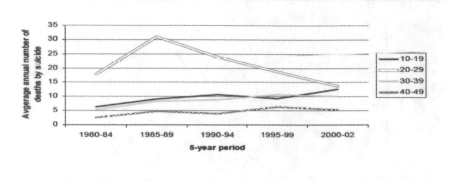

Figure 3.6: Rates of Death by Suicide by Persons Born in Greenland, by Sex, 1979-83 to 1999-2001

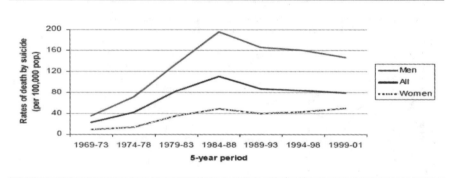

Figure 3.7: Rates of Death by Suicide by Persons Born in Greenland by Capital City and Coasts, 1970-75 to 1995-99

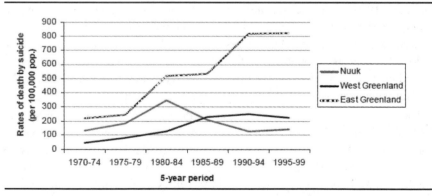

Figure 3.8: Rates of Death by Suicide by Nunavut Inuit, 1981-2003

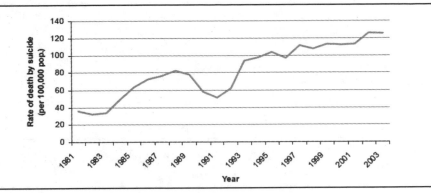

Note: 3-year moving averages

the suicide rate among males less than 25 years of age. Since 1986, Alaska has experienced a decrease in the rate of suicide in its Native population of males between 15 and 24 years of age (**Figure 3.4** – page 41).

In recent years, the rate of death by suicide among Alaska Natives living in the rural parts of the state (53 per 100,000 population) have been more than 3.5 times higher than the rate among Alaska Natives living in urban parts of the state (14.5 per 100,000 population), "urban" being defined as Anchorage, Kenai Peninsula Borough, Mat-Su Borough, Fairbanks Borough, and Juneau.

Data from Greenland

A record-level database on deaths by suicide has been maintained by the institution of the chief medical officer, and demographic data for this study was obtained from Statistics Greenland. The rate of death by suicide by persons born in Greenland rose sharply during the late 1970s and early 1980s, and has since leveled off at approximately 100 per 100,000. Greenlanders who are more than 30 years old have a higher rate of death by suicide than their Inuit peers in Canada. The rate of death by suicide by Greenlandic men in their twenties has decreased since the mid-1980s, while that of other cohorts have stayed more or less constant (**Figure 3.5**). This has resulted in the rate of death by suicide by men born in Greenland having decreased somewhat since the mid 1980s, while the rate for women has remained the same (**Figure 3.6**). There has been a significant and sustained decrease in the rate of death by suicide by residents of the capital, Nuuk, while the situation has worsened in East Greenland (**Figure 3.7**).

Data from Nunavut

Record-level databases on deaths by suicide have been maintained by the offices of the chief coroners of the Northwest Territories (1974–98) and Nunavut (1999–2005). Demographic data was obtained from Statistics Canada. Much of

Figure 3.9: Rates of Death by Suicide by Nunavik Inuit by Age, 1974-78 to 1990-2003

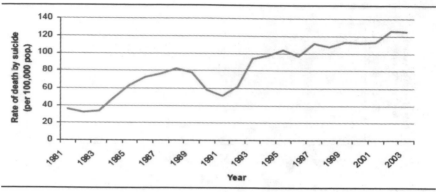

Note: 3-year moving averages

Figure 3.10: Increase in the Rate of Death by Suicide by Nunavut Inuit Less than 25 Years of Age, 1980-82 to 1990-2003

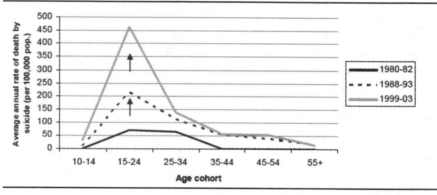

Figure 3.11: Rates of Death by Suicide by Inuit Men in Nunavut, and all Men in Canada

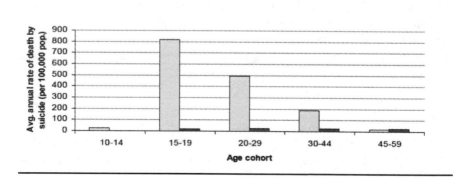

Figure 3.12: Rates of Death by Suicide by Inuit Men in Nunavut Inuit by Region and Sex, 1999-2003

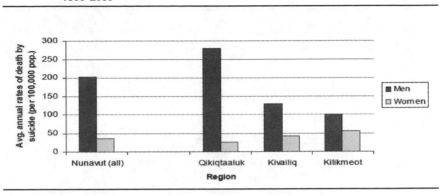

Figure 3.13: Rates of Death by Suicide by Nunavut Inuit by Community Where the Death Occurred, 1999-2003

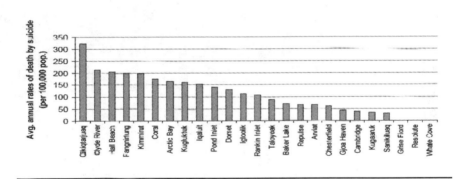

the following data presented is based on five-year time periods, with census years as the median year. The rate of death by suicide by Nunavut Inuit more than tripled during the 20 years beginning in 1983, and is currently ~120 per 100,000 (**Figure 3.8** – page 43).

In Nunavut, 85% of suicides are by Inuit men, with 60% being by Inuit men between 15 and 24 years of age. The increase in the rate of death by suicide is almost entirely the result of an increased number of suicides by Inuit less than 25 years of age (**Figure 3.9**), and the rate of death by suicide by Nunavut Inuit aged 15 to 24 has increased more than sixfold since the early 1980s (**Figure 3.10**). The rate of death by suicide in Nunavut by Inuit men is higher than among Inuit women, and the rate has increased more significantly in recent decades.

The most striking difference between Nunavut Inuit and non-Inuit Canadians is the suicide pattern for men (**Figure 3.11**). The rate of death by suicide by

Figure 3.14: Number of Deaths by Suicide by Nunavik Inuit by Age, 1974-78 to 1999-2003

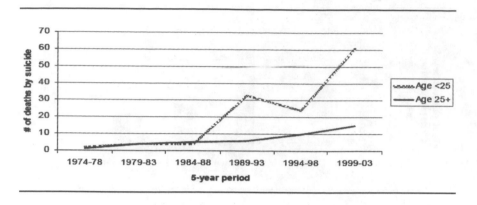

Figure 3.15: Increase in the Rate of Death by Suicide by Nunavik Inuit Less than 25 Years of Age, 1984-88 to 1999-2003

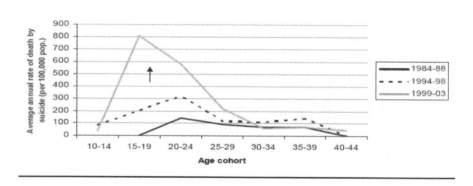

Figure 3.16: Increase in the Rate of Death by Suicide by Nunavik Inuit by Sex, 1978-83 to 1999-2003

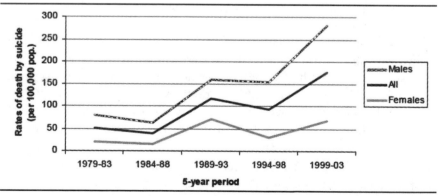

Figure 3.17: Number of Deaths by Suicide by Nunavik Inuit, Hudson vs. Ungava Coasts, 1974-78 to 1999-2003

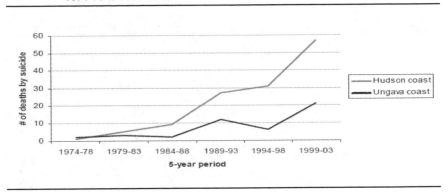

Inuit in the Qikiqtaaluk (formerly Baffin) region is higher than in the Kivalliq (formerly Keewatin) and Kitikmeot regions. The rate of death by suicide by Inuit men in the Qikiqtaaluk region is significantly higher than those of other groups (**Figure 3.12** – page 45). The suicide rate varies considerably by community; however, 10 of the 12 communities with the highest rates of death by suicide are communities in the Qikiqtaaluk region (**Figure 3.13** – page 45).

Data from Nunavik

A record-level database on deaths by suicide has been maintained by the Nunavik Regional Board of Health and Social Services. Demographic data was obtained from Statistics Canada. The rate of death by suicide by Nunavik Inuit has increased more than sixfold since the mid-1980s, and was ~160 per 100,000 during the period 1999–2003. Overall, 80% of suicides in Nunavik are by Inuit men, with 63% being by Inuit men between 15 and 24 years of age. The increase in Nunavik's rate of death by suicide is almost entirely the result of an increased number of suicides by Inuit less than 25 years of age (**Figure 3.14**). The rate of death by suicide by Nunavik Inuit aged 15 to 24 has increased dramatically since the early 1980s (**Figure 3.15**). The rate of death by suicide in Nunavik by Inuit men is higher than among Inuit women, and their rate has increased more significantly in recent decades (**Figure 3.16**). The rate of death by suicide by Inuit living in communities on the Hudson coast has risen much faster than that of Inuit living in communities on the Ungava coast (**Figure 3.17**).

Circumpolar Trends

As we have seen, the rate of death by suicide by Alaska Natives almost tripled in the late 1960s and early 1970s, eventually levelling off at a rate approximately 40 per 100,000. The rate of death by suicide by persons born in Greenland increased during the late 1970s and early 1980s and has since levelled off at ~100

Figure 3.18: Incidence of Tuberculosis in Alaska Natives, Greenlanders and Canadian Inuit, 1952-1961

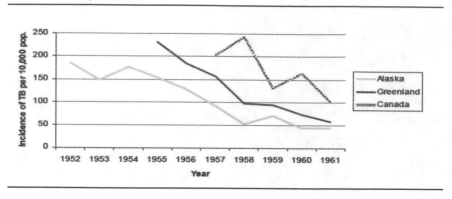

per 100,000. The present Inuit suicide pattern is characterized by an overwhelming percentage of younger male victims. It differs from the historical which was spread over the age cohorts. The new pattern developed later to the Eastern Arctic and involves more deaths. The rate of death by suicide for Canadians as a whole is included for comparative purposes (**Figure 3.18**).

As Upaluk Poppel, representative of the Inuit Circumpolar Youth Council, told the United Nations' Permanent Forum on Indigenous Issues on May 18, 2005:

> If the populations of "mainland" Canada, Denmark, and the United States had suicide rates comparable to their Inuit populations, national emergencies would be declared. But set aside the alarming statistics: every suicide is one too many. Across the Arctic, suicide rates are highest among young men. This is different than the case in most of the industrialized world, where it is older people who have the highest rates of suicide. At the same time, we see similar suicide patterns among most (but not all) Indigenous peoples. Suicide is one of the problems we need to look into not only as a problem in itself, but not least as a symptom. What are the causes, and what are the relations to the many faces of rapid change in our communities? How does suicide link to our culture, and to the cultural losses we face? I furthermore recommend that the UN should facilitate the development of suicide prevention strategies among Indigenous peoples and promote capacity building among Indigenous peoples' organizations to allow them to participate more effectively in national and international networking and research on suicide prevention.

Attempts at Explanation

A presentation by the Niutaq Cultural Institute in Igloolik to the 2003 conference of the Canadian Association for Suicide Prevention described the historical incidents that many Inuit and others believe have resulted in the pain that drives people to take their lives:

> Suicides started happening and were visible in early 1960s after the arrivals of non-Inuit and the taking away of their beliefs and introduced to none Inuit systems and beliefs

which were not recognized and not understood, introductions of alcoholism and heavily used by parents whose children are adults today and has been highly effected, children sent to residential school at the ages between 5–8 whose life were turned upside down due to physical, emotional, and sexual abuses that happens during the time in residential school and made to be ashamed of who they were and wiping away their own traditions and beliefs including driven away from their families, brothers and sisters due to not being allowed to talk to each other for some reason. (reported as delivered)

One of the most significant contributions to our understanding of suicide among Indigenous peoples is that made by Michael Chandler and Chris Lalonde (1998). They were the first to point out that it is an "actuarial fiction" to speak as if all First Nations and all First Nations communities suffer from high rates of death by suicide when they simply do not. This observation holds true for the Arctic as well—not all indigenous peoples in the Arctic have similarly high rates of death by suicide. Suicide is a less severe problem among the Sámi than it is among the Inuit, and in northern Québec the Cree have a far lower rate of death by suicide than their Inuit neighbours with whom they share a land claim. However, Chandler and Lalonde's methodology for assessing "cultural continuity"—which they see as a significant protective factor—in British Columbia First Nations communities does not appear to apply very well to the Inuit situation. Differences in rates of death by suicide among Inuit are not significant by community but rather by sex and by region (and sub-region). This can be seen very clearly in Nunavut, where the rates of death by suicide in almost all communities in the Qikiqtaaluk region are higher than they are in almost all communities in the two other regions. Additionally, the "factors" (i.e., variables) that Chandler and Lalonde employ to explain different rates of death by suicide do not vary at the community level for Inuit: self-governmental arrangements are structured at the regional rather than the community level, rates of language retention do not differ dramatically from community to community within each region, and so on.

To better understand Inuit suicide, we need to look more at the dynamics present at the regional and individual levels, and less at the dynamics present at the level of individual communities. One of the first attempts to theorize about suicide specifically by Inuit in Canada was Marc Stevenson's 1996 report for the national Inuit representative organization, at that time called the Inuit Tapirisat of Canada (ITC). Stevenson argued that "Inuit suicide is, in part, a function of economic realities" and that "the collapse of the seal skin market was one of the more significant factors contributing to Inuit suicide in the 1980s." He concluded that the collapse of the seal skin industry was "the 'trigger' that initiated an unprecedented rise in Inuit suicide within a few short years." While Stevenson's report was among the first to consider how macro-social forces and socio-economic realities might have contributed to increased suicide rates among Canadian Inuit, it did not attempt to explain how events such as the collapse of the seal market were mediated into suicidal behaviour by some individuals but not by others.

While Stevenson's remarks were considered to have the element of polemic in them, even more polemical was Frank Tester and Paule McNicoll's (2004)

Figure 3.19: Rates of Death by Suicide by Alaska Natives, Persons born in Greenland, and Eastern Arctic Inuit, 1960-2003

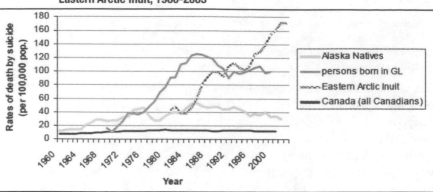

strongly worded assertion that "the impact of colonial relations of ruling has much to do with the current problem." However, the article made no attempt to explain how "colonial relations of ruling" have been (and are being) mediated into suicidal behaviour. Why would some people living under "colonial relations of ruling" and suffering from low self-esteem choose to end their lives, but not others? While analysis of the historic (and ongoing) processes of incorporation and colonization must be central to any serious understanding of the problem, Tester and McNicoll's approach is simplistic and disempowering in that it reduces Inuit suicide to a problem brought about entirely by outsiders and does not help communities figure out how best to heal themselves.

The Transition of Inuit Suicide Patterns as Seen from a Circumpolar Perspective

The transition from the historical Inuit suicide pattern to the present Inuit suicide pattern was first documented in Alaska by psychiatrist Robert Krauss. In a paper presented at a conference in 1971, he noted:

> In the traditional pattern, middle-aged or older men were involved; motivation for suicide involved sickness, old age, or bereavement; the suicide was undertaken after sober reflection and, at times, consultation with family members who might condone or participate in the act; and suicide was positively sanctioned in the culture. In the emergent pattern, the individuals involved are young; the motivation is obscure and often related to intense and unbearable affective states; the behaviour appears in an abrupt, fit-like, unexpected manner without much warning, often in association with alcohol intoxication; and unlike the traditional pattern, the emergent pattern is negatively sanctioned in the culture. (Krauss 1971)

These "suicide transitions" happened first in Alaska, later in Greenland, and still later in Canada's Eastern Arctic (in the Nunavik, and in the Qikiqtaaluk region of Nunavut). Each transition resulted in higher overall rates of death by suicide and, in each case, it was the rates of death by suicide by young men (<30 years of age) which increased most dramatically. And, in each case, there were sub-regions with particularly and persistently high suicide rates—the Bering Strait and Northwest Arctic regions in Alaska, East Greenland, the Hudson Bay coast of Nunavik, and the Qikiqtaaluk region of Nunavut. (There is also one case where the rate of death by suicide has *decreased:* the suicide rate in Nuuk, the capital city of Greenland, rose sharply in the 1970s and early 1980s but decreased considerably thereafter.) The temporal sequence in which these "regional suicide transitions" occurred is noteworthy.

Beginning in the 1950s, governments across the Arctic subjected Inuit to intense disruptions of the lifeways they were accustomed to—a process described as "active colonialism at the community level." The details varied considerably across the Arctic (see Yvon Csonka, 2005, on diverging Inuit historicities), but the fundamental economic, political, and social processes were similar. The wide-spread introduction of "southern" medical practices resulted in sharp decreases in the incidence of tuberculosis, first in Alaska, then in Greenland, and finally in Canada's Eastern Arctic. We can, therefore, use the decrease in incidences of TB as a historical marker of the early years of "active colonialism at the community level." The historical sequence in which Inuit rates of death by suicide *rose* across the Arctic (first in Alaska, then in Greenland, followed by Canada's Eastern Arctic) was the same order in which Inuit infectious disease rates *fell* (**Figure 3.19**).

Research in Greenland on the effect of adverse childhood experiences on suicidal behaviour later in life suggests that the socio-economic and structural characteristics of the home are less important than its emotional environment for the development of personality disorders. A logical sequence of trans-generational events would be that modernization leads to dysfunctional homes due to poor parental behaviour (alcohol and violence). This, in turn, results in suicidal thoughts, suicides, and probably also in incidences of substance abuse among the children of these parents. As Peter Bjerregaard and Inge Lynge (2006) noted:

> Most authors agree that the increase in suicide rates, the high incidence and the regional differences, are somehow causally related to the rapid social change since World War II, and that the upbringing of children and turbulent childhood conditions are central to the problem.

Our hypothesis is that a significant social determinant of elevated rates of Inuit youth suicide is the intergenerational transmission of historical trauma, much of which is rooted in processes and events which occurred (or were particularly intense) during the initial period of "active colonialism at the community level." The temporal sequence in which these "internal colonial" processes affected Inuit across the Arctic was replicated some years later by significant and rapid increases in suicidal behaviour by young Inuit men "raised in town" rather than "raised on the land." This hypothesis allows the important research contributions of Robert Krauss in Alaska, Inge Lynge and others in Greenland, and Laurence

Kirmayer and his collaborators in Nunavik to be understood in a new historical and geographic framework.

While the modernization process overall has been injurious to Inuit mental health to a significant degree, it should be noted that it is the sub-regions which have experienced the *most* "development" in recent decades that have generally experienced the *lowest* rates of death by suicide. Furthermore, the circumpolar data summarized in this presentation suggests that the *later* a region (or sub-region) underwent the transition from the historic Inuit suicide profile to the modern Inuit suicide profile the *higher* the resulting rate of death by suicide would be. This suggests that a "time compression" factor exists as well. It is our hope that these and other research results will contribute to the development of more effective suicide prevention efforts in the future.

References

Bertelsen, Alfred. 1935. Grønlandsk medicinsk statistik og nosografi I: Grønlands befolknings-statistik 1901–30. [Greenlandic medical statistics and nosography I: Greenland population statistics 1901–30.] *Meddelelser om Grønland* 117(1): 1–83.

Bjerregaard, Peter. 2004. *Folkesundhed i Grønland.* [Population health in Greenland.] Nuuk: Forlaget Atuagkat.

Bjerregaard, Peter, Tine Curtis, and the Greenland Population Study. 2002. Cultural change and mental health in Greenland: The association of childhood conditions, language, and urbanization with mental health and suicidal thoughts among the Inuit of Greenland. *Social Science & Medicine* 54 (1): 33–48.

Bjerregaard, Peter, and Inge Lynge. 2006. Suicide—a challenge in modern Greenland. *Archives of Suicide Research* 10(2): 209–20.

Boas, Franz. 1888. The Central Eskimo. In *Sixth annual report of the Bureau of Ethnology to the Secretary of the Smithsonian Institution,* 399–669. Washington DC: Government Printing Office.

CBC Archives. 1991. *An Inuit education: Honouring a past, creating a future.* "Clip 8 – Linking school and suicide—Did You Know? 3/5." <**archives.cbc.ca/IDC-1-69-529-2675/life_society/inuit_ education/clip8**>

Chandler, Michael J., and Christopher E. Lalonde. 1998. Cultural continuity as a hedge against suicide in Canada's First Nations. *Transcultural Psychiatry* 35(2): 191–219.

Csonka, Yvon. 2005. Changing Inuit historicities in West Greenland and Nunavut. *History and Anthropology* 16(3): 321–34.

Goldney, Robert D. Is Aboriginal suicide different? A commentary on the work of Colin Tatz. *Psychiatry, Psychology and Law* 9(2): 257–59.

Kirmayer, Laurence J., Cori Simpson, and Margaret Cargo. 2003. Healing traditions: Culture, community and mental health promotion with Canadian Aboriginal peoples. *Australasian Psychiatry* 11, suppl.: 15–23. (See also the research reports available on-line at <**www.mcgill.ca/tcpsych/ research/cmhru/workingpapers/**>)

Kraus, Robert F. 1971. Changing patterns of suicidal behaviour in North Alaska Eskimo. *Transcultural Psychiatric Research Review* 9(1): 69–71.

Kraus, Robert F., and Patricia A. Buffler. 1979. Sociocultural stress and the American Native in Alaska: An analysis of changing patterns of psychiatric illness and alcohol abuse among Alaska Natives. *Culture, Medicine and Psychiatry* 3(2): 111–51.

Leineweber, Markus, and Ella Arensman. 2003. Culture change and mental health: The epidemiology of suicide in Greenland. *Archives of Suicide Research* 7(1): 41–50.

Lynge, Inge. 2000. *Psykiske lidelser i det grønlandske samfund.* [Psychological suffering in Greenlandic society.] *Psykiatrisk Hospital I Århus, Institut for Psykiatrisk Grundforskning,* Århus.

Rasmussen, Knud. 1929. The intellectual culture of the Iglulik Eskimos. *Report of the Fifth Thule Expedition, 1921–24.* 7(1). Copenhagen: Gyldensalske Boghandel, Nordisk Forlag.

Steckley, John L. 2003 Aboriginal voices and the politics of representation in Canadian introductory sociology textbooks. Ed.D. diss., University of Toronto.

Stevenson, Mark G. 1996. *Inuit suicide and economic reality.* Report prepared for the Inuit Tapirisat of Canada.

Tester, Frank J., and Paule McNicoll. 2004. *Isumagijaksaq:* Mindful of the state: Social constructions of Inuit suicide. *Social Science & Medicine* 58(12): 2625–36.

4

A Regional Model for Ethical Engagement: The First Nations Research Ethics Committee on Manitoulin Island

Marion A. Maar, Mariette Sutherland,
and Lorrilee McGregor

Introduction

As do many Indigenous people and cultural minority populations worldwide, Aboriginal[1] people in Canada have, on average, poorer health status and lower income and education levels in comparison to the broader population. For Indigenous people and minority populations, the roots of this inequality are generally found deep within an existing socio-economic and political power imbalance (Geiger 2001, 1699). Ongoing research is necessary to gain a better understanding of how best to address this reality.

In the health sector, the circumstances that lead to poor health in Aboriginal communities need to be understood in order to develop appropriate services and programs that will address local health issues effectively. Aboriginal communities, government agencies, and academic institutions all require good data sources in order to develop effective interventions; however, conducting research on Aboriginal health issues has become an immensely complex endeavour that requires special knowledge and training in the areas of Aboriginal health, participatory research methodology, and research ethics. In order to address pressing and immediate health issues properly, researchers must also consider the effects of colonization on Aboriginal community health, including societal power imbalances, the loss of culture and a traditional way of life, and the experience of forced assimilation; many of these health determinants are still poorly understood in the health sciences. The historical circumstances that have shaped Aboriginal health issues also have had a profound impact on acceptable approaches to Aboriginal community research and contemporary Aboriginal research ethics.

A Century of Aboriginal Health Research

Much research has been conducted on the health of Aboriginal people in Canada over the past century, but the results generally have had only a limited positive impact on Aboriginal health and social conditions. As early as 1907, Peter Bryce, the general medical superintendent of the Department of Indian Affairs (DIA) conducted an investigation into Aboriginal health, which revealed deplorable conditions (Waldram, Herring, and Kue Young 1997, 156). While his report documented extremely high rates of child mortality and infectious diseases, and of a lack of medical care for Aboriginal people, there was no follow-up on the report, or any expansion of service provisions to improve the Aboriginal health situation (Bryce 1914). In fact, evidence shows that while considerable rates of infectious disease continued to exist in Aboriginal communities, funding for Aboriginal health services underwent significant financial cutbacks during this time (Kue Young 1988, 87–88). Many government reports documenting poor Aboriginal health status[2] have followed on the general medical superintendent's report; however, the collected information has, arguably, never been used to develop a comprehensive strategy to deal more effectively with Aboriginal health and mental health issues.

Just as with government-sponsored research, much of the existing academic research on this subject has also failed to impact positively on Aboriginal community health.[3] It is not surprising that most of the government-sponsored and academic research that has been conducted over the last century has had little impact on poor health conditions for Indigenous Canadians, since Aboriginal people have had little or no involvement in the research projects conducted in their communities. Rather, outside experts, often with little knowledge of the realities of Aboriginal community life, were commonly in a position where they controlled all aspects of the Aboriginal research projects. These experts decided which research questions warranted investigation, which methods should be used to collect data, and how the data should be interpreted and disseminated. The resulting research projects gave little consideration to the insider perspective of Aboriginal community members, existing Indigenous knowledge, the cultural competence of the research methods used, or to collaborative interpretations. Data and results were rarely accessible to community members. Knowledge transfer strategies geared to support community action on a particular problem were absent. Commonly, at the end of a project, outside experts would recommend inappropriate or unworkable solutions to community problems.

The health profile of Aboriginal people has changed dramatically over the past century. Chronic illnesses such as diabetes and heart disease, as well as health conditions related to the consequences of colonization such as mental health problems, family violence, addictions, and unintentional injuries, have emerged as major health concerns; unchanged, however, is the fact that the Aboriginal population has much poorer health status in comparison to the broader Canadian population. Increasingly, it has come to be accepted that, in order to improve Aboriginal health, Aboriginal people must be actively involved as leaders and collaborators in the development of solutions to local health problems. In light of this situation, it is encouraging to know that some successful collaborative health research projects have been documented in the literature, mainly since the 1990s.[4]

Addressing Aboriginal Concerns Related to Research

The shortcomings of past research have resulted in extreme research fatigue in many Aboriginal communities, which often have come to see government and academic research as an extension of mainstream colonialism, seen as the cause of much ill health in Aboriginal communities. Consequently, it now is common for Aboriginal people to resist participation in research projects. Research initiated by outsiders raises many concerns, some of which were succinctly summarized during the feasability consultation workshops for the 1996 First Nations and Inuit Regional Health Survey (FNIRHS).

Aboriginal people have become highly critical of governmental or university interests behind the research on their communities. Participants in the workshop had the perception that, despite decades of research on social problems in Aboriginal communities, not much has been improved as a result. They also expressed the concern that the research seems to benefit non-Aboriginal researchers alone by advancing their careers, for example, and providing them with employment. Additionally, participants felt that much of the research on Aboriginal people over the last several decades has asked questions that seem inappropriate in the community context (First Nations and Inuit Regional Health Survey National Steering Committee 1998, A-45).

Aboriginal people commonly see the lack of collaboration and community focus in research design and implementation as an ethical issue. Researchers who work in Aboriginal communities often come in contact with communities and individuals who have participated in research projects and have felt harmed or violated as a result, despite the fact that the research protocols for the projects received ethics approval from a university or hospital-based research ethics board (REB). Clearly, appropriate models for ethical Aboriginal research based on Aboriginal values need to be established and monitored through ethics review processes.

Over the past decade, the mainstream research community has become increasingly aware that ethical review of research topics and methods and dissemination strategies related to Aboriginal research must go beyond what is normally required for academic study in order to address issues like power imbalances and Indigenous knowledge in the research process (First Nations and Inuit Regional Longitudinal Health Survey National Steering Committee 1998, A-45). The Royal Commission on Aboriginal Peoples (RCAP) had a profound impact on raising awareness. The RCAP was established to conduct an in-depth investigation into the issues faced by Aboriginal people in Canada in 1991. The commission's work began against a backdrop of anger and upheaval: an ongoing national debate about the place of Aboriginal people in the Canadian Constitution; First Nations' blockades and protests over resources and rights-based agendas; and, most significantly, the armed conflict between Aboriginal and non-Aboriginal forces at Kanesatake (Oka) a year earlier, which drew international attention to the situation of Aboriginal people in Canada. The media began to focus more attention on the disturbing inequities in many Aboriginal communities. Statistics portrayed high rates of suicide, substance abuse, incarceration, unemployment, welfare dependence, low educational attainment, poor health, poor housing, and family breakdown. On the positive side, for many Aboriginal people, it was also a period of renewed hope as more and more people were openly reconnecting to their cultural heritage and identity as the foundation upon which to build solutions to community problems.

The RCAP completed its work in 1996, with over 350 research projects commissioned as part of this work (Royal Commission on Aboriginal Peoples 1996a). New ethical guidelines for research had been adopted by the commission as a best practice in order to help ensure that, in all research sponsored by the RCAP, appropriate respect was given to the cultures, languages, knowledge, and values of Aboriginal people (Royal Commission on Aboriginal Peoples 1996b). This was an important national turning point for the processes by which research was conducted within Aboriginal communities. Also, the RCAP report strongly supported the growing recognition that Aboriginal cultures, values, and world views differed fundamentally from the organizing principles of mainstream North American society, and, consequently, that Aboriginal people must formulate their institutions in ways consistent with these values. The RCAP gave voice to what had been a long-held understanding among Aboriginal people: that all Aboriginal people have the right of self-determination by virtue of international law and basic principles of morality.

The RCAP, thus, has had a strong influence on further national developments pertaining to the recognition of Aboriginal research ethics and respect for Aboriginal knowledge.[5] The Tri-Council Policy Statement on Ethical Conduct for Research Involving Humans (TCPS), adopted by the Canadian national research councils in 1998, acknowledged that research with Aboriginal people requires special consideration and that consultation needed to take place in order to establish policy in this area (Medical Research Council of Canada (MRC), Natural Sciences and Engineering Research Council of Canada (NSERC), and Social Sciences and Humanities Research Council of Canada (SSHRC) 1998, Section 6). In 2002, the Interagency Advisory Panel on Research Ethics (PRE), with the mandate of supporting the development and evolution of the TCPS, "identified as a priority the development of TCPS guidelines for research involving Aboriginal people, based on respect for Aboriginal knowledge, research modalities, and rights and needs" (Government of Canada 2006). The Aboriginal Research Ethics Initiative was expected to complete these guidelines in 2006, but they are currently still in draft form. Through a parallel process, the Canadian Institutes of Health Research

(CIHR) began development of Aboriginal-specific health research guidelines through consultations with Aboriginal communities and researchers in 2004, and published a set of draft guidelines in 2005 (CIHR 2005).

While all of this work is currently underway at a national level, it is important to stress that Aboriginal cultures in Canada are very diverse and much work remains to be done at the Aboriginal community level to develop regional, culturally specific Aboriginal frameworks for community-based research and ethical research conduct.

Aboriginal Community-based Research

In concert with the growing respect for Aboriginal research ethics, there has been a strong movement towards Aboriginally defined and Aboriginally controlled research approaches, along with the increased politicization of Aboriginal research, over the past decades (Jackson 1993, 49). This is especially true in the area of health services, where "researchers, government officials, and corporations (including those that are Aboriginal) may or may not understand, support, or even be aware of the aspirations of First Nations. They may not prioritize and may even be at odds with community interests (Schnarch 2004)." Thus, in order to advance their own communities' interests, Aboriginal people have begun to initiate more of their own research projects in an effort to better inform and support the effectiveness of decision making, advocacy efforts, and program design and management.

Among the First Nations of the Manitoulin Island area in Northern Ontario, there was a growing realization during the 1990s that it was important for First Nations to lead the development of all community research projects. To do so would, first and foremost, require the development of a local vision for research, and of locally developed guidelines to steer research. In the following section, we will discuss the development of a community-based Aboriginal research ethics committee on Manitoulin Island, the work of this committee, and the necessary support mechanisms required to support such a committee.

Mobilizing Community Resources on Manitoulin

Manitoulin Island is a large, fresh-water island located on Georgian Bay, in Lake Huron, in Northern Ontario. The closest urban centre, Sudbury, is about 160 kilometers away. The Manitoulin district is home to about 11,000 residents, made up of approximately 4,500 Aboriginal people and 5,500 non-Aboriginal people. The largest community, Wikwemikong Unceded Indian Reserve, has an on-reserve population of about 2,800, while the smallest community, Zhiibaahaasing First Nation, has an on-reserve population of less than 50 people.

On Manitoulin, many Aboriginal people who were working in the health sector had concerns for years about the uncoordinated approach to health research in the area and the lack of knowledge at the community level about research projects that were being run by outside researchers. Community frustrations culminated in 2000, when the two First Nations on Manitoulin Island who were involved decided to terminate two research projects initiated by academic researchers after ethical concerns about them were raised. The concerns expressed were significant and included problems such as the lack of free and informed consent of research participants, unauthorized linking of collected interview data with patient health information, potential psychological harm to research participants, culturally inappropriate research methods, a lack of community consultation, and the lack of a strategy for knowledge uptake. These serious ethical flaws were present despite the fact that these academic studies had received clearances from hospital and university-based research ethics boards (REBs).

In the aftermath of the terminations, local health agencies took the lead to mobilize and sponsor a regional community workshop (M'Chigeeng First Nation on Manitoulin Island, March 2001) to discuss local Aboriginal attitudes towards research, to create a vision for Aboriginal research, and to take control of local research initiatives. The ensuing two-day event brought together community members and leaders, health care workers, Elders, traditional healers, Aboriginal and non-Aboriginal researchers, and university students. On the first day, participants were invited to share their experiences, their concerns, and their views of potential benefits and drawbacks of health research among First Nations. Informal presentations were made by health care workers, community members, Elders, practitioners of Aboriginal medicine, and Aboriginal and non-Aboriginal students and academics. On the second day, participants broke into small groups and brainstormed about what makes research ethical from a First Nations perspective and how the goal of ethical health research could be realized for the Manitoulin area.

Despite the diversity of the participants' background, many common themes emerged. The most important theme was that community members wanted to become proactive in the area of research, build local research capacity, and develop a process to take control of research in their community. The main recommendation of this meeting was that a regional research committee be formed to bring community representatives together on a regular basis to advance these goals. Thus, a working committee was formed to facilitate the development of community-based research ethics guidelines for the Manitoulin area. Noojmowin Teg Health Centre, a regional Aboriginal service organization, was charged with coordinating this work, since this health centre had a research mandate and research staff.[6]

Over the following months the research committee began to meet on a regular basis to draft the guidelines, to plan further community consultations as necessary, and to promote the initiative with local decision makers. Committee members presented the initiative to health boards and Band Councils,[7] seeking formal support for the work of the committee and to incorporate feedback from local First Nations leadership into the development of the guidelines. During these follow-up consultations with community leaders, common themes emerged once again. Recommendations were made that the research committee should do more than evaluate research proposals, and that their work should include:

- To review and evaluate research proposals for cultural competence and the potential to create credible results; and to determine whether the research fits with local research priorities and Aboriginal values
- To create a strategic plan for research that encouraged research on topics relevant for the planning of local services
- To create a library of locally conducted research in order to discourage duplication of research and to identify gaps in research
- To support ongoing community capacity building in research
- To expand the health research focus to include other research areas that are of interest to local communities

A shared vision for Aboriginal research on Manitoulin Island began to emerge. People agreed that all health research conducted in First Nations communities should reinforce and respect the cultural values of First Nations organizations and communities, and that all research should be owned by the local First Nations communities and organizations. People also agreed that health research should have practical value for First Nations peoples, and should enhance information for decision making and development of local health programs. Under no circumstances should research lead to harm, or violate the privacy and confidentiality of patients or the community as a whole. Research proposals should be reviewed for their ability to respect communities Aboriginal and traditional knowledge and reaffirm First Nations culture, values and ethics; additionally, people stressed the importance to adhere to national guidelines such as the TCPS and privacy laws as well (Manitoulin Area Aboriginal Health Research Review Committee 2003).[8] There was also consensus that any proposed research projects should contribute to First Nations community empowerment and include the following properties.

- Be designed to directly benefit the community
- Respect the diversity between and within communities
- Produce documents which are useful for communities and agencies
- Respect that the collected data is owned by local communities and agencies
- Respect traditional Aboriginal knowledge and culture
- Build local capacity for research
- Research topic should fit into a local strategic plan for research and/or be directly relevant to local communities

Operationalizing Community-based Aboriginal Ethics Review

After community support for this project was established, the committee began a process to develop community-based guidelines for health research, established on the information collected during the consultations. To implement these guidelines, two important tasks had to be completed: first, documenting local Aboriginal values related to research; and second, developing a fair and empowering process for reviewing, evaluating, and monitoring research projects at the community level.

Documenting Aboriginal Values Related to Research

To document local Aboriginal values related to research, the committee conducted several discussion groups with respected community members and Elders to discuss their views on Aboriginal research values. The Elders emphasized that the Indigenous knowledge they shared was based on their unique culture and experience and stressed that these values were part of the local Aboriginal culture in the Manitoulin area and not intended to apply to other Aboriginal communities. Because Aboriginal cultures are unique and diverse, it is not appropriate to transplant local ethics and values and apply them to other Aboriginal nations.

Aboriginal research values for the Manitoulin area are based on the Seven Grandfather Teachings: respect, wisdom, love, honesty, humility, bravery, and truth. These teachings are interconnected, and it is difficult to separate them into individual "categories." However, in order to share the meaning of these teachings with respect to research, the Elders decided to provide interpretations by discussing concrete examples of how these values can be incorporated into research projects. These practical examples describe how the spirit and intent of the teachings can be actualized through specific actions and attitudes to achieve ethical research in local communities. The interpretations of the Seven Grandfather Teachings with respect to research became an important part of the Manitoulin research guidelines and a teaching tool for culturally appropriate research on Manitoulin. Two examples of the Elders' discussion on respect and honesty respectively are provided below:

> Respect the diversity in spirituality, beliefs, and values of First Nations people within each of their communities ... Being clear on what is to be done with data and what is not to be done with it ... Spending time with participants, to appreciate and respect the person's level of knowledge to ensure a mutual understanding of the proposed collaboration. Always have an interpreter with Elders who are more comfortable in their language. (Manitoulin Area Aboriginal Health Research Review Committee 2003)

The teaching of honesty brought on the following discussion and interpretation:

> Within the history of our communities, trust has been broken many times. As a result one often encounters reluctance towards research. The researcher needs to work towards a trust-based relationship with the community and the individuals and families who participate in research. To do this, you may have to visit more often than just once to do a survey. Particularly with Elders, gather the information bit by bit. It may not be appropriate to write things down continuously or tape record. This may be different for

the younger generation. Again it is important that the researcher is aware of the diversity in the community. Approach Elders with tobacco to build a relationship when appropriate. Ask yourself: "Were people happy that you have come to them?" (Manitoulin Area Aboriginal Health Research Review Committee 2003)

Developing a Process for Review

The research committee members recognized the importance of supporting and emphasizing the autonomy of all First Nations when choosing to engage in research projects. For this reason, it was decided that researchers must gain the support of local Aboriginal leadership or organizations before they request an ethics review of a research protocol. As the first part of the review process, the research committee would determine if any proposals under consideration were unethical from an Aboriginal perspective. After the ethics review process, the committee would be encouraged to review the proposal with an eye to the suitability of the research topic and how it fits in with current community priorities. The committee would also provide recommendations on how to maximize community benefit from the project, and the results would then be communicated to the Band Councils and other local leadership.

The evaluation process is designed to help communities to make an informed decision about their involvement in a research project. The committee also offers to provide support to communities during the implementation process by helping to form a local steering committee to guide the day-to-day operation of projects.

In order to ensure a well-functioning and transparent review process, the committee members developed an ethics application workbook with standard questions to be completed by researchers (Maar and McGregor 2005). Committee members have all received formal REB training from the National Council for Ethics in Human Research (NCEHR).

Lessons Learned

The process of documenting Aboriginal research values and developing a community-based REB is rewarding, yet very time consuming. In the Manitoulin area, it took four years to build community support, to develop guidelines and a review process, and to train committee members to review research proposals. Commitments from committee members and support from many community stakeholders are required to establish the process, and the process undoubtedly benefits from a community champion who is able to consistently allocate time to this project to coordinate activities.

It is very important to keep community organizations updated on the process and milestones achieved through ongoing presentations. Gaining and maintaining community support has been the key to the many accomplishments of the Manitoulin research committee. Throughout the research process, it was important to have knowledgeable community participants who had an interest in research methods and research ethics. Fortunately, a number of resource persons and individuals on the committee had post-graduate educations, health services experience, and/or traditional Aboriginal knowledge. Recruiting Aboriginal people with these types of expertise and experience was essential in making it possible to provide Aboriginal perspectives on research processes and ethics. These individuals also helped to build confidence and credibility in the committee's work within the First Nations communities on Manitoulin. Representation from First Nations communities and organizations was another key consideration in developing the research committee. Many of the representatives participating on the committee were appointed by their respective communities' Band Councils or health boards. These individuals were instrumental as a voice within each community and health agency by being the committee's "ears to the ground." Most importantly, they were experts on topics like community issues, demographics, community and leadership dynamics, as well as the overall priorities and aspirations of the community. They also understood their communities' experiences with research projects in the past and their communities' vision for research in the future. An important issue that was emphasized was that all conducted research must lead toward or result in a tangible benefit or action within the participating communities.

Linkages across sectors within the community were also very important because health issues are intertwined with many other social and economic determinants within communities. Representatives from the local band administrations, Band Councils, and the local tribal councils, were involved in a working group to provide broad policy perspectives. This political representation also helped to raise awareness of the importance of the guidelines and the potential benefits to all sectors in the community.

Ongoing consultation with the seven First Nations communities on Manitoulin Island, through presentations to leadership and health boards, was another key success factor in the development of these guidelines. It was important to continually inform, engage, and seek endorsement from all these groups by seeking their input, advice, and feedback throughout the development of the guidelines. When organizing community information sessions, the research committee felt strongly that community ownership of this process would be reinforced if the local community representatives of the committee were involved in presentations in their communities. This approach worked very well because the local community representative had an intimate understanding of local issues. The community representative was able to illustrate the issues and benefits of the initiative with local examples and could answer questions pertaining to the particulars of that community's situation. The presentations to community leaders were invaluable in terms of the advice and direction provided to the committee's work and the guidelines. Without exception, all presentations were well received and later supported with official Band Council resolutions. More importantly, communities began to see the research guidelines as the beginning of an evolving process of taking charge of research, rather than an endpoint. The following feedback illustrates this:

> Can you make sure that training is provided to our people and include our health staff and board members—We want to make sure they understand how this works and how it benefits the community and we want the skills and knowledge to be provided to our people as well as our committee representative.

> Will there be training that our post-secondary students can take part in as well? We should be building this knowledge in our budding scholars so that they can be the ones taking on the research projects for us. There are already many who are graduating with advanced credentials whom we can start calling on as resource people and researchers.

Engaging leadership in this manner was important to the overall process, not only in setting the direction for the committee's work, but also as a reminder of the importance of building local capacity and setting strategic directions for research topics.

After receiving many requests, the committee began to share its research on Aboriginal research ethics more widely through conference presentations and publications with the purpose of both educating researchers and health service providers and providing information to help other Aboriginal communities to take control over research projects in their communities. These dissemination activities have brought greater awareness to the work of the committee, both locally and nationally.

Funding to support this kind of initiative was difficult to find. The committee had to find creative ways to access funds and relied frequently on the support of local organizations. Sustainability is an ongoing issue for discussion at committee meetings.

The most important attribute of the Manitoulin research guidelines is their embodiment of traditional values and teachings of Aboriginal people in the Manitoulin Island area. The guidelines were built on a framework of original ethics or "teachings" passed down from generation to generation, which could only be gained from personal discussions with traditional knowledge keepers. Cultural sensitivities had to be carefully observed when this perspective was researched.

The work of the committee has had a tremendous impact on local research capacity A fully functioning, community-based REB now operates on Manitoulin Island. Guidelines and a workbook have been developed that serve as educational tools for researchers, research participants, and community members. The committee has also been able to network and exchange knowledge with other Aboriginal research committees outside of their region and with Aboriginal researchers and health professionals.

Future Areas of Development

The development of a community-based research ethics committee, research guidelines, and an ethics review process are not end points; ongoing policy and community research is necessary to keep this process alive and to ensure that it continues to evolve and respond to First Nations needs. In the case of Manitoulin Island, the committee has identified several future initiatives, They include the development of resource materials about ethics, participants' rights, and confidentiality in the Anishnaabe (Ojibwa) language. These materials are required to empower Elders who participate in research projects by eliminating the language barrier and informing them of their level of involvement and rights related to research.

Another long-term goal is to continue to build research capacity by forging academic partnerships based on community research needs and providing ongoing training opportunities. The committee is also interested in developing a model for long-term sustainable funding for this committee by assessing various funding sources and exploring diverse operational models. Most importantly, the committee recognizes that guidelines are living documents and will continue to evolve to support the changing needs of local First Nations communities.

Acknowledgements

This paper is based on the work of many people over the past five years, including the members of the research ethics committee, the Chiefs and Councils of the First Nations on Manitoulin, the four area health boards and the Elders Advisory Committee. This research received financial support from the Indigenous Health Research Development Program, the Interagency Advisory Panel on Research Ethics, the National Council on Ethics in Human Research and Noojmowin Teg Health Centre on Manitoulin Island.

Endnotes

1 The terms "Aboriginal" and "First Nations" are not used interchangeably in this paper. The term "Aboriginal" is defined in the Canadian Constitution Act and includes all people of Indigenous descent: Status Indians, Inuit, and Métis. The term "First Nations" is used to refer to Status Indians and their communities since it is preferred by many Aboriginal people.

2 See, for example, the report of the Ewing Commission (1934); T. Berger(1980). the Royal Commission on Aboriginal Peoples National Round Table on Health Issues (1993); and the Royal Commission on Aboriginal Peoples (RCAP)(1996a).

3 For a more detailed review of this topic, see M. Maar (2005).

4 Some examples of collaborative projects can be read in S. Abonyi (2001), A.C. Macaulay et al. (1999), and S. Peressini et al. (2004).

5 For example, see National Aboriginal Health Organization (NAHO) (2003).

6 The position of research coordinator was filled by one of the authors (M. Maar).

7 A Band Council is a council made up of the elected officials of a nation of Status Indians.

8 Manitoulin Area Aboriginal Health Research Review Committee. 2003. Guidelines for ethical Aboriginal research within the First Nations communities of Manitoulin, Document on file at Noojmowin Teg Health Centre, Aundek Omni Kaning, Ontario.

References

Abonyi, S. 2001. Sickness and symptom: Perspectives of diabetes among the Mushkegowuk Cree. PhD diss., McMaster Univ.

Berger, T. 1980. *Report of the Advisory Commission on Indian and Inuit Health Consultation*. Ottawa: Medical Services Branch, Department of National Health and Welfare Canada.

Bryce, P. 1914. The history of the American Indian in relation to health. Ontario Historical Society 12: 128–42.

CIHR. 2005. Guidelines for health research involving Aboriginal peoples. Draft for consultation. <**www.cihr-irsc.gc.ca/e/e29339.html**>

Ewing Commission. 1934. *A Royal Commission on Métis health*. Calgary: Government of Alberta.

First Nations and Inuit Regional Longitudinal Health Survey National Steering Committee. 1998. *First Nations and Inuit regional longitudinal health survey national report*. Ottawa.

Geiger, H.J. 2001. Racial stereotyping and medicine: The need for cultural competence. *Canadian Medical Association Journal* 164 (12). 1699–1700.

Government of Canada. Interagency Advisory Panel on Research Ethics. 2006. <**www.pre.ethics. gc.ca/english/workgroups/aboriginal.cfm**>

Jackson, T. 1993. A way of working: Participatory research and the Aboriginal movement in Canada. In *Voices of change: Participatory research in the United States and Canada*, ed. P. Park et al. Toronto: OISE Press. 47–64.

Kue Young, T. 1988. *Health care and cultural change: The Indian experience in the Central Subarctic*. Toronto: Univ. of Toronto Press.

Maar, M. 2005. From self-determination to community health empowerment: Evolving Aboriginal health services on Manitoulin Island, Ontario. PhD diss., McMaster Univ.

Maar, M. and L. McGregor. 2005. *Ethics review workbook*. Document on file, Noojmowin Teg Health Centre, Aundek Omni Kaning, Ontario

Macaulay, A.C., L.E. Commanda, W.L. Freeman, N. Gibson, M.L. McCabe, C.M. Robbins, and P. L. Towhig. 1999. Participatory research maximizes community and lay involvement. *British Medical Journal* 319:774–78.

Manitoulin Area Aboriginal Health Research Review Committee. 2003. *Guidelines for ethical Aboriginal research within the First Nations communities of Manitoulin*, Document on file at Noojmowin Teg Health Centre, Aundek Omni Kaning, Ontario.

National Aboriginal Health Organization (NAHO). 2003. *Ways of knowing: A framework for health research*. Ottawa: NAHO.

Medical Research Council of Canada (MRC), Natural Sciences and Engineering Research Council of Canada (NSERC), and Social Sciences and Humanities Research Council of Canada (SSHRC). 1998. *Tri-council policy statement: Ethical conduct for research involving humans*. Ottawa: Public Works and Government Services Canada.

Peressini, S., J.L. Leake, J.T. Mayhall, M. Maar, and R. Trudeau. 2004. Prevalence of early childhood caries among First Nations children, District of Manitoulin, Ontario. *International Journal of Pediatric Dentistry* 14:101–110.

Royal Commission on Aboriginal Peoples (RCAP). 1996a. *Report of the National Royal Commission Round Table on Aboriginal Peoples*. 5 vols. Ottawa: Supply and Services Canada.

Royal Commission on Aboriginal Peoples (RCAP). 1996b. Appendix E: Ethical guidelines for research. In *Renewal: A twenty-year commitment*. Vol. 5 of *Report of the National Royal Commission Round Table on Aboriginal Peoples*. Ottawa: Supply and Services Canada.

Royal Commission on Aboriginal Peoples National Round Table on Health Issues. 1993. *The path to healing: Report of the National Round Table on Aboriginal Health and Social Issues*. Vancouver: Canada Communications Group.

Schnarch, B. 2004. *Ownership, control, access and possession (OCAP) or self-determination applied to research: A critical analysis of contemporary First Nations research and some options for First Nations communities*. Ottawa: First Nations Centre, National Aboriginal Health Organization.

Waldram, J, D.A. Herring, T. Kue Young. 1997. *Aboriginal health in Canada*. Toronto: Univ. of Toronto Press.

5

Healing Historic Trauma: A Report From The Aboriginal Healing Foundation

Marlene Brant Castellano and Linda Archibald

Editor's Note:
The following chapter differs from others in this volume. Rather than being an individual research presentation, it is an overview of the findings from six presentations given at the Aboriginal Policy Research Conference (2006).
—Jerry White

Introduction

The Aboriginal Healing Foundation (AHF) hosted two sessions at the Aboriginal Policy Research Conference in 2006 to profile its final report and the research underpinning its findings. This paper brings together selected content from six presentations[1] at those sessions that, together, provide insight both into the traumatic legacy of the residential school system, and into interventions directed towards interrupting the transmission of that hurt through successive generations. Over the seven years of its first mandate, the AHF has taken direction from its board of directors, many of them residential school Survivors,[2] and those affected directly and indirectly by the residential school experience. This paper proposes that a new paradigm of healing is emerging, one that takes into account successive waves of trauma that were experienced by Aboriginal communities in the past, which continue to reverberate and may be repeated in diverse forms in the present. The paradigm draws on cultural resources, as well as the therapies of Western culture, to mobilize the inherent resilience of community members.

The Aboriginal Healing Foundation was established in March 1998 as a self-governing agency to manage the distribution of a $350 million, one-time grant from the Government of Canada for community-based healing of the legacy of physical and sexual abuse at residential schools. The healing fund was a concrete governmental response to volume 1 of the *Report of the Royal Commission on Aboriginal Peoples* (1996), which documented the damaging effects the schools had on Aboriginal culture and people. The fundamental aims of the residential school system had been to separate Aboriginal children from their families and communities, to erase their languages and identities as Aboriginal people, and to absorb them into Euro-Canadian society (337–44). Survivors who launched law suits seeking reparations emphasized that the emotional, cultural, and spiritual

Figure 5.1: Historic Past

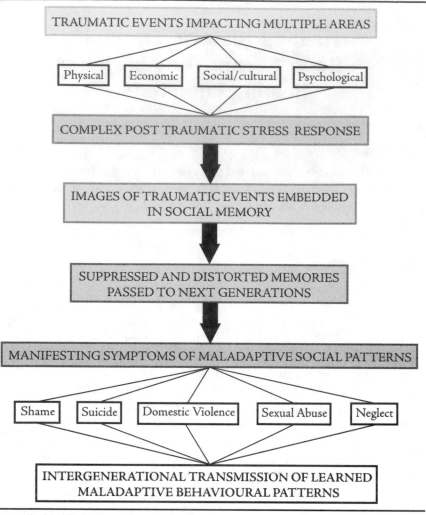

Source: Aboriginal Healing Foundation

damage they suffered as a result was common to all and which made the physical and sexual abuse suffered by some of their numbers even more devastating.

Prior to the establishment of the Aboriginal Healing Foundation, residential school Survivor groups had formed to support one another, particularly during the painful process of taking criminal and civil court actions relating to physical and sexual abuse through the justice system. Clinicians had begun to associate symptoms displayed by former students with post-traumatic stress disorder (PTSD). Still, little was known about the complexities and extent of trauma resulting from the residential school experience. Even less was known about interventions that would promote healing in Survivors and in their families, who also were affected by those experiences.

The Aboriginal Healing Foundation launched a two-pronged research program to create a knowledge base for its initiatives in community healing. The first prong was an effort to engage scholars and practitioners in searching out relevant practice experience and literature that would shed light on trauma and recovery in Aboriginal contexts. The second prong was a plan to involve personnel in projects funded by the foundation to provide systematic data, both quantitative and qualitative, and to document what was being done to deal with trauma and recovery issues in communities, and with what effects.

Research reports, evaluations, and a survey of promising practices formed the evidence base for the three-volume final report, released in January 2006 (*Report of the Aboriginal Healing Foundation*).[3] At the APRC, authors presented highlights of three research reports and each of the volumes of the final report. Synopses of the presentations make up the bulk of this paper, with sections on historic trauma, resilience, strategies for healing men, measuring progress, promising healing practices, and the healing journey. References for the original papers and reports are provided, and copies can be obtained from the Aboriginal Healing Foundation.

Historic Trauma[4]

In her presentation, Cynthia Wesley-Esquimaux utilized work from her jointly authored study, "Historic Trauma and Aboriginal Healing," to propose a theory of "historic trauma transmission," to explain the origins of social malaise in Aboriginal communities and the dynamics of interventions particular to Aboriginal contexts. The research drew on historical, social science, and therapeutic sources to develop core concepts.

Aboriginal peoples have lived through an unremitting series of traumatic events: demographic collapse resulting from early influenza and smallpox epidemics and other infectious diseases, conquest, warfare, slavery, colonization, religious proselytizing, famine and starvation, the residential school period from the 1890s to the late 1960s, and continuing assimilative pressures. These experiences have left

Figure 5.2: Historic Present

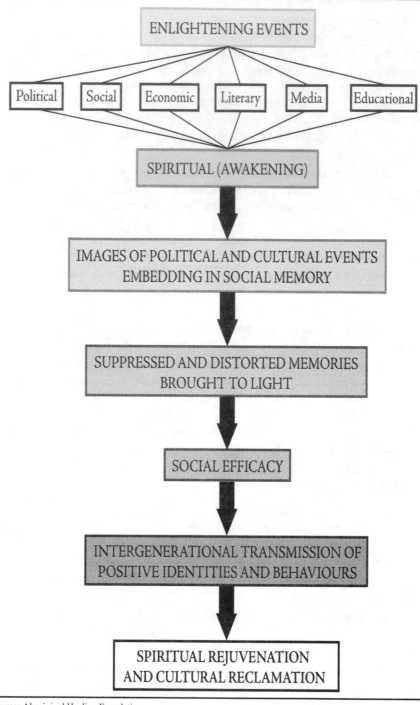

Source: Aboriginal Healing Foundation

Indigenous cultural identities reeling with what can be regarded as a pervasive and complex form of PTSD.

Figure 5.1 (page 70) depicts a model of historic trauma transmission whereby traumatic events in the past have implications and consequences for how Aboriginal peoples function in the present, both culturally and socially. In this model, symptoms of social disorders exhibited in the present are not only caused by immediate trauma; the memories and images of past traumatic events are being passed, from generation to generation, disrupting adaptive patterns of behaviour and diminishing social efficacy.

The traumatic events that accompanied the process of colonization and assimilation of Aboriginal peoples have been grouped into four categories, depending on their area of impact. These are physical impacts (introduction of infectious diseases and their consequences), economic impacts (such as forced removal of people from their familiar territories and changes in subsistence patterns), cultural/social impacts (such as changes brought by religious proselytizing, changes in social structures and cultural norms), and psychological impacts (including changes in perceived locus of social control). In the last case, individuals, families, and communities lost all sense of being able to control their lives, livelihoods, territories, and, in the case of residential schools, the care and education of their children. Multiple stressors over time elicit a response that is being named in the therapeutic literature as Complex Post-Traumatic Stress Syndrome (CPTSS).

Images and memories of traumatic events are passed on to following generations through cultural (storytelling, community discourse, myth), social (types of parenting), psychological (memory processes), and biological (e.g., hereditary predisposition to PTSD) modes of transmission. Over time, and with each generation, these images and memories of suffering become selectively distorted and not fully remembered but are still present, even if people may not be fully aware of the influence these stressors have on their own perceptions and ways of adapting. Recurrent recollections of trauma experienced by individual members of a society will, sooner or later, enter into a social narrative of the group and become transmitted to subsequent generations. Individual memories are recounted and enter into cultural collections of symbols and meanings, into rituals and ceremonies, and into the group's shared cultural memory and behavioural patterns.

Generations of people who have never experienced actual trauma may develop maladaptive patterns of behaviour and symptoms of social disorders by having memories of trauma passed on to them from their grandparents' or parents' generations. These patterns and symptoms are passed on again to their sons and daughters in the same way as the traumatic memories were to them. At this point, we can talk about an inheritance of socially learned, maladaptive behavioural patterns: addictions, helplessness, neglect.

Historic trauma is understood as both a cluster of traumatic events and a disorder in itself. Suppression of memories of painful events is a common defensive

Figure 5.3: Risk Pile Up

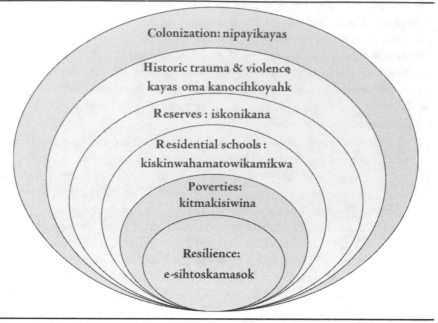

Source: Aboriginal Healing Foundation

response. Hidden collective memories of trauma, or a collective non-remembering, are passed from generation to generation, as are associated maladaptive social and behavioural patterns. There is no "single" historic trauma response; rather, there are different social disorders with respective clusters of symptoms. Historic trauma transmission disrupts adaptive social and cultural patterns and transforms them into maladaptive ones, manifesting in symptoms of social disorder. In short, historic trauma causes deep breakdowns in social functioning that may last for many years, decades, and even generations.

At the present time, many Aboriginal communities are re-engaging in positive social and cultural activities, which can be viewed as "enlightening events" (see **Figure 5.2** – page 72). Aboriginal people are revisiting their past, and making connections between the traumatic events from the past and disruptive social behaviours in the present. They are becoming aware of their memories of suffering and understanding the meaning behind the images of loss and grief. They are revitalizing their political, social, and economic spheres, and their participation in a collective enterprise of bringing wellness to their communities is creating positive changes. Good things are happening to people and communities more and more often and, one by one, these good experiences serve as competent guides for how to deal with the future.

When these experiences accumulate, people feel more competent, empowered, rejuvenated, and ready to participate in life. These very images of "enlightening events" and successful attempts to regain control become embedded in social memory and they are passed to successive generations, enabling members of the community to participate in self-healing, reclaim their spirituality and culture, and break through the interconnected bonds of loss, grief, and sadness. Using their reclaimed culture as a "healing tool," clusters of healthy, revitalized people are fostering community renewal, reforging their identities, and asserting their place within the wider Canadian society.

Resilience

The research in the present paper on Native People's historic trauma was undertaken in a broad historical and societal framework. The work that Madeleine Dion Stout reported on turned a more specific focus on human resilience in the context of residential school experience. The conference presentation elaborated on a study she authored jointly for the Aboriginal Healing Foundation (Dion Stout and Kipling 2003).

The original study on which Dion Stout's presentation was based contained no Cree words, but she included some Cree in order to locate the concept of resilience in the context of her personal knowledge. For Aboriginal people who have undergone and survived residential schooling, the memories of that experience are visceral. Dion Stout, herself a Survivor, used the Cree language (in which she is fluent) to help dislodge popular views of residential school students as passive victims and to elaborate on a culture-specific interpretation of adaptive responses. The stories told in Cree contain messages of warriorhood and survival as well as hardship, with words full of strength in adversity. By telling these stories and knowing these words, resilience and healing are tied to one's sense of identity, and retaining or recovering fluency in an Indigenous language is an assertion of agency contesting attempts to erase identity with harsh resocialization and routine corporal punishment.

Expressing concepts in Cree in a presentation on the residential school legacy, as Dion Stout has done, recognizes the intergenerational trauma and losses this legacy has inflicted on Survivors, their families, and their communities. Most importantly, words spoken in Cree or any other Indigenous language strengthen a sense of self, family, and community, while at the same time affirming all other relationships.

The presentation provided an overview of the literature, which defines resilience as the capacity to spring back from adversity and have a good life outcome despite emotional, mental, or physical distress. The definition was adapted to describe the innate capacity of Survivors to get along, get through, and get out of the risk position created by residential school experiences. The interplay between risk and protective factors is complex and fluid, and crosses lifespans and generations. Undue emphasis on risks reinforces deficits and reveals little about the human agency of residential school Survivors.

Figure 5.4: Protective Defences

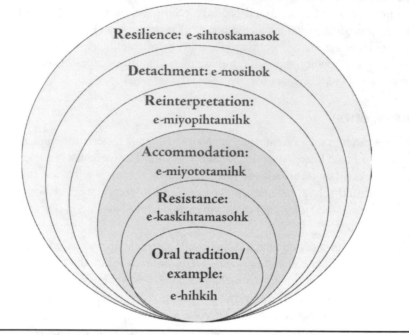

Source: Aboriginal Healing Foundation

Reframing the issue to examine risks and protective factors as understood by Aboriginal people in terms of their language and culture creates a narrative that is healing as well as explanatory. The analytical task remains the same: to consider the factors that increase the probability of a negative outcome and those that help to counteract risk and decrease individual vulnerability to adverse conditions. **Figure 5.3** (page 74) illustrates the reality that risk increases exponentially with each additional stressor. Starting from a core of resilience, the Cree expression for each layer of risk expands our understanding of the corresponding English term reaching the extreme condition of colonization of body, mind, and spirit.

- **resilience**—capacity to spring back from adversity and have a good life outcome despite emotional, mental or physical distress
- **e-sihtoskamasok**—the will and ability to stand up for one's survival
- **poverties**—multiple unmet basic human needs, leading to pathology
- **kitmakisiwina**—any action or inaction that causes deprivation of the body, mind, and spirit
- **residential schools**—the residential school system in Canada attended by Aboriginal students, including industrial schools, boarding schools, homes for students, hostels, billets, residential schools with a majority of day students, or a combination of any of the above

- **kiskinwahamatowikamikwa**—the structure where schooling takes place; the setting for an opportunity
- **reserves**—land measured out for "Indians"
- **iskonikana**—leftover land
- **historic trauma and violence**—the cumulative wounds inflicted on Aboriginal people over their lifetime and the lifetime of their ancestors, resulting in chronic symptoms that range from depression and psychic numbing to hyperglycemia and substance abuse
- **kayas oma kanocihkoyahk**—a long, visceral threat and assault
- **colonization**—the process by which local populations are displaced and subjugated
- **nipayikayas**—the deadly or extreme past

Some individuals are able to achieve a good life, despite the pile-up of adversity, by adopting protective defences. **Figure 5.4** represents layers of adaptation that build on the core of oral tradition. Resilience is the encompassing response, which includes the capacity to let go of defences when a place of safety is reached. Healing initiatives in the present need to take into account that people who have been severely traumatized in the past may be locked into rigid defences that undermine their capacity to respond flexibly to present opportunities for relationships and a good life.

- **oral tradition and example**—time-tested means of knowledge transfer and exchange that build and transform character
- **e-hihkih**—being and becoming
- **resistance**—provides opportunities to register opposition to an oppressive system. Direct resistance is overt—for example, stealing from pantries, defending younger children from mistreatment, and running away. Indirect resistance is covert—for example, wearing a "mask" to hide one's true feelings.
- **e-kaskihtamasohk**—one's self-deliverance
- **accommodation**—involves currying favour with those in power by working harder; co-operating with school personnel and feeling that giving in to the advances of staff members will provide protection
- **e-miyototamihk**—restoring peace and goodwill
- **reinterpretation**—recasting negative situations in positive ways—for example, maintaining strict composure during beatings, living out fantasies about present and future circumstances, idolizing those who ran away from school
- **e-miyopihtamihk**—aligning with order and balance
- **detachment**—distancing oneself from the source of hurt by "shutting down," not speaking or hearing, or laughing about the source of pain

- **e-mosihok**—an intuitive response to a sense of foreboding
- **resilience**—capacity to spring back from adversity and have a good life outcome despite emotional, mental or physical distress
- **e-sihtoskamasok**—the will and ability to stand up for one's survival

This framework for understanding resilience in residential school survivors can provide a basis for policy responses. Planning and research should include identifying risk and protective factors that operate in individuals and communities, conducting longitudinal and ethnographic research to map the healing of deep-rooted distress as it manifests and is relieved in particular persons and environments, and developing a resilience enhancement strategy.

Interventions should be targeted to identifying risk and protective factors at each life stage and to carrying out culture-based initiatives that acknowledge a historic trauma framework. Particular attention should be directed to Survivor populations who have been most directly affected by the residential school experience and youth who are most vulnerable to risk pile-up.

Quantitative and qualitative evaluations of progress in coping skills and adjustment levels will help to gauge success, and such evaluations should directly involve the perspectives and judgment of those who have a stake in increased personal and community resilience.

Healing of First Nations Men

The APRC presentation by Bill Mussell, a social worker, educator and mental health advocate, drew on a paper he prepared for the AHF (Mussell 2005). The paper incorporated a review of the limited literature, key informant interviews with social service and community workers, including one Elder, and Mussell's own extensive cultural and professional experience.

Fewer men than women become engaged in healing activities. This knowledge provided the impetus behind the exploration of challenges associated with healing men. A review of the sources suggests that men in general, and First Nations men and boys in particular, face a number of significant challenges.

Reports focusing on men and boys with problematic life adjustment indicate that boys, more than girls, are less likely to graduate from high school or to pursue higher education. Boys are expected to be tough and to look after themselves. They are not expected to be good students and, at home, little is done to facilitate success in the school system. In fact, they tend to learn more from their peers than from parents and caregivers. At the same time, boys are not expected to learn life skills associated with caring for and maintaining the home, and few boys are taught to make a living and provide for a family.

As adults, men are less connected in supportive ways to family and community than women. Men have difficulty expressing and addressing emotions and are less likely than women to seek professional help or to ask for assistance, especially in personal matters. They pay less attention to their physical health and are prone to deny violence and abuse in their lives. When things go wrong, both men and boys tend to blame others or they blame conditions, such as fetal alcohol spectrum disorder (FASD), addictions, the effects of residential school, and abuse.

Historically, colonization diminished the role of men as providers and protectors, and racism often prevented men from getting jobs or developing businesses that would allow them to be self-supporting. Today, too many men are no longer important role models or teachers of traditions and values for their sons and daughters. In light of the scarcity of positive models for First Nations males in many communities, the concept of the Warrior-Caregiver, introduced by Bill Mussell in healing and educational venues, is striking a responsive chord.

The concept of Warrior-Caregiver synthesizes the multiple roles and responsibilities filled by effective males at all stages of development within healthy family and community life. It represents an ideal, rather than a picture of one individual; it draws upon traditions, but speaks to the contemporary world in which First Nations men live their lives.

A Warrior-Caregiver is defined as a family and community member who cares about his environment and all things within it. He enjoys inner peace and relates well to the life forces in his world. As an adult, he takes pride in being responsible and accountable. He values safety and security, knows the importance of acceptance, understanding, and love, and enjoys relationships with people of all ages and in all stages of life. In family and community, he provides well, enjoys his work, volunteers to assist others, and is pleased to discuss needs and challenges when occasions present themselves. He has clear beliefs, stands on principle, and is alert and prepared to resolve conflict when in the presence of injustice, unfairness, and violence. He knows humility and genuine pride and believes in the ability of people to modify their outlook and behaviour. A "good" upbringing is not a necessary background to become a Warrior-Caregiver.

Warrior-Caregivers help enrich the identity of persons they interact with and the community itself. They know and facilitate awareness of connections between the past and the present and contribute to building optimism for the future. This vision of the Warrior-Caregiver as a healthy, responsible, connected First Nations' man has guided the development of practical strategies for healing historical damage. Before detailing these strategies, however, it is necessary to have a short discussion of teaching/learning models.

Prior to the introduction and imposition of formal Western education, knowledge and culture were transmitted in less formal ways among Indigenous peoples. While there were no physical institutions, learning was purposeful and took place in formal and informal settings and experiential modes. Strategies for catching game, constructing dwellings, making snowshoes, and building canoes, for example, were learned in non-formal ways. Informal learning happens when a parent, Elder, or other caregiver takes advantage of a "teachable moment" to help someone discover on their own what they need to know.

In residential schools, children did not learn anything about their family, community history, or culture, nor did they learn how to learn. Methods employed in the classrooms were designed to implant what the teacher taught as facts into the students. When these young people returned to their communities, common language and nurturing relationships to facilitate the sharing of knowledge were mostly absent. Extended families and community networks were stressed by grief at the loss of their children and by the poverty and powerlessness of their lives. Conditions for the transmission of knowledge, history, and culture from family and community to their children were impossible to create in these circumstances. These constraints on knowledge transmission between family and young people persisted when the residential school system ended.

Mediated learning is a process whereby a mediator (teacher, parent, grandparent, counsellor, healer, etc.) creates conditions that promote the integration of received information and lived experience. Connecting new information with life experience transforms it into personal knowledge, mitigating the malaise associated with formal learning, especially for boys. This learning/teaching model is designed to increase feelings of self-worth and self-esteem in learners. Whether the learning takes place in a structured environment, such as a healing program or a school, or informally within the family and community, it is especially important for men and boys who are not well prepared by prior socialization to take on the roles of caregivers and warriors.

The integration of culture and family and community history is essential to the learning process. Building upon the strengths of the family and extended family and incorporating culture, history, and traditional teachings creates an environment where boys can be nurtured and taught in a way that motivates them to become healthy, responsible, nurturing adults. Evidence is accumulating that shows how this type of learning can take place through storytelling and dialogue or during talking circles, informal and formal get-togethers, and ceremonies.

Practical strategies for healing men can be embedded in strategies for supporting healthy families and communities. One of the findings from key informant interviews is that a great many young families live with male violence. Men have major roles to fill in healing the effects of such experience and developing safe, secure, nurturing, and inspirational environments so that infants, young children, and youth can grow into healthy, strong, intelligent, and wise adults who value family and community life.

There are numerous practical strategies that can support and guide work with men. These include:

- Building upon values that reflect an Aboriginal world view and relate to the life experience of the learner

- Paying attention to family and community history, including institutionalization and posing issues in ways that connect to the learner's experience
- Offering cultural activities that speak to the learner
- Appealing to the person's intelligence
- Focusing on hands-on activities or "learning by doing"
- Focusing on the learner/client, not the practitioner; tailoring the nature and timing of interventions to fit the needs of participants
- Valuing the richness of lived-life experience.

The AHF Final Report

The final report of the AHF is published in three volumes and builds on insights derived from more than three dozen commissioned studies, including 13 case studies of community healing projects. *A Healing Journey: Reclaiming Wellness* (volume 1) presents a narrative covering the formation, activities, and accomplishments of the AHF over seven years; major findings are documented more fully in volumes 2 and 3, along with implications for future healing initiatives. *Measuring Progress: Program Evaluation* (volume 2) presents quantitative data from successive evaluations and interprets project impacts. *Promising Healing Practices* (volume 3) reports on in-depth survey responses from community projects.

Volume 2: Measuring Progress: Program Evaluation

Kim Scott, evaluator and author of volume 2, highlights evidence of the impact that the program has been having. The most significant question asked in the evaluation of AHF program activity during the period 2000 to 2005 is "What difference does it make?" Methods of inquiry included a review of project files, three national mail-out surveys in 2001, 2002, and 2004, respectively, telephone interviews with AHF board members and personnel, five national focus groups, 13 in-depth case studies, and 1,479 individual participant questionnaires (IPQs) that captured information about individuals' experiences in the therapeutic heal-ing process.

An estimated 111,170 individuals have participated in healing and, of these, almost two-thirds had never previously participated in a similar program. AHF-funded organizations hired and trained large numbers of Aboriginal people: 4,833 employees (91% of full-time and 85% of part-time workers are Aboriginal people), and 28,133 participants in training programs. Over time, projects demonstrated an increased capacity to meet the need for healing and they facilitated, through training, an increased connection between those in need and those able to help. At the same time, project teams identified increasing numbers of people with special needs who required access to longer-term individual treatment or specialist services, such as addiction treatment. Participants rated the following healing services as most effective: Elders, ceremonies, individual counselling, healing/talking circles, and traditional medicine. Western therapies were rated least effective.

Overall, people who participated in healing projects felt that they were better prepared to handle difficult issues (72%), to move beyond past traumas (76%), to handle future trauma (79%), and to find ways to get support once the project was over (69%). Project teams, however, noted a wide variability in "success" between individuals. This was attributed primarily the individual's "readiness to heal" and the fit between participants' needs and the intervention offered.

Readiness to heal or "fit" was sometimes assessed through a vigorous intake process, but most projects worked with a variety of priority-setting strategies. Some placed Survivors and their descendants at the top of the list and accepted them without assessment. Other projects identified those at greatest risk as a top priority, or specific target groups (gender, Aboriginal identity, sexual orientation, age), or those who self-initiated enrolment. However, there was recognition among some of the projects, expressed in the case studies or by focus group participants, that an individual's readiness to heal had an impact on their success in the program.

In assessing readiness, projects are determining who is likely to benefit most from the program being offered. For example, readiness to participate in therapeutic intervention is indicated in individuals who are self-motivated, interested, and willing to participate, as well as in those with a track record of regular, ongoing, or previous participation in healing. Other indicators include having a reasonably stable lifestyle and being alcohol- and drug-free. Individuals should be prepared to be accountable for their past and their present behaviour and have a source of outside support before, during, and after the program.

Recognizing that there are gradations of readiness, great flexibility and a variety of strategies were outlined to engage those who were not yet ready. For example, communities used public awareness campaigns, including education on the legacy of residential schools, and program promotion; they engaged in outreach to individuals and specific target groups; and they organized feasts and other social events and invited the community to participate.

Communities also exhibited varying degrees of readiness to engage in and support healing. High local demand for services, as opposed to high need, is a prime index of community readiness. Communities are generally ready when they exhibit an ongoing commitment to wellness, when whole groups are interested in or attending addictions programs, and community leaders support these efforts.

One significant piece of learning that emerged in the evaluation is that the nature and extent of Survivor involvement in projects are indicators of community readiness for healing. For example, in the early stages, the fact that Survivors want healing services is an important indicator. This demand for services is very different from situations where a high need for healing programs is evident but there is little desire on the part of community members and leaders to act.

Community progress along a continuum can be tracked in four stages. A demand for healing services often emerges along with a growing awareness of residential school history and its impacts on individuals, their families and previous generations. In the early stages of healing, progress is indicated by the creation of opportunities for Survivors to meet, connect, support each other, and encourage one another to heal. Survivors groups may meet informally or formally, with the support of a local, regional, or national organization.

During the second stage of community healing, as Survivors continue to meet, momentum gathers, and groups are more formally established. Indicators of success include the extent to which Survivors are involved in decision making in a formal healing project, the level of support of local leadership, Survivor involvement in the design of programs and services to meet their needs, and their involvement in hiring decisions for members of healing teams.

These indicators continue to be tracked in the third and fourth stages of community healing, with increased levels of Survivor action and involvement being expected as more and more community members, other Survivors, and leaders become involved. By the fourth stage, many Survivors have moved from wanting help to giving help.

It is interesting to note the dual role Survivors play in the healing process; evidence from project surveys, case studies, and IPQs reveals that those who are seeking healing and those who can facilitate healing are often the same people at different stages of their journey. It is clear that the qualities and attributes of healers/helpers[5] can have a profound impact on success. Identifying the range of skills and qualities possessed by effective healers/helpers was one of the tasks presented to focus groups.

In general, formal training and post-secondary education are valued, as are traditional training and experience, and knowledge of the local culture, language, and the community itself. A good healer/helper has a solid track record of ethical conduct and is recognized and respected by the community. People are advised to be wary of self-proclaimed healers.

Other qualities include evidence of stable recovery; that is, Survivors have worked through their own issues, including grief and anger, and are willing and able to share their experiences with others. Well-established personal boundaries protect them from burnout and harm. They are fearless and unflappable leaders who are comfortable with and knowledgeable about the residential school Legacy. They have an open mind, are free from the need to control people and situations, and have a clear understanding of their own limitations. When necessary, they make knowledgeable and appropriate referrals. Spiritually grounded, they have a

Figure 5.5: Promising Healing Practices

Source: Aboriginal Healing Foundation

respectful relationship with the land and are comfortable leading or participating in traditional ceremonies.

Skills of effective healer/helpers include the ability to listen attentively, process intense emotion, diffuse negativity, and differentiate between the need for crisis intervention and long-term therapy. In a crisis, they respond quickly and effectively and they have the skills to intervene in and prevent suicide. They understand the connection between the physical, mental, emotional, and spiritual aspects of self and know where trauma is stored in the body.

Skilled healers/helpers understand and dissipate lateral violence, counsel sexual abuse victims and/or perpetrators, and are comfortable discussing healthy sexuality openly. They have access to a variety of techniques and interventions, either as part of their own skill set or as a member of a multi-skilled healing team. They use traditional medicine themselves or partner with a traditional healer, and their commitment to ongoing learning includes working with clinical supervision.

In summary, three significant contributions to our collective learning about healing from the residential school Legacy have been highlighted: the link between readiness/fit and outcomes of interventions; the participation and leadership of Survivors as an indicator of success; and the qualities and characteristics of the good healers/helpers. Other learning, not addressed here, relates to the extent and complexity of the healing journey and the need to devote sufficient time and resources to sustain progress over the long term.

Volume 3: Promising Healing Practices in Aboriginal Communities

Linda Archibald, researcher and author of volume 3, reported on healing programs designed by and with Aboriginal people that make innovative use of both traditional and contemporary therapies. Research into promising healing practices[6] has led to the development of a framework for understanding trauma and healing, a framework which is based on the experiences of AHF-funded projects and which can be used to guide the development of new programs and services.

This study was based on responses by 103 AHF-funded projects to a questionnaire about healing programs and practices that are working well, supplemented by information gathered through five focus groups held throughout 2003–2004 (two in Ottawa and one each in Montreal, Winnipeg, and Iqaluit), internal file review, and workshops held at a national gathering in Edmonton.

Diversity is the word that best describes the healing methods and approaches found to be working well in Aboriginal communities. Promising healing practices share a number of key characteristics that are interrelated and mutually reinforcing, as portrayed in **Figure 5.5**.

In this figure, Aboriginal values, personal and cultural safety, and capacity to heal are viewed as necessary in the development of successful healing programs. The programs themselves are built around three intervention strategies: reclaiming history, cultural interventions, and therapeutic healing. The first three characteristics can be viewed as necessary elements of effective healing programs. The last three—referred to as the three pillars of healing—represent components of a holistic healing strategy.

In the figure, historic trauma theory is positioned across the top, providing a context for understanding that the residential school system represents only one of many historical assaults on Aboriginal people. At the socio-political level, the accumulated effects of oppression and dispossession are viewed as a root cause of the compromised social, economic, and health status of Aboriginal populations. At a personal level, they underlie the need for healing. However, we also recognize that individual and community experiences vary greatly and, therefore, the nature and extent of their losses will vary accordingly.

Situated below "Historic Trauma" are the program elements that support the healing process:

Aboriginal Values/World View. Successful healing programs reflect the values, underlying philosophy and world view of the people who design them. For healing programs designed by and with Aboriginal people, this includes values of wholeness, balance, harmony, relationship, connection to the land and the natural environment, and a view of healing as process and a lifelong journey.

Personal and Cultural Safety. Establishing safety is a prerequisite to healing from trauma. Promising healing practices ensure the physical and emotional security of participants. Moreover, for Aboriginal people whose cultures and beliefs have been under attack, creating safety extends beyond establishing physical and emotional security to building a culturally welcoming healing environment. Cultural safety includes providing services consistent with and responsive to Aboriginal values, beliefs, and practices, as well as creating a physical setting that reflects and reinforces the culture and values of participants.

Capacity to Heal. Skilled healers, therapists, Elders, and volunteers guide promising healing practices. Respondents expressed high regard for the skills, dedication, and capabilities of their healing teams. This is consistent with the best practices literature, which consistently identifies committed, skilled staff, and volunteers as characteristic of successful projects. Healing teams that include Aboriginal people and Survivors, especially people from the home community, were recognized as contributing to success.

The next level of the framework addresses intervention strategies. Healing is posited as a three-pronged process, and referred to in the framework as the *three pillars of healing*: reclaiming history, cultural interventions, and therapeutic healing. Participants can move back and forth among these interventions, concentrate their efforts in one area, or participate in two or all three at the same time.

Reclaiming History. This first pillar includes learning about the residential school system, its policy goals and objectives, and its impacts on individuals, families, and communities. It also includes delving into family and community histories as well as Canadian history from an Aboriginal perspective. This is a form of psycho-education, an intervention with recognized benefits with respect to preparing participants for the healing journey. Moreover, work in the fields of post-traumatic stress, historic trauma, and decolonization all recognize the need to acknowledge and mourn individual and collective losses, including losses that occurred in previous generations. The process allows personal trauma to be understood within a social context and serves to reduce self-blame, denial, guilt, and isolation. Understanding history can be a catalyst for healing and pave the way for mourning what was lost, a recognized stage in the trauma recovery process.

Cultural Interventions. The second pillar includes activities that engage people in a process of recovering and reconnecting with their culture, language, history, spirituality, traditions, and ceremonies. Such activities reinforce self-esteem and the development of a positive cultural identity. These are powerful, empowering experiences that provide a secure base from which to launch personal healing. They also contribute to individual and community healing. The evidence suggests that culture is good medicine. It also promotes a sense of belonging that can support individuals in their healing journey.

Therapeutic Healing. The third pillar encompasses the wide variety of therapies and healing interventions used by communities to facilitate recovery from trauma.

Practitioners use a broad range of traditional therapies, often in combination with Western or alternative therapies. In fact, more than half (56.3%) used traditional therapies coupled with Western and/or alternative methods The approaches chosen are holistic and culturally relevant and they recognize that healing from severe trauma, especially sexual abuse, can be a long-term undertaking.

Multiple interventions were standard among the projects participating in this study: 86.4% identified promising healing practices that include interventions in more than one area. The most popular approach involved a combination of therapeutic healing and cultural interventions (42.7%). This was followed closely by approaches falling into all three areas—reclaiming history, cultural interventions, and therapeutic healing (33%). The use of multiple intervention strategies is consistent with Aboriginal values, and it suggests that projects are implementing a holistic approach to healing.

Situated below the three pillars of healing in **Figure 5.5**—and in many ways determining a particular individual's need for healing—are factors related to their personal, family, and community history. These include an individual's particular experiences, strengths, motivations, resources, and relationships within the family, as well as the social, political, and economic conditions in which they live. Other factors also have an influence, such as the community culture, language, history, and resources, and the community's capacity to support healing. These individual and community characteristics represent a series of variables that impact upon both the need for healing and the success or failure of the healing process.

Healing programs and strategies for specific target populations, such as women, men, and youth, are built around the realities and experiences relevant to each group. Similarly, programs for Inuit and Métis, like that of First Nations, are rooted in distinct cultures and take account of differences in the experience of colonization. Still, the framework for understanding trauma and healing applies to each of these groups.

Among Inuit, for example, the experience of colonization and the introduction of residential schools are relatively recent phenomena. Traditional approaches to healing placed a strong emphasis on talking through one's problems. Land-based activities, talking therapies, drumming, singing, and prayer are incorporated into promising healing programs.

Métis' experiences with the residential school system and its intergenerational impact are only beginning to be documented. Breaking the silence and recovering Métis identity and pride are recurring themes. Oral history gathering, Survivor support groups, parenting classes, gatherings, and traditional and Western therapies are all techniques that support healing.

In urban centres, the mixture of cultures, languages, people, and backgrounds leads to an approach inclusive of First Nations, Metis, Inuit, and diverse Aboriginal people. A number of projects attempt to utilize resource people and Elders from a variety of Aboriginal cultural groups so that the clients' backgrounds are represented. Medicine wheel teachings, healing circles, smudging, and sweat lodge ceremonies are available in cities across Canada, often in combination with Western and alternative therapies. It is especially noteworthy that more than 80% of urban programs place an emphasis on spirituality.

Women have been at the forefront of the healing movement and have partici-pated in AHF-funded projects to a greater degree than men. For many women, safety is a major concern and this is often best addressed in women-only groups. Engaging men in healing has been challenging for many projects but success has been enhanced by adopting a male-centred approach, which reframes healing as an act of courage and provides both hands-on and land-based activities and access to male healers, counsellors, team members, facilitators, and role models. Psycho-education that includes exploring ideas about masculinity, gender roles (tradi-tional and Western), and the impact of colonization on traditional male roles work well, as do experiential therapies, such as psychodrama, and providing a variety of support services.

Among youth, a strategy that focuses on strengths rather than problems is preferred. Promising approaches include healthy peer modeling, peer support, cultural activities, teachings, learning aboriginal history, connecting with Elders, active non-verbal activities such as sports and crafts, and working in partnership with schools.

Volume 1: A Healing Journey: Reclaiming Wellness

A Healing Journey (volume 1) takes a narrative approach to the work, impact, and future of the AHF. The volume provides a brief organizational history describing its origins and early initiatives, and the structures and processes established to fulfill the AHF mandate as detailed in the funding agreement that set parameters for distributing the grant of $350 million. Results of evaluations and promising practices research reported more fully in volumes 2 and 3 are profiled. The volume concludes with lessons for the ongoing work of healing in communities and argues for renewal of the AHF mandate and funding.

The APRC presentation by Marlene Brant Castellano, author of volume 1, focused on evidence from research and evaluations that the AHF has mapped new territory in community healing, setting down guideposts for future Aboriginal-specific healing initiatives.

The healing needs uncovered in the course of the AHF's work make it clear that one-on-one therapies delivered by mental health professionals are by themselves inadequate to respond to the pervasiveness and depth of trauma that continue to reverberate in Aboriginal communities The distress that requires healing interven-tion is not limited to the span of an individual's life. Aboriginal communities have suffered repeated shocks from epidemics, displacement, and loss of control over their lives. The loss of children to residential schools laid down another layer of trauma and its distorting effects. When children returned from residential school lacking language and relationships and practical skills that would enable them to reintegrate into the community, the capacity of extended families to support recovery from abusive and demeaning experiences was compromised by their own grief over multiple losses.

First Nations, Inuit, and Metis communities and urban Aboriginal communities of interest seized the opportunity provided by AHF funding to submit 4,612 proposals and sign 1,346 contribution agreements for self-directed healing projects over the seven years covered by the final report. They made it clear that everyone who attended residential school was impacted, not only those who were subjected to physical or sexual assault while there. The need for healing extends to families who suffered alienation from their children, communities who saw the removal of large proportions of their children over decades, and subsequent generations who inherited distorted memories and battered self-esteem. Although healing the legacy of residential schools was necessarily the focus of community projects, those experiences were only one dimension of the risks that overwhelmed the resilience of individuals and communities.

Project reports consistently demonstrated that healing takes time. The work of healing starts with outreach and the breaking of self-imposed silences. The motives for keeping silence are diverse. Some Survivors believe they can protect their children by withholding knowledge of what they had endured. Others adopt a common response to trauma by suppressing memories and avoiding triggers that bring the past to consciousness. Still others hide shame at complicity with their tormentors or Survivor guilt that they live while their relations and peers have died. When the silence is broken, a tide of remembrance and pain is unleashed requiring skilled, persistent, and supportive responses over time.

Along with the depth and extent of need, deep currents of resilience were also discovered. Survivors of residential schools are themselves a key resource in healing. As they embark on their healing journey and uncover their innate resilience, they want to help others. In fact, some of the most prominent leaders and role models in contemporary Aboriginal life are Survivors of residential schools. Survivors who take on the role of healer/helper continue to carry vulnerabilities that need to be balanced with team support to protect them from overtaxing their emergent strength.

Professional therapies have a role in community healing and are almost always supplemented and modified by cultural approaches. Creating cultural safety in concert with personal safety for trauma survivors requires particular competencies on the part of healer/helpers. These competencies include familiarity with the history and protocols of the local community and the strengths and vulnerabilities of family networks, along with experience that can call into play the words, gestures, and symbols that heal rather than hurt. Because the impacts of trauma reverberate through extended family networks and across generations, healing initiatives must rebuild community support networks as well as reinforce individual resilience.

Reports from communities have advanced understanding of the many ways that spiritual healing is mediated as an essential dimension of holistic healing. Spiritual healing involves the discovery or recovery of meaning in existence. Spiritual healing facilitates connection with a life force that is greater than personal strengths, flaws, and circumstances. It puts individuals on the path of right living, where they have something to give and freely share it. It is often mediated through prayer and ceremony, healing circles, and a relationship with an Elder or mentor, and may include Christian practice or traditional teachings. Living on the land, feasting, and sharing traditional foods and stories that awaken awareness all play a part in spiritual healing, depending on the cultural context. Skilled practitioners who themselves have undergone rigorous apprenticeship guide individuals through stages of healing and awareness at a pace that allows integration of learning in daily life. The insights revealed in community reports confirm that spiritual healing is congruent with the most ambitious goals of psychotherapy.

Overall, the story of the Aboriginal Healing Foundation is one of hope and resilience set, nevertheless, against a background of massive risks to wellness that have accumulated over generations. The final report presents evidence of the effectiveness of AHF-funded interventions, estimates the extent of unmet needs, and argues that time is required to peel back the layers of risk that still tax the capacity of individuals and communities to achieve good life outcomes.

Conclusion

Media coverage of the tsunami in Southeast Asia and of Hurricane Katrina in the southern United States has created public awareness of how whole communities are affected by massive shocks. Aboriginal communities across Canada are engaged in recovery from a succession of disasters comparable in magnitude to a flu epidemic, followed by a hurricane, followed by occupation of their homelands, and the removal of thousands of their children.

Political agency and economic vitality in Aboriginal communities are necessary complements to interventions that support healing from historic trauma. As recovery proceeds on all fronts, documentation from community-directed healing initiatives funded by the AHF presents compelling evidence of how community healing can be pursued most effectively.

The healing paradigm that is emerging places healing interventions in the context of historical experience and cultural diversity. Interventions engage the energy and capacity of local personnel who bring cultural competence and growing expertise as they partner with western-trained professionals, local agencies, and community leaders. Vulnerable individuals who have started the journey to wellness are recognized as offering inspiration and support to those further back, with responsibilities appropriate to their strengths and team support in areas and periods of fragility. Community-led healing gives substance to the ideal of holistic healing involving body, mind, emotions, and spirit. Training of healer/helpers draws on both traditional wisdom and scientific knowledge.

As the first mandate of the AHF was winding down, communities made urgent pleas that the work of healing must continue to bring a degree of closure for those who had come forward for help, and to reach out to those who were just becoming aware of the possibility of healing.[7] Project personnel also underlined the need for specialized training to address the complex needs being presented.

Personnel in community projects made an extraordinary commitment to participating in research to report on participation and outcomes and to map promising healing practices. The healing approaches presented at the APRC are derived from analysis of self-reports from projects and participants, and are detailed more fully in research papers and the final report available from the AHF. These approaches require further testing and refinement to articulate a paradigm of community healing that can be incorporated into educational materials and training programs.

Advancing knowledge of healing modalities for Aboriginal people and others living with the intergenerational impacts of trauma will be a research challenge for the next mandate of the Aboriginal Healing Foundation.

Endnotes

1 The speakers in the APRC sessions, in addition to the two authors, were Cynthia Wesley-Esquimaux, Madeleine Dion Stout, Bill Mussell, and Kim Scott, all of whom gave access to their speaking notes for this paper. The authors also acknowledge the contribution of Gail Valaskakis, Director of Research for the Aboriginal Healing Foundation, in conceiving and directing the research on which this paper is based.

2 The term "Survivor" was adopted by the Aboriginal Healing Foundation to refer to former students of residential schools and in some contexts those who were intergenerationally impacted.

3 Report of the Aboriginal Healing Foundation (2006a,b,c). An interim extension of the AHF mandate with an additional grant of $40 million was announced in the federal budget in 2005.

4 This section draws on Wesley-Esquimaux and Smolewski (2004).

5 The term "healer/helper" encompasses members of project teams directly engaged in therapeutic healing work, including counsellors, therapists, traditional healers, circle keepers, Elders, etc.

6 The term "promising healing practices" is used because it suggests movement along the healing path, and acknowledges the likelihood of success without implying that only a particular practice or approach will succeed. Yet, like best practices, promising practices encourage learning, information sharing, innovation and adaptations in other settings.

7 In May 2006 the Minister of Indian and Northern Affairs announced an agreement providing compensation to former residential school students and a further grant of $125 million to support community healing initiatives for an additional five years.

References

Dion Stout, Madeleine, and Gregory Kipling. 2003. *Aboriginal people, resilience, and the residential school legacy*. Research report, Aboriginal Healing Foundation, Ottawa, ON.

Kishk Anaquot Health Research, 2006. *Report of the Aboriginal Healing Foundation*. 2006b. Volume 2: *Measuring progress: Program evaluation*. Ottawa, ON: Aboriginal Healing Foundation.

Mussell, Bill. 2005. *Warrior-Caregivers; Understanding the challenges and healing of First Nations Men*. Research report, Aboriginal Healing Foundation, Ottawa, ON.

Report of the Aboriginal Healing Foundation. 2006a. Vol. 1: *A healing journey: Reclaiming wellness*. Ottawa, ON: Aboriginal Healing Foundation.

Report of the Aboriginal Healing Foundation. 2006c. Vol. 3: *Promising healing practices in Aboriginal communities*. Ottawa, ON: Aboriginal Healing Foundation.

Royal Commission on Aboriginal Peoples. 1996. *Looking forward, looking back*. Vol. 1 of *Report of the Royal Commission on Aboriginal Peoples*. Ottawa: Royal Commission on Aboriginal Peoples.

Wesley-Esquimaux, Cynthia, and Magdalena Smolewski. 2004. *Historic trauma and Aboriginal healing*. Research report, Aboriginal Healing Foundation, Ottawa, ON.

6

A Cultural Approach to Aboriginal Youth Sport and Recreation: Observations from Year One

Janice Forsyth, Michael Heine, and Joannie Halas

Introduction

In the early 1990s, the Royal Commission on Aboriginal Peoples (RCAP) consulted with Aboriginal youth throughout Canada about the context of their lives and what they needed in order to flourish. The youth consulted spoke passionately and intelligently on a wide range of social issues, including the need for more sport and recreation programs in rural and urban settings. A holistic perspective emerged from their concerns, emphasizing the important ways organized sport and recreation contribute to individual health and community well-being, and reflecting their frustrations with existing delivery systems, in which access and equity issues severely limited the positive role sport and recreation played in their lives (Government of Canada 1996).

In the final report, published in 1996, the Royal Commission praised Aboriginal youth for the quality and relevance of their input, and for energizing the political struggles of Aboriginal peoples in Canada:

> We were encouraged to see that Aboriginal youth, when presented with a problem, imme-
> diately tend to look for solutions that are practical and feasible and that will work at the
> community level. It became clear that for young Aboriginal men and women, community
> development is not about infrastructure, but about people and about building a stronger
> community. (Government of Canada 1996, 148)

These statements, while calling attention to the positive potential in Aboriginal youth, also highlight two key weaknesses that impede advances in the organizational structure of Aboriginal sport and recreation programs in Canada. First, Aboriginal youth have limited involvement in the development and implementation of programs designed to meet their needs. Second, existing delivery systems generally do not meet the needs of Aboriginal youth. For example, the Aboriginal youth consulted for the RCAP identified the need for a cultural basis to sport by incorporating Aboriginal youth perspectives in program development and delivery. This lack of understanding and awareness of a cultural basis to sport ensures that Aboriginal and non-Aboriginal organizers will continue to be frustrated with their inability to engage Aboriginal youth in physical activities and serves to extend and legitimize paternalistic attitudes when designing policies and programs for them.

The Research Project

We are currently entering the second year of a three-year study, based in Winnipeg, to explore how the positive potential in sport and recreation can be mobilized to provide Aboriginal youth with opportunities to participate in physical activity programs that will improve their overall health and well-being and expand their leadership skills in ways that respect and enhance their cultural identities. At the completion of the three-year study, our ultimate goal will be to have fostered relationships across groups that will strengthen the long-term efficacy and sustainability of a culturally relevant Aboriginal sport and recreation community in Winnipeg.

Underpinning the practical implications of the study are four academic and policy objectives. Currently, the research literature identifies barriers to participation (e.g., Reid, Tremblay, Pelletier, and McKay, 1994), and provides *atheoretical* examples of successful practice that are too often short term and unsustainable. In this project, existing sport, recreation, and education groups collaborate with a research team to apply theoretically driven models as a means to effectively engage Aboriginal youth in culturally relevant ways. A description of the process to initiate and develop such collaborations is one of the intended outcomes and will be used to inform policy directives that can be used in other jurisdictions and social contexts.

Next, the research literature informs us of the important health and wellness outcomes of daily physical activity, yet it provides very little information on how to design culturally relevant interventions that will increase physical activity levels, particularly for Aboriginal youth. While there is some evidence concerning the design of meaningful and relevant sport, recreation, and physical education programs (Fox et al. 1998; Halas 2002), research in this area tends to raise more questions than it answers.

Third, the incorporation of Indigenous research methodologies is rare in the research literature, although it holds the potential to add much to the knowledge base of qualitative, community-based, action research. Finally, development of a model for delivering a culturally relevant sport and recreation program in an urban environment will empower Aboriginal youth to exert control over their own health and wellness issues, thus providing a "counter story" (Solorzano and Yosso 2002) to the discourse of pathology that pervades much of the research literature on Aboriginal youth.

Framework

We recognize the obstacles that constrain the participation of Aboriginal youth in sport and recreation, and to offset the debilitating implications of the discourse on pathology, we have chosen to work from a "strengths" perspective. It is based on the premise that "disadvantaged" or "at-risk" groups possess strengths that often go unrecognized and underutilized by researchers engaged in community development initiatives (Saleebey 1996). In their review of health and wellness programs in urban Aboriginal communities in Canada, Davidson, Brasfield, Quressette, and Demerais likewise conclude that projects initiated from a deficit perspective "failed to provide holistic and culturally appropriate solutions" (1997, 38) for Aboriginal peoples because they tended to neglect existing structural barriers that limit Aboriginal people from gaining access to human and financial resources that could help them to build better lives. The pervasiveness of this approach should not be underestimated. As Chapin (1995) points out, the findings of research projects founded on deficits are regularly translated into social policies that directly affect people's lives. Often, the results can be devastating, as complex social problems are reduced to individual pathologies that identify individuals (and their families) as the sole cause of his or her own failings (Halas and Hanson 2001).

Far from denying existing realities, a strengths-based approach offers a different starting point for asking questions, engaging in strategic partnerships, and finding appropriate solutions. Projects such as ours are founded on the premise that Aboriginal youth possess many *strengths* that adults need to recognize and respect—they are passionate, driven, and highly committed; they want to help, but often need the opportunity to express their ideas and display their skills in a positive and supportive environment, that is to say, what is really required is a strategy for seeing what is already available (Weick et al. 1989, 354). Within the context of our study, the strengths approach begins by inviting the participants to identify meaningful physical activities in which they may already be engaged or wish to pursue. Pre-existing strengths are thereby identified and can be built upon. The strengths perspective provides a positive means to evaluate, enhance, and (re)construct sport and recreation opportunities because it encourages people and communities themselves to identify their greatest assets and to recognize what they already do well. They are not merely asked to improve their lot by fitting better into the mainstream system.

Furthermore, our understanding of the various ways in which power relations can influence research practices, combined with our interest in collaborating on relevant undertakings with Aboriginal community members, has led us to adopt an Indigenous research methodology so as to privilege Indigenous concerns and practices in the research process (Smith 1999). We connect our interpretation of Indigenous methodology with traditional Native educational practices as described in the "Circle of Courage" (to name but one relevant example), which promotes belonging, independence, responsibility, and generosity as the central, unifying values from which to frame educational and youth work (Brendtro, Brokenleg, and van Bockern 1990). We use these values to guide our pedagogical interactions with young people in the study, as well as to inform our analysis of the cultural meaning of sport and recreation, particularly when Aboriginal perspectives are compared with mainstream approaches. For example, in one after-school physical activity program, we engage with and learn from Aboriginal high school students who have volunteered as mentors to design and deliver once-weekly recreation programming for early-years' students at a nearby school. As ethical research practice, this mentorship program (along with the after-school programming in our second school) provides immediate, tangible outcomes (enhanced access to physical activity opportunities) for all our research participants.

Context

The timing of this study coincides nicely with the convergence of growing public interest in the quality and quantity of daily physical activity programs available for youth in Winnipeg. Three documents, in particular, shaped our understanding of the field in which we are operating. First, the *Public Use Facilities Study* (Economic Research Associates 2004) provides an inventory of facilities in high- and low-income neighbourhoods, and examines several options for improving local recreation programming. Second, a detailed report on this study appeared in the *Winnipeg Free Press* in the winter of 2005. The findings of this public investigation clarified the possible ramifications of the various policy options identified in the *Public Use Facilities Study*. Third, the Healthy Kids, Healthy Futures Task Force, established in 2004, included a large-scale community consultation process, in which Manitobans were asked to provide their views on how to keep children and youth active and healthy into their adult lives. The *Healthy Kids, Healthy Futures Task Force Report* (2005) outlined the need for more quality, daily physical activity among youth and identified community strategies on how to achieve that goal.

In addition to its contemporary relevance, this study is strengthened by already existing relationships between education officials in two school divisions and one of the researchers (Halas), as well as graduate and undergraduate students who have been working with Aboriginal youth on a participatory action research (PAR) project since 2004. Results from this study have identified some key barriers that inhibit Aboriginal youth participation in high school physical education and sport (e.g., lack of cultural understanding between mainstream teachers and youth, students "opting out" of participation based on perceptions of exclusion, minimal opportunity to compete with other groups of Aboriginal youth). To offset the constraints on effective youth engagement represented by issues of race, class, power, and privilege (Halas 2004), our research team works as allies (Bishop 1994) with school officials, who are deeply committed to improving the educational lives of their Aboriginal students through physical education.

Year One activities focused on re-energizing our relationship with the two school divisions, familiarizing school officials with the current project, and establishing after-school physical activity programs at each research site. Year Two activities will focus on data collection with the youth at the two schools and building relationships with community partners. Year Three will include another round of data collection at each school, as well as hosting a large forum in which student participants will work with local allies and share their ideas on how public policy can better meet the sport and recreation needs of urban Aboriginal youth. Using a participatory action research model, a community-based, youth-driven sport and recreation agenda will be identified as a means to address barriers and enhance access in an important Canadian urban environment for Aboriginal youth.

Methods

A number of different information-gathering approaches, including participant observation, individual and small group interviews with Aboriginal youth, social mapping, and photovoice (participant visual auto-ethnography), have been incorporated into the project. A broad range of methods was selected in order to help illuminate the complex social experiences that shape Aboriginal youth involvement in sport and recreation. For example, the graduate, undergraduate, and older high school students who run the after school programs keep daily journals in which they record their observations in the gym and reflect on their own practices as mentors. As such, the journals function simultaneously as a form of participant observation and as means for critical reflection.

Social mapping and photovoice form the cornerstone of our data collection methods. Maps can be used for a wide variety of reasons. In this study, social mapping—that is, developing visual representations of community-use patterns and social dynamics in an urban setting employing cartographic metaphors—will be used to communicate important social information in an effort to "reclaim the commons" and depict "strategies of resistance" (Aberly 1993, 4): "What you are being encouraged to do is honestly describe what you already know about where you live in a manner that adds momentum to positive forces of change" (5). Maps that depict this type of social information show the "flow of life," which is seldom examined before it is disturbed (27). Thus, "a map becomes more than a series of lines; it becomes a visual agenda for action, a turf to defend, a series of memories that remind of action and pleasure and history" (73). Maps visually demonstrate that boundaries, far from being fixed and permanent, are always evolving and can be pushed back or changed. Researchers who seek to help local populations reclaim communal spaces and offer alternative visions for the possibilities of public policy development might find social mapping of benefit:

> If images of our neighbourhoods, our communities, and our regions are made by others, then it is *their* future that will be imposed. But if maps are made by resident groups and individuals who have quality of life as a goal, then images of a very different nature will predominate. Locally made maps will hang on the walls of community halls, town offices, and in school corridors. They will communicate layers of interconnected alternatives that can be implemented by persistent and courageous local action. The wisdom that this alternative vision speaks—sustainability, self-reliance, social justice—an incorruptible, decentralized power that is almost impossible to divert: the first step toward abandoning a status quo based on globalized corporate control, the commoditization of life, and institutionalized exploitation. (130–31)

There are a number of different ways to do social mapping. The method varies depending on the desired outcomes. In our study, for example, we are using 1) large- and small-scale maps of Winnipeg to plot physical spaces, 2) a sketch mapping technique with youth to plot their personal physical biographies in map form, and 3) photovoice to add visual representations and narrative meaning to the maps (Wang and Burris 1997). In addition to identifying the "active spaces" where youth engage in healthful physical activities, the maps call attention to the symbology of "empty spaces," those areas youth cannot access for a variety of reasons (e.g., costs, safety, regulated times, private interests, etc.).

Social mapping fits well with the underlying assumptions of the strengths perspective in that it does not merely provide a site inventory, it creates a dynamic visual representation of the strengths and experiences of Aboriginal youth (Strack, Magill, and McDonagh 2003). A map cannot change the neighbourhood, but it can be a window, rendering visible the options for change. The purpose of this research study is to demonstrate, visually, where urban Aboriginal youth, in their own view, spend time engaged in healthful recreation practices. The overall goal is to improve access to those spaces in order to encourage greater physical activity among urban Aboriginal youth.

Training and Mentorship

At the foundation of the entire research project is the training and mentoring of graduate, undergraduate, and high school students. At present, the project consists of an 11-member research team, including one coordinator, four graduate students, four undergraduate students, one high school student, and one community member. Ten of the team members are Aboriginal (First Nations and Métis) and one is non-Aboriginal. The team is divided evenly by gender. The demographics are important because of the need to build capacity among Aboriginal people as they work to rebuild their communities and establish new ones in urban environments. Consistent with the ethics of a participatory action research model, we also view our many youth participants and adult partner groups as co-researchers within the study. Through our collaborations, we seek to promote the value of community-based research as a tool for capacity building.

Not only do the student team members who carry out the day-to-day operations of the project have to be able to coordinate after-school programs, interact respectfully with urban Aboriginal youth, and liaise with non-Aboriginal administrative and educational personnel, they are also required to apply the broad range of qualitative information-gathering methods described above, carry out data coding, and assist with analyzing findings using computer-based tools. Beyond such pragmatic concerns, they should be sympathetic towards the political intents of community-based, participatory action research, and be positively interested in the uses of academic research for purposes of social activism and community empowerment—in other words, in the principal goals of Indigenous methodology capacity development and the enabling of political empowerment and self-determination.

Such a wide array of objectives and intents tends to place considerable stress on the human and material resources of any research project. Considerable personal commitments on the part of all concerned, and not inconsiderable material resources as well, are required to sustain such ambitious project goals. The objectives of the recently launched SSRHC Aboriginal Research Grants Program map well to the intents of our present project. The SSHRC support has enabled us to define—and, for now, sustain—the (perhaps) bold scope of our project. Our project's ultimate acceptance in the Aboriginal community remains to be determined, but to the extent that the intent of the SSHRC Aboriginal Research Grants Program is to increase the relevance of university-based research for Aboriginal communities, it has, we believe in our case, already proven its value.

Conclusions

Communities can be a tremendous source of strength, even if they lack the financial and material resources that are often taken for granted in less marginalized areas (Banerjee 1997). Aboriginal youth have acknowledged the importance of resolving issues and empowering people from community-based perspectives. Collectively, their ideas on the important connection between the individual and community led the RCAP to describe the process of empowerment as a holistic endeavour in which everyone participates and benefits. Empowerment tends to create an awareness of individual agency and power that, in turn, can have positive implications for the mental, physical, emotional, and spiritual well-being of people who come to recognize themselves as valuable members of the community. They work to make their community stronger, and in doing so they help other members of the community empower themselves (Government of Canada 1996, 149).

Acknowledgements

The authors gratefully acknowledge the financial support provided for this project by the Social Sciences and Humanities Research Council (SSHRC), Aboriginal Research Initiatives Grants Program.

References

Aberly, D. 1993. *Boundaries of home: Mapping for local empowerment*. Gabriola Island, BC: New Society Publishers.

Banerjee, M. M. 1997. Strengths in a slum: A paradox? *Journal of Applied Social Sciences* 22(1): 45–58.

Bishop, A. 1994. *Becoming an ally. Breaking the cycles of oppression*. Halifax: Fernwood Publishing.

Brendtro, L., M. Brokenleg, and S. Van Bockern. 1990. *Reclaiming youth at risk. Our hope for the future*. Bloomington, IN: National Education Service.

Chapin, R. K. 1995. Social policy development: The strengths perspective. *Social Work* 40(4): 506–15.

Davidson, S., C. Brasfield, S. Quressette, and L. Demerais. 1997. What makes us strong: Urban Aboriginal perspectives on wellness and strength. *Canadian Journal of Mental Health* 16(2): 37–50.

Economic Research Associates. 2004. *Public Use Facilities Study*. Report prepared for the City of Winnipeg, Department of Community Services, Public Works, Property, Planning, and Development.

Fox, K., S. Ryan, J. van Dyck, B. Chivers, L. Chuchmach, and S. Quesnel. 1998. Cultural perspectives, resilient Aboriginal communities, and recreation. *Journal of Applied Recreation Research* 23(2): 147–91.

Halas, J. 2002. Engaging troubled youth in physical education: An alternative program with lessons for the traditional class. *Journal of Teaching in Physical Education 21*: 267–86.

Halas, J. 2004. Interrupting the "isms" that influence the quality of qualitative research. International Qualitative Health Conference, Banff, May 2004.

Halas, J. and L. Hanson. 2001. Pathologizing Billy: Enabling and constraining the body of the condemned. *Sociology of Sport Journal:*18(1): 115–126.

Healthy Kids Healthy Futures All-Party Task Force. 2005. *Healthy Kids Healthy Futures Task Force Report*. Winnipeg: Government of Manitoba.

Reid, I., M. Tremblay, R. Pelletier, and S. McKay. 1994. *An analysis of the impact and benefits of physical activity and recreation on Canadian youth at risk*. Joint Initiative of the Interprovincial Sport and Recreation Council, the Fitness Directorate of Health Canada, and the Canadian Parks and Recreation Association.

Royal Commission on Aboriginal Peoples. 1996. *Perspectives and Realities*. Vol. 4 of *Report of the Royal Commission on Aboriginal Peoples*. Ottawa: Royal Commission on Aboriginal Peoples.

Saleebey, D. 1996. The strengths perspective in social work practice: Extensions and cautions. *Social Work* 41(3): 296–306.

Smith, Linda Tuhiwai. 1999. *Decolonizing methodologies: Research and Indigenous Peoples*. Dunedin, AUS: Univ. of Otago Press.

Solorzano, D., and T. Yosso. 2002. Critical race methodology: Counter-storytelling as an analytical framework for education research. *Qualitative Inquiry 8*(1): 23–44.

Strack, R., C. Magill, and K. McDonagh. 2003. Engaging youth through Photovoice. *Health Promotion Practice 5*(1): 48–58.

Wang, C., and M. Burris. 1997. Photovoice: Concept, methodology, and use for participatory needs assessment. *Health Education and Behavior* 24(3): 369–87.

Weick, A., R. Charles, P. Sullivan, and W. Kisthardt. 1989. A strengths perspective for social work practice. *Social Work* 34(7): 350–54.

Part Two:
Governance

7

The Reconstruction of Inuit Collective Identity: From Cultural to Civic

The Case of Nunavut[1]

André Légaré

Introduction

The negotiations that were conducted from 1976 to 1993, and the subsequent creation of Nunavut in 1999,[2] have attracted a flurry of publications on the subject of Inuit self-government in the Canadian central and eastern Arctic (Légaré 1999). A survey of writing on Nunavut since 1976, when the Nunavut project was first put forward (ITC 1976), reveals five main themes explored by scholars. First, there is the historical research done by anthropologists and historians, which recounts the ancestral history of Inuit from pre-contact up to the 1960s when the Inuit were forced by government to settle into villages. The second area contains works that focus on the Nunavut negotiation process and, in fact, this is where most of the academic literature on Nunavut is found. Third, there are publications that deal with the Nunavut political system and the Nunavut Land Claims Agreement (NLCA). Most recent publications have concentrated on this theme. As with the second theme, these scholarly works have been the domain of political scientists. Fourth, the construction of Nunavut geopolitical boundaries, based on traditional Inuit land use and occupancy, has given rise to some academic research done mainly by geographers. Finally, literature on Inuit identity has been published by anthropologists as well as by sociologists.

Nunavut-related publications show that the last two themes have not been treated as extensively as the previous three. However, they are of crucial importance to understanding how Nunavut was constructed and how the establishment of Nunavut has impacted Inuit collective identity in the Canadian central and eastern Arctic. This paper contains a review of the writings about Nunavut by exploring each theme, with a particular emphasis on the last two themes. In addition, I explore the concepts surrounding the construction of geopolitical boundaries and their linkage with Inuit collective identity and attempt to answer how the establishment of Nunavut boundaries has impacted on Inuit collective identity in the Canadian central and eastern Arctic. Finally, I examine the role of socio-political actors (i.e., governments, Inuit organizations, local medias) in the construction and in the promotion of a new form of collective identity in Nunavut from "Inuit" (cultural) to "Nunavummiut" (civic).

Nunavut: A Historical Background

Early History

Scholars (Damas 1984; Smith-Siska 1990; McGhee 2004) have divided the early history of Inuit in the Canadian Arctic into three distinct phases: the Pre-Dorset, Dorset, and Thule periods. Research into the pre-contact period is largely based on oral history and also on archeological research (Bennett and Rowley 2004). The first inhabitants of the Canadian central and eastern Arctic were the Pre-Dorset, whose ancestors crossed the Bering Strait into North America around 10,000 years ago. According to scholars (Burch 1986; Damas 1984), the Pre-Dorset arrived in the eastern Arctic from Alaska at around 4,000 BCE The Dorset succeeded them in 1,000 BCE. However, with the arrival of the Thule, the ancestors of today's Inuit, around the year 1,000 CE, the Dorset people vanished. There is still much debate among academics as to the reasons behind the disappearance of the Pre-Dorset and Dorset societies.

Aside from a brief Viking contact interlude with the Dorset people, around 1,000 CE, early contact between Inuit and Europeans started with Martin Frobisher's visit to Baffin Island in 1576. The story of his arrival, as well as those of subsequent British explorers also in search of the Northwest Passage, has been recounted by a number of scholars (Berton 2001; Fossett 2001; McGhee 2004). Yet, contact between Europeans (later Euro-Canadians) and the Inuit remain limited until the early twentieth century. The establishment of Hudson's Bay Company's trading posts and the arrival of the Catholic and Anglican churches in the region increased European contact with Inuit people. Damas (1993) depicted those early contacts as "harmonious" (Damas 1993, 5). In fact, until well into the early twentieth century, the Inuit continued to live a nomadic life in small groups.[3]

Canadian Government Intervention in the North

Regular contact between Euro-Canadian society and Inuit culture started only after the Second World War (Brody 1991). Canadian government intervention in the North was largely based on concern for the living conditions of the Inuit (Weissling 1991). Damas (2002) and Clancy (1987) illustrated how, in order to facilitate the delivery of government services (health, education, social services) and to improve the Inuit living condition, Ottawa established villages along the Arctic coast.[4] Inuit were settled into those villages where the government could provide health, social services, and education for them.

A number of authors (Creery 1993; Damas 2002; Brody 1991; Fossett 2001) describe this form of interventionism by Ottawa as "internal colonialism." Indeed, the move off the land, in the 1950s and 1960s, changed Inuit lives dramatically. The sedentary life in the villages increased the Inuit feeling of alienation from their land and their traditional way of life (Fletcher 2004). This forced settlement soon gave birth to dependency on government social services (e.g., housing, welfare). Inuit had become wards of the federal government (Colin 1988). Billson (1990) described how social ills (alcoholism, family violence, drugs, unemployment, inadequate housing, etc) became prevalent in the newly created villages.

At the end of the 1960s, having recently come from a tradition of governing themselves in almost all aspects, the Inuit were trying to reacquire control over their lives and their traditional lands (Dickerson 1992). Billson (2001) and Mitchell (1996) maintain that the search for Inuit political autonomy stems from the Euro-Canadian domination of Inuit, which started with the settlement initiative of the 1950s. The Inuit political revolution and the birth of the Nunavut project can be understood only within the context of this dramatic shift from the land to village life (Billson 2001, 284). In July 1971, the Inuit formed a political organization, Inuit Tapirisat of Canada, to regain control over their political and economic destinies in the eastern and central Arctic.

The Nunavut Proposal: The Negotiation Process

Most academic literature on Nunavut (Abele 1987; Bell 1992; Billson 2001; Gray 1994; Légaré 1996, 1998a) has focused on the negotiation process that led to the conclusion of the NLCA in 1993, and the subsequent creation of the government of Nunavut in 1999. In addition, people involved in the negotiations, such as consultants, lawyers, and negotiators (Jull 1982, 1988; Fenge 1992; McPherson 2004; Merritt and Fenge 1989; Merritt 1993; Molloy 1993), have also published on the subject.

Put forward by Inuit Tapirisat of Canada (ITC)[5] in 1976, the Nunavut proposal sought an agreement with Canada on land claims and on self-government. The Inuit of the Northwest Territories (NWT) hoped that by signing such an agreement, they would establish a new and respectful political relationship between themselves and the federal government. As demonstrated by Weller (1988) and Hamley (1995), the appeal of Nunavut meant that ITC expected that the proposed government would be closer to the people, both physically and culturally. Decentralization that had already started in the NWT (Dacks 1990; Légaré 1997) was not sufficient to quench the desire of the Inuit to have their own government.

The creation of Nunavut had to be negotiated as part of Canada's policy on Aboriginal outstanding land claims (INAC 1973).[6] Purich (1992) and Légaré (1996) examine the negotiation process at length and describe the events surrounding the three stages (i.e., proposal, elaboration, approval) that led to the signing of the final agreement. At the proposal stage (1976–81), ITC submitted to Ottawa three versions of the Nunavut project (1976, 1977, 1979). Ottawa accepted the third proposal as basis for negotiation. It contained four objectives:

1. Ownership rights over portions of land
2. Decision-making power over the management of land and resources
3. Financial compensation and royalties from non-renewable resources developed in the area
4. Commitment from Ottawa to create the government of Nunavut

In exchange for the settlement of their claim, the Inuit would have to surrender their ancestral Aboriginal rights to all lands in the North.

Duffy (1988) and Purich (1992) provide an excellent description of the elaboration stage (1981–91). This stage was the longest and most important phase of the negotiation process. At that stage, Tungavik Federation of Nunavut (TFN)[7] and federal government officials drafted the NLCA (INAC 1993). Cameron and White (1995) argue that the dominant issue of the elaboration stage focused on discussions regarding the boundary location that would divide the NWT in two halves.

Two separate, territory-wide plebiscites were held on the question of the boundary (Cameron and White 1995). The story surrounding these plebiscites can be found in Abele and Dickerson (1982) and in Parker (1996). They recount how, in the end, a majority of NWT residents supported the creation of Nunavut, thereby forcing the Canadian government through their democratic vote to support division. The first referendum took place in April 1982 and asked if people were interested in dividing the NWT into two political entities: to the west, Denendeh,[8] to the east, Nunavut. The plebiscite received the support of 56% of the residents. A second referendum on the subject of division took place in April 1992, once the final land claims agreement had been completed and once the parties (i.e., TFN and Canada) had agreed on the location of a boundary line to cross the middle of the NWT. This time, 54% of NWT residents supported division.[9]

Finally, Dacks (1995) and Légaré (1997) relate the story that led to the Nunavut Political Agreement, which confirmed the scheduled of the Territory of Nunavut for 1999. Both the Nunavut Political Agreement (Canada 1992) and the NLCA (INAC 1993) were approved by NWT Inuit through a referendum held in November 1992 (69% voted in favour) and later by the Canadian government through Parliament in June 1993. This constituted the approval stage (1991–93).

The Political Institutions of Nunavut

The academic literature that illustrates the political system of Nunavut comprises the highest percentage of recent scholarly material. Some authors have explored the components of the 41 chapters of the NLCA (Hamley 1995; Kersey 1994; Rodon 1998; Tulloch and Hust 2003), while others have examined the political structures and inner workings of the new Nunavut government (Gray 1994; Henderson 2004; Hicks and White 2000; Légaré 1997).

Tulloch and Hust (2003) argue that the NLCA establishes clear rules of ownership and control over land and resources in a settlement area covering one-fifth of Canada's land mass (1,963,000km²). Hamley (1995), Légaré (2003), and Rodon (1998) provide an overview of the provisions contained in the NLCA. The agreement gave to the Inuit of the Canadian central and eastern Arctic ownership over an area of 353,610 km², of which 36,257 km² includes subsurface mineral rights. In addition public boards, composed equally of Inuit and government representatives, were created to manage the lands and resources over the Nunavut settlement area. Inuit also obtained royalties from all current and future non-renewable resource development up to $2 million a year. Finally, the Inuit were to receive from Canada $1.15 billion, over a 14-year span (1993–2007), as compensation for extinguishing their Aboriginal land rights. However, scholars (Kersey 1994; Cherkasov 1993) point out that the NLCA does not take into account social and cultural items. Those are contained in the Nunavut Political Accord.

The Nunavut Political Accord provides a blueprint for Nunavut's political structure. Légaré (1997, 1998a) explores how this blueprint was later refined by the Nunavut Implementation Commission (NIC 1995, 1996).[10] Hicks (1999) and White (2001) depict the similarities between the political systems of Nunavut and of the NWT. The Nunavut territorial government enjoys the same political powers as the government of the Northwest Territories. These powers and jurisdictions are similar to those held by the provinces except that in Nunavut, the Yukon, and the Northwest Territories, the Canadian federal government owns and manages public Crown lands and non-renewable resources. Nunavut has the same political institutions as the NWT and the Yukon: i.e., a commissioner, an executive council, a legislative assembly, a public service sector, and tribunals.

Nunavut is a non-ethnic public government. However, since Inuit comprise the majority of the population (82%), Nunavut is often characterized by scholars (Gray 1994; Henderson 2004; Légaré 1997; Walls 2000) as a de facto Inuit government. Nunavut legislative authority rests in the nineteen elected members of the Nunavut Legislative Assembly. There is no party system in Nunavut, so each elected member sits as an independent. Hicks and White (2000) argue that the consensus legislative system of the Nunavut assembly should be described as "a non-partisan Westminster cabinet-style regime" (Hicks and White 2000, 69). It is interesting to note that the Nunavut Implementation Commission (NIC) proposed, in 1996, the idea of a gender-equal legislature for Nunavut. The proposal was ultimately defeated by a 57% "no" vote in a Nunavut-wide plebiscite held on the issue in May 1997. Dahl (1997), Young (1997), and Gombay (2000) have recounted the events that led to the proposal and the reasons behind its defeat.

Researchers (Abele 2000; Billson 2001; Henderson 2004) argue that the establishment of the Nunavut government has put in the hands of Inuit, who compose the majority of the population in Nunavut, powers over social and economic issues (e.g., language, culture, health, housing, education, social services) that would have been absent in a simple land claims agreement. To ensure that as many villages in Nunavut[11] as possible could benefit from government jobs, a decentralization initiative (Nunavut 2000, 2004a, 2004b) has been imple-mented with mixed results. Thus, the head offices of a number of departments (e.g., housing, justice, culture and language) are now located outside the capital Iqaluit.[12]

Seven years after its installment, Nunavut remains a political challenge. Authors (Abele 2000; Légaré 2001a; Walls 2000; White 2000) have highlighted some of these challenges:

- A lack of affordable housing
- Low education levels
- High unemployment rates
- Numerous health and social woes
- Financial deficiencies

Indeed, Nunavut's heavy dependence on federal funding[13] limits its spending power and curtails its effort to solve internal challenges. Only the future will bring us clarity as to the political success or failure of this de facto Inuit self-govern-ment experiment. Nunavut is still in its infancy. It is too early to draw any formal conclusion. Undoubtedly, though, to this day, Nunavut's biggest success has been its contribution in creating a civic regional identity consciousness among the Inuit of the Canadian central and eastern Arctic. This new identity, as we shall see, has been largely built around the construction of Nunavut's boundaries and the ensuing regionalization of Inuit collective identity.

Boundaries and Identity: Different Sides of the Same Coin

In traditional political geography, the link between territory and boundaries is usually taken for granted (Glasner and Fahrer 2004). Boundaries are understood as neutral lines: fixed, absolute, almost material entities. This paper argues that the study of boundaries needs to transcend the notions of static territorial lines so as to become more contextual. Paasi (1996, 2002) points out that geopolitical bound-aries are human creations manipulated by various socio-political groups who attempt to control certain spatial areas. In this context, boundaries have meaning as part of the production of territory. So, the important question here is not only where a boundary is located, but also how this boundary is established and then ritualized in the process of constructing a collective identity.

Anderson and O'Dowd (1999) interpret geopolitical boundaries as encapsu-lating a history of struggle against outside forces and as marking the limit of a society. Boundaries by definition constitute lines of separation or contact. The drawing of any regional border represents arbitration and a simplification of complex political and socio-cultural struggles between various groups who have interests as to the location of the border. Anderson and O'Dowd (1999) explain that once boundaries are drawn, they generate a dynamic for internal homogenization among residents located within the boundaries. Boundaries both shape and are shaped by what they contain: they look inwards as well as outwards, and simultaneously unify and divide, include and exclude.

As demonstrated by Newman and Paasi (1998), geopolitical boundaries usually fail to coincide precisely with the extent of a socio-cultural region and are rarely contiguous with the socio-cultural boundaries of a group of people. Geopolitical boundaries, therefore, become inherently contradictory, problematic, and multifaceted. As explained by Bone (1999), boundaries separating socio-cultural regions should be best viewed as transition zones rather than as finite limits. Thus, at its boundary, a region characteristic will become less distinct and merge with characteristics of the neighbouring region.

Paasi (1999, 2003) and Newman and Paasi (1998) have pointed out the importance of political boundaries in the construction of a collective identity for a group of people. Paasi (1996) argues that the bounded territory of a region is the primary focus of collective identification for its citizens. Boundaries penetrate society through numerous practices and narratives and help to construct a civic regional identity. Boundaries both create identity and are created through identity. As I will demonstrate, the link between boundaries and identity is particularly strong.

Identity is a concept that is hard to define. It is, in essence, a social construct: one's own conscious identity is a product of one's meeting with different forms of others' identities (Barth 1969; Hall 1990). A collective or group identity is but one of many identities in an individual's repertoire. As members of a society, each individual occupies a number of positions and plays a variety of roles which helps them shape several forms of identity (Barth 1969; Brah 1996). One can position himself/herself on many identity "axes" (Dorais and Watt 2001). Identity is also hard to define as a category. An examination of the literature that deals with the concept of identity reveals many forms of identity: cultural, gender, ethnic, religious, and others (Castells 1997; Driedger 1989; Roosens 1989).

Scholars (Brah 1996; Roosens 1989) have generally established that a person may identify himself or herself with others at three levels. The first is on an individual level, where one may identify oneself with some important persons in one's life (e.g., family, friends, co-workers). The second level is social, where one may identify with certain social roles (e.g., a gender, an economic activity, a religion, a language, etc.). The third is the collective level, where one may identify oneself with a broad category of persons (e.g., a cultural group, a political unit) at different spatial scales (i.e., local, regional, national, international).

Breton (1984) and Driedger (1989) have identified at least two forms of collective identity. One is cultural or ethnic identity, which refers to a person's attachment to a particular cultural group, i.e., the Inuit; another is civic or political identity, which refers to a person's attachment to a political unit. It is understood that there are several levels of civic identity in one's repertoire (local, regional, national, international), but this particular paper is concerned with identity at a regional level (i.e., Nunavut). Regional civic collective identity rests largely on certain historical, cultural, and political characteristics attached to a region (Albert et al. 2001; Hakli and Paasi 2003).

The Construction of Nunavut Geopolitical Boundaries

Scholars (Dacks, 1986; Hick and White 2000; Weller 1988, 1990; Wonders 2003) have noted that the most challenging issue of the negotiation process that led to the signature of the NLCA surrounded the discussions about the location of Nunavut's boundaries. Where to put the line which would serve to divide the Northest Territories in two parts was the dominant question throughout the 1980s. In the NWT, the Constitutional Alliance, composed of Dene, Métis, Inuvialuit, and Inuit representatives, was founded in July 1982. It had the challenging task of determining a western boundary line upon which all affected Aboriginal groups could agree: the Dene-Métis of the MacKenzie valley, the Inuvialuit of the MacKenzie Delta, and the Inuit of the Canadian central and eastern Arctic. To the south, the Denesuline of Saskatchewan and of Manitoba also voiced concerns in regards to the southern boundary of Nunavut (Usher 1990).

To assert its claim over the Canadian central and eastern Arctic, ITC initiated a land use and occupancy study in 1973. The purpose of the three-volume study (Freeman et al. 1976) was to prove to government that Inuit, and their ancestors, had used and had occupied virtually all of the land and oceans in the Canadian central and eastern Arctic for more than 4,000 years. The study was guided by Canada's policy on Aboriginal land claims (INAC 1973). The policy states that in exchange for proof of continued use and occupancy of the land, an Aboriginal group that had not yet surrendered its ancestral title to the land to the government may negotiate a comprehensive land claims agreement with the Canadian government (Saku and Bone 2000; Usher 2003). Such an agreement provides to the claimant Aboriginal group certain land ownership and land management powers over a defined region called a "settlement area."

The *Inuit Land Use and Occupancy Project* (Freeman et al. 1976) assembles more than 1,600 maps (such as biography maps) portraying the journeys travelled by Inuit hunters, on the land and on the sea ice, in search of game animals. In addition, the maps pinpointed the locations of Inuit outpost camps, cairns, burial grounds, and place-names. These socio-cultural traits and activities based on Inuit cultural identity helped trace an Inuit socio-cultural region. Research done by Freeman et al. (1976), Freeman (1984), Keller (1986), Riewe (1988, 1991), and Wonders (1984, 1985, 1990) presents excellent maps of current and traditional Inuit land use in the Canadian Central and Eastern Arctic. In addition, Collignon (1993), Lester (1979), and Wonders (1987) have shown the importance of Inuit place-names in determining the possible extent of the Inuit claim area in the Canadian Central and Eastern Arctic.

The biography maps and their contents were used by ITC and later by TFN·
to assert Inuit land interests (Wonders 1990). The biography maps became the
building blocks in the delimitation of the Nunavut territorial shape (Brody 1991).
TFN attempted to design geopolitical boundaries that were as closely contiguous
as possible to those of Inuit traditional use and occupancy of the land (i.e., their
socio-cultural region). Thus, TFN insisted that the Nunavut western boundary
should follow the tree line and should include the Inuvialuit communities and the
rich oil and gas fields of the MacKenzie delta.

However, Wonders (1984) and Usher (1990) have demonstrated that very few
land areas in the NWT are uncontested or homogeneous. There are significant
overlapping areas with a number of Aboriginal groups. Watkins et al. (1986) noted
that some areas along the tree line were contested by the Dene-Métis who had
also traditionally hunted and trapped in the area. The Dene-Métis socio-cultural
region (Ash et al. 1978) also extended north of the treeline as hunters searched
for caribou. The area was uninhabited, but both sides had hunting and trapping
interests to the area. Similar contested, overlapping claims lay along the proposed
southern boundary of Nunavut with Saskatchewan and Manitoba. Usher's land
use research (Usher 1990), on behalf of the Denesuline, showed continued use of
the land, located in the NWT along the Saskatchewan and the Manitoba borders,
by the Denesuline. However, Canada had said that it would deal with the Denesuline's overlapping claim in a separate process and that the Denesuline, being
non-residents of the NWT, would not be entitled to influence the negotiations in
the NWT (Molloy 1993).

As for the Inuvialuit, in July 1985 they decided not to join their Inuit counterparts (Keeping 1989). Their economic and transportation links along the
MacKenzie valley were attached to the western part of the NWT. They preferred
not to embark on a claim that focused largely on the eastern and central Arctic
(Wonders 1988, 1990). So, by the end of the 1980s, the only outstanding issue
was how to draw the boundary between the claim areas of the Dene-Métis and the
Inuit. Progress on this matter was not made until February 1987 when both sides
agreed, through the Constitutional Alliance, on a compromise boundary (Constitutional Alliance 1987).

However, the agreement broke down a few months later when Dene chiefs
refused to endorse the proposal (Dickerson and McCullough 1993; Merritt and
Fenge 1989). The heart of the problem lay in the ongoing harvesting activities
of both groups on a hundred-kilometre-wide area around the treeline limit. Both
groups argued that the whole of the hundred-kilometre-wide area should be on
their side of the boundary. Having failed to settle the boundary issue, the Constitutional Alliance was disbanded in July 1987. Negotiations on this boundary
issue were stalled for the next three years. In April 1990, Ottawa designated the
ex-Commissioner of the NWT, John Parker, with the task of solving the boundary
dispute. After consulting with all parties, Inuit and Dene-Métis, Parker recommended a compromise boundary (Parker 1991) largely similar to the border upon

which the Dene-Métis and the Inuit had agreed three years earlier, but which was rejected by the Dene-Métis. The "Parker Boundary Line" was later approved[14] (May 1992) in a NWT-wide plebiscite. It now served to divide the NWT in two halves.

In the end, Nunavut's geopolitical boundaries largely reflected the Inuit socio-cultural region in the Canadian central and eastern Arctic. However, other important factors also had to be taken into account in the delineation of Nunavut's boundaries. Thus, TFN did not claim land jurisdiction beyond the southern border of the NWT, even though some Inuit groups had in the past travelled down to Churchill, Manitoba. Rather, they chose to respect the existing provincial Manitoba border (Molloy 1993; Fenge 1992; Merritt 1993).[15] They also respected the existing settlement area boundaries of the Inuvialuit who had signed a comprehensive land claim agreement with Canada in 1984 (INAC 1984). Finally, once Canada had accepted the idea of creating Nunavut, it supported an eastern border for the Nunavut Territory that follows the NWT's existing geopolitical boundaries (Molloy 1993).[16] Those borders extend around James Bay, even though the waters and the islands in James Bay had never been used or occupied in the past by the Inuit.

In sum, the construction of Nunavut's geopolitical boundaries was determined by:

- The spatial localization of certain past and present Inuit cultural traits and activities

- The pre-existing borders of provinces, administrative districts, and settlement areas

- Canadian sovereignty in the Arctic through the meridian approach to the geographic North Pole

- By the land use interests of other Aboriginal groups (i.e., NWT Dene-Métis)

Today, the western boundary of Nunavut cuts into part of the socio-cultural region of the Dene-Métis (Ash et al. 1978), who now find some of their traditional hunting grounds within Nunavut. In addition to the Dene-Métis, the Denesuline of Saskatchewan and Manitoba, the James Bay Cree, and the Inuit of Northern Quebec have also been affected, since they also use some of those lands, now within Nunavut, for harvesting purposes. For all of these affected Aboriginal groups, the creation of Nunavut, and the location of its boundaries in particular, has signified a loss of their socio-cultural region.[17] Indeed, one may now expect that the newly created Nunavut government will redefine these lands as part of the heartland of the Inuit socio-cultural region in an attempt to fuse the socio-cultural region with the newly created political region of Nunavut. Obviously, like any other province or territory, Nunavut will jealously guard its geopolitical integrity.

The Reconstruction of Inuit Collective Identity in Nunavut

Research on identity in the Arctic has been conducted mainly by anthropologists and sociologists (Briggs 1997; Dorais 1995, 2001, 2005; Dybbroe 1996; Searles 2001). They have focused on Inuit social and individual forms of identity. They have explored particularly the themes of language (Dorais and Sammons 2000; Shearwood 2001), religion (Laugrand 2002), and harvesting activities (Doubleday 2003; Gombay 2005; Rasing 1999; Searles 1998; Wenzel 2001) as building blocks for Inuit identity. A few scholars have examined contemporary Inuit collective identity (Billson 1988; Dahl 1988; Dybbroe 1996; Muller-Wille 2001) but have done so from an ethnic or cultural (e.g., Inuit identity) perspective rather than on a civic or political basis (e.g., Nunavut residents' identity). To my knowledge none has looked at the connection between the construction of geopolitical boundaries and the re-definition of Inuit collective identity.

The reconstruction of collective identities is mediated and invented by various actors (i.e., TFN, Government of Canada) who will subjectively use symbols and geopolitical borders in order to highlight the differences between one group from other neighbouring groups (Massey 1994; Paasi 1999). During the construction of a region's borders, symbols, resting on an Aboriginal group's socio-cultural and physical environment, are established through which the group learns its distinctiveness and its uniqueness in relation to neighbouring regions (Paasi 1986, 1991). Once a region's boundaries are determined, symbols are reinforced and are used as components of an emerging regional collective identity. Symbols manifest themselves in the field of communication (advertisements, television, newspapers, books, sculptures, paintings, memorials, etc.).

Symbols have been shaped and manipulated by TFN through the local medias, during a land claim process, in an attempt to communicate their vision of political and social development to other actors (e.g., the government of Canada, Dene-Métis of the NWT, Denesuline, etc.). Symbols are "invented tradition": they are simple to understand and may change their meanings over time. They are continually reinvented by actors, who often use them to gain certain socio-political claims (Dybbroe 1996). In sum, symbols legitimize and celebrate the existence of a common regional consciousness or civic identity within a political unit. In Nunavut these socio-cultural symbols rest on the Arctic climate and wildlife as well as on socio-political traits, and manifest themselves in three forms: (1) rituals (e.g., the Nunavut holiday —a statutory holiday in Nunavut); (2) pictorial graphics (e.g., Nunavut's flag, logo-map, arctic wildlife, igloos, inuksuit, etc.); and (3) socio-political names (e.g., Nunavut, Nunavummiut).

Boundaries have an important role in the construction of a regional identity as symbols of the region (Paasi 1997), becoming instruments of communication (i.e., narratives) through which social distinctions are constructed. Scholars (Anderson and O'Dowd 1999; Newman and Paasi 1998; Paasi 2002, 2003) have

Figure 7.1: The process leading to the reconstruction of Aboriginal identities

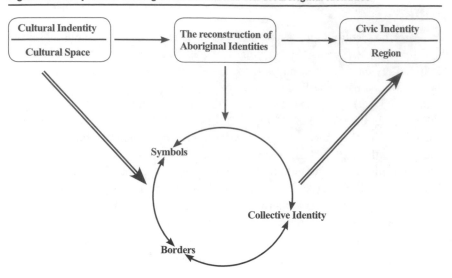

demonstrated that collective identities are constituted in relation to differences. Boundaries are symbols and manifestation of such differences. They are critical elements in establishing common consciousness within the borders, the "Us," and excluding those outside the borders, the "Others." A major part of the process of producing a common regional civic identity consists of presenting the residents of a region as being as united as possible, and of pointing out socio-cultural differences with people living outside the existing political boundaries of the region.

Meanings and symbols can be attached to borders. These are then exploited, often by political elites, to mobilize people and to construct a civic identity. Indeed, according to Paasi (1997) and Pickles (1992), regional civic identity is often associated with the narratives of a region's boundaries and carried through the media by socio-political actors (e.g., TFN in Nunavut). So, regional civic identity becomes, basically, a form of categorization, where boundaries are used to distinguish one spatial domain and social collectivity (e.g., Inuit) from another (e.g., Dene-Métis). These boundaries are then used to further define all residents as regionally united through a common civic form of identity, as TFN has done with both Inuit and non-Inuit in Nunavut by using the term Nunavummiut.[18] In sum, one may say that regional identity and geopolitical boundaries are different sides of the same coin.

Conclusion

A review of the academic literature on Nunavut shows that a significant number of scholarly works have focused on the history and on the politics of Nunavut. Even though one may argue that the greatest success of Nunavut has been the emergence of a new regional self-consciousness among the Inuit of the Canadian central and eastern Arctic, few articles have explored this important subject matter (Dorais and Watt 2001; Légaré 2001b).

I have indicated that, as the boundaries of Nunavut were being constructed, Inuit collective identity was being (re)defined on a civic-regional scale (i.e., Nunavummiut) and less and less in solely cultural terms (i.e., Inuit). This regionalization of Inuit collective identity is based on Inuit socio-cultural traits and activities. Since the socio-cultural region is the source of Nunavut's geopolitical boundaries, the regionalization process attempts to incorporate all Inuit of Nunavut, as well as non-Inuit residents, into a common civic identity: Nunavummiut. Obviously, as demonstrated by Dahl (1988) in the case of Greenland, this civic identity inherits strong Inuit cultural foundations since the vast majority of Nunavut's residents are Inuit.

In Canada, Inuit collective identity is being redefined around large-scale political units born through the land claims/self-government processes so as to incorporate Inuit and non-Inuit people into a common civic identity: e.g., Nunavummiut, Nunavimmiut, Nunatsiavummiut. Obviously the Nunavummiut identity portrayed by various socio-cultural symbols will inherit strong Inuit cultural foundations.

Through the reconstruction of Inuit collective identity from cultural to civic one can see the interconnection between borders, symbols and collective identity. Their construction occurs simultaneously and is mediated by actors (**Figure 7.1**). In the case of Nunavut Inuit cultural factors helped to define the borders of Nunavut. The symbols born from the spatial construction of Nunavut became the cornerstone of an emergent Nunavummiut civic collective identity. To sustain itself this new civic identity reinforces the symbols and highlights the borders of Nunavut.

With the continued emergence of new Nunavut institutions (e.g., the Department of Education, Department of Culture and Language, etc.), one should expect the progressive growth of regional civic identity i.e., Nunavummiut. In time, as illustrated by Dahl (1988),[19] one may suppose that the Inuit of the Canadian central and eastern Arctic will identify themselves more and more as Nunavummiut. This regionalization of Inuit collective identity has yet to receive broad attention by scholars. Ultimately, we can only hope that more scholars will explore the concepts of regional identity and boundary construction and its impact on Inuit collective identity in Canada's Arctic.[20]

Acknowledgements

The author is grateful to Kate Duncan at INAC, who chaired the session on "Impact of Claims on Culture," for her crucial help in preparing the logistical arrangements for the workshop session. The author also wishes to thank INAC, Claims and Indian Government Division, for allocating travel funds to the conference and making it possible for the author the attend. The text expresses solely the author's opinions. Any inaccuracies are solely the responsibility of the author.

Endnotes

1 This paper is based on the author's speaking notes for a presentation entitled "The Reconstruction of Aboriginal Identities: From Cultural to Civic. The Case of Nunavut," presented at the Aboriginal Policy Research Conference, Ottawa, March 21–23, 2006.

2 On April 1, 1999, the Canadian government officially proclaimed the Nunavut Territory and government. Nunavut, an Inuktitut word that means "our land," was carved out of the Northwest Territories to become the most recent member of the Canadian federation. Nunavut is inhabited by only 28,000 people, 82% of whom are Inuit.

3 There were approximately 50 Inuit "tribal" groups in the Canadian Arctic whose size varied between 30 to 100 individuals (Damas 1984; McGhee 2004).

4 Today, there are 28 communities in Nunavut.

5 In 2004, Inuit Tapirisat of Canada was renamed Inuit Tapiriit Kanatami.

6 The story surrounding the origins of Canada's Aboriginal land claims policy is described in detail by Weaver (1981).

7 In July 1981, TFN replaced ITC as the responsible Inuit negotiating body for the Nunavut claim. TFN represented solely the Inuit of the central and eastern Arctic. ITC felt at the time that it had to pull away from the Nunavut negotiations to concentrate more on Canada-wide issues.

8 Denendeh was a political project somewhat similar to Nunavut (Watkins 1986; Smith 1992). Ultimately, the project was rejected in 1991 by the Dene-Metis Chiefs of the NWT (Légaré, 1998b).

9 While the Inuit of the eastern Arctic strongly supported the line, the Dene-Metis of the western NWT disapproved of the proposed line. This explains the low approval level.

10 The NIC functioned from December 1993 to July 1999. It was composed of nine members equally nominated by Canada, the Northwest Territories, and TFN.

11 There are 28 communities in Nunavut. Twelve were targeted to benefit from decentralization. However, many employees refused to move outside the capital, Iqaluit. Today, in smaller communities, many job positions have yet to be filled.

12 About 500 of the 1400 government employees work outside the capital region.

13 About 95% of Nunavut's 750 million dollar annual budget is financed by Canada.

14 In the eastern Arctic, the support for the boundary was strong. However, in the western NWT, most people voted against the proposed boundary.

15 Indeed, any changes of the location of a provincial boundary require the approval of the province concerned. It also requires an amendment to the Canadian constitution, a task that is particularly challenging.

16 By taking this position Canada avoided the perennial debate over the provincial offshore boundaries in Hudson Bay and in James Bay (Québec, 1972).

17 Although affected Aboriginal groups could continue to hunt, fish, and trap within Nunavut, their Aboriginal rights may have been affected by the creation of Nunavut. Thus, any land claims or harvesting right claims by these groups within Nunavut would be complicated, since the newly created Nunavut government will defend the integrity of its newly acquired laws and powers within the borders of Nunavut.

18 The term "Nunavummiut" means in English "the inhabitants of our land."

19 Dahl asserts that the 1979 introduction of home rule in Greenland has helped to reshaped Inuit collective identity. The Inuit of Greenland now identify themselves collectively primarily as Greenlanders. The term also applies to the non-Inuit Danish inhabitants of Greenland.

20 One may add that there is also a similar regionalization process among the Inuit of the Quebec-Labrador peninsula, who now identify themselves collectively as Nunavimmiut on the Quebec side and as Nunatsivummiut on the Labrador side. As for the Inuvialuit of the western Arctic, such a regionalization process is currently absent. They have yet to negotiate a self-government component to their land claim agreement. Only persons with Inuvialuit ancestry can identify themselves as "Inuvialuit."

References

Abele, Frances. 1987. Canadian contradictions: Forty years of northern political development. *Arctic* 41(4): 310–20.

-----, 2000. Best chance, perilous passages: Recent writing about Nunavut. *International Journal of Canadian Studies* 21:197–211.

Abele, Frances, and Mark O. Dickerson. 1982. The plebiscite on division of the Northwest Territories: Regional government and federal policy. *Canadian Public Policy* 11(1): 1–15.

Albert, Mathias, et al., eds. 2001. *Identities, borders, orders*. Minneapolis: Univ. of Minnesota Press.

Anderson, James, and Liam O'Dowd. 1999. Borders, border regions and territoriality: Contradictory meanings, changing significance. *Regional Studies* 33(7): 593–604.

Ash, Michael, et al., eds. 1978. Dene mapping project. Yellowknife: Indian Brotherhood of the Northwest Territories.

Barth, Frederick, ed. 1969. *Ethnic groups and boundaries: The social organization of culture differ- ence*. Boston: Little Brown.

Bell, Jim. 1992. Nunavut: The quiet revolution. *Arctic Circle* 2(4): 12–21.

Bennett, John and Susan Rowley. 2004. *Uqalurait: An oral history of Nunavut*. Montreal and Kingston: McGill-Queen's Univ. Press.

Berton, Pierre. 2001. *The Arctic grail. The quest for the Northwest Passage and the North Pole*. Toronto: Anchor.

Billson, Janet M. 1988. Social change, social problems, and the search for identity: Canada's Northern Native Peoples in transition. *The American Review of Canadian Studies* 28(3): 295–315.

-----, 1990. Opportunity or tragedy: The impact of Canadian resettlement policy on Inuit families. *The American Review of Canadian Studies* 20(2): 187–218.

-----, 2001. Inuit dreams, Inuit realities: Shattering the bonds of dependency. *The American Review of Canadian Studies* 31(1–2): 283–99.

Bone, Robert M. 1999. *The regional geography of Canada*. Toronto: Oxford Univ. Press.

Brah, A. 1996. *Cartographies of diaspora*. London: Routledge.

Briggs, Jean L. 1997. From trait to emblem and back: Living and representing culture in everyday Inuit life. *Arctic Anthropology* 34(1): 227–35.

Brody, Hugh. 1991. *The People's land: Inuit, whites and the Eastern Arctic*. Toronto: Douglas & McIntyre.

Burch, Ernest S. 1986. The Eskaleuts—A regional overview. In *Native peoples: The Canadian Experi- ence*, eds., B.R. Morrison and R.C. Wilson. Toronto: McClelland.

Cameron, Kirk, and Graham White. 1995. *Northern government in transition. Political and constitu- tional development in the Yukon, Nunavut and the Western Northwest Territories*. Montreal: Institute for Research on Public Policy.

Canada. 1992. *Nunavut political accord*. Ottawa: Government of Canada.

Castells, Manuel. 1997. *The power of identity*. Oxford: Blackwell.

Cherkasov, Arkady I. 1993. Nunavut: The Canadian experiment in territorial self-determination for the NWT. *Polar Geography and Geology* 17(1): 64–71.

Clancy, Peter. 1987. The making of Eskimo policy in Canada, 1952–62: The life and times of the Eskimo Affairs Committee. *Arctic* 40(3): 191–97.

Colin, Irwin. 1988. *Lords of the Arctic: Wards of the State*. Ottawa: Health and Welfare Canada.

Collignon, Béatrice. 1993. The variations of a land use pattern: Seasonal movements and cultural change among the Copper Inuit. *Études/Inuit/Studies* 17(1): 71–90.

Constitutional Alliance. 1987. *Boundary and constitutional agreement for the implementation of division of the Northwest Territories*. Yellowknife: Constitutional Alliance.

Creery, Ian. 1993. The Inuit (Eskimo) of Canada. In *Polar peoples: Self-determination and develop- ment*, ed. Minority Rights Group. London: Minority Rights Group Publication.

Dacks, Gurston. 1986. The case against dividing the Northwest Territories. *Canadian Public Policy* 12(1): 202–13.

-----. ed. 1990. *Devolution and constitutional development in the Canadian North*. Ottawa: Carleton Univ. Press.

-----. 1995. *Nunavut: Aboriginal self-determination through public government. A report prepared for the Royal Commission on Aboriginal Peoples*. Ottawa: RCAP Notes.

Dahl, Jens. 1988. From ethnic to political identity. *Nordic Journal of International Law* 57(3): 312–15.

-----. 1997. Gender parity in Nunavut? *Indigenous Affairs* 3–4:42–47.

Damas, David. 1984. Copper Eskimo. In *Handbook of North American Indians, Arctic*. Vol. 5, ed. D. Damas. Washington: Smithsonian Institution.

-----. 1993. Shifting relations in the administration of Inuit: The Hudson's Bay Company and the Canadian Government. *Études/Inuit/Studies* 17(2): 5–28.

-----. 2002. Arctic migrants, Arctic villagers: The transformation of Inuit settlement in the Central Arctic. Montreal and Kingston: McGill-Queen's Univ. Press.

Dickerson, Mark O. 1992. Whose North? Political change, political development and self-government in the Northwest Territories. Vancouver: UBC Press.

Dickerson, Mark O., and Karen M. McCullough. 1993. Nunavut (Our Land). *Information North* 19(2): 1–7.

Dorais, Louis-Jacques. 1995. Language, culture and identity: Some Inuit examples. *The Canadian Journal of Native Studies* 15(2): 293–308.

-----. 2001. Inuit identities. *Études/Inuit/Studies* 25(1–2): 17–35.

-----. 2005. Comparing academic and aboriginal definitions of Arctic identities. *Polar Record* 41(216): 1 10.

Dorais, Louis-Jacques, and Susan Sammons. 2000. Discourse and Identity in the Baffin Region. *Arctic Anthropology* 37(2): 92–110.

Dorais, Louis-Jacques, and Robert Watt. 2001. *Inuit identities in the third millennium*. Quebec: Association Inuksiutiit Katimajiit Inc.

Doubleday, Nancy C. 2003. The nexus of identity, Inuit autonomy and Arctic sustainability: Learning from Nunavut, community and culture. *British Journal of Canadian Studies* 16(2): 297–308.

Driedger, Leo. 1989. *The ethnic factor. Identity in diversity*. Toronto: McGraw-Hill Ryerson.

Duffy, Quinn R. 1988. *The road to Nunavut. The progress of the Eastern Arctic Inuit since the Second World War*. Montreal and Kingston: McGill-Queen's Univ. Press.

Dybbroe, Susanne. 1996. Question of identity and issues of self-determination. *Études/Inuit/Studies* 20(2): 39–53.

Fenge, Terry. 1992. Political development and environmental management in Northern Canada: The case of the Nunavut Agreement. *Études/Inuit/Studies*, 16(1–2): 115–41.

Fletcher, Christopher, 2004. Continuity and change in Inuit society. In *Native peoples. The Canadian experience*, ed. B. Morrison and R. Wilson. Oxford: Oxford Univ. Press.

Fossett, Renee. 2001. *In order to live untroubled. Inuit of the Central Arctic*. Winnipeg: Univ. of Manitoba Press.

Freeman, Milton M R . 1984. Contemporary Inuit exploitation of sea-ice environment. In *Sikumiut: The People who use the sea ice*, ed. P. Wilkinson Ottawa: Canadian Arctic Resources Committee.

Freeman, Milton, M.R., et al., eds. 1976. *Inuit Land Use and Occupancy Project*. 3 vols Ottawa: Indian and Northern Affairs Canada.

Glasner, Martin, and Chuck Fahrer. 2004. *Political geography*. New York: John Wiley & Sons.

Gombay, Nicole. 2000. The politics of culture: Gender parity in the legislative assembly of Nunavut. *Études/Inuit/Studies* 24(1): 97–124.

-----. 2005. Shifting identities in a shifting world: Food, place, community and the politics of scale in an Inuit settlement. *Environment and Planning D: Society and Space* 23: 415–33.

Gray, Kevin R. 1994. The Nunavut Land Claim Agreement and the future of the Eastern Arctic: The uncharted path to effective self-government. *University of Toronto Faculty of Law Review* 52: 300–44.

Hakli, Jouni, and Anssi Paasi. 2003. Geography, space and identity. In *Voices from the North*, ed. J. Ohman and K. Simonsen. London: Ashgate.

Hall, Stuart. 1990. Cultural identity and diaspora. In *Identity: Community, Culture, Difference*, ed. J. Rutherford. London: Lawrence and Wishart.

Hamley, William. 1995. The Nunavut Settlement: A critical appraisal. *International Journal of Canadian Studies* 12: 221–34.

Henderson, Ailsa. 2004. Northern political culture?: Political behaviour in Nunavut. *Études/Inuit/Studies* 28(1): 133–54.

Hicks, Jack. 1999. The Nunavut land claim and the Nunavut government: Political structures of self-government in Canada's Eastern Arctic. In *Dependency, autonomy, sustainability in the Arctic*, ed. H. Petersen and B. Poppel. Brookfield: Ashgate.

Hicks, Jack, and Graham White. 2000. Nunavut: Inuit self-determination through a land claim and public government? In *Nunavut: Inuit regain control of their lands and their lives*, ed. J. Dahl, J. Hicks, and P. Jull. Copenhagen: IWGIA.

INAC (Indians and Northern Affairs Canada). 1973. *Indian Affairs Policy Statement*. Ottawa: Supply and Services.

-----. 1984. *Western Arctic Land Claim. Inuvialuit Final Claim Settlement*. Ottawa: INAC.

-----. 1993. *Nunavut Land Claims Agreement*. Ottawa: INAC.

ITC (Inuit Tapirisat of Canada). 1976. *Nunavut. A proposal for the settlement of Inuit lands in the Northwest Territories*. Ottawa: ITC.

-----.1979. *Political development in Nunavut*. Ottawa: ITC.

-----.1980. *Parnagujuk: Basic objectives of the comprehensive blueprint for the North*. Ottawa: ITC.

Jull, Peter. 1982. Nunavut. *Northern Perspectives* 10(2): 1–8.

-----.1988. Building Nunavut: A story of Inuit self-government. *The Northern Review* 1(1): 59–72.

Keeping, Janet. 1989. *The Inuvialuit Final Agreement*. Calgary: Univ. of Calgary, Faculty of Law.

Keller, Peter C. 1986. Accessibility and areal organizational units: Geographical considerations for dividing Canada's Northwest Territories. *The Canadian Geographer* 30(1): 71–79.

Kersey, Alexandra. 1994. The Nunavut Agreement: A model for preserving Indigenous rights. *Arizona Journal of International and Comparative Law* 11(2): 429–68.

Laugrand, Frederic. 2002. Écrire pour prendre la parole: Conscience historique, mémoire d'aînés et régimes d'historicité au Nunavut. *Anthropologie et Société* 26(2–3): 91–116.

Légaré, André. 1996. The process leading to a land claims agreement and its implementation: The case of the Nunavut Land Claims Settlement. *The Canadian Journal of Native Studies* 16(1): 139–63.

-----. 1997. The government of Nunavut (1999): A prospective analysis. In *First Nations in Canada. Perspectives on opportunity, empowerment, and self-determination*, ed. R.J. Pointing. Toronto: McGraw-Hill Ryerson.

-----.1998a. An assessment of recent political development in Nunavut: The challenges and dilemmas of Inuit self-government. *The Canadian Journal of Native Studies* 18(2): 271–99.

-----.1998b. *The Evolution of the government of the Northwest Territories (1967–1995): The debate over its legitimacy and the emergence of Nunavut and Denendeh*. Québec: GETIC, Université Laval.

-----. 1999. *Nunavut. A bibliography*. Québec: GETIC, Université Laval.

-----. 2001a. Our Land. *Hemisphere*, 9(3): 28–31.

-----. 2001b. The spatial and symbolic construction of Nunavut: Towards the emergence of a regional collective identity. *Etudes/Inuit/Studies* 25(1–2): 141–68.

-----. 2003. The Nunavut Tunngavik Inc.: An examination of its mode of operation and its activities. In *Natural resources and Aboriginal People in Canada*, ed. R.B. Anderson and R. M. Bone. Concord, ON: Captus.

Lester, Geoffrey S. 1979. Aboriginal land rights: The significance of Inuit place-naming. *Études/Inuit/studies* 3(1): 53–75.

Massey, Doreen. 1994. *Space, place, and gender*. Cambridge: Polity Press.

McGhee, Robert. 2004. *The last imaginary place. A human history of the Arctic world*. Toronto: Key Porter.

McPherson, Robert. 2004. *New owners in their land. Minerals and Inuit land claim*. Calgary: Univ. of Calgary Press.

Merritt, John. 1993. Nunavut: Canada turns a new page in the Arctic. *Canadian Parliamentary Review* 16(2): 2–6.

Merritt, John, and Terry Fenge. 1989. *Nunavut: Political choices and manifest destiny*. Ottawa: Canadian Arctic Resources Committee.

Mitchell, Marybelle. 1996. *From talking chiefs to a Native corporate elite. The birth of class and nationalism among Canadian Inuit*. Montreal and Kingston: McGill-Queen's Univ. Press.

Molloy, Tom. 1993. Negotiating the Nunavut agreement—A view from the government's side. *Northern Perspectives* 21(3): 9–11.

Muller-Wille, Ludger. 2001. Cultural identity among Sami and Inuit: Issues of ethnic groups and boundaries. *Études/Inuit/Studies* 25(1–2): 285–94.

Newman, David, and Anssi Paasi. 1998. Fences and neighbours in the postmodern world: Boundary narratives in political geography. *Progress in Human Geography* 22(2): 186–207.

NIC (Nunavut Implementation Commission). 1995. *Footprints in new snow*. Iqaluit: Nunavut Implementation Commission.

-----. 1996. *Footprints 2*. Iqaluit: Nunavut Implementation Commission.

Nunavut . 2000. *The Bathurst Mandate Pinasuaqtavut: That which we've set out to do*. Iqaluit: Government of Nunavut.

-----. 2004a. *Iqqanaijaqatigiit: Government of Nunavut and Nunavut Tunngavik Inc. Working together*. Iqaluit: Government of Nunavut.

-----. 2004b. *Pinasuaqtavut 2004 2009: Our commitment to building Nunavut's future*. Iqaluit: Government of Nunavut.

Paasi, Anssi. 1986. The institutionalization of regions: A theoretical framework for understanding the emergence of regions and the constitution of regional identity. *Fennia* 164(1): 105–46.

-----. 1996. *Territories, boundaries and consciousness*. New York: John Wiley & Sons.

-----. 1997. Geographical perspectives on Finnish national identity. *GeoJournal* 43:41–50.

-----. 1999. Boundaries as social processes: Territoriality in the World of Flows. In *Boundaries, territory and postmodernity*, ed. D. Newman. Portland, OR: Frank Cass.

-----. 2002. Bounded spaces in the mobile world: Deconstructing regional identity. *Tijdschrift voor Economische en Sociale Geografie* 93(2): 137–48.

- . 2003. Region and place: Regional identity in question. *Progress in Human Geography* 27(4): 475–85.

Parker, John. 1991. *The Boundary between comprehensive claims settlement areas of the Inuit and Dene-Metis of the Northwest Territories*. Ottawa: Indian and Northern Affairs Canada.

-----. 1996. *Arctic power. The path to responsible government in Canada's North*. Peterborough: Cider Press.

Pickles, John. 1992. Text, hermeneutics and propaganda maps. In *Writing worlds. Discourse, text and metaphor in the representation of landscape*, ed. T. Barnes and J.S. Duncan. New York: Routledge.

Purich, Donald. 1992. *The Inuit and their land. The story of Nunavut*. Toronto: James Lorimer & Co.

Québec. 1972. *Commission d'étude sur l'intégrité du territoire du Québec. Les frontières septentrionales*, Québec: Éditeurs officiel du Québec.

Rasing, Willem C.E. 1999. Hunting for identity. Thoughts on the practice of hunting and its significance for Iglulingmiut identity. In *Arctic identities. Continuity and change in Inuit and Sami societies*, ed. J. Oosten and C. Rennie. Leiden: Leiden Univ. Press.

Riewe, Rick. 1988. Land use mapping and regional variations within Nunavut. In *Polar science, technology and information*, ed. P. Adams and F. Duerden. Ottawa: Association of Canadian Universities for Northern Studies.

-----. 1991. Inuit land use studies and the Native claims process. In *Aboriginal resource use in Canada. Historical and legal aspects*, ed. A. Kerry and J. Friesen. Winnipeg: Univ. of Manitoba Press.

Rodon, Thierry. 1998. Co-management and self-determination in Nunavut. *Polar Geography* 22(2): 119–35.

Roosens, Eugeen E. 1989. *Creating ethnicity. The process of ethnogenesis.* London: Sage.

Saku, James C., and Robert M. Bone. 2000. Looking for solutions in the Canadian North: Modern treaties as a new strategy. *The Canadian Geographer* 44(3): 259–70.

Searles, Edmund. 1998. The crisis of youth and the poetics of place: Juvenile reform, outpost camps, and Inuit identity in the Canadian Arctic. *Etudes/Inuit/Studies* 22(2): 137–55.

-----. 2001. Fashioning selves and tradition: Case studies on personhood and experience in Nunavut. *The American Review of Canadian Studies* 31(1–2): 121–36.

Shearwood, Perry. 2001. Inuit identity and literacy in a Nunavut community. *Études/Inuit/Studies* 25(1–2): 295–307.

Smith, David M. 1992. The dynamics of a Dene struggle for self-government. Anthropologica 34:21–49.

Smith-Siska, Heather. 1990. *People of the ice. How the Inuit lived.* Toronto: Douglas & McIntyre.

Tulloch, Shelley, and Victoria Hust. 2003. An analysis of language provisions in the Nunavut Act and the Nunavut Land Claims Agreement. In *Arctic economic development and self-government*, ed. G. Duhaime and N. Bernard. Québec: GETIC, Université Laval.

Usher, Peter J. 1990. *Recent and current land use and occupancy in the Northwest Territories by Chipewyan-Denesuline bands.* Prince Albert, SK: Prince Albert Tribal Council.

-----. 2003. Environment, race and nation reconsidered: Reflections on Aboriginal land claims in Canada. *The Canadian Geographer* 47(4): 365–82.

Walls, Denis. 2000. Aboriginal Self-Government in Canada: The Cases of Nunavut and the Alberta Métis Settlements. In *Vision of the Heart: Canadian Aboriginal Issues*, ed. D. Long and P.O. Dickason. Toronto: Harcourt.

Watkins, Mel, ed. 1986. *Dene Nation. The colony within.* Toronto: Univ. of Toronto Press.

Weaver, Sally M. 1981. *Making Canadian Indian policy: The hidden agenda, 1968–1970.* Toronto: Univ. of Toronto Press.

Weissling, Lee E.. 1991. Inuit life in the Eastern Canadian Arctic, 1922–1942: Changes as recorded by the RCMP. *The Canadian Geographer* 35(1): 59–69.

Weller, Geoffrey R. 1988. Self-government for Canada's Inuit: The Nunavut Proposal. *The American Review of Canadian Studies* 18(3): 341–57.

-----. 1990. Devolution, regionalism and division of the Northwest Territories. In *Devolution and constitutional development in the Canadian North*, ed. G. Dacks. Ottawa: Carleton Univ. Press.

Wenzel, George W. 2001. Nunamiut or Kabloonamiut: Which identity best fits Inuit (and does it matter)? *Études/Inuit/Studies* 25(1–2): 37–52.

White, Graham. 2000. Public service in Nunavut and the Northwest Territories: Challenges of the Northern frontier. In *Government restructuring and creating public services*, ed. E. Lindquist. Toronto: Institute of Public Administration of Canada.

-----. 2001. And now for something completely Northern: Institutions of governance in the Territorial North. *Journal of Canadian Studies* 35(4): 80–99.

Wonders, William, C. 1984. *Overlapping land use and occupancy of Dene, Metis, Inuvialuit and Inuit in the Northwest Territories.* Ottawa: Indian and Northern Affairs Canada.

-----. 1985. Our land, your land—Overlapping native land use and occupancy in Canada's Northwest Territories. In *Environment and human life in Highlands and High Latitudes zones*, ed. A. Leidemain and K. Frantz. Innsbruck: Brucker Geographische Studien.

-----. 1987. Native claims and place names in Canada's Western Arctic. *The Canadian Journal of Native Studies* 7(1): 111–20.

-----. 1988. Overlapping Native land claims in the Northwest Territories. *The American Review of Canadian Studies* 28(3): 359–68.

-----. 1990. Tree-line and politics in Canada's Northwest Territories. *Scottish Geographical Magazine* 106(1): 54–60.

----. 2003. Canada's new Arctic territory. In *Canada's changing North*. Montreal and Kingston: McGill-Queen's Univ. Press.

Young, Lisa. 1997. Gender equal legislatures: Evaluating the proposed Nunavut electoral system. *Canadian Public Policy* 23(3): 306–15.

8

Perceptions of Implementation: Treaty Signatory Views of Treaty Implementation

Jean-Pierre Morin

The views expressed in this communication are those of the author, and not necessarily those of the Government of Canada.

Introduction

Since the rebirth of the Indian Rights movement, Treaty First Nations and the Government of Canada have agreed to disagree. Both sides have radically different perspectives of the same issue: the implementation of the Numbered Treaties. On the one hand, Treaty First Nations have argued that the Numbered Treaties have not been fully implemented and that the Government of Canada continues to refuse to honour to its treaty obligations. The Government of Canada, on the other hand, counters that it has substantially implemented and fulfilled its treaty obligations. For cases in which First Nations groups have maintained that treaty terms remain unfulfilled, the specific claims process has been created to address their allegations. This disagreement on the degree of implementation of the Numbered Treaties is a major underlying cause of conflict between Canada and Treaty First Nations on Numbered Treaty issues, which, in turn, is affecting the implementation of modern initiatives, programs, and agreements—not to mention increasing the financial and resource costs associated with them through such delays.

This is, however, not a modern debate. Immediately after the signing of Treaties 4 and 6 in 1874 and 1876, it was clear that both parties to the treaties had different understandings of how the treaties would be implemented. To the Crown, the terms of the treaties were clearly spelled out in the text, and it was understood that the written terms were to be strictly adhered to. Treaty chiefs, however, argued that the treaty terms as described were incomplete and insufficient to help them cope with a changing living environment. To understand the modern Numbered Treaty debate, it is useful to examine the origins of the conflict—specifically, how the treaty signatories' views of treaty implementation were expressed in the first 20 years after the treaty signings, and how these views had an impact upon the relations between the Government of Canada and First Nations peoples. It was clear from the first year after the treaty signings that the Crown and Aboriginal signatories did not share the same view of the treaties. While Treaty chiefs repeatedly called upon the Department of Indian Affairs and Ottawa to fulfill their promises through letters and petitions, the government steadfastly stuck to its policy of strict adherence to the terms of the text. As hardship befell the bands in the northwest, they pushed for fulfilment and some even asked to renegotiate the treaties. Through all this, Ottawa continued to reject all complaints about the treaties and increased the pressure on bands to settle on reserves. A clash between the two was inevitable.

While it would have been useful to examine all treaty areas in the Northwest Territories, such an expansive study is not practical in this instance. In order to develop a better, representative understanding of the issues at hand and the evolution of the growing conflict between the Government of Canada and First Nations in the Northwest, two treaty regions will be used as a type of case study of the Northwest. The areas included in Treaties 4 and 6, covering what is now southern and central Saskatchewan as well as central Alberta, are the best to represent the conflict because of the large volume of correspondence from bands in these areas to the Crown expressing their opinions regarding the implementation of the treaties. Furthermore, the Department of Indian Affairs saw several of the chiefs in these two areas as "troublesome," and kept substantial record of their opinions on these particular tribes and their claims. Finally, departmental officials also responded to the claims being made by the Treaty 4 and 6 chiefs, in which they elaborated and debated the Crown's obligation and its fulfilment of treaty promises.

Treaty Signings

Shortly after the transfer of Rupert's Land to the Dominion of Canada in 1869, Canada undertook the negotiation of a series of treaties across the Northwest Territories. Obligated by the terms of the *Rupert's Land Act* and the *Northwest Territories Act*, the Dominion wanted to secure the Aboriginal title to the lands in the Northwest so as to facilitate settlement and development of the Territories. Furthermore, events in the United States, such as the Indian Wars and calls for the annexation of the Northwest Territories, pushed Canada to quickly establish its authority and sovereignty over its newly acquired territories. As the Indian Wars raged south of the border, the Dominion was concerned that, without treaties, the violence would spread north and engulf the bands in Canada. Over the span of 50 years, 11 treaties were negotiated and signed, covering northern Ontario, all of the Prairies, northeastern British Columbia, and the MacKenzie Valley, and involved territory covering some three million square kilometres.

In the case of Treaties 4 and 6, the negotiation and conclusion of the treaties were only done after a considerable number of requests from the Aboriginal populations of the North and South Saskatchewan rivers. After initially refusing to do so, the government conceded to increasing demands and appeals from the area's Aboriginal population and the Northwest Territories Council and sent Commissioners to negotiate Treaty 4 at Fort Qu'Appelle. Alexander Morris, the lieutenant-governor of the Northwest Territories, along with David Laird, Minister of the Interior, and other commissioners negotiated a treaty with the Aboriginal peoples throughout the Qu'Appelle Valley and in the vicinity of the Canada-United States border.[1] In September 1874, after negotiations at Qu'Appelle and Fort Ellice, the treaty commissioners and the chiefs agreed to use the same terms as those in Treaty 3 with little variation (Taylor 1985, 28).

After the geological survey team, which was exploring and mapping the Territories, and a telegraph construction crew were stopped by Aboriginal people in the untreated areas in the summer of 1875, the Dominion government decided to undertake the negotiation of Treaty 6, with Morris heading the commission (Taylor 1985, 7). Treaty meetings were held in August and September 1876, at Fort Carlton, and further west at Fort Pitt on the North Saskatchewan River. While there was considerable dissent among the different assembled bands, Morris and the other commissioners managed to secure a treaty, but only after conceding some significant additions to the treaty terms (Morris 1881/1991, 176-77). These concessions were criticized by Ottawa, but the criticisms were allayed by Morris' reassurances that it was the only deal acceptable to the chiefs.[2]

While Canada's stated goal in the treaty process was to secure its authority and sovereignty over the Northwest, Aboriginal signatories had different goals and intents. It was central for them to secure some compensation for the inevitable loss of their land to growing settlement, and they needed assistance in making the transition towards an agricultural lifestyle. During the negotiations for both Treaties 4 and 6, the chiefs called for more assistance, more food, more seed, more cattle, and more implements. The treaties also promised to avoid any possible violent conflicts between the Aboriginal population and white settlers, a concern especially in light of the Indian Wars in the United States. As Blair Stonechild states, "it was ... this sentiment for peace that the Indian leaders were receptive to the signing of treaties in the 1870s. Not only had Indians never been at war with whites in the Northwest, but they also sought to prevent such a thing from ever happening" (1986). For these chiefs, the treaties created a relationship between the Northwest's Aboriginal population and Canada that ensured not only peace in the Territories, but also the survival of the area's original inhabitants.

Initial Reaction to Treaty Terms and Implementation

As the officials of the Department of Indian Affairs settled into the administration of Ottawa's policies and the fulfilment of the Crown's treaty obligations, problems with the treaties were becoming apparent. At both signings, a significant number of bands were absent. It has been estimated that, during the negotiations at Qu'Appelle in 1874, nearly half of the Aboriginal population either was not present at the signing or refused to sign at that time. These included some of the most influential chiefs, such as Piapot. In his historical study of the implementation of Treaty 4, Raoul McKay reports that most of the Assiniboine bands between the Cypress and the Touchwood Hills refused to adhere to the treaty (McKay 1973, 41). Morris himself, in his report of the treaty negotiations, recognized that not all the bands were present at the signing of the treaty. At his stop at Fort Ellice, Morris added to the number of adherents when he convinced two Saulteaux chiefs also to sign the treaty (124). Even with this second signing of 1874, there were still some 600 to 700 Crees, Saulteaux, and Assiniboine who had not yet signed.

A similar situation existed during the negotiations for Treaty 6, during which several prominent chiefs were absent during the Fort Pitt negotiations. When Morris and the Treaty Commission arrived, some one hundred lodges were gathered to meet them. A large number of Cree and Saulteaux were out on a hunt, as a herd of buffalo had been spotted in the vicinity (Taylor 1985, 23). While messengers were sent out to fetch some chiefs, such as Sweet Grass, others were ignored or forgotten. Two such prominent chiefs were Big Bear and Little Pine, who controlled some 85 lodges between them (Dempsey, 1984, 71). Morris believed that Sweet Grass was the principal chief of the district and that, with his presence, there was no need to wait for the other chiefs to arrive (Morris 1881/1991, 179). This decision would have dire consequences for the relations between the Treaty 6 bands and the Crown.

The absence of a large number of bands at the 1874 signing of Treaty 4 became a serious issue during the first treaty annuity payment. Two members of the original treaty commission, W.J. Christie and M.G. Dickieson, arrived at Fort Ellice in 1875 to find twice the number lodges that had been present a year previous. A council had been held prior to the arrival of the government officials, and Christie and Dickieson were surprised to discover that the assembled bands wanted new terms for the treaty. In his report to David Laird, Minister of the Interior and Treaty 4 Commissioner, Christie warned the chiefs that a refusal of the terms of the 1874 treaty would result in a report to the government that the chiefs had "broken the agreement." In her study of the agricultural policies of the Department of Indian Affairs in the Northwest, Sarah Carter states that "officials saw the treaty as a 'covenant' between the Indians and the Government; therefore it was impossible to comply with new demands" (Carter 1990, 74). While Christie agreed to hear the chiefs' demands and report them back to Ottawa, Christie and Dickieson did not include the demands in the official report of the adhesion and annuity payment. Rather, they included them in a separate letter to Laird. In their letter, the commissioners indicated that they explained the main premises of the treaty to the bands, that all bands be treated equally. They also had stressed to the assembled bands that the original agreement should be respected. For their part, the assembled First Nations had made three demands: more money, more implements, and more assistance. The annuity set in Treaty 4 was regarded as insufficient, and the chiefs asked for the annuity to be increased from $5 to $12 a person. They also requested an increase in the amount spent on ammunition and twine from $750 for the entire treaty area to $250 per year per band. In regard to agricultural implements, they demanded a blacksmith and a forge, mowers, and mills for every reserve, as well as the implements offered in 1874. The most important demands they made dealt with assistance to the bands. The chiefs recognized that they needed assistance to make the transition to agriculture. They asked for more rations, medicines, and someone to teach them how to farm and build houses.[3] In reply to these demands by both Treaty and non-Treaty bands, Christie and Dickieson stated that none of these concerns and demands had been brought up at the Qu'Appelle signing in 1874. They followed up by saying that these demands could not be considered rights, but if they were fulfilled they would only be considered "favours." Dickieson and Christie reported that they had made it clear to the chiefs that they did not believe that these demands would be granted: "At the same time, we held out no hope that any would be granted except that a man might be sent possibly to shew them how to use their tools."[4]

Christie and Dickieson's reaction to the chiefs' demands for a renegotiation of treaty terms was typical of the position that the Department of Indian Affairs held regarding calls for new terms for the treaties. Over the next 10 years, all calls for new treaties or terms were answered in the same way: The treaty terms were established at the time of signing and those terms could not be changed. Not only could the terms not be changed, the exact wording of the text had to be strictly followed. The federal government had intended the Numbered Treaties to be their main tool for securing Canada's interests to the lands of the Northwest at the lowest possible cost (Dyck 1986, 122). Treaty commissioners and the officers of the Department of Indian Affairs saw the treaties as once and for all agreements to exchange Aboriginal interests to the Crown for benefits. The interpretation of the terms, in the eyes of the government, was under no circumstances to be left to the Aboriginal signatories. As no provisions in the treaties allowed for any type of arbitration in the case of disagreement, the department maintained that its interpretation of the written text was the most accurate (McKay 1972, 39). Ottawa also believed itself to be in a position of strength, both legally and morally, compared to the bands. Indian policy in the late nineteenth century was largely guided by the civilization projects of the department, and officials, politicians, and the public at large maintained that it was their responsibility to bring the Indian towards the more "civilized," British Victorian way of life. Furthermore, the treaties bound the Treaty bands to the law of Canada, as well as binding them to fulfilling their half of the treaty promises—"yielding, ceding and surrendering" their interests and title to the land (39). But while the government had a legal system to enforce Aboriginal fulfilment of the treaty terms, there was no such mechanism to enforce a mutually acceptable interpretation of the Crown's obligations.

As demonstrated by the 1875 requests for renegotiation of the terms of Treaty 4, the fulfilment of the clauses regarding agricultural implements and assistance was one of the central grievances of Treaty bands. As several historians have shown, the Crown was not willing to commit fully to the lifestyle transformation of the Plains Indians, regardless of its own rhetoric. The Department of Indian Affairs was not prepared to undertake the logistics of establishing an administrative infrastructure or providing practical assistance to bands attempting to farm (Dyck, 1986 125). In addition to the logistical nightmare of transferring some 60,000 people from a nomadic to a settled agricultural lifestyle, the department was hampered by constant financial shortfalls and budgetary restrictions. As McKay's study of the implementation of Treaty 4 suggests, the terms of the treaties themselves did not allow for sufficient funds or rations to allow bands to gain a foothold in their new lives as agriculturalists (McKay 1972, 131).

The terms of the treaties were to be followed exactly and precisely. This strict adherence to the text not only limited the extent of the Crown's treaty obligations, but was also fiscally prudent for the government. In both Treaties 4 and 6, the agricultural benefits were only to be issued to bands that had first settled on a reserve and broken the ground. Treaty 4 states that "It is further agreed between Her Majesty and the said Indians that the following articles shall be supplied to any band thereof who are now actually cultivating the soil, or who shall hereafter settle on their reserves and commence to break up the land."[5] To departmental officials, both this clause and the similar one in Treaty 6 limited the Crown's responsibility for issuing implements and cattle only to those bands that were settled on a reserve and who had already broken up soil prior to receiving implements, although this does lead to the question of how the agricultural implements clauses of the treaties would assist the bands to adopt agriculture if implements were only issued to bands already engaged in farming. Furthermore, departmental officials stated that implements were not to become the property of the bands or chiefs. Rather, the tools, and even the cattle, remained the property of the government and any damage to them could be judged as vandalism of Crown property. Departmental officials were reluctant to replace damaged tools because of the cost, but also because some believed that it would serve little purpose to do so.

At the time of the implementation of the treaties, an economic slowdown was having a serious impact upon the business of the Canadian government. The worldwide recession, later a depression, lasted some 20 years, and severely reduced the federal government's revenues, which were based on excise taxes and duties. At the same time, a new deputy superintendent general of Indian Affairs was taking charge, centralizing decision making and changing the administration of the department. Lawrence Vankoughnet, a high-ranking Tory from Cornwall, Ontario and a long-time supporter of Sir John A. Macdonald, was a micro-manager of the highest order. Vankoughnet centralized all decisions into his own hands and removed nearly all the discretionary powers of Indian agents, including those of the Indian commissioner in the Northwest (Carter 1990, 51). He seldom took the advice of men in the field and relied almost entirely upon his own opinions. Vankoughnet was also renowned for his frugality and efforts to minimize costs; his efforts created a slow and largely inefficient administration.[6] Vankoughnet's administration made no distinction between the funds spent for treaty implementation and those spent for general assistance to bands, such as the issuing of rations. To him, all were expenses that needed to be cut. After his 1881 tour of the Northwest, during which he met with several chiefs and visited reserves, Vankoughnet dramatically cut $140,000 from the departmental budget, dismissed clerks and agents, and ordered the reduction of rations (Dempsey 1984, 121).

The deputy superintendent also was interested in reducing costs. Laird's replacement (as of 1876) as minister of the Interior and ex officio superintendent general of Indian Affairs was David Mills, who believed that more than enough had been done in the few years since the signing of the treaties to encourage the transition of First Nations people to agriculture. He also held the notion that, during Laird's ministry, the government had been far too generous in issuing implements, tools, and cattle (Carter 1990, 69). With the goal of reducing costs, the department was to limit the distribution of tools and implements. Along with Vankoughnet and Mills, other officials in Ottawa had begun to develop, along with their desire to cut spending, a view that Canada was being too generous towards the Treaty bands, and that such "charity" was detrimental to the civilization of Aboriginal people.

While it is true to state that the Department of Indian Affairs was spending far more than was required by the terms of the treaties for rations, implements, and cattle, these expenditures were still insufficient to permit a proper transition from hunting to farming. Reports of bands killing their cattle for food were frequent, as were accounts of individuals begging at the doors of white settlers. These incidents did not lead departmental officials to recognize problems with the agricultural policy or the insufficiency of the rations being issued. Instead, politicians and bureaucrats saw these incidents as examples of laziness, or a refusal to become self-sufficient. This opinion was widespread throughout Indian Affairs. In a letter to Alexander Morris in 1873, Edward McKay stressed that the transition to an agricultural way of life would not be easy for the Plains people: "The Plains Indians accustomed to an easy, free, and lazy existence will not in the present generation take to farming unless compelled to do so."[7]

By the end of the 1870s, the belief that treaty bands had no desire to make the transition to agriculture because they preferred to live by government handouts was the dominant view of officials, and this opinion coloured all subsequent relations with First Nations. With the desired goal of compelling Aboriginal people to adopt farming, in concordance with the government's underlying goal of civilizing the Treaty bands, and influenced by the Victorian belief that charity leads to laziness, the Department of Indian Affairs adopted a ration policy of "food for work." The issuance of rations became directly tied to the work Aboriginal bands undertook, and their adoption of agriculture, treaty benefits, and government assistance were rolled into the central issue of rations. Rations were issued to individuals who were working on their reserves, for their agents, or, after the creation of instructional farms, for the farm instructors. Agents were instructed to feed only those who were willing to work and to criticize openly those who did not (McKay 1972, 114). The issuance of rations was not only used to encourage farming. On several occasions, officials such as Indian commissioner, Edgar Dewdney, used the issuance of rations as tool for Aboriginal compliance. When trying to get bands to stay on their reserves, Dewdney ordered that rations were only to be issued on a band's respective reserve.[8] The department's rations policy quickly became a major complaint for Treaty bands.

The government's interpretation of the treaty terms, and the desire to reduce expenditures as well as the growing administrative structure of the department, had a severe impact on its ongoing relationship with Treaty chiefs. In her paper "Magnificent Gifts," Jean Friesen explains that "to the Indians, disillusioned with the government's unilateral interpretation, increasingly confined in their economic opportunities, and ruled by the federal *Indian Act* to which they had never consented, the treaties came to be seen in the words of a Saskatchewan chief as merely 'sweet promises' " (Friesen 1999, 212). Only a few years after the signing of the treaties, chiefs were beginning to believe that the treaties had serious shortcomings and that the Indian Affairs department did not see the treaties in the same way as they did. Because the buffalo disappeared much more quickly than anyone had expected—the conservative estimates at the time had been 10 or more years before their total disappearance—Aboriginal populations lost not only their main food staple but also their main economic staple within five years of the signing the treaties (McKay 1972, 110). While Morris and Laird had promised that the treaties would allow the bands to prosper and adapt to the new realities of the Northwest, in reality the Aboriginal population had begun a steady economic and social regression from their pre-treaty lives.

The annual treaty annuity payments, which were made at a gathering of bands on the site of the treaty negotiations until 1879, were a popular occasion for chiefs to express their dissatisfaction with government policy and treaty implementation. At the first treaty payment after the signing of Treaty 6 at Fort Carlton, complaints and concerns about the treaty culminated in the drafting of a petition that stated that the government had broken the treaty because of its non-fulfilment of the terms. The petition further called upon the governor general to reopen the negotiations so as to make it more generous towards the bands.[9] This incident created much concern for the Indian agent, Captain James Walker, who was completely taken aback by the complaints. Walker, who had been at Carlton but returned to Battleford, attributed the reason for the petition upon the late arrival of treaty goods and provisions to Fort Carlton. He reported to G.M. Dickieson that all the assembled chiefs had signed the petition and already sent it to Ottawa.[10] This petition referred to the treaty of 1876 as nothing but "sweet promises" to the bands so that they would surrender their lands. In an effort to resolve the situation, Walker called a council of the chiefs and explained why the presents had not been distributed at the time of the payments. Through the influence of Mistowasis and Ah-kha-ta-koop, two chiefs who had led the campaign for the adhesion of the bands to the treaty in 1876, Walker was able to convince the chiefs to rescinded their petition, and sign a letter of apology. The letter stated:

> We the undersigned chiefs of the Cree Nation who signed the Treaty that was made at Carlton last summer wish you to express to our Good Father, the Governor of this Country our entire, and complete content and satisfaction with the terms and conditions of that treaty; and to thank our good Mother the Queen in our own manners, for the governors way in which she has fulfilled the promises they made to us ... We want also to tell you that we are well pleased with the way in which you have dealt with us, for the patience you have borne with our many questions and the kindness you have shown in explaining the articles of the Treaty that we do not quite understand.[11]

There are two remarkable points that must be noted regarding this incident. First the bands, when confronted by Walker, acquiesced to the demands of the departmental official and apologized for their actions. In the early years of the treaty, chiefs were quick to rescind their earlier demands when confronted and asked for specifics. Another point of interest is in the last sentence of the letter signed by the chiefs. In it, the chiefs say that they were thankful for the agent's explanation of the treaty terms. By doing so, they not only admitted that their interpretation of the terms was different to that of the Department of Indian Affairs, but that they may not have fully understood the treaty terms or, at the very least, not understood the government's interpretation of the terms. This would not be the last reference of this nature.

In the following year, 1878, another incident attracted the attention of the department. Chief Pasqua, an original signatory to Treaty 4 in 1874 and a leader in the call for Aboriginal people to make the transition to agriculture, travelled to Winnipeg to meet with Lieutenant-Governor Cauchon. In the account drafted by Cauchon's interpreter, Pasqua presented a series of complaints about the inadequacies of the treaties. Seeing the lieutenant-governor as a more direct representative of the Queen than the officials of the Department of Indian Affairs, Pasqua asked that Cauchon call upon the Queen to rectify the inadequacies of the treaties. The report stated that the chief believed that the department was not fulfilling its promises even though his band had cleared 30 acres of land for planting, adding that "they were neither supplied with cattle to break and work the land; seed to sow it; nor provisions to feed them while at work."[12] Pasqua also stated that specific promises, made by Laird, to be supplied with rations were not being carried out and that his people were starving and forced to eat their dogs while at work. He closed his meeting with Cauchon by stating that he had come to Winnipeg as a sign of his friendship with the representative of the Queen, but that the Indians were "subject at time to an irritation of feeling against the white race who while establishing themselves in comfort on their broad domain have directly or indirectly caused such havoc in the Northwest and that without assistance there was nothing left for them to do but suffer and die."[13]

When Cauchon's office forwarded a report to the Department of Indian Affairs, Laird was quick to refute Pasqua's claims and question the value of his character.

While sources prior to this incident cited Pasqua as an industrious and valuable leader amongst the Cree who had already adopted farming prior to the Treaty, Laird dismissed his complaints as baseless and stated that Pasqua "is the most untruthful chief whom I have met in this Superintendency and though not really so poor as many others, he is a great beggar."[14] In regard to Pasqua's statement that he had made promises to feed the bands during planting, Laird refuted the claim and returned to the letter of the text of the treaty, stating that "there is no stipulation to that effect in Treaty no. 4."[15] Because Laird refuted Pasqua's claims, the department saw no need to address the claims and ignored them. Pasqua, however, was no longer considered a good chief, but rather as a troublesome one, a typical conclusion made by the department towards any chief who dared complain.

David Laird's dismissal of Pasqua's complaints as frivolous and exaggerated was typical of the "outside service," the Indian agents scattered across the Territories, and of the department. In late 1877, the Indian Department in Ottawa sent a circular to all agents in Manitoba and the Northwest from the superintendent general of Indian Affairs. The circular asked that reports of the status of Indian affairs by agency be sent to Ottawa. One question in particular related to the implementation of treaties: "Are the Indians satisfied with the manner in which the treaty are [sic] being carried out; if not, what are the grounds of their dissatisfaction?"[16] On the whole, the agents stated that the bands in their agencies were largely satisfied with the implementation of the treaties and that there were but a few complaints regarding the quantity of stock animals and implements due to them.[17] David Laird, as the highest ranking departmental official, rejected any possibility of complaints: "The Indians of this superintendency [the entire Northwest Territories] have no reason to be dissatisfied with the manner treaty obligations are carried out."[18] He further stated that the only complaint he received pertained to the quantity of provisions being distributed at the time of treaty payments. As there was no provision to issue rations at the treaty payments in the treaties, this could not be considered a complaint about the fulfilment of the treaty terms. Laird added that the issuance of rations was "a necessity forced upon the Government in order to enable the Indians from the Plains to subsist while away from their hunting grounds," and he saw such complaints as unreasonable considering the massive government expenditure.

Without a single agent reporting any general dissatisfaction among the bands and Laird's categorical rejection of complaints, one must question the purpose of the reports in light of Pasqua's meeting and the 1877 petition of the Carlton chiefs. As the Indian Affairs department was also using these reports as a measure of the agents' management of their agencies, agents themselves appear to downplay the complaints made by bands. In several instances, the agents stated that the bands were satisfied, but had a few minor complaints and proceeded to list several specific complaints dealing with the fulfilment of promises for stock animals and implements.[19] Agents replied that the bands were asking more than the treaty entitled them to receive. Any possible complaints were explained away not as any mismanagement on the part of the agent, but rather as excessive and unreasonable demands by the bands.

Indian Activism and Government Refusals

The reports of departmental officials are, thankfully, not the only source of information regarding complaints of treaty non-fulfilment made by bands. Chiefs were quick to use the available resources at their disposal to press the government to look into their complaints. The letters, petitions, and delegations were so numerous as to lead government officials to view Aboriginal peoples as chronic complainers. While it is impossible to review every single complaint made, two occasions merit special review: the interview of chiefs by the governor general, the Marquis of Lorne, in 1881, and the letter to the prime minister printed in the Edmonton *Bulletin* in 1883.

As part of his general tour of Western Canada, the Marquis of Lorne travelled throughout the Territories and large-scale meetings with chiefs were held in the different treaty areas. For the Aboriginal population, the news of the coming of the governor general was seen as an occasion for a grand council where their concerns could be expressed to the direct representative of the Queen. In a society so closely linked by family relations, the fact that the Marquis was also the Queen's son-in-law signified to the assembled chiefs the importance of his status and influence. During his tour, Lorne held meetings with the chiefs at Qu'Appelle in the Treaty 4 area and at Fort Carlton in the Treaty 6 region. Not fully understanding the somewhat symbolic role of the governor general, the chiefs of Treaties 4 and 6 believed that the Marquis of Lorne could undertake steps to address their grievances. Over the course of the two meetings, the governor general was addressed by numerous and influential chiefs and headmen.

At both meetings, the chiefs presented three specific arguments: the insufficiency of the treaty terms, the need to renegotiate, and the need for more assistance. At Qu'Appelle, Chief Kanasis told Lorne that they could not "make [their] living by what was given to [them] by the Treaty."[20] This sentiment was repeated by Yellow Quill and Louis O'Soup. The chiefs explained that their people were without horses because they had been forced to eat them, and that they did not know how to farm because no one had taught them how to use their tools. Yellow Quill's statements regarding the nature of the treaties are a good representation of the other chiefs' comments. He openly stated that he did "not understand the Treaty" and that a new treaty was necessary because "we cannot live by the first treaty: we shall die off ... They [the government] cannot hold the treaty that was made before."[21] The chiefs called upon the governor general to reopen the treaties and negotiate more generous terms for the Aboriginal signatories. Chiefs such as Poundmaker, the influential Cree leader from the Battleford district, recalled Alexander Morris's words at the treaty negotiations in 1876 when it was stated that the Indian would live like the white man. Poundmaker told Lorne that the treaty terms did not permit him to live like the white settlers and that better tools and implements, similar to those used by the settlers, should be provided to him.[22]

In response to these constant calls for a new treaty and more assistance, the Marquis de Lorne responded in a manner typical of the federal government and white society as a whole. Lorne saw the bands as lazy and idle with no real desire to adapt to the new reality of the Northwest (Carter 1990, 144). Lorne stressed that the treaties had brought peace to the Territories and that it was because of the benevolence of the Queen that such a thing was possible. He also underlined the fact that the chiefs had already signed a treaty and that such agreements must be respected. He reminded them that the Queen would respect her promises and that the "red men" must do the same. He also expressed some displeasure at the constant calls for a new treaty and said, "I hope to hear nothing more of breaking treaty for the treaty was made for them and their children's good. And no good man among them need fear that he will not be as well off as the white man."[23] The chiefs came away from their council with the governor general with nothing more than a few presents and statements that the treaties must be maintained as they were negotiated. Their experience with the Queen's son-in-law proved to be similar to every other meeting with government officials.

The other incident that garnered considerable attention was a letter to the prime minister that appeared in the Edmonton *Bulletin*. Signed by nine chiefs, including all of the chiefs of the Hobbema agency south of Edmonton, the letter is a striking complaint of their treatment since signing Treaty 6. The chiefs argued that the treaty was only favourable for the federal government—"the white man had it all his own way. He made the conditions both for himself and for us"—and that the Department of Indian Affairs treated the bands like groups of children. They stressed that, at the signing, the treaty was said to be inviolable and binding upon both parties, but that only the Indian was required to follow the treaty while the federal government did what it wished and ignored its promises and obligations. As did the chiefs who met with the governor general, the letter referred to the promises made by the Treaty commissioners that the treaties would help the Indians survive and prosper. Since the treaty, the bands had become poverty-stricken and starving, and the chiefs feared that their people would eventually disappear from the Plains. They closed by warning that their complaints should be addressed or they "shall conclude that the treaty made with us six years ago was meaningless matter of form and that the white man had indirectly doomed us to annihilation, little by little."[24]

Despite the chiefs' warnings, the department paid little heed to the letters' complaints and accusations. Rather, Lawrence Vankoughnet, the deputy superintendent general, and Edgar Dewdney, the Indian commissioner, spent the next several months trying to find whom had written the letter for the chiefs. When Father C. Scollen, a Catholic missionary in the Edmonton district and a man highly critical of the Indian department, was finally identified, they accused him of acting in a treasonous manner and of causing great harm to the bands by raising their expectations and spreading lies.[25] The archival files of the Department of Indian Affairs contain a copy of the original letter printed in the *Bulletin*, and some 20 pages worth of correspondence relating to the department's efforts at identifying Scollen, but not a single document disputes or even addresses the complaints presented in the letter.

As letters, petitions, and delegations proved to be largely ineffectual, other chiefs chose different routes in attempts to enforce the fulfilment of treaty terms. Poundmaker, Piapot, and Big Bear, all very influential and powerful chiefs in their own right, each chose a different tactic: Poundmaker refused to work; Piapot refused to take a reserve; and Big Bear refused to take treaty. Each had his own reasons for discontent. During the Fort Carlton negotiations, Poundmaker, at the time a headman and not a chief, openly opposed the treaty and demanded that the chiefs wait for better terms. In the years after the treaty, he routinely challenged the authority of Indian agents and demanded more implements and more sophisticated machinery, all the while demanding rations for his band (Department of Indian Affairs, 1882, 195). Piapot, while not present at the 1874 signing of Treaty 4, was one of the leading chiefs who demanded that the treaty be modified during the 1875 treaty payment at Qu'Appelle. As with many chiefs in the Treaty 4 area, Piapot wanted his reserve to be in the Cypress Hills, a location rejected by the department (Morin 2003). Told to take a reserve near Indian Head, Piapot refused to select a specific site until 1882, when the department agreed to his selection and provided rations and transportation to the reserve.[26] As for Big Bear, his band's hunting expedition cost him the chance to speak at the Fort Pitt negotiations for Treaty 6, and he staunchly believed the treaty terms to be meagre and insufficient to meet the needs of the Plains people. Big Bear continually refused to sign the treaty and travelled across the Prairie in search of buffalo, often crossing into Montana. He met with various chiefs and Aboriginal leaders trying to garner support for a renegotiation of the treaties (Dempsey 1984, 122). Only after starvation and desertions to other bands had severely reduced the number of his followers did Big Bear take treaty at Fort Walsh in 1882.

Of the three chiefs, Big Bear was considered by far the most influential and potentially dangerous leader on the Prairie. As has already been stated, Big Bear had one of the largest followings among the Plains Cree in the Treaty 6 area, and was well respected as a wise man not only for his council but also for his medicine. While starvation forced him to adhere to the treaty, Big Bear was still determined to continue to press the Department of Indian Affairs for better treaty terms. Refusing to take a reserve, or by asking for land that he knew would be rejected by officials, he travelled across the region, calling upon the other chiefs to stand united with him against the federal government. By 1884, Big Bear had considerable support from among the different bands. In his report to Edgar Dewdney about Big Bear calling upon the department to fulfil the treaties, Agent J.A. McRae stated that "a year ago, [Big Bear] stood alone, in making these demands; now, the whole of the Indians are with him."[27] Big Bear encouraged other chiefs to stand together when confronting agents and other government officials, a tactic adopted by Louis O'Soup in the Treaty 4 area.[28] For his refusal to take treaty and a reserve, as well as his constant meetings with chiefs, the higher-ranking officers of the department viewed Big Bear with considerable suspicion. Hayter Reed, one-time Indian agent and assistant Indian commissioner for the Northwest, described Big Bear as "an agitator and always has been and having received the moral support of the half-breed community he is only too glad to have the opportunity of inciting the Indians to make fresh and exorbitant demands."[29] Every statement and meeting Big Bear made was closely monitored by the department. While Big Bear was getting the attention that he wanted, it was for the entirely wrong reasons. The Department of Indian Affairs continued to dismiss his claims as gross exaggerations of the treaty terms and his actions as nothing more than troublesome behaviour. The officials of the Department of Indian Affairs continued to be blind to any link between the claims and complaints being made and their own implementation of the treaties.

The general feeling of dissatisfaction with the department's policies and practices, and Big Bear's efforts to unite the bands across the Northwest, coalesced in 1883 and 1884 in a series of councils. Sponsored by some of the chiefs considered by Dewdney and Reed to be the most troublesome, the department looked upon these gatherings with suspicion. The focus of these councils, which also included the traditional thirst or sun dance, was to decide how best to deal with the federal government's non-fulfilment of the treaties and what tactic should be employed to negotiate new agreements with the Crown. Piapot and Big Bear were, again, central figures in this latest attempt to organize the bands. As both chiefs were of the same mind regarding the need to stand united against the federal government, Piapot and Big Bear wanted the councils to give them the authority to represent the other chiefs and present their grievances and complaints to Dewdney and Macdonald. In Piapot's case, a council and dance was held on his reserve in the fall of 1883 with attendance by most of the Treaty 4 chiefs. During the meetings, Piapot had little difficulty convincing the others to change their stance towards the government officials. Recognizing the need for wider representation, the council concluded with a call to hold a grand council of the Northwest where representatives from the Cree, Assiniboine, and Blackfoot bands would attend to plan an appropriate strategy to deal with the federal government in a united manner (Dempsey 1984, 123).

As messengers travelled between reserves calling the bands together, the Department of Indian Affairs, thinking that these councils were the prelude to a violent uprising, began to flex its muscles in response. Senior officials were also very much aware of the purpose of the councils. In March 1884, J.M. Rae, Indian agent for the Carlton district, stated in a letter to Edgar Dewdney that "messengers are being sent all over the Country and that the chiefs all over the Country are to join those B/ford rascals next summer in asking for better terms."[30] As Rae notes, the chiefs' dissatisfaction with the treaty terms was well known. Because the department saw the terms of the treaties as fixed and non-negotiable, officials perceived these councils as fomenting dissent and, therefore, to be prevented. Rae gave a clear representation of the Crown's position in his same letter to the Indian commissioner:

> A firm stand must be taken and the answer no given to all their demands, for if they succeed this time, years will not undo the work of one day. At the present they think they can do anything they like—and they must be disabused of this idea even by force if necessary—the Chiefs from below here will take and active part in the matter unless they see what a grave turn affairs are taking here. [emphasis in original][31]

As there were a relatively small number of North West Mounted Police in the Territories, agents had few coercive powers. The only true method of influence at Indian agents' disposal was the refusal of rations. When a chief came to ask for rations for the trip to a council in 1884, Indian Agent Rae was quick to refuse the request, stating that the federal government disapproved of the council meeting, while trying to dissuade the chief from attending.[32]

The councils were, on the whole, very well attended. The biggest council of 1884 was hosted by Big Bear and Poundmaker, on Poundmaker's reserve near Battleford. These meetings of the chiefs proved to be constructive and accomplished Big Bear's goal of unifying the bands. The final outcome of the council was instruction for a delegation led by Big Bear to travel first to see Piapot in Treaty 4, then to Dewdney in Regina, and finally onward to Ottawa to meet with Vankoughnet. Their goal was to express the concerns and desires of the chiefs to the highest possible officials; specifically, to the superintendent general of Indian Affairs, Sir John A. Macdonald (Dempsey 1984, 123). Any possible success the proposed delegation might have had, however, was ruined before the council was concluded. During the council, a farm instructor named Craig was assaulted by a small group from the Yellow Quill band, who stopped by his house asking for provisions. When Craig refused, he was struck by one of the men and subsequently lodged a complaint with the nearby North West Mounted Police post. When the constables arrived at the council to arrest the man in question, a large confrontation occurred and violence was only averted by the intervention of Big Bear and Poundmaker and the voluntary surrender of the suspect by the council to the NWMP a few days later.[33] This incident completely overshadowed the rest of the council and dance. The near outbreak of violence put the Department of Indian Affairs and the NWMP on the defensive. Dewdney was no longer willing to meet with any delegations, and all the blame for the incident was placed on Big Bear and Poundmaker for having organized the council in the first place. The incident, however, led to a review of the department's policy regarding rations and the discretionary powers of agents.

With a growing number of incidents between departmental officials and Indians occurring across the Northwest, Dewdney, Hayter Reed, and Deputy Superintendent General Lawrence Vankoughnet began to focus their attention on the influence of specific chiefs as being at the root of the problems. Reed, the assistant Indian commissioner, was an ever-increasing presence in Indian Affairs. After Dewdney's assumption of the role of lieutenant governor of the Northwest Territories, Reed took on an ever-growing amount of responsibility. As he personally investigated incidents between officials and bands, his views and perspective of Indian-government relations became more and more important. Reed maintained the view that the bands were generally content with their treatment by the department, and that certain chiefs, namely Big Bear and Poundmaker, were stirring up dissent. He investigated a petition presented to Agent Macrae in the fall of 1884, which listed 18 items of complaint about the implementation of the treaties. Reed's report dismissed all the complaints.[34] He had in the past responded to complaints by saying that they were based on "false statements being made by them [the chiefs] and constantly repeated until they become a matter of belief as no one was ever present capable of giving them a denial."[35] Reed based his opinion on his direct experiences with individual chiefs. During those meetings, he pressed chiefs to show how the treaties had not been fulfilled and explained away the basis of every complaint with examples of the Crown's fulfilment of its obligations. Reed reported that Big Bear's involvement in the petition was further proof of his role as a "troublemaker" in the district.[36] As a sign of Reed's growing influence on Indian policy, in a reply to Reed's report from the Department of Indian Affairs, likely from Vankoughnet, the department stated that "it would appear from Mr. Reed's report that the Indians have no good grounds for serious complaint in any respect."[37] The memorandum goes on to instruct all Indian agents to explain to the bands that the treaties were being fulfilled and that the federal government was giving them far more than what was stated in the treaties.

As they were seen as the most disruptive influences to the proper administration of Indian affairs in the Northwest, senior departmental officials wanted to remove these "troublesome" chiefs from their positions. Vankoughnet, in a February 1885 letter, asked Dewdney for his opinion on how best to deal with Big Bear, Little Pine, and Poundmaker, calling them "Indians [who] incite or stir up other Indians ... to act in a riotous, disorderly or threatening manner."[38] Vankoughnet suggested that such people should be used as examples to the general Aboriginal population through their arrest and imprisonment. Dewdney agreed whole-heartedly with his superior's plan but noted that the territorial judicial system did not view the matter in the same way. Where the Department of Indian Affairs wanted convictions and imprisonment of chiefs for "disloyalty" and stirring up discontent, the magistrates and the North West Mounted Police only arrested and convicted people for specific crimes as listed in the Criminal Code.[39] Dewdney went so far as to suggest the code itself be amended to make the prosecution of chiefs easier. No modification to the Criminal Code was ever made in this regard.

As Dewdney and Vankoughnet debated how to rid themselves of the chiefs, the North West Mounted Police was growing increasingly concerned with the policies of the Department of Indian Affairs. Throughout 1884, police inspectors and constables were reporting on the state of Indian affairs from a police perspective. In his report of the 1884 incident during Big Bear and Poundmaker's council, Inspector W.W. Crozier of the Battleford detachment placed the blame for the incident not on the chiefs, but rather on the department's policies. He stated, "if the government wish to conduct Indian affairs peacefully, their policy should be, as it has been in the past, one of conciliation." He roundly condemned Indian policy by questioning the very nature of the civilization program: "It does not seem to me reasonable to expect a lot of pure savages to settle down and become steady farmers all at once—or even within a few years—and even if they do not do much work for some time, it should not be considered extraordinary."[40] He continued by suggested that the refusal of the bands' demands would lead to further confrontation. He also warned that the bands were prepared to resist any attempts interfere with them, and that further confrontation would adversely affect the whole of the Territories. The inspector's words had little impact upon the administration in the Northwest. Agents did not receive more discretionary powers to issue rations, the work for food policy was continued, and discontent among the bands continued to increase. Crozier's warnings of possible future violence became reality in the spring of 1885.

Rebellion and the End of the Treaty Movement

On April 2, 1885, Big Bear's attempts at negotiating new treaties with the federal government came to a quick and violent end. Shortly after the Métis victory at Duck Lake, and while Big Bear was absence from his camp, several warriors from his band and the neighbouring Wood Cree band attacked the settlement of Frog Lake, looting the Hudson's Bay Company store and killing nine people, including the Indian agent, Thomas Quinn; the farm instructor, John Delaney; and two Catholic priests (Morton 1979, 77). Bolstered by additional warriors from Bobtail's Reserve and the Cold Lake Chipewyans, the bands moved down the Saskatchewan River towards Fort Pitt, where they met Little Poplar and his followers from Battleford, who had been waiting before the fort (Dempscy 1984, 168). On April 14, 1885, Fort Pitt surrendered and then was pillaged by the Cree for war plunder. After receiving news that Poundmaker was under attack by soldiers and police, the camp was moved to Frenchman's Butte. On May 28, 1885, the Cree warriors ambushed the militia forces of General Strange, who was tracking the Cree from Fort Pitt (Beal and Macleod 1984, 284). During the battle, the Chipewyans deserted, prisoners escaped, and the Cree warriors began to fall back. Fleeing towards Loon Lake, the Cree were again attacked by the militia on June 3, 1885. The Wood Cree left the group to take refuge in the forests and others headed towards Batoche, while a number of warriors held out until the end of June. Big Bear's son, Imasees, avoiding patrols and the militia, led more than a hundred Cree south across the border to take refuge in the United States. On July 4, 1885, Big Bear, alone, abandoned by his band, surrendered to the militia at Fort Carlton (Dempsey 1984, 180). Big Bear, Poundmaker, and nearly 45 other "rebel Indians" were put on trial, along with Louis Riel and other Métis arrested after the battle of Batoche (Dickason 2002, 311). Big Bear was sentenced to three years imprisonment, as was Poundmaker, although their sentences were reduced to 18 months after both developed serious illnesses. Big Bear was released in early 1887, and, having never taken a reserve, joined his daughter on Poundmaker's reserve.

As the events on the North Saskatchewan unfolded, numerous chiefs across the region refused to participate in the uprising. The concerns of the North West Mounted Police and government officials, such as Reed and Dewdney, that the uprising would spread to all the bands in the Territories, proved to be unfounded. From the first instances of violence, several chiefs attempted to distance themselves from the bands in revolt and made overtures of peace to the Crown. Chiefs such as George Bear, Pasqua, and Piapot, all sent letters and telegrams to Ottawa stating their loyalty to the Crown. They all referred to the treaties as the source of their loyalty, as did a group of chiefs from the Wolf Creek region of Alberta: "At the Treaty, we were promised peace, not war, and we wish to remain loyal till death."[41] Piapot, once considered one of the more "troublesome" chiefs in Treaty 4, also referred to his promise of loyalty by stating, "It is eleven years since I gave up fighting. When I took the Government Treaty, I touched the pen not to interfere with the white man and the white man not to interfere with me ... I promise you [Macdonald] as I have promised our Governor that I will never fight against the white man."[42] All the while promising their loyalty, the chiefs used the occasion of their communication to stress again for the fulfilment of the treaty promises. Chiefs Ochapascoopeeasis and Rock Chief both reminded the federal government that they remained loyal, even though all the treaty provisions had not been fulfilled.[43] In his letter, Pasqua comments on the poor state of his band by saying, "We depend on promises by Governor Morris to us because of our keeping faith, and hope when trouble is ended that she [the Queen] will extend some help to us on our reserves to make a better living than before."[44] Interestingly, Prime Minister Macdonald responded directly to the telegrams and letters, stating that "the Government will do everything that they properly can to forward the interests and improve the conditions of the red man. All treaty promises will be faithfully carried out and loyalty of these chiefs is fully appreciated."[45] As it had been prior to the uprising, however, the treaty promises were "carried out" according to the federal government's understanding of its obligations.

In the aftermath of the defeat of Riel and the Métis at the battle of Batoche, the Department of Indian Affairs attempted to ascertain why part of the Aboriginal population had rebelled. Again relying on reports by Hayter Reed, Lawrence Vankoughnet placed the blame squarely on the shoulders of Riel, Poundmaker, and Big Bear, describing them as disloyal troublemakers who had always been opposed to Canada's administration of the Northwest. Following the line of argument that had been presented prior to the events of the spring of 1885, Reed and Vankoughnet saw Big Bear and Poundmaker as the leaders of the Indian rebellion, disregarding several eyewitness accounts to the contrary. As leaders of disloyal bands, they were to bear the brunt of the blame.[46] As a result of their involvement, the rebellious bands were considered to have violated the treaties they had signed, and their treaty rights were to be suspended until such time as the department saw fit to restore them. On Reed's recommendation, the department instituted a series of punitive measures against any rebellious Indians, such as withholding annuities, a pass system, and breaking up bands.[47] While Vankoughnet's memorandum stated that loyal bands would not face any such restrictions, certain measures, especially the pass system, were applied to all bands in the Northwest.

One of the major consequences of the rebellion was a hardening of the Department of Indian Affairs's position towards complaints. In the first years after the uprising, any chief that dared complain about missing treaty cattle or not having received his full complement of implements was accused of disloyalty. The department continued to keep a close watch on bands, and appointed regional officials to tour reserves and report on the level of discontentment among the bands. An example of one such tour was the one made by the Anglican bishop of the Northwest Territories, J.A. MacKay, to the Battleford bands. While he found most of the bands fairly complacent, the bishop noted that some bands were disgruntled and that only the constant presence of troops in the area was preventing a repetition of the events of the previous year.[48]

As the Department of Indian Affairs began to enforce its new restrictive policies, its general handling of the Aboriginal population in the Northwest and, specifically, its respect of the treaties, was being questioned in Ottawa. The member of Parliament for Huron-West, Malcolm Cameron, presented a strong criticism of the department's handling of the treaties and the rebellion. Using first-hand accounts from prominent figures in the Northwest Territories, such as Father Scollen, and the reports of the department itself, Cameron presented the case that the root causes of the rebellion were the non-fulfilment of the terms of the treaties and the refusal of the Department of Indian Affairs to acknowledge its mistakes. He went on to criticize every aspect of Indian administration, from the quality of the implements and cattle to the morality and character of Indian agents and the Indian commissioner. Cameron was adamant that the blame of the uprising had to rest with the department's officials.

> The conduct of the officials of the North-West Territories, more than any thing else, created dissatisfaction and discontent among the Indians; I say that the misconduct and the mismanagement of the Administration in connection with the Indian Affairs in the North-West Territories, as much as anything else produced uneasiness, dissatisfaction and discontent among the Indians, which ultimately broke out into open rebellion.[49]

Cameron also accused the federal government of breaking the promises made in the treaties, what he called "solemn covenants entered into with the Indians ... shamefully, openly, persistently and systematically broken by this Government."[50] He concluded that "instead of dealing fairly and honestly by the Indian, as we ought to have done, instead of maintaining unbroken our treaty obligations with the Indian, we pursued, and we still pursue that mad and reckless and inhuman policy of submission by starvation."

The MP's remarks in the House of Commons were a surprisingly accurate representation of the arguments being made by Treaty chiefs in the 10 years following the signing of the treaties. As usual, the Department of Indian Affairs responded to Cameron by outlining how the government had endeavoured to fulfil the treaties. In a 60-page document, the officials of the department, specifically Lawrence Vankoughnet, refuted every single claim made in Cameron's speech to the House of Commons. The departmental report refuted Cameron's claims on two fronts: first, by showing that it had implemented the treaties according to the letter of the text and more so; and second, that Treaty bands had not properly understood the nature of the federal government's obligations under the treaties. In response to the claims that the bands had not receive all the implements and cattle they asked for, the report states that all that was entitled to by the treaties had been issued to the bands. The department added that the issue at hand was not what was promised in the treaty but, rather, what the chiefs demanded beyond the terms of the treaty (Department of Indian Affairs 1886, 37). The department stated that while it could have limited itself to the terms of the treaty, it had been in fact far more generous, reporting that the bands "certainly have received far more than they were entitled to under their treaties. Let it not be forgotten that with a single exception [Treaty 6] not one of the treaties stipulates that the Government shall supply the Indians with food" (5). The rationing of Aboriginal people was done "as a measure of humanity" and that food was issued so as to encourage the bands to become self-sustaining. The overarching policy goal of civilization was reinforced again, while refuting the claims of a starvation policy: "The provisions supplied them are so distributed as to encourage industry. Men who absolutely refuse to work are certainly not encouraged in their idleness."

The departmental report attributed the Treaty bands' incomprehension of the federal government's treaty obligations largely to their "primitive condition" and childish manner. The report stated that the Treaty bands "have very imperfect notions of the duties of the Government towards them, and of their claims upon the Government. They desire to get all they can; and they are deeply incensed when they think they have been wronged" (Department of Indian Affairs 1886, 3). Moreover, the report accuses of Cameron of spreading the same "exaggerated notions of their rights" as had been claimed by leaders such as Big Bear, Piapot, and Poundmaker. The department stated that it was its responsibility to care for the bands while they were in a state of "simplicity" and "ignorance." Further-more, it saw itself as the ultimate arbiter of what was required for their advance-ment and what was beyond their capabilities (5). The department's rebuttal of Cameron's allegations brought the matter to a close. While there was a short debate in the Senate regarding Cameron's presentation later that year, the issue of treaties and the fulfilment of treaty obligations never returned to the floor of the

House of Commons. The unmediated implementation of the Department of Indian Affairs' policies and their effect on the lives of Aboriginal people in the Northwest remained largely unchallenged for the next 70 years. Over the course of that time, successive amendments to the *Indian Act* brought ever-tighter controls over the daily lives of Treaty bands.

In the past 130 years, the confrontational positions of Treaty First Nations and the federal government have remained largely unchanged, although the conflict was suppressed. First Nations still claim that the treaties have remained largely unfulfilled while the Crown's position is that treaty obligations have been respected in accordance to the letter of the text. While Indian and Northern Affairs Canada maintains a largely similar position to the one it held back in the late nineteenth century, the Treaty First Nations have modified their position. In the 1870s and 1880s, treaty leaders continuously remarked that the treaties they had signed were not sufficient to allow them to either continue their traditional way of life or to adapt to the new agricultural lifestyle being advocated by the department. This perception of the insufficiencies of the existing treaties led to a series of calls for a renegotiation of the treaties, and attempts to get better terms.

Today, Treaty First Nations are looking for new agreements that would build upon their existing treaties. While the replacement of the treaty was an aspect of the earlier Yukon Umbrella Agreement and some comprehensive land claim agreements in the Northwest Territories, more recent negotiations have stalled or broken off, such as the Akaitcho negotiations, because the agreements on the table did not reflect the earlier treaty. The same has happened in Saskatchewan with the long-standing self-government negotiations between Canada and the Federation of Saskatchewan Indian Nations. In this case, Grand Chief Alphonse Bird linked the rejection of the final agreement at the referendum level to the failure to see any clear references to the Numbered Treaties. As self-government and comprehensive land claim negotiations continue, the respect accorded to the Numbered Treaties and the need to reflect them in modern agreements are becoming central issues, aggravated by the continuing gap that exists between Crown and Treaty First Nations' perceptions of the implementation of the treaties themselves.

Endnotes

1 National Archives of Canada (hereafter NAC), MG 27 I-C-8, Alexander Morris Papers, Morris to Minister of the Interior, June 8, 1874.

2 PAM, M12B1 Morris Papers (KC), Morris to the Minister of the Interior, March 27, 1877.

3 RG 10, vol 3625, file 5489, W.J. Christie and M.G. Dickieson to David Laird, October 7, 1875.

4 Ibid.

5 Treaty 4 between Her Majesty the Queen and the Cree and Saulteaux Tribes of Indians at Qu'Appelle and Fort Ellice, 15 September, 1877.

6 For a more detailed account of the administration of Lawrence Vankoughnet, see Douglas Leighton (1983:104–19).

7 Morris Papers, Lieutenant-Governor's Collection, Report of Edward McKay to A. Morris, 18 May 1873.

8 RG 10, vol 3741, file 288856, E. Dewdney to Superintendent General of Indian Affairs, April 22, 1881.

9 RG 10, vol 3654, file 8855, James Walker to Dickenson, August 28, 1877.

10 Ibid.

11 Ibid. This petition was signed by several of the prominent chiefs of the Fort Carlton area.

12 RG 10, vol 3665, file 10094, Report of meeting with Chief Pasqua and Lieutenant Governor of Manitoba, 1878, unsigned.

13 Ibid.

14 RG 10, vol 3665, file 10094, David Laird to Minister of the Interior, August 11, 1878.

15 Ibid.

16 RG 10, vol 3654, file 8904, Circular to David Laird and all agents in Manitoba and the North-West Territories, November 6, 1877.

17 See RG 10, vol 3654, file 8904 for a complete listing of all the reports by Indian agents. There are some 35 reports from agents in Manitoba, the NWT, and Keewatin.

18 RG 10, vol 3654, file 8904, David Laird to Minister of the Interior, December 31, 1877.

19 For detailed examples, see RG 10, vol 3654, file 8904, reports by H. Martineau, November 26, 1877; R.J.K. Pither, January 3, 1878; and George McPherson, January 3, 1878.

20 RG 10, vol 3768, file 33624, Governor General's meeting with chiefs at Qu'Appelle, 1881.

21 Ibid.

22 RG 10, vol 3768, file 33624, Governor General's meeting with chiefs at Carlton, 1881.

23 RG 10, vol 3768, file 33624, Governor General's meeting with chiefs at Qu'Appelle, 1881.

24 RG 10, vol 3673, file 10986, Edmonton *Bulletin*, January 7, 1883.

25 RG 10, vol 3673, file 10986, C. Scollen to Edgar Dewdney, March 17, 1884; Unsigned memo [likely from L. Vankoughnet] to Edgar Dewdney, May 21, 1884.

26 RG 10, vol 3686, file 13168, MacDonald to Dewdney, July 8, 1884.

27 RG 10, vol 3697, file 15423, J.A. MacRae to Edgar Dewdney, August 25, 1884.

28 RG 10, vol 3697, file 15423, A. MacDonald to Indian Commissioner, May 14, 1884.

29 RG 10, vol 3697, file 15423, Hayter Reed to the Superintendent General of Indian Affairs, January 23, 1885.

30 RG 10, vol 3741, file 28856, J.M. Rae, no recipient noted, 28 March 1884.

31 Ibid.

32 Ibid.

33 RG 10, vol 3576, file 309, part B, W.W. Crozier to Edgar Dewdney, June 25, 1884.

34 RG 10, vol 3697, file 15423, J.A. Macrae to Indian Commissioner, August 25, 1884.

35 RG 10, vol 3668, file 10644, Hayter Reed to Indian Commissioner, December 28, 1883.

36 RG 10, vol 3697, file 15423, Hayter Reed to Superintendent General of Indian Affairs, January 23, 1885.

37 RG 10, vol 3697, file 15423, Memo to E. Dewdney but likely from L. Vankoughnet, February 4, 1885.

38 RG 10, vol 3576, file 309, part A, L. Vankoughnet to E. Dewdney, February 5, 1885.

39 RG 10, vol 3576, file 309, part A, Comms [Dewdney] to Superintendent General of Indian Affairs, February 12, 1885.

40 RG 10, vol 3576, file 309, part B, W.W. Crozier to Edgar Dewdney, June 25, 1884.

41 RG 10, vol 3709, file 19550, part 2, Report of letter sent to Prime Minister by chiefs at Wolf Creek.

42 RG 10, vol 3709, file 19550, part 2, Telegram from Piapot to Sir J. Macdonald, April 30, 1885.

43 RG 10, vol 3709, file 19550, part 2, Telegrams from Rock Chief and Oochapascoopeeasis to Macdonald, April 30, 1885.

44 RG 10, vol 3709, file 19550, part 1, Pasquah, Muscowpeting, and Charles Ashault to Macdonald, April 21, 1885.

45 RG 10, vol 3709, file 19550, part 2, John Macdonald to Lieutenant Governor Dewdney, May 11, 1885.

46 RG 10, vol 3709, file 19550, part 3, L. Vankoughnet to Sir John Macdonald, August 17, 1885.

47 Ibid.

48 RG 10, vol 3598, file 1364, J.A. MacKay to Indian Commissioner, February 16, 1886.

49 Debates of the House of Commons, 5th Parliament, 4th Session, April 1885, Mr. Cameron, Huron West, 719.

50 Ibid.

References

Beal, Bob and Rod Macleod. 1984. *Prairie fire: The 1885 North-West Rebellion*. Edmonton: Hurtig Publishers.

Carter, Sarah. 1990. *Lost harvest: Prairie Indian reserve farmers and government policy*. Montreal and Kingston: McGill-Queen's Univ. Press.

Dempsey, Hugh. 1984. *Big Bear: The end of freedom*. Toronto: Douglas and McIntyre.

Department of Indian Affairs. 1886. *The facts respecting Indian administration in the North-West*. Ottawa: Queen's Press.

Dickason, Olive Patricia. 2002. *Canada's First Nations*. Toronto: Oxford Univ. Press.

Dyck, Noel. 1986. An opportunity lost: The initiative of the reserve agriculture programme in the Prairie West. *In 1885 and after: Native society in transition*, ed. F. Laurie Barron and James B. Waldram. 121–138. Regina: Univ. of Regina Press.

Friesen, Jean. 1999. Magnificent gifts: The treaties of Canada with the Indians of the Northwest, 1869–1876. In *The spirit of the Alberta Indian treaties*, ed. Richard T. Price. 203–213. Edmonton: Univ. of Alberta Press.

Leighton, Douglas. A Victorian civil servant at work: Lawrence Vankoughnet and the Canadian Indian Department, 1874–1893. In *As long as the sun shines and water flows*, ed. Ian A. L. Getty and Antoine S. Lussier, 104–19. Vancouver: UBC Press.

McKay, Raoul J. 1973. A history of Indian Treaty Number Four and government policies in its implementation, 1874–1905. MA thesis, Univ. of Manitoba.

Morin, Jean-Pierre. 2003. Empty hills: Aboriginal land usage and the Cypress Hills problem, 1974–1883. *Saskatchewan History* 55(1), Spring: 5–20.

Morris, Alexander. 1991. *The treaties of Canada with the Indians of Manitoba and the North-West Territories*, Originally published 1881. Saskatoon: Fifth House Publishing.

Morton, Desmond. 1979. *Rebellions in Canada*. Toronto: Grolier Ltd.

Stonechild, A. Blair. 1986. The Indian view of the 1885 uprising in the Prairie West. In *1885 and after: Native society in transition*, ed. F. Laurie Barron and James B. Waldram. Regina: Univ. of Regina Press.

Taylor, John Leonard. 1985a. Treaty research report: Treaty 4, 1874. Treaties and Historical Research Centre , Indian and Northern Affairs Canada.

Taylor, John Leonard. 1985b. Treaty research report: Treaty 6 1876, Treaties and Historical Research Centre, Indian and Northern Affairs Canada.

9

Inuit Women Reach a Deadlock in the Canadian Political Arena: A Phenomenon Grounded in the Iglu[1]

Carole Cancel

Introduction

Inuit political representatives constitute an integral part of the Canadian political life. Long negotiations in various regions of Arctic Canada, such as Nunavik (Northern Quebec), Nunavut, the Northwest Territories, and Nunatsiavut (Labrador), have allowed them to be active at all levels of politics.[2] Even though some Inuit women have managed to make their way into the public sphere, their numbers remain very low in comparison to those of men. The Legislative Assembly of Nunavut, for example, currently has only two women out of a total of 19 members. Still, many Inuit women are involved in local and community councils and associations.[3]

Since the 1980s, a few Canadian Inuit women have publicly denounced the barriers they face in their attempt to be part of the political arena (Flaherty 1994a, 1994b; Goo-Doyle 1989; *Nunatsiaq News* Nov. 9, 2001). Interestingly, while the male-dominated Inuit political elite officially espouses an open position towards female participation in politics, these declarations of openness have been contradicted in practice by disrespectful behaviours that some of these women have pointed out.[4] While various reports released in Canada have revealed that most Canadian women face analogous obstacles, such as the difficulties in combining family and political life as well as paternalistic attitudes from male counterparts (Royal Commission on the Status of Women in Canada 1970; Purdon 2004), there are two reports which deal specifically with the case of Inuit women in politics (Archibald and Crnkovich 1999; Pauktuutit 1991). The case of Inuit women is unique and deserves to be analyzed.

Recent research conducted about the role of Inuit women in the public sphere (Finland Ministry of Social Affairs and Health 2002) often consists of chronological observation of Inuit women's potential access to political power from pre-contact social organization to the initiation of the Canadian political model (Minor 2002). In a complementary approach to that research, we will focus here on recent political events in Nunavut.[5] Our work analyzes and compares the tensions between the inclusive rhetoric within the political arena towards women, and the difficulties women actually face. In order to find out how much tension there is, we conducted a field work project, interviewing Inuit people close to the public sphere. Field work took place in Ottawa and Montreal in the spring of 2005. At first, we only intended to gather data on the working conditions of these women. As the interviews progressed, however, we realized that the recollections of the interviewees who had been participants in the campaign meeting for the 1997 referendum on gender parity in Nunavut were a valuable source of information.[6] We also collected memories concerning the reactions of the public to the campaign, which provided us with salient insights into the real condition of Inuit women's participation in politics.

The results of the interviews we conducted provided us with insights into the difficulties previous research has shown to be faced by Inuit women who want to be involved in politics. These difficulties include characteristics of the cultural background of the Inuit, the consequences of the introduction of the Inuit to the Canadian political model of governance (Minor 2002), and the influence of some religious beliefs. Rather unexpectedly, statements collected during field work allowed us to glimpse a sort underground aspect to the phenomenon which was not evident at first. Several responses we received to our questions urged us to focus on the campaign for the 1997 gender parity referendum in Nunavut, a crucial episode in the history of Canada. A closer look at the various attitudes and reactions by the Inuit of Nunavut to this event reveal the key role played by the idea of the traditional Inuit household. Further research on the cultural concept of the couple (the basic entity of Inuit identity) is instrumental in understanding the difficulties faced by Inuit women in politics today.

Resistance in the Political Sphere

Inuit women, as individuals or a group have decried the negative attitudes and behaviours they have experienced in the political arena, such as in the various statements made by Martha Flaherty, President of Pauktuutit[7] in the early 1990s (Flaherty 1994a, 1994b; Pauktuutit 1991). The "code of conduct for leaders" proposed by Pauktuutit in 1994 was an attempt to make the actors on the political stage more accountable and respectful toward one another and the individuals they represent. At the time, Flaherty (1994b) said:

> Inuit leaders must work on behalf of their people in a way which reflects this tradition of respect and concern. This means putting the good of the people before personal gain ... Inuit leaders should be responsible for ensuring that women, youth and Elders are adequately represented in their organizations ... Inuit leaders have additional responsibilities as public figures and role models. These include not engaging in conduct which hurts other people, breaks laws, or is harmful to Inuit society ... Acts of violence against women and children, including sexual assault, child abuse, child sexual abuse, and wife battering are absolutely unacceptable, and any leader who engages in such conduct should immediately step aside.

Beside its primary message, this proposal clearly reveals a malaise within the Inuit political sphere. Flaherty's proposal was not discussed at the time but rather put aside, probably because it could have been a subject of dissension if it had been debated publicly. Internal quarrels certainly would have marred the impression of cohesion which the Inuit have been trying to reinforce for decades in their dealings with the Canadian political system. Was the silence surrounding this proposal due to the urgent need to give priority to more critical topics for the Inuit or due to the fear that Inuit values regarding women would be misunderstood on the Canadian stage?

In the end, the subject was not publicly discussed or debated until the Nunavut Implementation Commission proposed a unique model based on gender parity for the Legislative Assembly of Nunavut. The campaign for the referendum necessary to implement the proposal revealed another form of resistance, rooted in the electorate, to the inclusion of women in the political arena.

The Campaign for the Gender Parity Referendum

The referendum was a confusing time for the electorate, probably because the most vehement opponent of the gender parity proposal was a prominent Inuit woman, Manitok Thompson, Minister of Municipal and Community Affairs and Minister Responsible for the Women's Directorate in the Northwest Territories, at that time. According to Jackie Steele and Manon Tremblay (2005), Thompson dramatically influenced the outcome of the ballot:

> The fact that, as a woman, [Manitok Thompson] could protest so vehemently against the proposal, threw people into confusion about who legitimately held the feminine viewpoint with regards to equality. (37)[8]

Thompson argued that the proposition was paternalistic towards women and discriminatory towards men. Moreover, she challenged the accounts of Inuit women who had reported systemic barriers in the political arena. Thompson may not have experienced, in fact, any significant barriers to political participation herself, yet she showed no sign of solidarity with women who pointed out difficulties.

On the other hand, John Amagoalik, who defended the proposition, emphasized the need for the political arena to be more inclusive, enabling it to benefit from the specific contributions of men and women:

> Yes, women have made great strides in recent times. But they still face systemic barriers. One of them is an attitude that women need to prove themselves first. Women don't need to prove themselves to me. I believe in women's abilities and strengths and look forward to their positive contributions. I do not want to wait until someone has judged women to be "ready" ... A gender-equal Legislative Assembly is a picture of tolerance and mutual respect. (Amagoalik 1997)

The campaign was one-sided. Apart from an organized group of opponents from Kaniqliniq (Rankin Inlet) named "Qauliqtuq," challengers to the referendum proposal did not organize committees to present their views at the meetings. The vast majority of floating voters did have an opportunity to attend a formal debate; however, they were faced with an uneven debate between pugnacious and articulate defenders of the proposal and a few isolated angry members of the public. Describing the situation, Jens Dahl (1997) said:

> [The] plebiscite results do not evidence that these visits had any positive effect for their cause—in fact the opposite is true. This can be explained by the fact that many people felt intimidated by the one-sided campaign. Why didn't you bring representatives from the opposition? Who has paid for your campaign? These and similar questions were repeatedly asked during the meetings and by the media. (46)

According to one of our informants, who attended several of the meetings, few women dared to speak up, thereby depriving the debate of their point of view.[9] Interestingly, strong reactions from the public reveal an underlying animosity towards associations such as Pauktuutit (representing Inuit women in Canada).[10]

> A man spoke up, he was very angry "that women shouldn't be given advantages like that ... he said ... that the women have stupid associations like Pauktuutit or women's group who are getting so powerful.[11]

The meetings for the referendum turned into a forum for some people in the audience to express their complete discomfort with a women's association becoming too influential.

This criticism leads us to consider the issue of the visibility of female representatives in the public sphere in the light of certain features of Inuit culture. In her work on Inuit female writers of autobiography, an activity that places women at the centre of public life, Robin McGrath draws our attention to the attitude of restraint that is required for women in Inuit culture: "Inuit women appear to observe taboo against drawing attention to themselves as mature adults."[12] This social behaviour, part of a code of conduct dictated by custom, seems difficult to reconcile with the role expected of a political representative according to the Canadian political model. The latter requires visibility and grants more prestige to people with a high-level, and therefore highly visible, position in the hierarchical system. Thus, the Canadian political model indirectly gives way to patronizing attitudes.

Oral data that we collected which dealt with the campaign for the referendum on gender parity in Nunavut, outlines a potentially embedded structure of this phenomenon. This structure directs us to consider the possibility that the gender tensions within the political sphere may be rooted in tensions in the private sphere of the Inuit household.

The Inuit Household under Scrutiny

During the 1997 campaign for the referendum on gender equality, supporters of the proposition considered the arguments of equality as being complementary to, and rooted in, Inuit culture. These supporters presented the proposition for gender parity as a way of helping to reinforce these notions. They wanted to recreate the interaction between men and women, as recommended by their interpretation of certain Inuit values, in the Legislative Assembly.

> [Rita Arey, Status of Women Council] said gender parity is a reflection of what has always been part of traditional Inuit culture. "Women's opinions were respected and sought out because they provided balance and harmony in decisions affecting the well-being of the community as a whole ... We must regain this balance by making sure that women's voices are equally heard in the legislature. (Bourgeois 1997)

The debate on equality did not take place, but the initiative unveiled a latent form of anxiety rooted in the notion of the family unit.

The settlement of the Inuit in communities had challenged the integrity of male status, and a social malaise began to be detected in Canadian Inuit society as early as in the mid-twentieth century.[13] Meanwhile, women had managed to make their way into the education system.[14] The omnipresence of women in schools and, consequently, their success in the world of work were considered a threat to the social order and balance within the traditional unit of the couple. Traditional gender roles are reversed when the woman becomes the breadwinner, and this leads to uncertainty about the respective responsibilities of the man and woman in the household. As a result, many young Inuit men find it difficult today to fit into society as it is proposed to them.

> Because of their presence, even sporadic, at school, they [young men] cannot follow hunters on the ice floe, or on the land. Paradoxically, these young people have attended school too much to be able to become excellent providers (seal, caribou, fish), and not enough to expect living well as salaried employees. Thus, they feel humiliated, downgraded, without future prospects and the suicide rate or suicide attempt rate give cause for concern. (Therrien 1992)[15]

Consequently, men and women, as couples, need to re-create a fragile balance within their household. This new balance within the couple, thus re-formed, is often maintained by Christian beliefs, which have a strong influence in the North. Redefinition of the roles of men and women in each household is left to individual discretion and influences. The Pentecostal Church, for instance, proposes rather fixed roles for men and women, placing strict boundaries on the sphere of influence acceptable for women and confining them to the domestic sphere.[16] The gender parity proposal, however, implied the equal representation of men and women in the political arena. Negative reactions to this proposal reveal a need on the part of many Christians among the Inuit to cling to a stable definition of male and female relationships in the household, a definition based on an interpretation of Holy Scripture.

> And there was a man who was so angry, he was even talking about his Bible. [Laugh.] He said that according to his Bible it should be the man to be the head of the house [low voice], according to the Bible ... I finally said "in these years 1900, I think you and I have a different Bible."[17]

According to Manon Tremblay, the referendum was, in fact, asking the population in Nunavut to choose which version of their tradition was most relevant:

> The debate aroused by the proposal on gender equality was such that the population was actually asked to choose which version of Inuit tradition (meaning before or after contact with the Christian civilization, or a combination of both periods) constituted the foundation of relations between the sexes and democratic practices. (Steele and Manon 2005, 36)

Concerning these "democratic practices," Françoise Héritier, a French anthropologist, considers that the theoretical universal equality between the sexes emphasized in democratic states, such as in Canada, reaffirms a latent transcendental inequality between the sexes.[18] In the case of the Nunavut Inuit, the public had to reach a decision, taking into account discriminatory, unspoken rules derived from an exogenous political model on top of the cultural and religious issues with which they were familiar and that only few Inuit women had questioned so far. In the end, the debate mainly concerned different understandings of tradition, but the resulting answers created more instability within the couple relationship, generating fear and anxiety. Many people in the electorate may have even considered the restrictions on the involvement of women in the public arena as a method of maintaining a fragile balance within the household and society.

According to Jens Dahl, the strong opposition from many women towards the proposal was grounded in a desire to protect the integrity of their household.

> Any initiative which can be interpreted as a threat to the family will be rejected out of fear for more social problems. Regardless of who has the best solutions, in Nunavut there is a strong ideological desire to strengthen close family relations—even if there are many indications in everyday life that point in the opposite direction. (1997, 47)

The strong will to protect the family arises from a context in which women are exposed to high rates of domestic violence, and men are at a high risk of attempting suicide.[19] This further implies a lack of confidence towards women and, especially, towards their ability to share power with their male counterparts.

Mary Wilman, from the Nunavut Implementation Training Committee, attempted to find out more about the failure of the proposal. She concluded that the massive success of women in school, and their chances of becoming the next elite in Inuit society, might have influenced the ballot.

> Some people have indicated to me perhaps that it is because men don't know how to cope with the women and power and at the same time women perhaps don't know how to balance power. It is that we, as women, should take the power for granted, that we should use it well, in partnership with the men. Because we have power doesn't mean that we should disrespect the men.[20]

In the aftermath of the referendum, what is left of the definition of the roles of men and women on the political stage? At first glance, it seems that the entire debate was given a new twist when it took on a symbolic dimension. When the Chamber of the Legislative Assembly was conceptualized and presented to the public in 1999, officially it was meant to represent the iglu, the Inuit household, in which man and woman share equal authority. For example, when the house is in session, the mace of Nunavut rests in a carving depicting the hands of a man and a woman, fashioned in granite and labradorite. When the mace was unveiled, it was clear that the Government of Nunavut intended the mace to symbolize "the equal respect for both genders of the population."[21] Is this symbol a politically correct way of displaying the image of unity among Inuit men and women? Is it a message advising families to apply this pattern of equality to themselves, taking the Assembly as a model, an embedded image of the iglu? Does this symbolic dimension present equality and partnership as a reality, or as an image of Inuit politics that the Inuit political elite wants to establish towards the population and towards the world?

The silent crisis in Canadian Inuit politics, where men and women oppose one another, is rooted in a broader social malaise that was unspoken for decades. Interestingly, as a result of the need for the couple to re-establish trust at different levels, some female representatives in Greenland have shown a cautious attitude towards the issue. In an interview recorded in 2004, Henriette Rasmussen, Minister of Culture, Education, Language, Science and Ecclesiastical Affairs in the Greenlandic Home Rule Government, describes such a stand:

> I am aware that as a woman who has been struggling for the women's rights in Greenland before, I see now that in education there are more women in education than men. Maybe one day, there will be more women educated then men and it is a bad thing for our society ... We have to be careful ... (because we have been educated, or whatever, we have power) that we should do this to men. No! We shouldn't! Now we are suddenly in a situation in Greenland that we have to be aware of the boy's identity not to get them to be minor, you know. We have to look at the men's rights, men's feelings.[22]

She encourages the enhancement of the role of men in society, with the side effect of re-establishing a balance in the household and, by extension, in the political sphere (the topic she was actually asked about).[23] Henriette Rasmussen demonstrates the necessity to share power and pay attention to men's feelings, which may be a way for the public to grant women legitimacy as leaders. According to this quote, there seems to be, in Greenland as well, a need for mutual respect within the couple in order to fend off the imbalance in Inuit society caused by the pre-eminence of women in the work force.

Inuit women in the Canadian political sphere, and especially in Nunavut, are under close scrutiny. They are paving the way for the next generation of women in politics. The way they deal with the male electorate and the concept of the couple may be the key to their finding their own legitimacy on the political stage.

Conclusion

This analysis has shown that balance on the Canadian Inuit political stage depends upon stability in the household within an embedded structure. In other sectors of the public sphere, such as the economy or art, discriminatory practices toward women persist. The research in this paper can be the basis for further study of this complex phenomenon, with a focus on the household and a more holistic approach, by comparing the various effects of this phenomenon on diverse sectors of the Inuit public sphere.

The way the Inuit Canadian elite deals with the sensitive topic of dissention between Inuit men and women in the political arena is worth a closer look. To what extent is Inuit political discourse concealing internal Inuit conflicts? What are the deep-seated motives of the Canadian Inuit decision-making elite?[24] How does the Inuit elite in Canada deal with topics of dissension that challenge the unity in the political discourse of the Inuit at all levels of politics, from local to international?

Acknowledgements

This presentation is based on the findings and fieldwork/collected data from a master's thesis in Inuit Studies under the supervision of Michèle Therrien. It was defended and validated at the Institut National des Langues et Civilisations Orientales (Paris) in July 2005.

Appendix A: Map of Inuit Settlement Areas in Canada.

Source: <www.makivik.org/images/map/11_inuit_settlement_areas.gif>

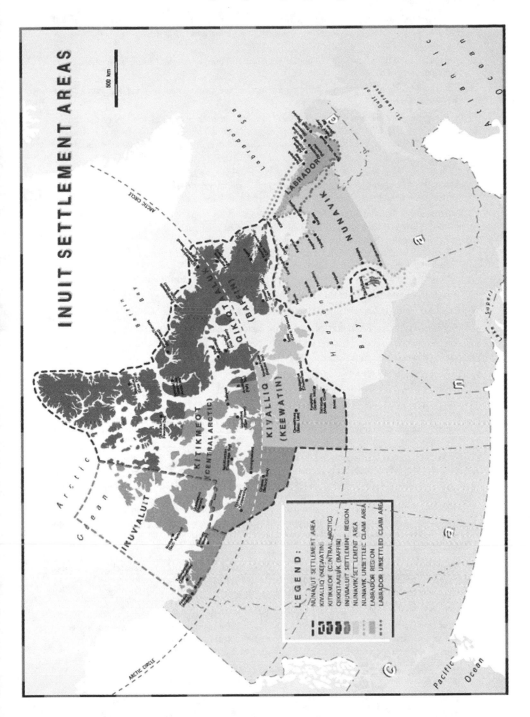

Endnotes

1 The Inuktitut term "iglu" is a generic term. It refers to various kinds of accommodation. In its most common use, it designates a house.

2 At the federal level, there are only two Inuit political representatives: Nancy Karetak-Lindell, Member of Parliament for Nunavut to the House of Commons, and Charlie Watt, who was appointed to the Senate in 1984.

3 For instance, at the Ottawa urban community centre Tunngasuvvingat Inuit, at least six of the eight members of the board are women.

4 It was made particularly obvious during the campaign for gender equality at the Nunavut Legislative Assembly in 1997.

5 Some researchers, such as Jens Dahl (1997) from the Department of Eskimology of the University of Copenhagen, as well as Jackie Steele and Manon Tremblay (2005) from the Research Centre on Women and Politics at the University of Ottawa, currently are focusing on analyzing these events.

6 At that time, the Nunavut Implementation Commission recommended that the Legislative Assembly of Nunavut would be composed of the same number of male and female MLAs. Each constituency would have been represented by a man and a woman.

7 Pauktuutit is a national non-profit association representing Canadian Inuit women. It was incorporated in 1984. It has various aims, such as "act and be recognized as the official representative for Inuit women," "work towards better conditions for Inuit women," "promote self-confidence and self-reliance amongst Inuit women," "promote the equality of Inuit women in all levels of Canadian governmental and non-governmental structures," and "encourage the involvement of Inuit women in all levels of Canadian society." See <**www.pauktuutit.ca/about_e.asp**>.

8 Translation was provided for the purpose of this article by Carole Cancel.

9 This observation is consistent with Jens Dahl (1997).

10 It is noteworthy that Pauktuutit, the national Canadian Inuit women's association, was involved in the campaign without having originally initiated it.

11 Interview with an informant, Spring 2005, Ottawa.

12 Robin McGrath (1990) insists on the restraint attitude expected from the woman as an obstacle for some of them to publish their autobiographies or get support from their relatives for doing so.

13 It is noteworthy that when the Canadian political model was gradually introduced in the North, the government encouraged the Inuit to get involved in local political representation. See Minor (2002).

14 In the 2001 census, the highest level of schooling is quite revealing. The percentage of Nunavut Inuit with a graduate certificate increased dramatically within the last 20 years, with very little difference between men and women. On the contrary, the percentage of Nunavut Inuit with a university certificate, diploma or degree has been gradually decreasing for the last 20 years, with a growing prominence of women, compared to men. For instance, in 1991, among the population aged 20 to 34 in Nunavut, 9.1% of women have such a degree compared to 6.7% of their male counterparts. See the 2001 census on the Statistics Canada website at <**www12.statcan.ca**>.

15 Translation of this article was provided to the author by Carole Cancel.

16 The role attributed to women by the Pentacostal Church requires further research, all the more so as evangelical Christianity is becoming quite influential in Northern communities. It will no doubt constitute a factor of deep change among the Inuit.

17 Interview with an informant, Spring 2005, Ottawa.

18 Françoise Héritier (2002) in French calls this transcendantal inequality between the sexes "valence différentielle des sexes." This expression could be literally translated as "differential valency between the sexes." Translation provided by Carole Cancel.

19 In her recent article, Karla Jessen Williamson (2004, 190–91) indicates that the suicide rate among Nunavut males is more than three times higher than women's.

20 Mary Wilman, on the radio program "Boréal hebdo," 31 May 1997.

21 Quotation from a leaflet entitled "Mace of Nunavut," distributed at the entrance of the Nunavut Legislative Assembly building.

22 Interview with Henriette Rasmussen, 19 October 2004, Paris.

23 It is noteworthy that recent research in Greenland has been focusing on Inuit men's experience in order to shed a new light on social phenomena such as domestic violence and difficulties in relationships between Inuit men and women. See Williamson (2004, 187–205).

24 The analysis of the new data we gathered in Iqaluit (Nunavut) in the autumn of 2005 will provide us with further insight on the Inuit political discourse in Nunavut.

References

Amagoalik, John. 1997. My little corner of Canada. *Nunatsiaq News*. March 21. <**http://www. nunatsiaq.com/archives/back-issues/week/70221.html#8**>

Archibald, Linda, and Mary Crnkovich. 1999. *Et si les femmes avaient voix au chapitre ? Étude de cas sur les Inuites, les revendications territoriales et le projet d'exploitation du nickel de la baie Voisey.* Case Study, Ottawa: Condition Féminine Canada (Status of Women, Canada).

Bourgeois, Annette. 1997. Assembly Plebiscite on May 26? *Nunatsiaq News*. Feb. 28. <**http://www. nunatsiaq.com/archives/back-issues/week/70221.html#1**>

Dahl, Jens. 1997. Gender parity in Nunavut? *Indigenous Affairs* 3-4:42–47.

Finland Ministry of Social Affairs and Health. 2002. *Taking wing conference report : Conference on gender equality and women in the Arctic.* Helsinki: 3–6 August.

Flaherty, Martha. 1994a. Aboriginal women and self-government. *Canadian Women Studies* 14(4): 112–14.

---1994b. Inuit women, equality and leadership. *Canadian Women Studies* 14(4): 6–9.

Goo-Doyle, Ovilu. 1989. The role of Inuit women in politics. *Northern Perspectives*. Canadian Arctic Resources Committee 17, no. 3 (Aug–Oct): n.p.

Héritier, Françoise. 2002. *Masculin/féminin II. Dissoudre la hiérarchie.* Paris: Odile Jacob.

McGrath, Robin. 1990. Circumventing the taboos: Inuit women's autobiographies. Paper from the Seventh Inuit Studies Conference at Fairbanks, Alaska. *Inuit Studies Occasional Papers* 4 (Aug.): 215.

Minor, Tina. 2002. Political participation of Inuit women in the government of Nunavut. *Wicazo sa Review* 17 (1) Spring: 65–80.

Nunatsiaq News. 2001. A Seat of One's Own. Nov. 9.

Pauktuutit. 1991. *Arnait: The views of Inuit women on contemporary issues.* Ottawa: Pauktuuti.

Purdon, Colleen. 2004. *Increasing women's participation in municipal decision making. Strategies for more inclusive Canadian communities.* Ottawa: Federation of Canadian Municipalities.

Royal Commission on the Status of Women in Canada. 1970. *Report of the Royal Commission on the Status of Women in Canada.* Ottawa:.Royal Commission on the Status of Women.

Steele, Jackie and Manon Tremblay. 2005. Paradis perdu? Référendum au Nunavut sur l'égalité des sexes. *Revue Parlementaire Canadienne* (Spring) 34–40.

Therrien, Michèle. 1992. L'identité bien construite des Inuit de l'Arctique oriental. In *Métamorphose d'une utopie.* Paris: Presses de la Sorbonne Nouvelle, Éditions Triptyque. 193–204.

Williamson Jessen, Karla. 2004. Do Arctic men and women experience life differently? In *Arctic Human Development Report*, 190–91. Akureyri : Stefansson Arctic Institute..

Wilman, Mary. 1997. *Boréal hebdo* (CBC). 31 May.

10

Organizing Indigenous Governance in Canada, Australia, and the United States

Stephen Cornell

Introduction

My purpose in this paper—a preliminary contribution to a larger project—is to raise a set of research and policy issues having to do with the organization of Indigenous governance in Canada, Australia, and the United States. I make the assumption, both in this presentation and in the larger enterprise of which it is a part, that there is value to be found in comparative work on certain Indigenous issues across these countries. While they differ in important ways, they have significant commonalities in political and legal heritage, in the historical displacement of Indigenous populations, and in the vigorous and contemporary Indigenous pursuit of self-determination.

One of the primary goals of Indigenous populations in all three countries is to establish and exercise the right to govern themselves, and the set of issues surrounding Indigenous governance is my concern here. While this paper is based on ongoing research, much of what I have to say at this point is impressionistic. This is, emphatically, a preliminary exploration.[1]

The Rise of Governance as an Indigenous Issue

The rise of governance as an Indigenous issue echoes to some degree a broader discussion of governance in the economic development community around the world. That community has paid an increasing amount of attention to governance issues in recent years, and to the link between institutions of governance on one hand and development outcomes on the other (see, among others, Bräutigam and Knack 2004; Doornbos 2001; Egnal 1996; Knack and Keefer 1995; La Porta et al. 1999; North 1990; Ostrom 1992). But that community has paid only occasional attention to Indigenous peoples and their often distinctive situations. Furthermore, in the development community, the focus on governance remains primarily a donor and academic concern over what less developed countries are not doing. In the Indigenous community—at least in the countries considered in this paper—the focus on governance is being driven as much by Indigenous initiatives, and reflects a somewhat different policy dynamic.

Nonetheless, the concern with governance on the part of central governments addressing Indigenous issues probably reflects some familiarity with the larger development discussion. At the very least, central governments, looking for solutions to seemingly intractable poverty among Indigenous peoples, saddled with discouraging histories of failed policies, and having tried almost everything else, would seem likely eventually to hit on a "governance" approach.

Real life has been given to the governance debate, however, by factors within the Indigenous arena. Three, in particular, seem important. The first is the *relative* success of the Indigenous rights agenda in all three countries. I emphasize "relative" because any account that describes the fight for Indigenous rights as successful must be carefully qualified. But in each of these countries the last few decades have seen some progress—admittedly mixed—on the rights front. This is apparent in a number of places, among them the self-determination policy dating from the 1970s in the United States; the 1997 *Delgamuukw* and 2004 *Haida* and *Taku River* decisions (among others) of the Canadian Supreme Court; the work of Canada's Royal Commission on Aboriginal Peoples; and the 1992 *Mabo* decision of the Australian High Court, the related Native Title Act of 1993, and various Australian co-management agreements.[2]

To be sure, these developments are hardly secure—recent Supreme Court decisions in the US, for example, have undermined much of what was earlier achieved (Williams 2006), while actions of the Howard government in Australia have stripped *Mabo* and Native title legislation of much of their effect (e.g., Behrendt 2003). But, in all three countries, Indigenous peoples have succeeded in increasing, to one degree or another, their control over at least some of the decisions that affect their lives.

Success—even modest success—in the pursuit of self-determination eventually leads to issues of governance. As Indigenous peoples increase their control over major decisions, how they make and implement such decisions are becoming, more and more, a topic of discussion, not least among those peoples themselves. As long as they had little or no governing power, such discussions were pointless. Now that Indigenous peoples have some governing power, both they and outside authorities look to the resultant governments for decisions and for capable execution of decisions, once made. Along with the shift in power, there is a shift in accountability—a point not missed by many Native communities now looking to their own leadership to address problems that outside governments have neglected or been incapable of solving.

Another source of the turn toward governance issues within the Indigenous arena is the need for funding. This is most apparent, probably, in the United States, where American Indian nations with ambitious nation-building agendas are faced with reduced federal support and the need to generate revenues of their own with which to operate. They have discovered, in some cases quite independently, the significance of governance as a critical factor in economic development. The result is that governance has joined economic development near the top of some Indian nations' lists of concerns.

Something similar is happening in Canada and Australia as well. As Indigenous peoples in all three countries begin to replace federal or other outside agendas with their own, they often are confronted with the realities of outside funding limits and the divergence, in some cases, between their priorities and those of funding bodies. In addition, many of them have recognized the difficulty and incongruity of governing in the name of self-determination while remaining substantially dependent for operating funds on decisions made by some other government that may be serving other interests.

Finally, there are research results. In particular, research generated over the last 20 years by the Harvard Project on American Indian Economic Development and its partner organization, the Native Nations Institute at the University of Arizona, has shown that the form and quality of Indigenous governance, assuming there is substantial and meaningful Indigenous jurisdiction, is a powerful predictor of success in economic and community development (see, for example, Cornell and Kalt 1997a, 1997b, 2000, 2003, 2005; Cornell 2005; Jorgensen 2000, forthcoming). Recent scholarship in Australia also is underlining the importance of governance in realizing Indigenous agendas (see Hunt and Smith 2006 for a summary).

There may be other factors involved as well. We have some evidence that a new generation of leaders and professionals in all three countries is less inclined to spend time blaming outsiders for current problems—however justified that blame may be—and more inclined to focus their energies on what steps Indigenous peoples themselves can take to regain control of their situations and generate their own solutions to pressing problems. Not all of these people are in community leadership positions; some are in NGOs of one kind or another, or are prominent in activist Indigenous networks.

Regardless of the exact combination of factors, however, the result has been to establish governance as a major issue in Indigenous policy debates—both among Indigenous peoples and in central governments—in all three countries. It has become a headline topic at major conferences, a leading agenda item for a number of organizations, and a growth topic in policy and academic dialogues.

Some Policy Questions

These developments raise a number of policy questions. I want to highlight four of them.

First, when states and Indigenous peoples talk about governance, they often seem to have different things in mind, and they consequently talk past each other. In Canada, and to some extent in Australia, the state often appears to conceive Indigenous self-government as self-management or self-administration.[3] The core idea seems to be that Indigenous communities can administer programs designed by central governments for their benefit. Much of the focus is on fiscal account-ability, process, and bureaucratic rules (see Cornell, Jorgensen, and Kalt 2002; Cornell, Curtis, and Jorgensen 2004, Table 1).

Indigenous conceptions of governance, on the other hand, often differ from those of the state in at least two ways. First, they conceive self-government as involving significant, substantive power over the decisions that shape Indigenous lives, from law-making to governmental design to resource management to intergovernmental relations. Second, the idea of governance is often consciously embedded in a more comprehensive set of concerns that get little attention from state actors.

For example, a former governor of a New Mexico Pueblo recently remarked, "Governance is ... multi-layered. One layer is maintaining the harmony of a community—its well-being. It is about maintaining all the things we cherish: the language, the culture, the ways we are with each other.... Another layer of governance is jurisdiction. It involves dealing with counties, states, school systems. This is a very different context. It is potentially a win-lose context, and it can be dangerous ... You have to work very carefully at this level, and the governance challenge is very different."

A retired judge with an American Indian tribal court, discussing governance over a meal, said, "We are dealing with two very different systems here. We have the customary system ... It is about how to live a successful life, a good life, a meaningful life. Then there is the Western system. It is a very different system, with different roots ... We have to figure out how to live in these two systems. It is not a matter of making a choice. And they do not mix easily ... What we face is how to live in this place where these two systems meet and still be ourselves." He indicated a bowl of stew in front of him. "The question is: how do you make this bowl of stew feed everybody? That's what governance is about."[4]

A second issue is related to the first. What will be the scope of Indigenous jurisdiction? Will it be limited to administrative decisions within a local legal and political context that is controlled by outsiders? Or will central governments give up enough jurisdictional power to enable Native peoples who are equipped with capable governing systems to have practical impacts on real-world problems?

This is a critical matter. A substantial body of research now demonstrates that Indigenous progress on economic and related community development depends substantially on jurisdiction. Indigenous nations need to have the authority—and the accountability that goes with it—to shape what happens on their lands and in their communities. Without jurisdiction, governmental reform is an exercise in futility: regardless of the resultant form, the government remains toothless.

This problem raises the third issue. What institutional form will Indigenous governance take? In all three countries, central governments have been eager to provide the answers to this question. This is apparent in the Indian Act in Canada and its various amendments; it also is apparent in the Indian Reorganization Act in the United States, which strongly encouraged American Indian nations to adopt governmental forms designed in the Solicitor General's office in the US Department of the Interior. And it has been a recurrent theme in the efforts of Australian governments to encourage Aboriginal community organization (see Morphy 1999; Rowse 2000; Smith 2004).

The danger in this approach is the lack of legitimacy that imposed governance solutions almost invariably have with the people being governed. People tend to respect governments that they view as genuinely theirs, regardless of whether they actually played a part in their design (although that is one way to build legitimacy). Governments are likely to perform better where they reflect Indigenous conceptions of how authority should be organized and exercised.

The last issue is a variation on the second and the third. It has to do with a particular aspect of both jurisdiction and form: scale. What should be the boundaries along which both jurisdiction and governing institutions are organized? To put it somewhat differently, who is the self in self-government? This is the topic I will pursue in the remainder of this paper.

Who Is the Self in Self-Government?

The answer to this question is more obvious in some situations than in others. For example, in much of the United States, the logic of what Sanders and Smith (2002) call "the social geography of governance" is readily apparent. While both the expropriation of Indigenous lands and the colonial administration of Native communities were enormously destructive, the organizational boundaries of many American Indian nations today coincide with Indigenous conceptions of peoplehood. In other words, a large number of Indian reservations in the United States are homes to more or less unitary peoples. The organizational and the cognitive dimensions of peoplehood coincide (Cornell 1988, ch. 5).

This is not everywhere the case, not even in the US. Not only were some nations forced together on single bodies of land (for example, the Shoshone and Arapaho on the Wind River reservation or the fourteen tribes and bands of today's Yakama Nation), but there are tensions in some nations that share language and culture between component village or kinship units with long traditions of autonomy and centralized structures empowered by the United States (for example, the Hopi Tribe and the Tohono O'odham Nation). In still other places, historical events or administrative or organizational boundaries sometimes separated groups who had seen themselves as a single people, while in Alaska, efforts to regionalize administration fly in the face of many Indigenous concepts of peoplehood and of appropriate organizational scale.

While such issues are more the exception than the rule in the United States, the fragmentation of peoples has been common in Canada. Aboriginal group organization was diverse. In parts of the country, such organization seldom reached beyond the extended family; in others, supra-familial units sustained coordination over extended periods of time through political structures of considerable complexity. As throughout much of the world, colonization had a leveling effect, reducing organizational diversity as colonial administrators reorganized Indigenous communities in ways that facilitated administration, land transfers, and assimilative programs. In Canada, it also had a fragmenting effect as Indigenous lands were taken and individual bands were restricted to tiny fragments of land: the reserves. The reserve structure then became the organizational structure of Indigenous affairs, with each reserve treated as a separate unit.

The effect of this, in many cases and in contrast to the pattern in the United States, was to pull apart the organizational and cognitive dimensions of peoplehood.[5] Bands sharing a sense of themselves as a people, based in kinship links, shared language and culture, and intimately shared histories, found themselves separated into multiple, small, heavily administered settlements and enclaves.

This has left a legacy that vastly complicates the challenge of Indigenous self-government. In 1996, the Royal Commission on Aboriginal Peoples estimated that Canada has approximately 1,000 Aboriginal reserve and settlement communities—many of them identified as First Nations—but that those communities make up only 60 to 80 nations, defined as "a sizeable body of Aboriginal people that possesses a shared sense of national identity and constitutes the predominant population in a certain territory or collection of territories" (1996, 25). Fragmentation and isolation have made it very difficult for these nations to organize self-government along national (as opposed to First Nation) lines. Meanwhile, small land bases and populations mean many First Nations have only limited human capital pools and limited assets that can be used in productive economic activity.

The "who is the self" issue is most complicated in Australia. Hugely diverse and widely dispersed across a vast landscape, most of the Indigenous peoples of Australia lived in small populations with few supra-familial political structures other than, in some cases, shared understandings of law. Such shared understandings shaped decisions, but in complex ways. Diane Smith comments, for example, that

> In Indigenous societies, certain scales of social aggregation are associated with "proper" authority and decision making about particular kinds of matters. But these aggregations are fluid in their composition and stability. For example, religious, economic and political interests in land are not held exclusively by primary owners. Rather, rights and responsibilities overlap and are dispersed across a range of people and interest groups. Extended families deal with particular domestic matters and localities; larger groups of extended kin may come together for particular economic activities; "clans" may meet across larger regions for ceremonial and dispute-resolution purposes; and responsibility for the conduct of particular ceremonies is distributed across kin categories of ownership and management resident in different locations. (Smith 2004, 18; see also Sutton 1995, ch. 4 and 5)

On top of this variability and fluidity came mid-twentieth-century federal policies that forced many of these Aboriginal groups to leave their territories and resettle at mission stations, where welfare and social services could be administered more economically and, supposedly, more effectively. The result was the creation of numerous central and outlying service centres with largely Aboriginal populations of great diversity in language and culture, concentrated on lands to which only one of these peoples may have a traditional claim. Economic, social, and ceremonial relationships may not at all coincide. Nonetheless, outside governments want these physically separate communities to make decisions; they want to know who speaks for them; and they want to know who will be accountable for what happens.

In such situations, unitary governmental structures may end up reflecting administrative realities but no Indigenous boundaries at all, either organizational or cognitive, or may have legitimacy in one domain of decision-making but no legitimacy in another. The challenge of building capable governing institutions under such circumstances is daunting (see discussions in Smith 2004; Taylor 2004, ch. 1; Morphy 1999).

Efficacy vs. Legitimacy

For Indigenous peoples, the significance of the "who is the self" issue is partly practical: many of the nations or communities involved are small and operate at the limit of their own human capital supply. They have to figure out how to exercise governmental functions effectively, and they have to consider potential economies; larger units may not only be easier to staff but, in some cases, are more effective at executing certain governmental functions and/or cheaper to run. They also may wield more political clout, not an insignificant consideration for many Native peoples.

But the issue is also a matter of legitimacy. The resultant governments must have the support of the people they govern. Imposed boundaries—however much administrative or economic sense they make—can fatally undermine processes of governance (Cornell and Kalt 2003).

The issue has significance for non-Indigenous governments as well. Where it remains unresolved or is inadequately resolved, the likely result will be Indigenous governments that are inefficient, abused by their own citizens, and conflict-ridden, leading to problematic intergovernmental relations and greatly increased costs.

Cornell and Kalt (2003, 2005) argue that the organization of Indigenous self-governance has to pay attention to both of these requirements—efficacy and legitimacy. This means that governance solutions have to be adequate to the practical, governmental challenges Indigenous nations currently face and have to be viewed, at the same time, by their peoples as appropriate ways of governing. As part of any governance solution, social geography is likewise subject to these same requirements. The boundary aspect of the organization of Indigenous self-government also has to address concerns both of efficacy and legitimacy. Of course, efficacy solutions and legitimacy solutions do not always coincide. Discontinuities between the two can produce pressure on Indigenous nations for cultural change, institutional innovation, or both.

Unfortunately, Native and non-Native governments often part company in their respective emphases when they consider Indigenous governance. Dominant governments tend to be much more interested in efficacy than legitimacy. Often overlooking legitimacy issues, they want to organize Indigenous self-governance—to the extent that they want it at all—for administrative convenience and efficiency: how we can deliver services to Indigenous peoples in cost-effective ways. Often operating within a self-administration or self-management framework, they have difficulty looking beyond efficacy as a governmental goal.

Indigenous nations, on the other hand, while not necessarily ignoring efficacy, tend to operate in a very different framework and to be more interested in legitimacy (perhaps only implicitly) insofar as their concerns, in part, are with the survival of Indigenous communities, not only as physical entities but as complexes of social relationships. For example, while economies of scale in service provision might matter to them, survival is as much a cultural and political issue as it is an economic one. Indigenous nations may be quite willing to accept higher economic costs for higher cultural and political returns to a specific form or scale of organization. These different emphases can produce divergent solutions to the "who is the self" question.

What's more, efficacy and legitimacy affect each other. Governments that have legitimacy with those being governed are likely to be less vulnerable to rent-seeking and internal conflicts, and consequently are more likely to perform well. Similarly, governments that perform well over time are more likely to maintain or establish legitimacy with those being governed. "This government works" and "this government is ours" may appear to be competing orientations, but they tend, ultimately, to support each other.

Governance Solutions

As one might expect, in all three countries, an assortment of nations and groups are developing governance solutions, sometimes within, sometimes outside of state-sponsored processes. Many of them directly address the "who is the self" issue, from the Ktunaxa Nation in British Columbia that links five First Nations in a unitary governance structure, to the Thamarrurr Regional Council that links twenty different clan groups in the Northern Territory of Australia, to intertribal courts and intertribal service organizations in the United States.

These solutions typically involve institution-sharing, bringing together previously separated parts of single nations or uniting multiple nations for some governmental tasks. In most cases, they rely on shared cultures, shared ecosystems, or shared histories as bases for building trust among entities that have become accustomed to operating independently. They also typically distinguish among governmental functions, with some functions remaining the primary responsibility of a component group, while others are deferred to the larger collectivity; in other words, many of these solutions are multi-scalar. More and more, these nations also are trying to learn from each other, sharing models and ideas that may have relevance across cultural and even international boundaries.

Effective approaches to this issue will require both Indigenous and non-Indigenous governments to abandon certain preconceptions. Central state approaches to Indigenous government typically indulge a one-size-fits-all fantasy that denies diverse Native nations the freedom to choose institutional solutions of their own design, including solutions that may depart from state ideas about what viable governance structures should look like. Meanwhile, Native nations often have a we-can-do-it-all fantasy that hesitates to cross political boundaries in search of more viable institutional solutions to governance challenges. Both preconceptions present obstacles to the kind of innovation that some of these challenges may require.

Preliminary Lessons

This is a preliminary presentation of these issues, but it suggests some equally preliminary lessons.

- In many cases, and for reasons outlined above, the current organization of much Indigenous government is ineffective.
- Capable governance will require change and, in some cases, innovation.
- Some innovations will necessarily involve adjustments in scale for at least some peoples and, for some governmental purposes, a rethinking of "who is the self."
- Not all governing institutions within a nation or community must have the same social or geographical scale.
- Governing institutions shared across communities or even nations can be a solution to size, asset, and isolation problems.
- Institution-sharing is an act of self-determination.
- Institution-sharing, because it often is a departure from recent practice, typically faces legitimacy challenges, but these challenges can be solved through:
    - Shared culture, ecosystem, experience, etc.
    - A deliberate "process of Indigenous choice" (Smith 2004, 27)

What We Need

How such lessons should be applied in practice is a major question and beyond the scope of this presentation. However, there is a research agenda that could be of considerable assistance to both Indigenous and non-Indigenous policy makers wrestling with these issues.

First, we need a better understanding of how Indigenous and non-Indigenous conceptions of governance differ, so as to facilitate more productive communication between the two about the governance challenges Indigenous peoples face.

Second, we need a systematic examination of what Indigenous governance requires in terms of both structure and scale. Such an examination will have to be sensitive both to the different requirements of various governmental functions—including functions that Indigenous peoples see as critical but that central governments fail to comprehend—and to the variable concerns and situations of diverse peoples.

Much of this second need could be met by the third: documentation of effective models and of how change toward those models takes place. We do not have, in any of these three countries, a shortage of Indigenous solutions to governance challenges. However, we are not very good yet at analyzing those solutions and making these emergent Indigenous models and the practical analysis of why they work available to Indigenous and non-Indigenous decision makers.

Finally, we need to know more about the sources of governmental legitimacy and about Indigenous processes of legitimation that can allow innovative governance solutions once again to emerge and endure in Indigenous communities.

Acknowledgements

This paper is an early product of a comparative project on Indigenous governance in the United States, Canada, Australia, and New Zealand. Several people have contributed substantially to my thinking on the topics covered here. I would like to acknowledge in particular extensive conversations with Fred Wien of Dalhousie University and Diane Smith of the Australian National University. I have benefited also from conversations with Miriam Jorgensen of the University of Arizona's Native Nations Institute, Jason Glanville of Reconciliation Australia, Satsan (Herb George) of the National Centre for First Nations Governance, and Joseph P. Kalt of Harvard University. Thanks also to the W. K. Kellogg Foundation, Reconciliation Australia, and the Native Nations Institute at the University of Arizona for their support of aspects of this work.

Endnotes

1 Much of the material in this paper applies also to New Zealand, which is included in the larger project of which this paper is a part. For further discussion of the grounds for comparative work across these countries, see Cornell (2005).

2 On the US, see Castile (1998), Cornell (1988), and Nagel (1996). On Canada, see Asch (1999), Cairns (2000), McNeil (1998), and the Royal Commission on Aboriginal Peoples (1996). On Australia, see Baker, Davies, and Young (2001), Behrendt (2003), Craig (2002), and Smith (2004).

3 This was at one time the case in the United States as well, and a similar view still surfaces in the federal bureaucracy and elsewhere, but over the last thirty years or so, it has been widely accepted that American Indian nations can exercise, among other things, significant law-making, enforcement, and judicial powers. The long-term security of those powers is another matter.

4 These comments are taken from my field notes on conversations about Indigenous conceptions of governance, November 2005.

5 As Satsan (Herb George) of the Wet'suet'en people in British Columbia put it, "they shredded our nations." Presentation at the University of Arizona College of Law, Tucson, Arizona, September 23, 2005.

References

Asch, Michael. 1999. From *Calder* to *Van der Peet*: Aboriginal rights and Canadian law, 1973–96. In *Indigenous Peoples' rights in Australia, Canada, and New Zealand*, ed. Paul Havemann, 428–46. Auckland: Oxford Univ. Press.

Baker, Richard, Jocelyn Davies, and Elspeth Young. 2001. *Working on country: Contemporary Indigenous management of Australia's lands and coastal regions*. Melbourne: Oxford Univ. Press.

Behrendt, Larissa. 2003. *Achieving social justice: Indigenous rights and Australia's future*. Sydney: The Federation Press.

Bräutigam, Deborah A., and Stephen Knack. 2004. Foreign aid, institutions, and governance in Sub-Saharan Africa. *Economic Development and Cultural Change* 52 (2): 255–85.

Cairns, Alan C. 2000. *Citizens plus: Aboriginal Peoples and the Canadian state*. Vancouver: UBC Press.

Castile, George Pierre. 1998. *To show heart: Native American self-determination and federal Indian policy, 1960–1975*. Tucson: Univ. of Arizona Press.

Cornell, Stephen. 1988. *The return of the Native: American Indian political resurgence*. New York: Oxford Univ. Press.

-----. 2005. Indigenous Peoples, poverty, and self-determination in Australia, New Zealand, Canada, and the United States. In *Indigenous Peoples and poverty: An international perspective*, ed. Robyn Eversole, John-Andrew McNeish, and Alberto Cimadamore. CROP International Studies in Poverty Research Series. London: Zed Books. 199–225.

Cornell, Stephen, Catherine Curtis, and Miriam Jorgensen. 2004. The concept of governance and its implications for First Nations. Joint Occasional Papers on Native Affairs no. 2004-02. Tucson and Cambridge: Native Nations Institute, University of Arizona, and Harvard Project on American Indian Economic Development.

Cornell, Stephen, Miriam Jorgensen, and Joseph P. Kalt. 2002. The First Nations Governance Act: Implications of research findings from the United States and Canada. A report to the Office of the British Columbia Regional Vice-Chief, Assembly of First Nations. Native Nations Institute for Leadership, Management, and Policy, University of Arizona.

Cornell, Stephen, and Joseph P. Kalt. 1997a. Cultural evolution and constitutional public choice: Institutional diversity and economic performance on American Indian Reservations. In *Uncertainty and evolution in economics: Essays in honor of Armen A. Alchian*, ed. John Lott, 116–42. London and New York: Routledge.

-----. 1997b. Successful economic development and heterogeneity of governmental form on American Indian reservations. In *Getting good government: Capacity building in the public sectors of developing countries*, ed. Merilee S. Grindle, 257–96. Cambridge: Harvard Institute for International Development.

-----. 2000. Where's the glue?: Institutional and cultural foundations of American Indian economic development. *Journal of Socio-Economics* 29:443–70.

-----. 2003. Alaska native self-governance and service delivery: What works? Joint occasional papers on Native affairs, no. 2003–01. Native Nations Institute for Leadership, Management, and Policy, and Harvard Project on American Indian Economic Development. Tucson: Udall Center for Studies in Public Policy, University of Arizona.

-----. 2005. Two approaches to economic development on American Indian reservations: One works, the other doesn't. Joint occasional papers on Native affairs, no. 2005–02. Native Nations Institute for Leadership, Management, and Policy, and Harvard Project on American Indian Economic Development. Tucson: Udall Center for Studies in Public Policy, University of Arizona.

Craig, D.G. 2002. Recognizing Indigenous rights through co-management regimes: Canadian and Australian experiences. *New Zealand Journal of Environmental Law* 6:199–255.

Doornbos, Martin. 2001. "Good governance": The rise and decline of a policy metaphor? *Journal of Development Studies* 37(6): 93–108.

Egnal, Marc. 1996. *Divergent paths: How culture and institutions have shaped North American growth.* New York: Oxford Univ. Press.

Hunt, J., and D. E. Smith. 2006. Building Indigenous community governance in Australia: Preliminary research findings. Working Paper no. 32/2006. Canberra: Centre for Aboriginal Economic Policy Research, Australian National University.

Jorgensen, Miriam. 2000. Bringing the background forward: Evidence from Indian country on the social and cultural determinants of economic development. Ph.D. diss, Harvard Univ.

-----, ed. Forthcoming. *Resources for Native nation building.* Tucson: Univ. of Arizona Press.

Knack, Stephen and Philip Keefer. 1995. Institutions and economic performance: Cross-country tests using alternative institutional measures. *Economics and Politics* 7(3): 207–27.

La Porta, Rafael, Florencio Lopez-de-Silanes, Andrei Shleifer, and Robert W. Vishney. 1999. The quality of government. *Journal of Law, Economics and Organization* 15 (April): 222–79.

McNeil, Kent. 1998. *Defining Aboriginal title in the 90's: Has the Supreme Court finally got it right?* Toronto: Robarts Centre for Canadian Studies, York University.

Morphy, Howard. 1999. The Reeves Report and the idea of the "region." In *Land rights at risk? Evaluations of the Reeves Report*, ed. J. C. Altman, F. Morphy and T. Rowse. Research Monograph no. 14. Canberra: Centre for Aboriginal Economic Policy Research, Australian National University. 33–38.

North, Douglass C. 1990. *Institutions, institutional change and economic performance.* Cambridge: Cambridge Univ. Press.

Nagel, Joane. 1996. *American Indian ethnic renewal: Red power and the resurgence of identity and culture.* New York: Oxford Univ. Press.

Ostrom, Elinor. 1992. *Crafting institutions for self-governing irrigation systems.* San Francisco: Institute for Contemporary Studies.

Rowse, Tim. 2000. *Obliged to be difficult: Nugget Coombs' legacy in Indigenous affairs.* Cambridge and Oakleigh: Cambridge Univ. Press.

Royal Commission on Aboriginal Peoples. 1996. *People to people, nation to nation: Highlights from the Report of the Royal Commission on Aboriginal Peoples.* Ottawa: Royal Commission on Aboriginal Peoples.

Smith, D. E. 2004. From Gove to governance: Reshaping Indigenous governance in the Northern Territory. Discussion Paper no. 265/2004. Canberra: Centre for Aboriginal Economic Policy Research, Australian National University.

Sutton, Peter. 1995. *Country: Aboriginal boundaries and land ownership in Australia.* Aboriginal History Monograph 3. Canberra: Australian National University.

Taylor, John. 2004. *Social indicators for Aboriginal governance: Insights from the Thamarrurr Region, Northern Territory.* Research Monograph no. 24. Canberra: Centre for Aboriginal Economic Policy Research, Australian National University.

Williams, Robert A., Jr. 2006. *Like a loaded weapon: The Rehnquist Court, Indian rights, and the legal history of racism in America.* Minneapolis: Univ. of Minnesota Press.

11

Successful First Nations Policy Development: Delivering Sustainability, Accountability, and Innovation

Jennifer Brennan,
on behalf of the Assembly of First Nations

Introduction

There is a profound need for a process that will afford Aboriginal peoples the opportunity to restructure existing governmental institutions and to participate as partners in the Canadian federation on terms they freely accept. This conclusion of the Royal Commission of Aboriginal Peoples (RCAP) (1996, 244) accurately identifies a central challenge for the Assembly of First Nations (AFN). The AFN, as the political representative for First Nations governments throughout Canada, has amassed a great deal of experience in dealing with the Government of Canada. Indeed, it is our perspective that a critical determinant of a successful outcome for the full range of engagement—from senior government-to-government negotiations to policy development and singular program considerations—lies in the initial process design.

This paper will provide a general overview of examples of interaction between First Nations and Canadian governments, as well as Indigenous peoples and state governments in other parts of the world. From these examples, both situations to avoid and best practices emerge. Based on this information and direction received from First Nations by way of our assemblies and policy forums, the AFN has designed a First Nations policy development model.

This paper presents the First Nations policy development model and fully describes its elements, considerations, and operating principles. We also provide examples of the utility of the model guiding the engagement of the AFN in critical intergovernmental fora, as well as on specific project initiatives currently underway with the Government of Canada.

Treaties: The Essential Starting Point

In addressing the question of appropriate interaction between the Government of Canada and First Nations peoples, the treaty-making process is the essential starting point. While this paper does not seek to fully describe the history of the treaty process, its clear purpose of establishing mutual protection and coordination, as is evident in the early contact and treaty-making processes, informs this discussion. By 1763, Aboriginal/English relations had stabilized to the point where they can be seen as grounded in two fundamental principles: recognition of the autonomous status of Aboriginal nations and acceptance of the fact that Aboriginal nations exercised full entitlement to territories unless, or until, they ceded them away (RCAP 1996, 114). Therefore, we can establish that the first period of interaction between First Nations peoples and what was to become the Government of Canada was characterized by recognition and respect, and the shared goals of co-operation and mutual co-existence.

This paper argues that, after two and half centuries of interaction, the central challenge to finding effective ways for both sides to engage in the new millennium is in finding mechanisms that accurately reflect this original point of interaction between the peoples of the First Nations and the Government of Canada.[1] Of course, we must be cognizant of change over this time and of the resultant implications, which may create different conditions than those anticipated during the early contact period. For the purposes of this paper, we seek to draw not from the content of these interactions but, rather, from the principles and processes of interaction.

Certainly, the time and space required to appropriately summarize First Nations—government relations from the treaty-making period to the present are beyond the scope of this paper. However, many excellent studies are available on this topic: the RCAP reports are particularly relevant, as are important studies such as Sarah Carter's *Lost Harvests: Prairie Indian Reserve Farmers and Government Policy* (1993). As these studies point out, the waning military importance of First Nations in the mid-1880s gave rise to new policy orientations on the part of the Canadian government. The central policy goal of ensuring alliance and military support from First Nations was gradually displaced by new goals aimed at cultural transformation and assimilation. Achievement of these goals allowed for greater access to First Nation territories that were required for the emerging settler economy. This transformation ushered in a long period of unilateral policy-making by the Government of Canada. By almost every measure, this phase of policy-making failed to achieve any desired outcome for First Nations people. Furthermore, it is the position of the AFN that this phase produced devastating effects[2] that are the direct causes of the current gap in socio-economic conditions between First Nations and the rest of Canada.

In reaching for sustainable solutions, the AFN believes that we must begin with a deliberate and careful plan. Such a plan must be based on the broad goals of reconciliation and respect that reflect the goals of the original relationship. Furthermore, it is believed that achieving sustainable solutions will require intense planning and effective processes to enable change to succeed.

Much can be learned from a summary of attempts at policy engagement in the recent past between First Nations and the Government of Canada. Beginning with the round of Constitutional talks that culminated in the Charlottetown Accord of 1992, First Nations and the various governments of Canada generally expressed some desire to find effective ways to work together. Despite this general agreement, a wide variety of attempts to arrive at policy change occurred. The following overview attempts to point out both the strengths and weaknesses of these attempts.

The Experience of Engagement

Royal Commission on Aboriginal Peoples (RCAP)

The RCAP process itself represents a unique and powerful mechanism to fully discuss and consider an appropriate strategy to move forward. First Nations thoughtfully and thoroughly participated in this process and the final report of the RCAP is now generally regarded by First Nations as the most comprehensive and accurate summary of the First Nations perspective. Yet, RCAP itself was not intended to be a vehicle for change. Rather, the RCAP report set the context necessary to enable both First Nations and the Government of Canada to respond and to act in an appropriate way to produce the changes required to address First Nations issues.

So, while the RCAP process itself was successful in meeting its own objectives, it is at the point of response and action that its limitations are revealed. While RCAP delivered hundreds of very specific recommendations, a coordinated, specific plan and process to effectively and practically move forward was not provided. First Nations governments and the federal and provincial governments of Canada had varied responses. While First Nation governments and organizations generally responded positively, they typically did not have the capacity, resources, or, perhaps, the leadership focus, to drive a plan for implementing change.

Gathering Strength

The response from the Government of Canada, entitled *Gathering Strength,* although viewed positively by some First Nations, was seen as a limited response to some portions of the RCAP report. Even the response itself admits limitations, as it indicates that the "RCAP report served as a catalyst and an inspiration" for setting "a new course in Federal policies for Aboriginal people,"[3] rather than directly informing a process to implement RCAP's recommendations. *Gathering Strength* expressed important values regarding partnership and reconciliation, which were important initial steps; however, by most accounts, it did not deliver the intended or anticipated change in the policy relationship.

Despite endorsement by the entire Cabinet, with a change in leadership both at the ministerial and senior administrative level at Indian and Northern Affairs Canada (INAC), *Gathering Strength* quickly lost influence and relevance. The most stunning evidence of this was found in the process leading to the introduction of the proposed First Nations Governance Act by Robert Nault, the new minister of Indian and Northern Affairs.

First Nations Governance Act

Despite the explicit objections of First Nations, Minister Nault unilaterally developed an approach and process that would have direct impacts on First Nation governments.[4] First Nations raised specific concerns with the orientation and content of the proposed legislation, but the most repeated and salient characteristics of the opposition were to do with the process.

> First Nations have opposed the process by which Minister Nault set about to achieve these ends. The majority of First Nations rejected the consultation process stating that the content was arbitrarily limited and the outcomes pre-determined. Those who did participate tabled serious concerns that the initiative did not provide sufficient consultation and that the content did not reflect the priorities of the First Nations.[5]

In the end, of course, the First Nations Governance Act also failed to meet its intended outcomes as it did not become law. The First Nations Governance Act died on the order paper due to the intense opposition of First Nations and the reluctance of the federal government to continue to pursue a measure that was so unpopular.

These two examples of government-initiated policy change, *Gathering Strength* and the proposed First Nations Governance Act, differ in many respects. *Gathering Strength* attempted to set a course of action based on key principles that would include First Nations. However, its potential to create lasting change appears to have been cut short by a lack of political will across the federal government, making it vulnerable to a change in leadership. By contrast, the First Nations Governance Act aimed to target specific policy and program irritants for INAC, as opposed to First Nations priorities for change, and sidestepped the development of a process of engagement almost entirely. In fact, as described above, the consultation effort associated with the First Nations Governance Act was largely seen as completely illegitimate by First Nations.

While clearly different approaches, both *Gathering Strength* and the First Nations Governance Act were developed and driven almost exclusively within INAC. Indeed, while these initiatives may have had other weaknesses (namely a lack of clear targets in the case of *Gathering Strength* and the complete lack of recognition and respect for First Nations in the case of the First Nation Governance Act), it is possible to conclude that a central factor in the failure of these efforts to produce change was that they did not allow for First Nations to drive the process from the outset. These examples, therefore, illustrate that First Nations must be engaged from the earliest stages of a process to establish principles and priorities, in order to produce change that can be sustained and produce desired results.

Still, such engagement does not provide the entire answer. An examination of two policy efforts in which First Nations did, in fact, play a key role from the outset of the process provides additional important information to consider as these efforts also failed to reach their intended outcomes.

AFN/INAC Joint Initiative For Policy Development

The AFN/INAC Joint Initiative for Policy Development (Lands and Trusts Services sector) was initiated jointly by the national chief of the Assembly of First Nations and senior officials within INAC in 1998. This initiative clearly included extensive engagement with First Nations. In fact, the first principle adopted as part of the process was that it would be driven by First Nations concerns. However, this process was limited to dealing with one sector within INAC and therefore, despite a broad commitment to general principles, AFN and the First Nations involved were limited by the constraints of departmental organization and a lack of department-wide commitment, let alone by the Government of Canada. Still, there are important lessons to be derived from this process.

In a paper released by the AFN,[6] both the strengths and weaknesses of this process were presented. First, it summarizes the Joint Initiative as containing the following positive procedural elements:

- Shared commitment
- Flexibility
- Clear principles
- Inclusive and open process
- Recognition of First Nation values

Several aspects of this process are worthy of note. First, the process was First Nations-driven, allowing for trust within First Nations to gradually evolve. Second, accessibility of senior level officials within INAC was deemed a critical element for progress. Third, careful consideration was given to ensure an effective evolution of policy. The AFN insisted that they must conduct extensive research on all subject matters and, further, that regional and national dialogues must be maintained at all critical stages of the initiative.

In this paper, the AFN also identified significant barriers—systemic, structural, and environmental—that threatened the Joint Initiative's progress. In the end, this assessment proved prescient, as a change in leadership at the ministerial level at INAC led to the swift termination of all funding for the initiative. This termination occurred despite rising expectations for change resulting from a national gathering, attended by hundreds of First Nations individuals from across Canada, and the production of specific implementation plans for anticipated change.[7]

Joint First Nations—Canada Task Force On Specific Claims Policy Reform

The Joint First Nations—Canada Task Force on Specific Claims Policy Reform provides another example of extensive First Nations engagement in a policy initiative with the Government of Canada. This exercise, which began in 1997, was based on the clearly shared desire and commitment of both the Government of Canada and First Nations to improve the existing claims policy.

Both Canada and First Nations agreed to use this task force to "find mutually acceptable means by which to settle claims." Importantly, the task force was a technical forum comprised of regional First Nations representatives and federal officials from both INAC and the Department of Justice. This process, therefore, benefited both from a clear focus as well as a degree of parity in terms of the human resources each side brought to the table. Legal expertise and research, from a First Nations perspective, were resourced through this initiative.

The recommendations of the Joint Task Force, tabled in 1998, were never acted upon. Despite commitment by the ministers involved, Cabinet did not approve the changes being sought. Instead, INAC brought forward a significantly different approach in June 2002: Bill C-60—the Specific Claims Resolution Act. The legacy of this process remains, however, as First Nations continue to advocate for adherence to the task force recommendations prior to the bill's receiving royal assent.

When we examine the broader international context, additional examples of Indigenous peoples interacting with state governments illustrate the importance of the process, and provide additional characteristics to successful engagement.

New Zealand

The failure of the so-called "Fiscal Envelope" proposals in New Zealand in the mid-1990s has been attributed largely to the fact that there had been no formal joint process or engagement leading to the release of the proposals. The Maori objected to the total lack of adequate consultation, the principles behind the proposals, the government's assumptions and claims of ownership over natural resources, and the billion-dollar cap. The Maori united against the proposal not only for what it proposed, but how it was developed and presented (Akiwenzie-Damm 2000, 24). They were angered by what they interpreted as "a slick and expensive public relations campaign designed to make the Government look like a reasonable and generous benefactor" (Orakei Research Unit for Maori Education 1995, 1:25).

Despite high expectations in the mid-1980s and the commitment to a "decade of Maori development," efforts on the part of the New Zealand government did not produce positive results. Commentators have suggested that "behind the rhetoric, Maori remained in essentially the same position they had been since 1840. Arguably, they were worse off'" (Kelsey 1990, 247). Additional studies reached similar conclusions—that despite the appearance of engagement between the New Zealand government and the Maori, very little changed and very little was accomplished. "In fact the neo-liberal reforms of the economy, state and civil society, which had begun in 1984 by the Fourth Labour Government and were continued by the national governments of 1990–1996 saw the position of the worst-off Maori become still worse" (Sharp 1997, 291).

Throughout this period, Maori leadership advocated for different processes and a formal engagement aimed at reconciliation and decolonization. Maori leaders and commentators identified that, while their engagement was being framed as a "partnership," the Crown and/or its agencies retained the power to develop documents, policies, and corporate plans which would affect the Maori without consultation them as a treaty partner" (Mahuika 1998, 216). Furthermore, Maori leaders stated that "the crucial issue for resolution has always been and remains Maori sovereignty" (Orakei Research Unit for Maori Education 1995, 26). As a result, the Maori identified that in order for there to be progress, the Maori needed to be fully and effectively engaged, and clear principles and formal processes for consultation had to be established.

United States of America

In the United States, despite uneven treatment in the past, significant steps towards effective collaborative relationships between governments and First Nations have been established. Most significantly, in 1994, former President Clinton issued a memorandum reaffirming the federal government's commitment to operate within a government-to-government relationship with federally recognized American Indian and Alaska Native tribes.[8]

On a practical level, the presidential directive has contributed to significant changes in the ways in which state governments interact with North American Indian tribes. Specific guidelines have been set, which direct regular and meaningful processes of consultation in the development of all federal policies that have tribal implications.

Based on emerging experiences of collaboration and joint policy development, the National Conference of State Legislatures and the National Congress of American Indians have confirmed a number of key principles for effective intergovernmental relationships. These include commitment to co-operation in areas that tribes and states can come together on: mutual understanding and respect; regular and early communication before policies are developed and conflicts arise; identifying a process and establishing accountability or addressing issues; and institutionalizing positive relationships. These principles are evident in examples of collaborative social policy initiatives in several states.

Policy Development from a First Nations Perspective

First Nations and the AFN have expressed a set of clear policy priorities; however, the critical question of how best to advance this policy agenda with the federal government has remained unanswered. Consequently, the AFN has set out to design a policy development model based on research and best practices.

The experience outlined in the preceding examples points to several important considerations necessary to build an appropriate, effective, and ultimately successful model of policy engagement between First Nations and Canadian governments.

Clearly, for a policy initiative to be successful, it must both respond to and be directed by First Nations. In other words, First Nations must have a central role in directing change in order to achieve sustainable solutions. Also, past experience has demonstrated that all parties involved in a process of change must secure clear political commitment and mandates for change. Finally, it appears that joint or shared discussions and dialogue are the necessary vehicles to arrive at innovative, accountable, and sustainable solutions.

Certainly, a range of processes for change has been tried. Generally, there are three broad processes for creating and implementing First Nation policy change: those controlled by other governments; those controlled by First Nations; and joint processes.

Essentially, processes led by other governments generally fail due to several factors, including First Nations mistrust and the fact that the changes suggested did not respond to First Nations desires or needs for change. Processes controlled by First Nations have been difficult to implement and sustain because of a lack of independent resources, and federal and provincial mistrust. Previous attempts at joint processes have not succeeded due to an imbalance between the parties involved and a lack of clear commitment to engage.

The best approach to First Nations policy change is a combination of these three general policy processes. The AFN has suggested that the best approach to achieving transformative policy change is one that contains the following general elements: First Nations leadership; national dialogue; independent research and expertise; clear mandates and commitment; and, finally, joint principled policy engagement to develop options for the consideration and adoption of First Nations governments.

1. First Nations Leadership

Policy initiatives must originate from strong First Nations leadership and advocacy. This will provide the policy proposal with First Nations political legitimacy and a mechanism to evaluate the costs and benefits of the proposed policy change through a case study or pilot project approach. Federal and provincial governments can assist in facilitating this kind of leadership through supporting pilot projects to establish capacity in a number of areas corresponding to the policy priorities articulated by First Nations.

2. National Dialogue

For any change to be effective, it is fundamental to have a process to share information widely throughout all sectors of First Nations society. While every initiative may not be relevant or of interest to every First Nation, there is a fundamental obligation to provide general information about any policy initiative. First Nations must, therefore, have reasonable access to information in order to create trust and confidence for any process of change. The Assembly of First Nations has a long-established tradition of community processes and reporting relationships to all First Nations. These processes are currently being strengthened by the AFN renewal exercise, which will result in expanded communication vehicles, as well as regularized policy and citizen forums.

3. Independent Research And Expertise

There is a clear need for independent policy research. This activity is necessary to create legitimacy for all parties involved in an exercise of policy change. Most importantly, First Nations seek to work directly with academic and other research entities to ensure an accurate reflection of First Nation priorities and perspectives.

In regards to specific policy advice and expertise, First Nations view such support originating from First Nations institutions or organizations under the clear direction of First Nations governments. These organizations and institutions must have a clear mandate and expertise with First Nations governments in a particular policy area. A best practice would be for the federal government to support, or to assist in the development of, First Nations institutions and organizations that provide specialized expertise and support to First Nations.

4. Clear Mandate For Change

Effective policy engagement requires all parties involved to have a clear mandate for policy change. Most importantly, federal and provincial government officials must seek and secure a comprehensive mandate in order for the effort of policy engagement to have a clear path to implementation. Too often, policy options are not acted upon because other governments do not have the authority or the mandate to explore these options. This lack of authority or mandate is an indication to First Nations that other governments are not serious. Changes to government machinery, such as those recommended through the RCAP process, will be necessary over the longer term to enable efficient mandating of such initiatives.

5. Joint Principled Policy Processes

Finally, there must be a forum for joint policy discussion and development, and non-prejudicial research. These forums would allow all parties to articulate and protect their interests and work on mutual interests through non-prejudicial research and option development. Further, they would create political legitimacy and establish momentum for proposed policy changes. First Nations governments must have the opportunity and capacity to fully participate in these processes, as the results will fundamentally impact their constituencies. A best practice would be to reach agreement on pre-specified objectives, principles, and timelines for these processes.

General operating principles should include the following:

- Most activities will involve both national and regional work. National level activities will be built from the ground up and regional level activities will reflect the priorities determined in the regions.
- All relevant information, including documents and data, shall be available to both parties to encourage an open and transparent environment, subject to each party's confidentiality requirements for internal decision making.
- Joint working groups shall operate on the basis of consensus.
- The focus and commitment of the joint working groups shall be to produce tangible outcomes.
- National discussions and activities will not prejudice ongoing community-based negotiations led by individual First Nations, and First Nations will have the opportunity to fully review and accept policy or legislative change.
- Resource requirements for the overall process and the working groups will be fairly and openly addressed.
- First Nations communities, organizations, and the general public shall be kept informed of progress on a regular basis.

Policy Considerations

Effective policy development must also take into consideration clear priorities for First Nations. The AFN is guided by the following key considerations when engaging in any policy development:

- Self-government is an inherent Aboriginal and treaty right as well as the necessary foundation for First Nation socio-economic development. The achievement of self-government is the primary consideration of any First Nation participation in federal policy, program, or organizational changes.
- Policy processes must respect the distinctive nature of First Nation interests, rights, and circumstances, and not be considered part of a pan-Aboriginal policy process.
- National policy dialogues cannot encumber local or regional processes but, rather, should facilitate and foster development at this level.

The First Nation Policy Development model can then be summarized as containing the following characteristics:

- An internal First Nation policy development process led by First Nations and supported by First Nation institutional and organizational expertise and a thorough national dialogue with all First Nations
- An internal process for other governments, providing them with a mandate for change
- A pilot project or case study mechanism to explore policy options in a non-prejudicial fashion
- A principled and objective-driven forum to discuss, design, and ultimately implement policy changes

First Nation Policy Development in Action

While still an essentially new concept, the First Nation policy development model has been utilized by the Assembly of First Nations since 2004. The Assembly of First Nations structured its engagement in the Canada-Aboriginal Roundtable process based on this model. For instance, the AFN sought to describe policy interests fully by way of thorough research and the presentation of background papers that resulted from national policy direction from resolutions and discussions at policy forums and Assemblies.[9] In addition, the AFN's engagement in the process leading up to the first ministers meeting in Kelowna, November 2005, also followed the First Nation policy development model. By all accounts, the AFN was recognized as leading the policy discussions through these forums, a situation indicative of both the strength and utility of the First Nation policy development model.

Recognition and Implementation of First Nation Governments

The most comprehensive policy engagement by the Assembly of First Nations in the recent past is found in the Recognition and Implementation of First Nations Governments initiative (RIFNG), started in 2004. By way of a thorough review of relevant studies, as well as an extensive, year-long process of dialogue among all First Nations, this initiative put forward a key report in 2005: *Our Nations, Our Governments: Choosing Our Own Paths*. The entire report has relevance to this discussion, and certain central considerations bear mention. In particular, the RIFNG further develops and articulates the necessary principles and broad processes and structures required to achieve change. The RIFNG report was presented in full to a special Chiefs assembly in March 2005. Following a full discussion among all regions, the Chiefs in assembly endorsed the report and mandated implementation of the initiative.

Based on the broad discussion among First Nations and intense research undertaken by RIFNG, key procedural requirements emerged as considerations for mapping a process forward. These considerations include:

- Attaining consent of First Nations
- Conducting joint development of any proposed legislation or policy
- Establishing independent monitoring and decision-making bodies to address the current imbalance in power
- Appropriate intergovernmental mechanisms, including appropriate consultation policies, financing, and dispute resolution mechanisms[10]

RIFNG directed that two key features of any process are required: an internal First Nation process which emphasizes the importance of community and regional level engagement, and a senior-level, principled process of engagement with the federal government. Further, RIFNG set in motion a joint steering committee at the ministerial level to oversee policy reforms, legal instruments, and arrangements, as well as the development of structures and processes to advance the recognition and implementation of the First Nation governments.

The RIFNG initiative and process positioned the AFN, and all First Nations, to effectively lead the discussions in preparation for the Federal Government Cabinet Policy Retreat with Aboriginal leaders on May 31, 2005. As a result of this preparation, the AFN and the Canadian government endorsed the First Nations-Federal Crown Political Accord on the Recognition and Implementation of First Nation Governments. This accord is a very significant achievement, as it confirms the appropriate context for engagement between First Nations and Canada on all policy matters.

The AFN continues to lead this agenda and has suggested principles and processes to guide interaction based on the political accord. In order to advance an agenda which includes mechanisms for managing and coordinating renewed and ongoing intergovernmental relationships, establishing timely and meaningful consultation and coordination, and strengthening the government-to-government relationship between Canada and First Nations, the AFN has suggested that the following principles be expressed by First Nations and Canada:

- The Crown in Right of Canada has a unique legal relationship with First Nations governments, and the inherent right of self-government is an existing right recognized and affirmed by section 35 of the Constitution Act, 1982.
- Federal departments shall respect the inherent right of self-government, honour treaty rights and strive to meet the responsibilities that arise from the fiduciary duty of the Crown.
- Federal officials shall be counselled on Canada's fidelity to section 35 of the Constitution Act, 1982, and a culture of respect in government for Aboriginal and treaty rights shall be encouraged.

- Before a proposed bill is introduced to Parliament or before a policy is presented to Cabinet, a minister, or other federal authority for federal approval, each policy or legislative proposal falling within the purview of this protocol shall be assessed from a viewpoint of compliance with section 35 of the Constitution Act, 1982, by requesting that the Department of Justice undertake a review and confirm that every proposed law and policy comports with section 35 of the Constitution Act, 1982, and the fiduciary duties of the Crown, and the opinion provided by the Department of Justice shall be shared with the Assembly of First Nations and an opportunity for the AFN to respond be provided.
- Before a legislative proposal is introduced to Parliament, the AFN and Canada shall meet to discuss their views concerning section 35 compliance and shall jointly determine a timeline and model for meaningful and timely consultation with individual First Nations in a manner consistent with the principles of the protocol.
- The AFN and Canada may agree to exempt any particular legislative proposal that is not national in scope from the above requirements.

Conclusion

The decades of failed policy and legislative initiatives must serve as a rallying cry for real change to address the basic injustices and socio-economic disparities facing First Nations peoples and their governments. This paper has demonstrated that First Nations must be fully engaged in driving policy change, that parties must express firm commitment to change, and that carefully planned processes for joint engagement are necessary.

First Nations seek change that renews the original relationship between Canada and First Nations governments. Through a process of reconciliation that embraces clear principles and sets about to transform existing processes and structures, real change can and will be achieved.

Endnotes

1 This position has been formally tabled previously as detailed in Assembly of First Nations (1993).

2 The Assembly of First Nations (AFN) has produced discussion and research papers, and the Chiefs in assembly have passed several resolutions articulating this position in regards to matters such as the Indian residential schools policy, the reserve system, and general effects of Indian policy causing displacement, injustice, and poverty throughout this period.

3 Government of Canada, Ministry of Indian Affairs and Northern Development (1997, 4).

4 For a full analysis of First Nation objections to the proposed First Nation Governments Act, see Assembly of First Nations (2002).

5 AFN analysis, June 2002, 1.

6 Assembly of First Nations (1999); AFN/INAC Joint Initiative for Policy Development (LTS) (1999).

7 AFN/INAC Joint Initiative for Policy Development (2001).

8 Presidential Executive Order 13175 of November 6, 2000, Bureau of Indian Affairs, Consultation and Coordination with Indian Tribal Government, December 13, 2000.

9 For full information and all background policy papers, see Assembly of First Nations (2005a).

10 Assembly of First Nations (2005b, 39).

References

Akiwenzie-Damm, Kateri. 2000. *Partnership arrangements between Maori and New Zealand governments.* Prepared for the AFN-INAC Joint Initiative for Policy Development (LTS).

Assembly of First Nations. 1993. *Reclaiming our nationhood, strengthening our heritage.* Report to the Royal Commission on Aboriginal Peoples.

Assembly of First Nations. 1999. *The Experience of building a partnership.* AFN/INAC Joint Initiative for Policy Development (LTS).

Assembly of First Nations. 2002. *First Nations Governance Act: Analysis.*

Assembly of First Nations. 2005a. *Getting from the roundtable to results: Canada Aboriginal Peoples roundtable process: April 2004–March 2005, Summary report.*

Assembly of First Nations. 2005b. *Joint Committee of Chiefs and Advisors on the recognition and implementation of First Nation Governments.* Final Report of *Our Nations, Our Governments: Choosing Our Own Paths*, Ottawa, 2005.

AFN/INAC Joint Initiative for Policy Development. 2001. *The voice of First Nations: Planning for change.* Ottawa: Assembly of First Nations.

Canada. Ministry of Indian Affairs and Northern Development. 1997. *Gathering strength—Canada's Aboriginal action plan.* Ottawa: Ministry of Public Works.

Hicks, Sarah and Kathryn Dyjak, "Happy together: The story of collaboration, policy and practice." *Policy & Practice of Public Human Services.* 62(3): 18-21.

Kelsey, Jane. 1990. *A question of honour? Labour and treaty 1984–1989.* Wellington NZ: Allen & Unwin.

Mahuika, Apirana. 1998. Whakapapa is the heart. In *Living relationships, kokiri ngatahi: The Treaty of Waitangi in the new millennium*, ed. Ken Coates and P.G. McHugh. Wellington NZ: Victoria Univ. Press.

Orakei Research Unit for Maori Education. 1995. *The fiscal envelope: Economics, politics & colonisation.* Vol. 1 of A Series of Readers Examining Critical Issues in Contemporary Maori Society. Auckland: Univ. of Auckland.

Royal Commission on Aboriginal Peoples. 1996. *Looking forward, looking back.* Vol. 1 of *Report of the Royal Commission on Aboriginal Peoples*. Ottawa: Royal Commission on Aboriginal Peoples.

————. 1996. *Restructuring the relationship*. Vol. 2 of *Report of the Royal Commission on Aboriginal Peoples*. Ottawa: Royal Commission on Aboriginal Peoples.

Sharp, Andrew. 1997. *Justice and the Maori: The philosophy and practice of Maori claims in New Zealand since the 1970s*. Auckland NZ: Oxford Univ. Press.

Part Three:
Housing and Homelessness

12

Urban Hidden Homelessness and Reserve Housing

Evelyn Peters and Vince Robillard

Introduction

> I don't know if they'd ever do it, but they promise natives education and housing
> in treaties. Why couldn't they give me a lot here? I'm a walking reserve. I'm a
> nation. (Hidden homeless Aboriginal male)

A number of studies have emphasized the over-representation of First Nations people in the homeless population (Beavis et al. 1997; Begin et al. 1999; Golden 1999). Attempts to count homeless individuals in particular cities—Toronto, Winnipeg, Saskatoon, Calgary, and Winnipeg—have found large First Nations homeless populations (Ambrioso 1992; Arboleda-Florez and Holley 1997; Caputo et al. 1994; Hauch 1985; Kinegal 1989; City of Calgary 1996). Most of these studies have focused on the population on the streets or in shelters of various kinds, rather than on the hidden homeless—people who use informal mechanisms (e.g., friends and family) to reduce absolute homelessness. The over-representation of First Nations people in the absolutely homeless population suggests that they will also be over-represented in the hidden homeless population. However, there is very little information available about this group (but see Distasio 2004; SIIT 2000).

This paper is based on a collaborative research project between the Prince Albert Grand Council Urban Services Inc. and the University of Saskatchewan.[1] The project (Exploring First Nations Hidden Homelessness in Prince Albert) is unique in that it involves a First Nations organization working with university researchers to explore urban First Nations issues. This paper is part of a larger longitudinal study that is exploring factors associated with change, or lack of change, in the housing situation of individuals over time. Here we will explore the relationship between the availability and conditions of reserve housing and the hidden homeless among urban First Nations band members.

The following section is a literature review that places this study in the context of work that addresses factors facilitating and constraining the movement of First Nations band members out of homelessness. We then provide some background with respect to housing conditions on reserves. The method used in the study is outlined, followed by a brief description of the participants. Finally, the paper describes participants' access to housing on reserves, their perspectives on their ability to obtain housing on reserves, and whether they would move to the reserve if they had access to housing there.

Movement out of Homelessness: A Review of the Literature

While there is relatively little research on First Nations people and hidden homelessness, there is some work on homelessness in other populations that helps to put First Nations experiences in context. The following paragraphs summarize some of this work, and identify material that speaks directly to the experience of First Nations people.

The literature on homelessness suggests that there are various personal factors enabling or acting as barriers to an individual's ability to exit from homelessness (Allgood and Warren 2002; Dworsky and Piliavin 2000; Piliavan et al. 1996; Wong et al. 1998; Zlotnick et al. 1999). Personal characteristics commonly associated in the literature with moving out of homelessness include human capital (education, training, employment history) and social networks (access to informal support). Personal characteristics commonly identified as barriers to becoming homed include personal disabilities (i.e., physical and mental health status, substance abuse) and acculturation to homelessness (i.e., a history of homelessness). Some of these elements have also been identified in literature on Aboriginal homelessness (Beavis et al. 1997). However, additional factors identified in work on homeless Aboriginal people include the effects of family violence, the lack of housing on reserves, and the process of making a transition to the city (Beavis et al. 1997; Distasio 2003; Golden 1999; LaPrairie 1994). Some research on service needs and service provision to urban First Nations populations emphasizes the fragmentation of services among different levels of jurisdiction and the lack of central sources of information (Hanselmann 2002; SIIT 2000).

These personal characteristics interact with interventions and opportunities that may act as catalysts for change in housing situations. Most of the literature focuses on the determinants of homelessness, rather than on the characteristics and events that precipitate exits from homelessness (Sosin 2003). Nevertheless, from some longitudinal studies and from studies of homeless individuals that also make policy recommendations, we can group interventions and opportunities that might facilitate movement out of homelessness. Available studies focus on three main areas of intervention (Allgood and Warren 2002; Early and Olsen 2002; CMHC May 2003; CMHC July 2003; Klodawsky 2003b; Orwin et al. 2003; Piliavan et al. 1996; Stojanovic et al. 1999; Zlotnick et al. 1999). The first area has to do with the provision of a variety of social support services to the homeless, including services that address physical and mental health and addictions, housing information and advocacy, anti-violence programs, and training and assistance with finding employment. A second area of intervention is the increase of individual and family income through employment or the availability or increased levels of social assistance. A third intervention addresses the increased provision of subsidized or affordable housing. While these factors are also identified in the limited literature on Aboriginal homelessness, this material adds the importance of culturally appropriate support services, spiritual healing from the effects of colonial histories, and the importance of increased First Nations control over housing initiatives (Beavis et al. 1997; Golden 1999; Lobo and Vaughan 2003; Obonsawin 1999; SIIT 2000).

This paper focuses on the last area of intervention and on opportunities that provide a context for homelessness—the provision of subsidized or affordable housing. However, this analysis is a departure from the focus of existing studies, as most of the existing work on the relationship between homelessness and housing characteristics assumes that the particular community being studied represents the appropriate locale for assessing housing availability. This may not be the appropriate scale for examining housing and homelessness for First Nations people, however. For them, the condition and availability of housing on reserves may affect their housing situations in urban areas.

As urban First Nations populations grow, and an increasing proportion of the First Nations population comes to live in cities, it might seem that reserves and rural areas are depopulating as Aboriginal people move to urban areas. However, analyses of migration patterns suggest that this is not actually what is happening. Since 1986, the proportion of Aboriginal people moving from urban areas to reserves and rural communities has been larger than the proportion moving from reserves and rural communities to urban areas (Norris and Clatworthy 2003). It appears that the pattern of migration for contemporary First Nations people is not one in which reserves and rural areas are depleted by movement to urban areas.

Early academic analyses of Aboriginal urbanization have demonstrated an expectation that Aboriginal migrants to cities would eventually become permanent urban dwellers (Frideres 1974, 1983, 1993). Contemporary patterns of mobility suggest that this is not happening for all First Nations people. Mary Jane Norris has identified a back-and-forth movement between urban and reserve areas that she called "churn" (Norris and Clatworthy 2003). A recent study of recent First Nations migrants to Winnipeg found that a substantial number had moved out of Winnipeg and back again within a six-month period (Distasio 2004). Strong patterns of movement back and forth between urban areas and reserve areas emphasize the continuing importance of these communities for urban First Nations people.

In this context, it is appropriate to think carefully about the geographic scale at which we consider the role of housing in affecting homelessness. It may be that the unavailability of housing on reserves influences the decisions of First Nations people to move to urban communities and, particularly for the purposes of this paper, their presence in the hidden homeless population. Here we will attempt to relate housing issues on-reserve to urban First Nations hidden homelessness.

Conditions of Reserve Housing in Canada

The housing situation on reserves has been a matter of concern for many decades. In 1996, the Royal Commission on Aboriginal Peoples (RCAP) found that First Nations housing conditions fell considerably below the standards for other Canadians. In 1991, 38.7% of housing on-reserve was in need of major repairs, compared to 6.8% of housing for other Canadians. On reserves, 11.5% of houses had no bathroom facilities and 19.4% had no flush toilets, compared to 0.6% and 0.5% for other Canadians, respectively. The Royal Commission noted that, on reserves, more than 39.2% of the needs of residents in housing were not being met and that 12.9% of residents were on waiting lists. The commission proposed a 10-year strategy to remove barriers to improved housing, and to make strategic investments to bring the housing stock to a level of adequacy (RCAP 2006, 365–78).

Ten years after the publication of the commission's report, there are still serious problems with housing on reserves.

> According to the most recent census, about 12% of houses in First Nations communities are overcrowded, compared to 1% elsewhere in Canada. Data, as of March 31, 2005, indicate that of the almost 96,800 houses in First Nations communities, more than 21,200 (21.9%) are in need of major repairs and about 5,500 (5.7%) need to be replaced. (Indian and Northern Affairs 2005. See also CMHC 2004, 2)

At the federal government's recent roundtable on Aboriginal housing, the Assembly of First Nations had this to say:

> The shortage of First Nations housing in Canada has reached crisis proportions. According to the April 2003 Auditor General's Report, there is a shortage of 8,500 units across the country. However, internal INAC [Indian and Northern Affairs Canada] figures suggest that the actual shortage is 20,000 units, with an additional 4,500 new units required annually simply to stop the backlog from increasing. (AFN 2004,1)

The Native Women's Association of Canada (NWAC) pointed out that the shortage of housing on reserves made it difficult for individuals who had regained their status under Bill C–31 to gain access to reserve housing.

Analyses of the implications of the conditions of reserve housing focus most often on the implications for reserve communities. For example, the Government of Canada's "Fact Sheet on Aboriginal Housing" (2005) states that "the limited supply of housing not only leads to unhealthy, overcrowded conditions but it also accelerates the depreciation of the housing stock. It affects the health and well-being of *Aboriginal people living on reserve*" (emphasis added). However, the condition of reserve housing raises some questions about housing conditions for First Nations people in urban areas. Do some of the individuals who have applied for housing live temporarily with friends and family in nearby towns and cities? Would the improvement of on-reserve housing make a dent in the urban hidden homeless population? Some of these issues will be explored in the remainder of this paper.

Methods

According to the census, the population of Prince Albert in 2001 was 34,291, with an Aboriginal identity population of 10,185. A large proportion of the Aboriginal population is made up of First Nations people, and represented by the Prince Albert Grand Council (PAGC). City planners and representatives of First Nations organizations suggest that the First Nations population in Prince Albert may be higher than that reported by the census because of the difficulty in documenting a mobile population, many of whom live with other households.

Exploring First Nations hidden homelessness in Prince Albert is a panel study that attempted to interview hidden homeless people three times over an 18-month period. Because the available literature suggested that gender, age, and family status affect the experience of homelessness, the study attempted to interview 25 individuals from each of five groups: male and female youth (15–19), male and female adults (20 and over), and individuals living with dependent children. The purpose of the study was not to obtain a representative sample of the hidden homeless population but to gain some understanding of the situation of these five groups. Moreover, the goal was not to focus on determinants of homelessness but to explore reasons for change over time. The first set of interviews was an attempt to gain some baseline information that could be compared with the situation of participants in subsequent interviews.

The initial set of interviews took place between June 13, 2005, and September 16, 2005. In total, 143 people participated. The data discussed in this paper are based on 109 interviews with individuals who indicated they were band members. This included 22 individuals who had dependent children living with them, 22 adult males, 22 adult females, 22 male youth, and 21 female youth.

Participants for this study were reached through various avenues. The assistance of organizations in Prince Albert was critical in reaching hidden homeless people because they had contact with clients who were living with others, and the ability to refer them to the study. Organizations also had an established rapport with, and the trust of, potential participants, on which researchers could draw to build the relationship between interviewer and interviewee. Over the summer of 2005, a total of 57 (39.9%) participants came to the study as a result of posters and pamphlets at organizations or referrals from organization staff. Information and interviewing sessions at organizations generated another 22 (15.4%) participants. There were also attempts to reach people who did not use organizations. Interviewers used direct recruiting on days when there were few interviews scheduled or when scheduled interviews fell through. The geographical scope of this recruiting was limited to downtown Prince Albert. Direct recruiting generated 27 (18.9%) participants. Nine participants (6.3%) were referred to the study by a friend or family member. Interviewers also drove to areas outside the downtown core to put up posters at apartment complexes, laundromats, corner stores, grocery stores, daycares, colleges, hospitals, health clinics, and street posts, in order to recruit city-wide. Overall, 28 (19.6%) respondents were reached by using posters around the city.

While there was an attempt to contact people from a spectrum of hidden homeless situations, it is likely that the project was biased towards individuals with more precarious socio-economic characteristics. Posters and recruitment materials used a variety of terms, including "couch surfing" and "can't afford your own place," but it is likely that individuals going to school, or working and rooming with friends or relatives to be able to afford rent, would not refer to themselves as "hidden homeless" or as "couch surfing." The aggregate characteristics of the participants described in **Table 12.2** suggest that many of these individuals were socio-economically marginalized. While the project did not attempt to obtain a representative sample, it is important to recognize that the methods employed meant that we probably interviewed a particular segment of this population.

Participants were screened with an initial question to establish if they identified themselves as First Nations and if their housing situation classified them as "hidden homeless." The majority of participants met the interviewer at the downtown offices of PAGC Urban Services Inc. Interviews were carried out at various locations, including restaurants, PAGC Urban rooms, and quiet areas in various organizations. The first step of the interview involved an explanation of the project, signing a consent form, and the collection of personal information so that participants could be contacted for the subsequent interview. Most interviews were taped and interview times varied from 45 minutes to 1.5 hours. Interviews combined qualitative questions with quantitative questions and scales. Participants received a cash honorarium for the time they spent on the project. They also received a contact card and a list of resources. In many cases, the interviewer pointed out specific organizations most useful to the participant, and some participants were referred to the front desk to apply for PAGC programs, such as ABE10, jobs, and transitional housing applications.

Characteristics of Participants

Before we discuss the social and economic characteristics of the population interviewed for this study, it is important to situate them within the larger urban First Nations population. In the context of the public perception that all urban First Nations people are poor and socio-economically marginalized, it must be emphasized that urban First Nations residents, increasingly, are coming to be represented in the employed, well-educated middle class (Wotherspoon 2003). The population interviewed for this project is not representative of all urban First Nations people. Participant characteristics are presented in order to provide a context for the analysis of reserve housing and urban homelessness that follows.

Except for male youth, most of the participants considered themselves to be homeless (**Table 12.1**). It is difficult to interpret male youth responses. It may be that most of the male youth interviewed are still living with family or kin at their

Table 12.1: Participant Characteristics

	Family* (n=22)	Adult Male (n=22)	Adult Female (n=22)	Male Youth (n=22)	Female Youth (n=21)
Define themselves as homeless (%)	72.20	81.80	80.00	27.80	66.70
Average number in household	6.60	3.70	4.90	5.00	5.80
Live in house/duplex/row house (%)	72.70	59.10	50.00	80.00	76.20
Average number of bedrooms	3.00	2.00	2.30	2.90	2.70
Housing unit rented (%)[1]	86.40	100.00	86.40	90.90	90.0
Have own bedroom (%)	68.20	36.40	36.40	50.00	42.90
Average health rating[2]	3.20	2.70	2.90	2.40	3.00
Average age	27.60	30.40	33.30	17.60	17.60
Age range	19-51	23-48	22-63	15-19	16-19
Single (%)	45.50	68.20	77.30	95.50	81.00
Grew up on reserve (%)	9.10	41.00	33.30	36.40	23.80
Average number of children[3]	2.70	2.50	3.10	0.00	0.02
Main income from social assistance (%)[4]	68.20	77.30	86.40	45.50	25.00
Average monthly income ($)	652.72	601.73	433.77	294.00	233.60
Employed (%)	22.70	9.30	13.60	13.60	14.30
Have less than high school certificate (%)	63.30	86.40	77.30	95.50	90.50

1 The unit was rented by someone other than the participant.
2 1=excellent; 2=very good; 3=good; 4=fair; 5=poor
3 Not all of these children were living with them.
4 This includes Saskatchewan social assistance, child benefits or employment supplements, federal child benefits, unemployment insurance, or training allowance, or social assistance that individuals received from their reserves.

Table 12.2: Relation to Reserve Housing[1]

	Family* (n=22)	Adult Male (n=22)	Adult Female (n=22)	Male Youth (n=22)	Female Youth (n=21)
Did not have their own place on reserve (%)	100.0	100.0	100.0	86.0	100.0
Had applied for housing on the reserve (%)	36.4	23.8	50.0	18.2	0.0
Would live on reserve if they had own house (%)	65.0	47.4	52.4	42.1	21.4

1 Percentages are of those who answered the questions. Some individuals did not answer every question.

age, and so these participants did not see their situation as unusual. Families and youth were more likely to live with other families, and therefore their average household size was slightly larger. Adult males were most likely to be living with other, unrelated individuals. Similarly, families and youth were more likely to be living in a detached house, row house, or duplex with a slightly larger number of bedrooms. Almost all of the units were rented by someone else living in the household. Family participants were most likely to have their own bedroom (rather than sleeping on the couch or the hallway), although many shared the

Table 12.3:Reasons Why Participants Did Not Apply or Receive Housing On-reserve (%)

No housing available	38.6
Not enough housing/families given priority	(21.5)
Band favouritism	(11.4)
Too young to apply	(5.7)
Not part of reserve community	27.2
Bad conditions on reserves	15.9
Personal reasons	10.2
No jobs or educational opportunities	8.0
Total	**88.0**

bedroom with their own children. About half of the male and female youth had their own bedrooms. Most of the adult males and females did not have their own bedroom and slept on the couch or in another room or shared with other non-family members.

Self-rated health was between very good and good, with male youth rating their health the best. The average age of participants was relatively young, with only two individuals over 50 years old. Except for family participants, most were single. Most of the participants had not grown up on a reserve. Almost all of the adults had children, although not all of them had children living with them. Except for the youth, many of whom received little income except what they received from family or through informal means, most participants' main source of income came from various kinds of social assistance sources, including Saskatchewan social assistance, child benefits or employment supplements, federal child benefits, unemployment insurance, training allowances, or social assistance individuals received from their reserves. Families had the highest average monthly income because many of those participants were eligible for social assistance for themselves and their children. Employment and education rates were low, with the lowest rates for adult males. Many of the youth were attending school at the time of the survey.

Relationship to Reserve Housing

Access to Reserve Housing

Almost all of the participants we interviewed indicated that they did not have their own place on-reserve (**Table 12.2**). Only two of the male youth said they had their own place, but in one case the youth's grandmother was leaving and had promised him her house. In other words, he was expecting to have his own place soon but did not actually have it at the time. The majority of individuals had not applied for housing on-reserve, although this varied between respondents. Youth were least likely to have applied for reserve housing, and many of them indicated that

Table 12.4: Unavailability of Housing

There's very limited housing available each year to reserve residents so you're like having 3–4 families, with 19–20 people living in a house and I think when you don't live at the reserve level or your Chief and Counsel are struggling to provide for on-reserve, I think, you know, that basically means that the off-reserve people are basically worse off than the band.

(Male head of family #0)

Because I needed a house out there but I still haven't gotten one so I decided to stay living with my ...Well, how does it go? I lived with my dad, then I lived with my sister for like, I lived with my sister for like 15 months and then I moved back with my dad and I couldn't stand my dad so I moved in with my cousin, and we get along good and we go half on everything.

(Female head of family #43)

And there's not, yah. On the reserve there's not that many houses. We need more houses and it's forced other people on [reserve] to live outside of the reserve 'cause there's families living in families. Like their kin and then their kin's, kins ... Yah. And they force them to live in Melfort, Kinistino and areas around the reserve and, you know, the cities too. It's up to the people if they wanna live on the reserve or live in P.A. ... But more houses would be better.

(Adult male #511)[1]

Bands give houses to people with bigger families. Single people can't get a house.

(Adult female #36)

Well I tried for the past two years but I didn't get it 'cause there's like a big list now.

(Male youth #120)

[You] can't get a house unless, unless you have kids.

(Female youth #112)

1 Questionnaire numbers were not consecutive.

Table 12.5: Band Favouritism

I could [apply] but I don't think they'd take me seriously. Because they would say like I'm not from there. It's strange. Even though I'm from there they would say "well you haven't lived here and like ever."

(Female head of family #56)

Like I was adopted growing up so I don't know a lot of my relatives and that and there's a process like to get housing you got to apply and got to be willing to live on the reserve. You gotta be living there for some time before they'll even give you any kind of financial help and that's just something I've never done.

(Adult female #18)

There's none. Well the way it is out there is you got the right family name you get a house ...You don't got the right family name you don't get nothing. That's the way it is out there. That's why I moved.

(Male youth #96)

they were too young. Adult males were slightly more likely to apply for housing than youth, followed by heads of families, and adult females (who were the most likely). At the same time, slightly less than half (48.9%) of the hidden homeless population in this survey indicated they would live on reserve if they had their own housing. In this context, it is important to pay some attention to the reasons individuals gave for not being able to obtain, or for not wishing to apply for,

Table 12.6: Do Not Feel Part of Reserve Community

'Cause P.A. is like where I mostly grew up in. I was about eight or well nine years old. That's where I mostly grew up so like I've been to my reserve. I've been to my town and now I never wanna go back there.
(Female head of family #99)
I don't really like the reserve life to be honest. I don't go with living out there ... I'm more of a city person. I grew up in the city, you know, but if it was my last resort I would move out but I, you know, I'm just not comfortable living out there.
(Adult male #54)
Yah, well I have friends but there's no way I'm gonna go out to the reserve ... Cause it's a reserve and it's depressing and you have a totally different environment. Spend my all days watching the day go by.
(Adult male #1001)
I just don't feel comfortable in a reserve. Although my family's from there, you know, like ... I don't know, I just don't feel comfortable out there.
(Adult male #49)
'Cause I don't wanna live on my reserve. I like to be somewhere where there's, where there people, lots of people because it pisses me off just sitting at home alone ... All bored and shit watching TV ... Well, well if you get to go out and go out and drink there's that to do, there's nothing else basically to do. There's no Macs, there's no Costco, there's no basketball court.
(Male youth #103)
Because I'm used to living in town. I'm used to living in the city. I'm not used to living walking out on dirt roads all the time. Not really having anything to do, you know. Just walk around the reserve. That's all I ever do when I'm there. It's not very interesting and I don't speak Cree. I try to get along with these people that speak Cree but they're always speaking it and they just leave me out and I feel too bucked out when I'm there.
(Female youth #45)

housing on-reserve, and also why individuals would stay on-reserve if they had their own housing unit.

Reasons for Not Living On-reserve

Table 12.3 (page 196) lists all of the reasons participants gave to explain why they did not apply for housing on the reserve, or why they did not live on the reserve even though they had applied for housing. Twenty-one participants did not answer. For the remaining participants, their answer was put into only one category and, in general, the answers focused on one main reason. Where there were two reasons, we classified the answer according to the main reason. So, for example, in the quote, "I could get a place on there if I want. I just don't wanna get one, it's too boring up there and no jobs. I like this 'cause I'm so used to the city" (adult male #9), the participant mentions employment, but his main emphasis is on liking the city more than the reserve. This quote was placed in the category "Not part of the reserve community." There were very few quotes that could be placed in more than one category.

Table 12.7: Bad Conditions On-reserve

Because personally I don't think that reserve is the most stable place. They say the city is worse than the reserve, but I would disagree because there is more alcohol, more drugs and more abuse on the reserve, that I think that your kids could be exposed to. And in town my kids aren't exposed to violence, alcohol, drugs, smoking, nothing like that. And on a reserve, all the families out there. I don't drink and if I was to drink, my family would probably be at my house spending time drinking. So I don't think it is, I would never live on my reserve.

(Female head of family #72)

I heard the water and stuff is pretty bad over there so ... I don't how to go about so I didn't apply for a house.

(Adult male #82)

It doesn't make a good place and I don't want to leave my children in an environment like that.

(Adult female #30)

Not really 'cause it's kinda going down hill. Crazy things go on there It's going crazy. It used to be a nice place but now it's just like kinda run down.

(Male youth #127)

Because if you see all of the like people drinking around there. There, it's, I don't like, I personally don't like the reserve because of all of the, like all the stuff it has on it like, you know, like ... negativity. Like when people talk about it and they make fun of it.

(Female youth #108)

The unavailability of housing was the single most important reason (36.8%) individuals gave for not being able to live on their reserve. This was followed by not feeling like they belonged on-reserve (27.2%), bad conditions on reserves (15.9%), personal reasons (10.2%), and no jobs or education on-reserve (8.0%).

People gave a variety of reasons for not having housing on reserves. The largest proportion indicated that because there was a shortage of housing, large families were given priority (21.5%). This included adult males who had lost their housing when they broke up with their female partner. Housing was unavailable to them because the housing for single individuals was limited. Heads of families were most likely to identify this reason, but some individuals in every category mentioned it. Aspects mentioned by individuals are summarized in **Table 12.4** (page 197). Participants recognized the difficulties bands faced in allocating housing in the context of severe housing shortages. People living off-reserve, single people, or people with small families had less of a claim to band housing, according to these participants.

Related to this situation was the sense of a number of participants that band councils tended to favour some people over others. Some participant comments appear in **Table 12.5** (page 197). Adult females and female heads of families were most likely to make this comment, probably because they were most likely to have applied for housing at some point in the past. Several individuals also indicated that they were too young to apply for housing. Not surprisingly, most of these individuals were male or female youth or young heads of families.

Table 12.8: Personal Reasons/No Jobs or Education

I would say yes to the urban reserve but not to the northern reserve ... I wouldn't have a job.
(Female head of family #56)
Me and my common-law we've been separated for like well maybe a month and a half, close to two months now so I've been struggling with this homelessness since then.
(Adult male #25)
There's no work on the reserve either eh. You have to be a councillor or something, related to a councillor before you can get a job out there and when you do get a job out there like it only lasts for about a week or two. Just one cheque isn't much, eh.
(Adult male #12)
Because my ex-husband lives in La Ronge and my other ex so it's, I feel more comfortable being in the city alone so that it's my private life.
(Adult female #234)
My mom asked me to leave.
(Female youth #34)

Participants gave a number of non-housing related reasons for not being able to live on-reserve (61.3%). The total number of these additional reasons was greater than the total number of housing-related reasons. The single largest category had to do with individuals not feeling as if they were part of the reserve community (27.2%). This included not speaking the language, having grown up in the city, and finding the reserve to be boring. Adult men made up almost half of this category, so **Table 12.6** (page 198) includes several of their responses. Male and female youth also mentioned these reasons, but adult females did not.

The next largest category of reasons, at 15.9%, concerned bad conditions on reserves. These reasons were most often mentioned by male and female youth, but individuals in every category mentioned them. **Table 12.7** (page 199) summarizes some of their comments. Individuals mentioned both social and physical conditions on reserves as reasons why they would not live there, even if they had their own housing. The second largest category of additional reasons had to do with preferring urban life, or not feeling like part of the reserve community.

Adult males and adult females were the most likely to list personal reasons. Male youth and heads of families did not give any reasons that fell into this category. In many cases, these reasons had to do with personal relationships that prevented individuals from returning to the reserve. However, some people also wished to stay away from reserves because of bad memories.

The unavailability of employment and higher levels of education comprised the smallest category of reasons individuals would not live on reserves. On the surface, this seems surprising because studies of why individuals move away from reserve often list education and employment as primary reasons. However, it is important to remember that a very small proportion of this population is employed, and many of the youth are in Prince Albert to finish high school. It makes sense that this would not be the main reason for living off the reserve.

Table 12.9: Reasons for Wanting to Live on the Reserve, if Housing Were Available

Family	Better Conditions
Because if it is a house of my own my kids will be there. That would be okay, you know, 'cause it'd be nice for me to stay. But if I end up staying in someone else's place, you know, paying for this and paying for that, you're ending up paying for everything there for them and there is nothing there for you. It's like I'm doing at my sister's right now.	I guess I've always wondered about that whether I would go back. With so much of my health problems right now I think that I would be better off on the reserve and I did think about this after the place I live now. I asked my sister if there were any houses available and she said the were none ... I would probably move back if I had housing because of the quiet, the serenity, family. I have family out there. And probably get better assistance then I do in town.
(Adult male #60)	(Female head of family #70)
Definitely. Because I'm from there and got family there and it'd be my house.	Because I know I wouldn't have to worry, have extra worry about like living, I don't want to be like in a city with my kids. I wouldn't have to, you know, worry about, you know, traffic and, you know, break-and-enter or whatever. I wouldn't have to worry about that ... To have my own place basically.
(Adult male #511)	(Female head of family #87)
Because, I get so, there's so many of us sometimes at my mom's house and sometimes I wish I had my own house, cause if I did have my own house over there I wouldn't be here, I'd be over there with my kids, I have kids eh ... My kids are over there [reserve] ya with my mom ... Yup and that's, where I would be, if I had my own home.	I think it's a better environment for my kids. If I was to move on the reserve I wouldn't have to worry so much of kids not getting into drugs, the alcohol or, you know, having been robbed in your own home and stuff like that ... It's also quiet like you know like it's probably safe, yah they do a lot of drinking there but if you're on your own little world nobody bothers you. You basically just, you'll be okay. All you have to worry about is the people driving drunk and half of the time they don't do any of that anyway so and when they, if they're drinking they're not drinking on reserve. They're either out if town, like country bars or city or whatever, you know. It's better that they stay over there.
(Adult female #10)	(Adult female #232)
I would like that it's away from the city and a lot of my family is there ... And it would be a good place for my son to grow up	Because I feel like if I was to get out of, out of P.A., you know, it would be a lot easier for me because I wouldn't have to feel like I'm, I wouldn't have to feel like I'm still like, I wouldn't have to feel pressured, pressured into things any more, you know, like say friends, you know, people that try to come in pressuring me to doing drugs with them, you know. Stuff like that.
(Female youth #116)	(Adult female #78)
	Like to stay out in the reserve ... More isolated. Less trouble out there.
	(Male youth #64)
	I like it. It's like peaceful. It's not like the city is. Less people around there. There's no traffic. It's quiet.
	(Male youth #120)

Table 12.8 (page 200) gives examples of participant responses having to do with these two categories.

Desire to Live on Reserve if Participants Had Their Own Housing

Of the ninety participants who gave an answer to the question, "If you had your own housing on-reserve, would you live there?" forty-four (48.9%) answered that they would. Not all of these individuals indicated why they would live on the reserve, but the available answers give some indication of what participants looked for from the reserve setting. A major theme was that if individuals had a place of their own, they would be able to live with family members. For some, both male and female, this meant that they would be able to live with their children. For others, it meant being closer to their family of origin. There was also a longing for a place of their own in these statements. Others saw conditions on reserves as providing a better place for both themselves and their children. In contrast to those who would not move to the reserve because of alcohol and drugs, some of these individuals saw reserve locations as a place where they could get away from these addictions. The answers emphasize the importance of understanding the variety of conditions on reserves and of not labelling reserves as homogeneous. Taken together, it seems clear that the housing situation on reserves has some effect on First Nations peoples' experiences of hidden homelessness.

Conclusion

While First Nations homelessness in urban areas has been linked to the process of urbanization (Beavis et al. 1997; Distasio 2003; Golden 1999), there is very little work that explores whether the ability of First Nations individuals to access housing on-reserve affects rates of homelessness in urban areas. Perhaps this reflects erroneous assumptions that there is a continuous and inevitable out migration from reserves to cities, and that urbanization reflects the choices of individuals to live in cities rather than on reserves (Norris et al. 2002, 2003). The responses from our participants suggest that this is not universally the case, and that some individuals who are relying on friends and family to obtain shelter in Prince Albert would not be there if the housing situation on the reserve were better. According to participants, there is a need for more housing for families, but there is also a need for housing for individuals and couples without children.

The proportion of participants who said they would live on the reserve if they had housing there is significant. Forty-four of ninety individuals (48.9%) would like to live in their own place on the reserve. Clearly, expressed preferences do not always translate into behaviour. The first quote under "better conditions" in **Table 12.9** (page 201), for example, is by a woman who has hardly spent any time living on the reserve. This raises some questions about whether she would actually move out to the reserve and stay there. For other individuals, though, it seems quite likely that their hidden homeless situation would be alleviated by more housing opportunities on the reserves. The literature on movement out of homelessness indicates that one element that might facilitate this change is the increased provision of subsidized or affordable housing.

In this paper, we have addressed mainly increased provision of housing on reserves. Our results suggest that this is important to participants, and this finding adds to the urgency of addressing the reserve housing situation. It has implications not only for reserve residents but also for the urban First Nations community.

Acknowledgements

We acknowledge the participants in this study who agreed to talk about their situation in the hopes that their experiences might lead to positive change. We also would like to thank the interviewers who worked on this project: Bobbi Jo Lafontaine, Raul Munoz, and Shauna Wouters. The people working at PAGC Urban were wonderfully supportive partners. We also express our appreciation for individuals in a variety of Prince Albert organizations without whose support this study would have been impossible. This research was supported through kind funding from PAGC Urban Services Inc., research grant funding from the Social Sciences and Humanities Research Council of Canada (SSHRC), and the National Housing Initiative (NHI).

Endnotes

1   PAGC Urban has been involved in a variety of initiatives to address First Nations homelessness in Prince Albert (City of Prince Albert 2001, 2004; PAGC 2000).

References

Allgood, S. and R.S. Warren. 2003. The duration of homelessness: Evidence from a national survey. *Journal of Housing Economics* 12(3): 273–90.

Ambrioso, E., C.D. Baker, and K. Hardill. 1992. The Street Health Report: A study of the health status and barriers to health care of homeless women and men in the City of Toronto. <**www.tdrc. net/HealthRpt_sec01.pdf**>

Arboleda-Florez, J. and H. Holley. 1997. Calgary homelessness study: Final report. Alberta: Alberta Health Report.

Assembly of First Nations. 2004. Background Paper on Housing. Canada-Aboriginal Peoples Round-table, Housing Sectoral Session. Ottawa, Ontario.

Beavis, M.A., N. Klos, T. Carter, and C. Douchant. 1997. *Literature review: Aboriginal Peoples and homelessness*. Ottawa: CMHC.

Begin, P., L. Casavant, and N. Miller Chenier. 1999. *Homelessness*. Ottawa: Library of Parliament, Parliamentary Research Branch.

Canada Mortgage and Housing Corporation (CMHC). 2004. Aboriginal housing background paper. Canada-Aboriginal Peoples Roundtable, Housing Sectoral Session. Ottawa, Ontario.

Canada Mortgage and Housing Corporation (CMHC). July 2003. *Family homelessness: Causes and solutions*. Socio-economic Series 03–006. Ottawa: CMHC.

Canada Mortgage and Housing Corporation (CMHC). May 2003. *A study of tenant exits from housing for homeless people*. Series 03–005. Ottawa: CMHC.

Caputo, R., R. Weiler, and K. Kelly. 1994. Phase II of the Runaways and Street Youth Project. Solicitor General of Canada, Police Policy and Research Division. Ottawa: Department of Supply and Services.

City of Calgary. 1996. Homeless count in downtown Calgary, Alberta, Canada, 1996. Calgary: Community and Social Development Department of Social Research Unit.

City of Prince Albert. 2001. Prince Albert Community Action Plan on Homelessness. Prince Albert, Saskatchewan: City of Prince Albert.

City of Prince Albert. 2004. Prince Albert Community Action Plan on Homelessness and Housing. Prince Albert, Saskatchewan: City of Prince Albert.

Clatworthy, S.J. and M. Cooke. 2001. Reasons for Registered Indian migration. Report prepared by Four Directions Project consultants for Indian and Northern Affairs Canada, Research and Analysis Directorate.

Cornet, W. and A. Lendor. 2004. Matrimonial issues on-reserve. In *Aboriginal policy research: Setting the agenda for change*. Vol. 2,, ed. J.P. White, P. Maxim, D. Beavon, 141–43. Toronto: Thompson Educational.

Distasio, J. 2004. First Nations/Métis/Inuit mobility study: Interim report one. Winnipeg: Institute of Urban Studies.

Dworsky, A.L. and I. Piliavin. 2000. Homeless spell exits and returns: Substantive and methodological elaborations on recent studies. *Social Service Review* 74, (2): 193–213.

Early, D.W. and E.O. Olsen. 2002. Subsidized housing, emergency shelters, and homelessness: An empirical analysis using data from the 1990 census. *Advances in Economic Analysis and Policy* 2: article 2.

Frideres, J. S. 1974. *Canada's Indians: Contemporary conflicts*. Scarborough: Prentice-Hall.

-----. 1983. *Native people in Canada: Contemporary conflicts*. Scarborough: Prentice-Hall.

-----. 1993. *Native people in Canada: Contemporary Conflicts*. Scarborough: Prentice-Hall.

Hauch, C. 1985. *Coping strategies and street life: The ethnography of Winnipeg's skid row regions*. Report No. 11. Winnipeg: Institute of Urban Studies.

Homelessness Action Task Force. 1999. Taking responsibility for homelessness: An action plan for Toronto. City of Toronto. Prepared by A. Golden.

Indian and Northern Affairs. 2005. First Nations housing. <**www.ainc-inac.gc.ca/pr/info/info 104_ e.html**>

Kinegal, J.W.N. 1989. Finding the way home: A response to the housing needs of the homeless women of the Downtown East Side, Vancouver. M.A. thesis, University of British Columbia.

Klodawsky, F., T. Aubry, and E. Hay. 2003. Panel study on homelessness in Ottawa: What have we learned so far? <**www.uottawa.ca/academic/socsci/crcs/homeless/Oct1–3–2003/presentation01_ files/v3_document.htm**>

La Prairie, C. 1994. *Seen but not heard: Native people in the inner city*. Ottawa: Department of Justice.

Lobo. S. and M.M. Vaughan. 2003. Substance dependency among homeless American Indians. *Journal of Psychoactive Drugs* 35 (1): 63–70.

Native Women's Association of Canada (NWAC). 2004. Aboriginal women and housing. Background Paper on Housing. Canada-Aboriginal Peoples Roundtable, Housing Sectoral Session. Ottawa, Ontario.

New Policy Institute. 2004. Estimating the numbers of people in housing need and at risk of homelessness in London: A report for the GLA. London: New Policy Institute.

Norris, M. J. and S. Clatworthy. 2003. Aboriginal mobility and migration within urban Canada: Outcomes, factors and implications. Paper presented at the Joint PAA/CPS Session on Demography of North American Aboriginal Populations, Annual Meeting of the Population Association of America, Minneapolis, Minnesota, April 30–May 3, 2003.

Obonsawin, R. 1999. Keynote presentation: An aboriginal homelessness strategy framework for Toronto. Meeting Summary, Nov. 24. Ottawa: CMHC Working Group on Homelessness.

Orwin, R.G., C.K. Scott, and C.R. Areira. 2003. Transitions through homelessness and factors that predict them: Residential outcomes in the Chicago Target Cities treatment sample. *Evaluation and Program Planning* 26 (4): 379–92.

Peters, Evelyn (principal investigator) and PAGC. (ongoing). Exploring First Nations Hidden Homelessness in Prince Albert. Funded by SSHRC and NHI.

Piliavan, I., B.R. Entner, R.C. Wright, and A.H. Westerfelt. 1996. Exists and returns to homelessness. *Social Service Review* (March): 33–57.

Prince Albert Grand Council (PAGC). 2000. Prince Albert Grand Council Homelessness Project. Feasibility Study. Prince Albert: PAGC.

Saskatchewan Indian Institute of Technologies (SIIT). 2000. Urban First Nations people without homes in Saskatchewan. Saskatoon: SIIT.

Stojanovic, D., B.C. Weitzman, M. Shinn, L.E. Labay, and N.P. Williams. 1999. Tracing the path out of homelessness: The housing patterns of families after exiting shelters. *Journal of Community Psychology* 27(2): 199–208.

Wong, Y.L.I, I. Piliavin, and B.R.E. Wright. 1998. Residential transitions among homeless families and homeless single individuals. *Journal of Social Service Research* 24 (1–2): 1–27.

Wotherspoon, R. 2003. Prospects for a new middle class among urban Aboriginal Peoples. In *Not strangers in these parts; Urban Aboriginal Peoples*, ed. D. Newhouse and E. J. Peters, 147–66. Ottawa: PRI.

Zlotnick, C., M.J. Robertson, and M. Lahiff. 1999. Getting of the streets: Economic resources and residential exits from homelessness. *Journal of Community Psychology* 27(1): 209–24.

13

Aboriginal Mobility and Migration: Trends, Recent Patterns, and Implications: 1971–2001

Stewart Clatworthy and Mary Jane Norris

Introduction

Many aspects of the mobility and migration of Aboriginal populations differ significantly from those of mainstream populations. Population movement between reserves, rural communities, and urban areas can play an important role in shaping the demand for a wide range of goods and services. This paper explores various aspects of Aboriginal population movement, including reserve and rural-urban migration, the role of migration in the growth of urban Aboriginal populations, residential mobility and population turnover, and related policy implications. Discussions will address and clarify some of the misinterpretations surrounding migration phenomena, including the impression that the demographic explosion of urban Aboriginal populations observed in the recent censuses of countries is the result of an exodus from Aboriginal communities.

Using data from the 2001 Census of Canada, this study examines several dimensions of the migration patterns between 1996 and 2001 of four Aboriginal subgroups: Registered Indians, non-Registered Indians, Métis, and Inuit. Migration patterns for this time period are compared to long-term migration trends for the 1981–1996 period. The study also examines the 2000–2001 patterns of residential mobility for Canada's Aboriginal populations living in major urban areas.

Several dimensions of the recent mobility and migration patterns of Aboriginal Peoples are explored using data from the 2001 and earlier censuses and the 1991 Aboriginal Peoples Survey (APS). Specific issues examined in this regard include five key areas:

1. An overview of the measures and patterns of Aboriginal migration, comprising migration flows by origin and destination and net migration flows and rates by location

2. The contribution of migration to population change, especially in relation to growth of the Aboriginal population in urban areas

3. Measures, patterns, and effects of residential mobility, particularly within urban areas

4. Reasons for moving, in relation to migration to and from reserves, and

reasons for residential moves

5. Implications of migration and residential mobility

In their analysis of the contribution of net migration to population change, especially in relation to growth of the Aboriginal population in urban areas, the authors ask a key question: *To what extent has migration contributed to the rapid increase in the Aboriginal population living off-reserve, especially that part living in large urban areas?* The ramifications of this question are explored not only for urban areas in general, but are examined in an analysis of the role of migration in growth for ten cities, selected on the basis of the largest Aboriginal populations from the 2001 Census.

In their examination of residential mobility, the authors address another key question that is extremely relevant to urban Aboriginal conditions: *To what extent do residential moves among the Aboriginal population result in acceptable housing situations?*

In looking at the broader picture of the repercussions of migration and residential mobility for Aboriginal people, the authors explore the policy implications and responses surrounding mobility and migration patterns of Aboriginal populations in Canada. They consider reasons for migration and residential churning of the population as a prelude to examining some of the consequences for policy and program development, and effective service delivery. The concept of "churn," or "turbulence," is borrowed from analyses of mobility in the context of the developing world, in which the pattern often involves movement between rural and urban areas. The implications and considerations address a number of areas, including the compositional effects on urban populations, their demographic and socio-economic characteristics; education program delivery and high mobility and student performance; housing on- and off-reserve; and social isolation and social cohesion.

Before proceeding to a discussion of the research findings, the authors provide a brief background on census migration data and definitions that underlie the analyses in this study.

Census Migration Data and Definitions

The Census of Canada collects mobility and migration data using two questions:

1. Where did you live five years ago?

2. Where did you live one year ago?

Data from either question can be configured to distinguish among three subgroups, including:

- *Non-movers,* who lived at the same residence at the outset of the reference period (i.e., either five years ago or one year ago)
- *Migrants,* who lived in a different community at the outset of the reference period

- *Residential movers,* who lived at a different residence in the same community at the outset of the reference period

Combined, these latter two groups comprise the total population of movers during the reference period.

The migration components of the analyses presented in this chapter use data from the five-year mobility question. Two population subgroups are excluded from the analysis, individuals who migrated to Canada from abroad and individuals who migrated from an Indian reserve that was not enumerated by the census.[1] Migration rates are presented as average annual rates computed for the five-year period.

The analysis of residential moves uses data from the one-year mobility question. Residential mobility rates presented in this study are calculated for the non-migrant population, and reflect annual rates for the 12-month period preceding Census Day.

While the census provides the most complete and consistent set of data concerning the mobility and migration patterns of Aboriginal peoples, census data are limited in several respects. First, the census is administered to a sample of the population and excludes individuals living in various institutions, including prisons, chronic care facilities, and rooming houses. Second, a significant portion of the population living on-reserve is not captured by the census due to under-coverage (i.e., individuals missed by the census) and incomplete or non-enumeration. Although under-coverage occurs both on and off-reserve, levels of under-coverage (including non-enumeration) are known to be substantially higher on-reserve. As a consequence, the geographic distribution of the Aboriginal population captured by the census is biased. The proportion of the population residing on-reserves is underestimated, while that off-reserve is overestimated. As Registered Indians form the vast majority of the population residing on-reserve, this population is most underrepresented in the census data. Third, the census migration and mobility data also present some conceptual limitations. For example, many characteristics of migrants (e.g., education, marital and family status, and socio-economic attributes) are known only at the end of migration reference period (i.e., at the time of the census). Migrant characteristics at the time of migration may differ. The census also does not capture multiple moves, migrants who leave and return to the same location, or those who die during the time interval.

Aboriginal Population Definitions

Recent censuses allow for the Aboriginal population to be defined according to several criteria, including ethnic origin (ethnicity), identity (self-reported affiliation with an Aboriginal group), Registered Indian status, and band membership.[2] The analyses presented in this chapter are based on the population that reported an Aboriginal identity (North American Indian, Métis, or Inuit) and/or reported registration under the Indian Act. According to the 2001 Census, this population numbered about 976,310 individuals, including 608,850 North American Indians (62.4%), 292,305 Métis (29.9%), 45,075 Inuit (4.6%) and 30,080 others who gave either multiple Aboriginal responses or did not report identity but did report Indian registration or band membership. The population reporting Indian registration numbered 558,175, representing about 57.2% of the total population reporting Aboriginal identity.

For purposes of this study, the Aboriginal identity population has been configured into four subgroups: Registered Indians, non-Registered Indians, Métis, and Inuit. Distinguishing the population on the basis of Indian registration status is important to any analysis of Aboriginal mobility or migration. Unlike other Aboriginal groups, those registered under the Indian Act have certain rights and benefits, especially if they live on-reserve. Among other things, these include taxation exemptions, access to funding for housing and post-secondary education, and land and treaty rights. Aboriginal populations living off-reserve, including those in Métis and Inuit communities, do not have legal access to the same rights and benefits as Registered Indians living on-reserve. The varying landscape of rights and benefits which exists between on- and off-reserve communities and between those registered and non-registered is important to gaining an understanding of the migration patterns of the four Aboriginal subgroups.

Geographic Distribution of the Population

As noted previously, the study's scope is restricted to internal migration. In this regard, mobility and migration are examined within the context of four mutually exclusive geographic areas: Indian reserves and settlements, rural areas, urban non-census metropolitan areas (urban non-CMAs), and census metropolitan areas (CMAs). CMAs are defined as urban areas with a minimum core population of 100,000. Urban non-CMAs include all other urban areas with a core population of at least 10,000. As defined for this study, both of these urban geographies exclude Indian reserves and rural fringe areas located within the broader boundaries of the urban areas. Rural areas comprise all remaining areas, including the undeveloped fringes of urban areas but excluding lands defined as Indian reserves and settlements.[3]

Figure 13.1 illustrates the geographic distribution of the four Aboriginal groups as captured by the 2001 Census. Comparative data are also presented for the total Aboriginal and non-Aboriginal populations. According to census data for 2001, about 29% of the total Aboriginal population resided on Indian reserves or settlements, 20% in rural areas, 22% in small urban centres (urban non-CMAs), and 29% in urban areas. The geographic distribution of the Aboriginal population contrasted sharply with that of the non-Aboriginal population, which was heavily concentrated in urban areas (80%), and especially in large urban areas (61%).[4]

The figure also illustrates that there were quite pronounced differences in the geographic distributions of the four Aboriginal groups. The non-Registered Indian

Figure 13.1: Distribution of Aboriginal and Non-Aboriginal Population by Geographic Location, Canada 2001

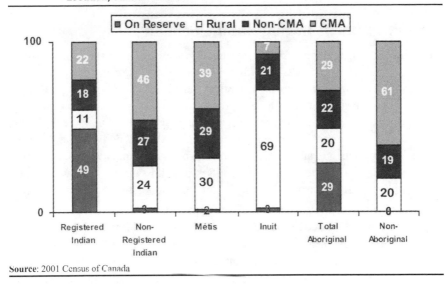

Source: 2001 Census of Canada

Figure 13.2: Growth in the Population Reporting Aboriginal Identity by Location of Residence, Canada 1996-2001

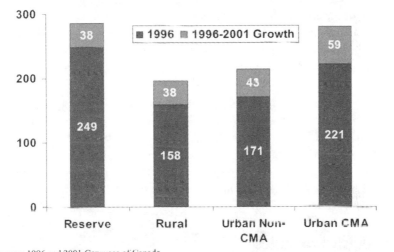

Source: 1996 and 2001 Censuses of Canada

and Métis populations were most heavily concentrated in urban areas, at 73% and 67% respectively, while a substantial majority of the Inuit population lived in rural areas (69%). The Registered Indian population differed from other Aboriginal groups in that close to one-half of the population identified by the census lived on-reserve (understated). In comparison to both the non-Registered Indian and Métis populations, Registered Indians were considerably less urbanized (40% [overstated]).

Recent Patterns of Population Growth

Many observers, including both researchers and those writing in the general media, have commented on the rapid growth of the Aboriginal urban population, especially in major urban areas. Measuring the extent of Aboriginal population change using census data is a highly problematic exercise, as census estimates are confounded by changes over time in concepts used to define the population, the wording of questions used for this purpose, levels of non-enumeration and survey under-coverage, and the population's propensity to identify their Aboriginal heritage and affiliation. These difficulties notwithstanding, census estimates can provide a rough measure of the scale of recent population changes.

Unadjusted census estimates of growth for the total Aboriginal identity population during the 1996–2001 time period are presented in **Figure 13.2** (page 211). The total population increase for the period numbered 177,300 individuals (about 22%). This figure reveals that substantial increases to the Aboriginal identity population occurred both on-reserve and in off-reserve rural and urban areas. The population on-reserve increased by about 38,000 individuals: an annual growth rate of about 2.8% during the period. Some portion of the reported growth on-reserve is associated with the lower number of reserves incompletely (or non-) enumerated by the 2001 Census. Most of the growth during the period, or about 77%, occurred off-reserve. The population in rural areas increased by about 38,000 individuals, representing an annual growth rate of about 4.3%. Growth in the urban Aboriginal population totalled about 101,800 individuals. Most urban growth occurred in large cities, where the average annual rate of growth approached 4.7% for the period.

The pattern and scale of population growth reported for 1996 to 2001 is similar to that identified for the 1986–1996 time period. The very high rates of growth for the urban Aboriginal population, which characterize the 1986–2001 time period, cannot be explained by natural increase (i.e., the excess of births over deaths). This situation raises a key question: *To what extent has migration contributed to the rapid increase in the Aboriginal population living off-reserve, especially that living in large urban areas?*

Gross Migration Rates

Between 1996 and 2001, 174,550 Aboriginal people, or about 20% of the population, changed their community of residence. As illustrated in **Figure 13.3**, the proportion of the population that reported migration during this period varied widely among Aboriginal subgroups, the highest proportion being among non-Registered Indians (23.7%) and Métis (22.2%), and the lowest among Inuit

Figure 13.3: Proportion of Population Aged 5+ Years Reporting Migration by Aboriginal Identity Group, Canada 1996-2001

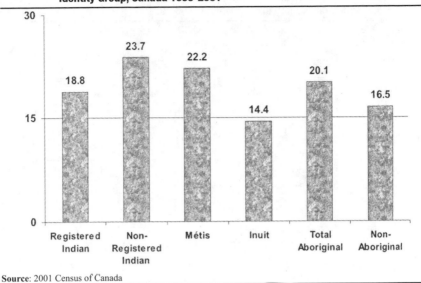

Source: 2001 Census of Canada

Table 13.1: Average Annual Gross Migration Rate (per 1,000 Population) by Aboriginal Identity Group and Location of Residence, Canada 1996–2001

Location	Population Group						Aboriginal/ Non- Aboriginal
	Registered Indian	Non- Registered Indian	Métis	Inuit	Total Aboriginal	Non- Aboriginal	
Reserve	34.1	na	na	na	35.9	na	na
Rural	116.1	83.5	77.2	38.1	84.7	63.1	1.34
Non- CMA	125.6	116.8	107.7	91.5	116.5	77.9	1.50
CMA	100.9	89.0	84.7	134.1	93.1	63.1	1.48

na – not available due to small population counts
Source: 2001 Census of Canada

(14.4%). About 18.8% of Registered Indians also migrated during the period. With the exception of the Inuit, migrants formed a larger segment of the Aboriginal, as opposed to non-Aboriginal, population.

Gross migration rates, which measure the combined in and out migrant flows in relation to the size of the population, can be used to provide a measure of the overall extent of population movement into and out of a geographic area. Average annual gross migration rates for the 1996–2001 period are presented in **Table 13.1** for each Aboriginal subgroup by geographic location. The data in the

Table 13.2: Distribution of Aboriginal Migrant Flows by Origin and Destination and Aboriginal Identity Group, Canada 1996-2001

Origin/Destination Flow	Registered Indian		Non-Registered Indian		Métis		Inuit	
	Number	%	Number	%	Number	%	Number	%
Urban to Urban	31,885	34.3	13.365	59.7	28,515	53.0	1,500	26.7
Urban to Rural	8,490	9.1	3,385	15.1	10,340	19.2	995	17.7
Urban to Reserve	16,940	18.2	515	2.3	630	1.2	100	1.8
Rural to Rural	3,080	3.3	1,240	5.5	4,105	7.6	1,385	24.6
Rural to Urban	12,365	13.3	3.255	14.6	8,920	16.6	1,200	21.4
Rural to Reserve	5,355	5.8	155	0.7	240	0.4	110	2.0
Reserve to Urban	9,960	10.7	345	1.5	660	1.2	150	2.7
Reserve to Rural	1,565	1.7	40	0.2	280	0.5	80	1.4
Reserve to Reserve	3,240	3.5	70	0.3	125	0.2	100	1.8

Source: 2001 Census of Canada

table reveal several additional features of the migration patterns of specific Aboriginal subgroups. For example, while the overall rate of migration among Registered Indians (18.8%) is lower than that of non-Registered Indians and Métis, this situation is the result of low rates of migration to and from reserves (34.1 migrants per 1,000 population). In fact, gross migration rates among Registered Indians living in off-reserve locations are significantly higher than those reported for the non-Registered Indian and Métis populations. Similarly, the low rate of migration recorded for the total Inuit population reflects quite low levels of migration to and from rural areas.[5] In major urban areas, the rate of gross migration among the Inuit population exceeds that of all other Aboriginal subgroups and the non-Aboriginal population.

While Aboriginal residents of reserves display much lower levels of migration than the non-Aboriginal population, rates of Aboriginal migration off-reserve are considerably higher than those of the non-Aboriginal population in both rural areas (about 34% higher) and urban areas (nearly 50% higher).

Migrant Origin and Destination Flows

Table 13.2 provides a summary of the migration flows during the 1996–2001 period between reserves and off-reserve locations for each of the four Aboriginal subgroups. Flows between urban areas (i.e., urban to urban) formed the largest component of migration among each of the four groups, and accounted for the majority of moves amongst non-Registered Indian and Métis migrants. Several other dimensions of the migration flows of the four groups, however, differ. These differences relate, in part, to variations among subgroups with respect to geographic distribution and degree of urbanization. For example, moves to and from Indian reserves and settlements are common only among the Registered

Figure 13.4: Net Migration Flows of Aboriginal Identity Population Aged 5+ Years, Canada 1996-2001

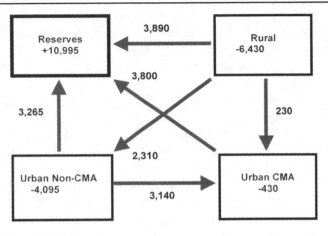

Source: 2001 Census of Canada

Table 13.3: Volume of Net Migrants by Aboriginal Identity Group and Location, Canada 1996-2001

Location	Registered Indian	Non-Registered Indian	Métis	Inuit
Reserves	10,770	285	-70	-20
Rural Areas	-7,665	15	1,460	-235
Urban Non-CMAs	-2,185	-360	-1,700	250
CMAs	-920	60	310	5
Net Migrants	16,100	1,150	2,580	395
% of Population	3.3	1.2	1.1	1.0

Source: 2001 Census of Canada

Indian population. Migrants originating from or relocating to reserves formed nearly 40% of all Registered Indian migrants during the period. Nearly two-thirds of Registered Indian moves between on- and off-reserve locations involved moves to reserves. More than three-quarters of the moves by Registered Indians to reserves involved migrants from urban areas. Reciprocal moves between reserves and urban areas constitute an important dimension of the migration patterns of Registered Indians.

For both the non-Registered Indian and Métis populations, three migration streams—urban to urban, urban to rural, and rural to urban—account for nearly nine out every ten migrants. These three migration streams are also common among Inuit migrants. Migration among the Inuit, however, is also characterized by significant flows between rural areas, a dimension that constitutes a minor component of migration for all other Aboriginal populations.

Net Migration Flows and Rates

Although nearly 20% of the Aboriginal population changed their community of residence between 1996 and 2001, the net effects of the relocations on the geographic distribution of the population was not large. Net changes among the four geographic areas during the period numbered only 21,950 individuals, or about 2.5% of the population aged five years and over. As revealed in **Figure 13.4** (page 215), the Aboriginal population living on reserves gained about 10,995 migrants as a consequence of net inflows from both rural and urban areas. All off-reserve geographic areas reported net outflows of migrants for the period. Rural areas lost 6,430 individuals through net outflows to all other areas. Although small urban centres (urban non-CMAs) experienced a net inflow of migrants from rural areas, this was offset by larger net outflows to both large cities (CMAs) and to reserves. For the period, Aboriginal population losses through migration for smaller cities totalled 4,095 individuals. Large urban centres recorded net inflows of Aboriginal migrants from both rural areas and smaller urban centres. Larger net outflows of Aboriginal migrants to reserves, however, resulted in a net migration loss in large urban centres of 430 individuals.

Aggregate data for the total Aboriginal identity population mask some important differences in the net migration patterns of the various subgroups. The volume of net migrants by geographic area is presented in **Table 13.3** (page 215) for each of the four Aboriginal groups.

The geographic pattern of net migration changes for Registered Indians is similar to that presented previously for the total Aboriginal population. Reserves gained about 10,770 Registered Indians through migration during the period, while all off-reserve geographic areas recorded net migration losses. Net migration losses of Registered Indians were significant only for rural areas (7,765) and smaller urban areas (2,185). Overall, net changes to the Registered Indian populations of the four geographic areas resulting from migration totalled only 16,100 individuals and represented only 3.3% of the Registered Indian population aged five years and over. The contribution of migration to changes in the geographic distribution of other Aboriginal groups during the 1996–2001 period was much smaller (about 1% of the population aged five years and over). Migration among the Métis population resulted in net gains in rural areas (1,460) and large cities (360), and losses in smaller urban areas (1,700) and reserves (70). For both the non-Registered Indian and Inuit populations, net migration flows for the period were quite small for all geographic areas.

Contribution of Migration to Population Change

Net migration rates can be used to measure of the impact of migration on changes in the size of the population in each geographic area. As illustrated in **Figure 13.5**, for most Aboriginal subgroups, net migration rates tend to be quite small for most geographic areas. Population size impacts were most significant for the

Figure 13.5: Average Annual Rate of Net Migration (per 1,000 Population) by Aboriginal Identity Group and Location, Canada 1996-2001

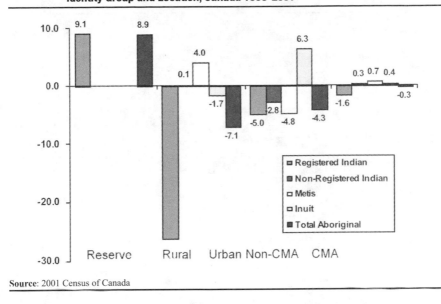

Source: 2001 Census of Canada

Figure 13.6: Average Annual Rate of Registered Indian Net Migration by Location and 5-Year Period, Canada 1966-2001

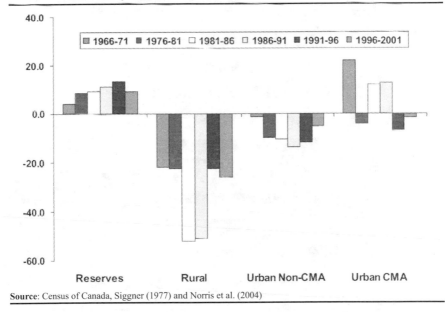

Source: Census of Canada, Siggner (1977) and Norris et al. (2004)

Figure 13.7: Aboriginal Population Growth in Select Major Urban Centres, Canada 1996–2001

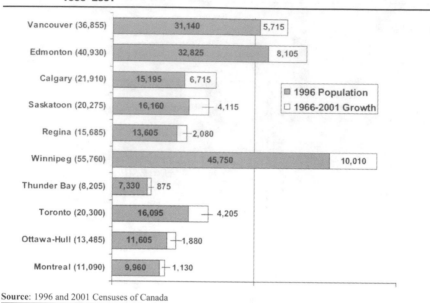

Source: 1996 and 2001 Censuses of Canada

Figure 13.8: Average Annual Rate of Gross Migration per 1,000 Population for Select Major Urban Areas, Aboriginal and Non-Aboriginal Population, 1996–2001

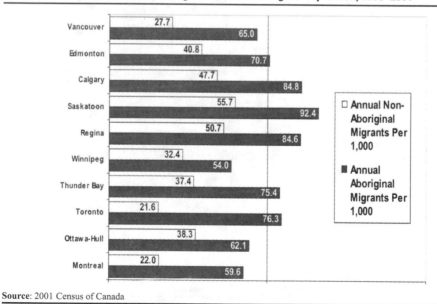

Source: 2001 Census of Canada

Registered Indian populations residing in rural areas and on-reserve. In rural areas, the net outflow of Registered Indian migrants averaged 26.2 per 1,000 population (or about 2.6%) annually. Net inflows of Registered Indians to reserves averaged 9.1 per 1,000 population (or 0.9%) annually. For all remaining Aboriginal groups and locations, average annual rates of net migration ranged between 6.3 and -5.0 per 1,000 population, implying that *migration did not contribute to significant changes in the distribution of the Aboriginal population during the 1996–2001 period.*

In many respects, the patterns of Aboriginal migration identified for the 1996–2001 period are similar to those reported for the previous five-year period (Clatworthy and Cooke 2001; Norris et al. 2004). Reserves continued to experience relatively small net inflows of migrants, who were almost exclusively Registered Indians. Rural areas experienced small net inflows of Métis and non-Registered Indian migrants, but much larger outflows of Registered Indian migrants. Urban areas also continued to record net outflows of migrants, most notably Registered Indians, although the impacts of migration on the size of the urban Aboriginal population remained quite small.

Due to changes in census population definitions, long-term migration trends are available only for the Registered Indian population. As revealed in **Figure 13.6** (page 217), net inflows of Registered Indian migrants to reserves, first reported for the 1966–1971 time period by Siggner (1977), have continued throughout the past 35-year period.

Net out-migration of Registered Indians from rural areas and smaller urban areas has also occurred consistently throughout this period. A more complex pattern of net migration exists for large urban areas. Large urban centres recorded net inflows of the Registered Indian migrants throughout most of the 1966–1991 time period. The net outflows of the Registered Indian migrants from major urban centres reported for both the 1991–1996 and 1996–2001 time periods reflect a reversal of the longer-term migration trend. Although migration has contributed to growth in the Aboriginal populations of large cities in the past, this no longer appears to be the case. In fact, recent evidence suggests that migration has tended to retard Aboriginal population growth in both small and large urban centres, as well as in off-reserve rural areas.

Although high rates of migration characterize all Aboriginal populations, especially those off-reserve, data for the 1991–2001 time period clearly suggest that migration has not played a major role in altering the geographic distribution of the Aboriginal population, nor has it served as a significant component of recent population growth in any of the geographic areas considered in this study. These findings clearly imply that the recent high rates of Aboriginal population growth must result from other factors. As noted by Clatworthy et al. (1997) and Guimond (1999), these other factors are both numerous and complex and include natural increase (i.e., the excess of births over deaths), changes in levels of census

Figure 13.9: Average Annual Gross Migration per 1,000 Population, Registered Indian and Other Aboriginal Populations, Select Major Urban Areas, 1996-2001

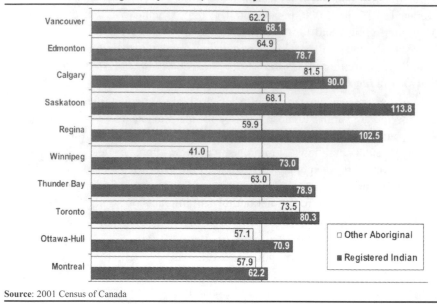

Source: 2001 Census of Canada

Figure 13.10: Average Annual Net Migration Rate per 1,000 Aboriginal Population, Select Major Urban Areas, 1996-2001

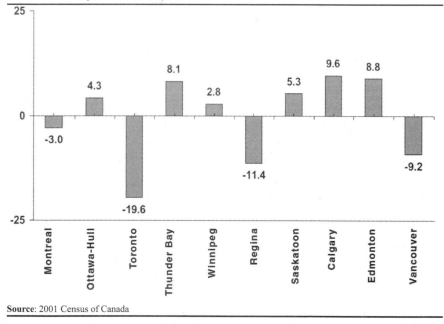

Source: 2001 Census of Canada

Figure 13.11: Average Annual Growth and Net Migration Rates per 1,000 Aboriginal Population, Select Major Urban Areas, 1996-2001

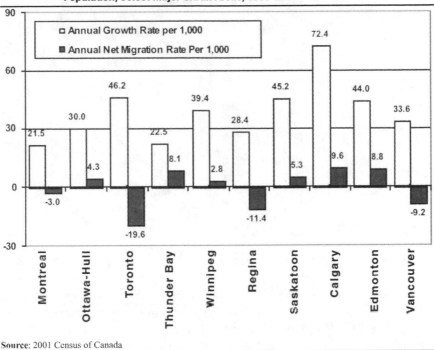

Source: 2001 Census of Canada

coverage, legislative changes (e.g., the 1985 amendments to the Indian Act), and changes in self-reporting of Aboriginal identity (ethnic mobility or ethnic drift). These latter two factors appear to account for much of the reported recent population growth reported for the Registered Indian, non-Registered Indian, and Métis populations, especially in off-reserve areas.

Aboriginal Migration and Major Urban Areas

As noted previously, movement to and from urban areas, especially large cities, forms a significant component of the recent migration patterns of all Aboriginal subgroups. Based on the 2001 Census, about 244,500 Aboriginal peoples (or about 25% of the total recorded by the census) lived in one of 10 CMAs that reported the largest Aboriginal populations. Estimates of recent Aboriginal population growth for these cities are presented in **Figure 13.7** (page 218). As revealed in the figure, each of these 10 cities recorded significant levels of Aboriginal population growth (in excess of 10%) between 1996 and 2001. Four of these cities—Toronto, Saskatoon, Edmonton, and Calgary—recorded Aboriginal population increases exceeding 20%.

Figure 13.12: Reasons for Migration to and from Reserves and Between Non-Reserve Areas, Registered Indians, Canada 1991 APS

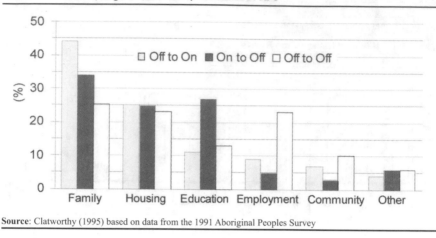

Source: Clatworthy (1995) based on data from the 1991 Aboriginal Peoples Survey

Average annual gross migration rates for the Aboriginal populations of these cities (**Figure 13.8** – page 218) ranged from 54.0 per 1,000 population (5.4%) in Montreal to 92.4 per 1,000 population (9.2%) in Saskatoon. In addition to Saskatoon, gross migration rates were also quite high among the Aboriginal populations of Calgary and Regina. In all of the highlighted urban areas, Aboriginal migration rates exceeded those of the non-Aboriginal population by a wide margin.

For all of the highlighted cities, high rates of gross migration are most typical of the Registered Indian populations (**Figure 13.9** – page 220). Average annual gross migration rates for Registered Indians ranged from 62.2 per 1,000 (6.2%) in Montreal to 113.3 per 1,000 (11.3%) in Saskatoon during the period. For other Aboriginal groups, average annual rates over the same period ranged between 41.0 per 1,000 (4.1%) in Winnipeg and 81.5 per 1,000 (8.2%) in Calgary. Differences between Registered Indians and other Aboriginal groups were most pronounced in Winnipeg, Regina, and Saskatoon. For these cities, Registered Indian migration rates rose sharply over those of other Aboriginal groups.

Net Migration and Urban Growth

As illustrated in **Figure 13.10** (page 220), Aboriginal net migration rates varied widely among the highlighted cities. Six cities reported net inflows of Aboriginal migrants for the period, although these were of significant scale only in Thunder Bay, Calgary, and Edmonton. Four cities reported net outflows of Aboriginal migrants. Net outflows of Aboriginal migrants were significant for Regina, Vancouver, and Toronto, in particular. Although several of the highlighted cities recorded significant net migration flows for the period, migration did not play a major role in Aboriginal population growth in any of these cities. The relationship between net migration and Aboriginal population growth is displayed in **Figure 13.11** (page 221) which presents the average annual population growth rate and net migration rate for each of the cities. As revealed in **Figure 13.11**, annual net migration rates account for only a small component of the total growth rates of cities recording net inflows of migrants. In addition, each of the four cities that recorded net outflows of migrants during the period also reported high rates of Aboriginal population growth. The situation of Toronto is most striking in this regard. During the period, Toronto recorded an annual net outflow of 19.6 migrants per 1,000 population, but an overall annual growth rate of 46.2 per 1,000 population, one of the highest rates of Aboriginal population growth among the cities highlighted.

Reasons for Migration

Migration factors differ among Aboriginal groups, communities, and reserves. As discussed earlier, variations in migration patterns reflect group differences, such as location, urbanization, and legal status (rights and benefits). For example, compared to other Aboriginal communities, reserves tend to have higher rates of in and out migration, and to experience net inflows of migrants, rather than net losses or no gain or loss, through migration flows (Norris et al. 2000). Reserves contribute to a unique set of push-pull factors that affect migration patterns related to the rights and benefits associated with Registered Indian status and residence on-reserve, as noted earlier (e.g., housing, post-secondary schooling, tax exemption, land/treaty rights). Still, it should be remembered that migration flows between individual communities and cities are the outcomes of particular sets of circumstances; reserve communities in Canada do differ widely in their economic, socio-cultural, and geographic characteristics.

The decision to move is the outcome of competing push-pull factors that influence migration, with "pushes" being the reasons to leave one's current place of residence, and the "pulls" being the benefits to be gained by moving to a potential destination. The pushes of reserves and cities as places of current residence can be many and varied, including socio-economic factors such as education, employment, and housing (availability, adequacy); institutional completeness; health facilities; and the political situation. In addition to any housing considerations, with respect to the pulls of reserves, Aboriginal communities and reserves can also serve as potential destinations for city dwellers with goals of preserving ties with the home community and maintaining cultural traditions and language. As destinations, they can provide a home base with a critical mass of friends and extended family support, and serve as a "cultural hearth" with culturally appropriate activities and services. In some cases, these communities have been cited by some migrants as their place of choice to raise children and for retirement (Cooke 1999).

Figure 13.13: Rate of Residential Mobility per 1,000 Population Aged 1+ Years by Age Group, Aboriginal and Non-Aboriginal Populations Living in Urban Areas, Canada, 2000-2001

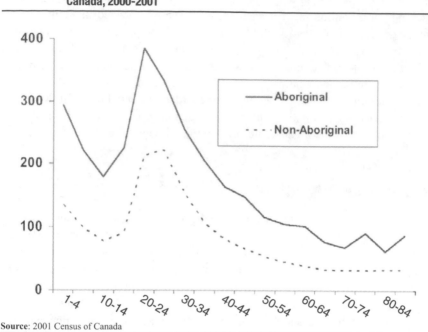

Source: 2001 Census of Canada

In an analysis of 1991 APS migration data, looking at the reasons for migration among Registered Indians, family and housing were cited as the major reasons for moving, regardless of destination, while education was a major reason for leaving reserves (**Figure 13.12**). Employment was also a major reason for moves between urban communities (Clatworthy and Cooke 2001).

It should be remembered that migration reflects the interplay among personal characteristics of potential movers, and the characteristics of communities of residence and those of potential destinations. The propensity to move is influenced by stages in the life cycle and personal attributes (e.g., education level, attachment to traditional culture). For example, differences associated with personal characteristics can include age-gender variation in migration rates by origin; destination (e.g., women have a higher rate of out-migration from reserves, while men have a higher in-migration rate to reserves); the fact that women are more likely to move for family or community-related reasons; and that female lone parents are more common amongst the urban in-migrant population. Community characteristics, such as location, are also known to affect migration. In the case of communities that are located either "near to" (within 60 km) or "distant from" (more than 300 km) urban centres, people are more likely to leave and less likely to return, as compared to communities at more moderate distances (Clatworthy and Cooke 2001).

Figure 13.14: Reasons Cited by Aboriginal Residential Movers for Last Move Off Reserve, Canada 1996-2001

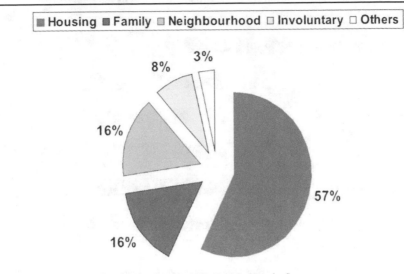

Source: Clatworthy (1995) based on data from the 1991 Aboriginal Peoples Survey.

Residential Mobility

Changing residence within the same community represents a specific dimension of mobility that has not been explored to any great extent for Canada's Aboriginal population. This aspect of mobility is important, as residential mobility represents the major process though which households and individuals adjust their housing consumption to reflect changes in needs and resources. Changes in housing needs may result from a variety of events such as marriage, the birth of a child, or a new place of work. Many events may also affect the resources available for housing, such as a rise in income, finding stable employment, or losing a job. This section provides some general indicators of recent residential mobility rates and reasons for residential moves among the Aboriginal population, especially the population residing in urban areas.

Residential mobility rates, as presented in this study, are defined as the proportion of the non-migrant population that changed residence in the previous 12-month period. The rates reflect moves made during the year preceding the 2001 Census, and are presented as the number of residential movers per 1,000 population aged one or more years.

For the 2000–2001 period, the overall rate of residential mobility among the non-migrant Aboriginal population was 152.1 per 1,000 population, a rate roughly 1.8 times higher than that reported for the non-Aboriginal population. Residential mobility rates, however, varied widely by location. Among the Aboriginal population, the rates of mobility on-reserve (85.2 per 1,000 popula-

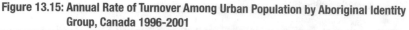

Figure 13.15: Annual Rate of Turnover Among Urban Population by Aboriginal Identity Group, Canada 1996-2001

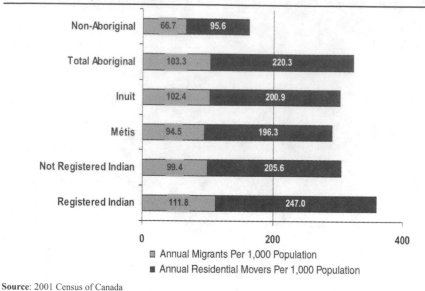

Source: 2001 Census of Canada

tion) and in rural areas (85.8 per 1,000 population) were of similar magnitude, but sharply below those reported in urban areas (220.3 per 1,000 population). In relation to the non-Aboriginal population, the rate of residential mobility of the Aboriginal population was about 2.1 times higher in rural areas, and about 2.3 times higher in urban centres.

High rates of residential mobility characterize all four Aboriginal groups in urban areas. In urban centres, annual rates among the groups ranged from about 198 per 1,000 population for the Métis population to 247 per 1,000 population for Registered Indians. By way of comparison, the annual residential mobility rate among the urban non-Aboriginal population during the period was about 96 per 1,000 population.

As many of the events that can trigger residential moves (e.g., marriage, family development, buying a new home) are associated with life cycle changes, residential mobility is strongly patterned over age groups. Additionally, most of these triggering events are associated with younger age groups, especially young adults. Given this situation, and the much younger age structure of the Aboriginal population, one would expect residential mobility to be more common among Aboriginal peoples. As illustrated in **Figure 13.13** (page 224), differences in residential mobility rates between the Aboriginal and non-Aboriginal populations in urban areas cannot be explained by differences in age structure. For all age groups, including older cohorts, rates for the Aboriginal population are significantly (at least 50%) higher than those of the non-Aboriginal population. Other factors, such as inadequate housing, low rates of home ownership, discrimination, and low incomes and poverty, are likely to be more important than age in explaining the high rates of residential mobility of the urban Aboriginal population.

Figure 13.13 also reveals that the general pattern of residential mobility over age groups is quite similar for the Aboriginal and non-Aboriginal populations. Mobility for both populations is highest among cohorts aged 20 to 34 years, and among children aged 1 to 9 years. This pattern most likely reflects the higher levels of mobility associated with younger families in the early stages of family development who are attempting to bring their housing consumption in line with the larger space needs of a growing family.

While the mainstream literature (e.g., Rossi 1955) tends to view a residential move as a voluntary response to changing household or individual circumstances, moving may also occur involuntarily as a consequence of events such as marriage dissolution, eviction, or the loss of the dwelling to fire or condemnation. The most recently available survey data concerning the reasons for residential moves among Aboriginal peoples derives from the 1991 Aboriginal Peoples Survey. The reasons cited by APS respondents living off-reserve are summarized in **Figure 13.14** (page 225).

As expected, housing-related issues were the largest category of reasons given by APS respondents (57%) for moving. Family-related reasons were cited by 16% of respondents. Factors related to neighbourhood circumstances (e.g., crime and safety) and accessibility (e.g., to schools or employment) were also cited by 16% of respondents. Involuntary moves were noted by 8% of all respondents. Most of these involuntary moves were linked to sub-standard housing. APS data on reasons for moving among Aboriginal peoples clearly identify efforts to improve housing situations as the primary motivation for residential moves. This suggests that the high levels of residential mobility among urban Aboriginal populations flow from inadequate housing situations.

The housing difficulties experienced by Aboriginal populations both on- and off-reserve have been well documented over the past 20 years (e.g., Clatworthy and Stevens 1987; Clatworthy 1980, 1983, 1995; Spector 1996). Little of this prior research, however, has examined the housing circumstances of Aboriginal movers and non-movers. According to widely accepted theory, moving represents an opportunity for the household or individual to bring housing consumption more in line with needs and resources. This raises a key question: *To what extent do residential moves among the Aboriginal population result in acceptable housing situations?* In this regard, recent research conducted for the Royal Commission on Aboriginal Peoples by Clatworthy (1995) found that a substantial majority of urban Aboriginal movers did not acquire housing that met Canada's standards for affordability (cost in relation to income), quality (condition), or suitability (adequate space). This research also found that, in relation to non-movers, recent Aboriginal movers were considerably more likely to experience one or more housing consumption deficiency (most commonly affordability and quality). For a significant segment of the urban Aboriginal population, the process of residential mobility does not appear to result in acceptable levels of housing consumption. Given this situation, the high levels of residential mobility that characterize the urban Aboriginal population are cause for concern, and may constitute an additional dimension of the housing difficulties experienced by the population.

Implications of Urban Population Turnover and Instability

Based on the findings of this study, the most important aspects of recent Aboriginal mobility and migration patterns relate not to population redistribution (as migration has played only a minor role in this regard) but, rather, to the high levels of population turnover off-reserve, especially in urban areas. In urban areas, high levels of residential mobility, in conjunction with high levels of in and out migration, result in Aboriginal populations that are in a high state of flux, or churn. As illustrated in **Figure 13.15** (page 226), nearly one in every three urban Aboriginal residents either migrates in or out of the city or changes residence within the city annually, a level of population turnover roughly twice that of the non-Aboriginal population. Among urban Aboriginal residents, population turnover is most pronounced for Registered Indians, who display higher rates of both migration and residential mobility. For Registered Indians, higher levels of migration to and from cities appear to be the result of high levels of movement between cities and reserves, a dimension of migration that is unique to this population. More severe socio-economic difficulties, including a higher incidence of inadequate housing conditions among Registered Indians (Clatworthy 1980, Clatworthy and Stevens 1987), may account for the higher levels of residential mobility associated with this segment of the urban Aboriginal population.

Although little research currently exists, evidence is building to suggest that high levels of population turnover among Aboriginal peoples in urban areas can have disruptive effects on individuals, families, communities, and service providers. For example, many social programs that provide services to urban Aboriginal populations, such as health, family support and counselling, and education, are designed on a neighbourhood basis to ensure a coordinated response to multifaceted family and individual needs. Frequent mobility among Aboriginal families can result in discontinuity or disruption of service provision, with negative consequences for the family and service provision agencies.[6] Discontinuity in service delivery can be especially pronounced among high-need families such as those of lone female parents, who are among the most mobile, yet often in the most need.

The provision of education services may serve to illustrate the challenges and implications associated with high levels of mobility. In a recent study of schools in central Winnipeg neighbourhoods, Clatworthy (2000) found a strong relationship between the Aboriginal share of the population and student turnover rates in central city schools. A 10% increase in the Aboriginal share of the neighbourhood population resulted in a 14% increase in student turnover. Among schools serving neighbourhoods where Aboriginal peoples formed more than 25% of the population, annual student turnover rates generally exceeded 50%, and were at least twice the central city average. High rates of residential mobility appear to translate into an unstable education environment for many Aboriginal children. Although Clatworthy's research did not explore the link between mobility and student performance, a recent US study by the Government Accounting Office (GAO) identified frequent mobility as a key, contributing factor to student academic underachievement.

> The GAO study ... revealed that of the nation's third graders who have changed schools frequently, 41% are below the grade level in reading, compared with 26% of third graders who have never changed schools ... Results are also similar for math ... Children who have moved often were also more likely to have behaviour problems.

Frequent moves may also serve to limit opportunities for individuals and families to establish meaningful and lasting social relationships within the Aboriginal and the broader urban community. If so, mobility may promote social isolation and act as barrier to the development of social cohesion in the urban context. As Beavon and Norris (1999) have suggested, "high mobility (or churn) could lead to a weaker social cohesion in communities and neighbourhoods and, as a consequence, people living in these areas could exhibit greater social problems (e.g., poorer educational attainment, divorce, crime, suicide), which in turn could lead to even greater levels of churn."

Implications for Policy Development

Clearly the most immediate consequences for policy arise from the bi-directional movement between reserves and urban areas, which are then combined with high mobility rates off-reserve, particularly in urban areas. As the analysis above demonstrates, there are considerable implications for policy and program development in service areas and outcomes. Also, compositional effects of high turnover on the urban population imply a difficulty in adapting services to the needs of a "changing" population. It is clear that policies need to be sensitive to cultural needs. Aboriginal people are confronted with the challenge of maintaining cultural identity and developing urban institutions that reflect Aboriginal values in urban areas. Reserves remain attractive destinations as a cultural hearth for Aboriginal people who feel socially or culturally isolated, if not economically marginalized, in urban settings. Furthermore, the high population turnover among Aboriginal people in urban areas poses challenges for developing social cohesion within communities.

This study has attempted to address and clarify some of the misinterpretations surrounding First Nations migration phenomena. This clarification process is essential to informed policy making, as misunderstandings concerning Aboriginal

migration, mobility, and ethnic mobility could adversely affect policy development. For example, by exploring the myth that reserves tend to experience large
net outflows of migrants to cities, this study has shown that reserves have tended
to gain population due to migration instead of the other way around. This is in
contrast to the predictions made by policy makers in the 1960s that there would
be a gradual loss of population from reserves. From a policy perspective, this
is significant because migration gains add to the already considerable need for
additional employment, housing, and infrastructure due to high natural increase,
and suggest other issues, such as the reintegration of return migrants to reserves.

For urban areas, the myth that the growth of urban Aboriginal populations is
largely due to migration from reserves leads to the belief that the characteristics
of urban Aboriginal populations are those largely associated with migrants. From
a policy perspective, the findings of high population turnover due to residential
moves both within and to and from cities, suggests that there is a need for identification of different requirements and services for different groups within urban
areas. Non-movers, residential movers, non-migrants, and migrants represent
different socio-economic, demographic, and cultural characteristics, origins,
and needs.

Impact of Policy and Program Delivery on Migration

While mobility and migration may affect program delivery, it is also the case
that policies and program delivery may affect migration, whether or not this
effect is intended. Some observers (Reeves and Frideres 1981; Bostrom 1984)
have claimed that, through the 1970s, the federal government actively curtailed
programs available on reserves as a way to encourage migration and reduce its
fiscal obligations. It has also been suggested that the decreasing effectiveness of
public service delivery to a growing urban Aboriginal population may have led to
less effective Aboriginal acculturation into urban communities, resulting, in turn,
in return migration to reserves (Norris et al. 2004). However, no real evidence has
yet been presented that the implementation of a policy to promote out-migration
from reserves, or that better service delivery in urban areas, would reduce return
migration.

The impact of policy and program delivery can be explored using the example
of housing as a related policy challenge in the area of migration—that is, the
provision of housing on and off reserves. As demonstrated earlier, housing is one
of the primary reasons for mobility on- and off-reserve. Housing responsibilities differ by government levels, so that the federal government is traditionally
responsible for housing on reserves, while provinces and territories have been
accountable for social housing off reserves since the late 1990s. With respect to
the situation regarding Aboriginal housing policies and programs in Canada, the
federal government's role in Aboriginal housing off-reserve mainly has been one
of cost-sharing with provinces, and not of actual policy development or administra-

tion. Furthermore, no urban Aboriginal housing policy exists at the national level. Policy and administration tend to be decentralized at provincial and municipal levels, a reflection of the diversity of regional and local housing needs off-reserve. Policies and programs have not been developed in a consistent fashion across cities. Municipal governments often deal directly with housing using ad hoc programs and services—frequently in the absence of a policy framework.

Housing-related commitments were contained in the federal government's response to the recommendations of the 1996 Royal Commission on Aboriginal Peoples, as outlined in Indian and Northern Affairs Canada's report *Gathering Strength* (Canada 1997). These various commitments included improving the conditions of all Aboriginal populations, including Registered Indians on and off-reserve, non-status, Métis, and Inuit; improving housing and social services; building economic capacity in reserve communities; and discussions with Métis and urban Aboriginal organizations to frame new models and approaches regarding funding, policy making, and self-government.

Such institutional arrangements could affect population movement, and might thereby reduce the level of population churn—whether or not this effect is intended.

Conclusion

The fact that population mobility remains high is central to understanding many of the social, economic, and political development issues that face Aboriginal people in Canada. High mobility churn has significant implications for the building of institutional completeness and capacity within all communities.

Looking ahead, it seems that housing and employment situations in communities, potentially, could increase pressures to migrate from reserves, especially given the rapid growth projected in the working-age population. On the other hand, the process of an aging Aboriginal population may reduce mobility because individuals are less inclined to relocate at older ages.

As for the present, it is the frequency of population movement among reserves and cities (and within), not an exodus from the former, that has the greatest implications for the well-being of Aboriginal people and their communities.

Endnotes

1   As the census collected data only for residents of Canada, it is not possible to fully examine international movement patterns of Aboriginal peoples. Data on Aboriginal migrants moving to Canada suggest that this component of Aboriginal migration is quite small and of little consequence to changes in the national Aboriginal population. For the 1996–2001 time period, Aboriginal migrants from abroad numbered 3,065 individuals, and represented less than 1.8% of all migrants aged five or more years.

    Although the census captures migrants from non-enumerated reserves, migrants into these reserves are not captured. To avoid bias in the estimation of flows and rates, all migrants originating from non-enumerated reserves have been excluded from the study.

2   The census also allows for the population to define themselves according to specific cultural, band affiliations (e.g., a particular Cree First Nation in Manitoba) or a particular linguistic group (e.g., Cree).

3   Settlements include Crown land and other communities with Aboriginal populations as defined by Indian and Northern Affairs Canada. This category, which is grouped with Indian reserves in this study, includes some, but not all, Métis and Inuit communities.

4   The extent of differences in the geographic distribution of the Aboriginal and non-Aboriginal populations is actually greater than that depicted by the census data, due to higher levels of non-enumeration and under-coverage on-reserve.

5   To some extent the low rate of migration reported among Inuit in rural areas may result from the configuration of census geography in northern rural areas. The census sub-divisions (CSDs), which are used to define rural Inuit communities, may be much larger geographically than those of the communities of other Aboriginal populations. The possibility exists that some Inuit moves within the same rural CSD may, in fact, involve quite distant relocations. Such moves would not be recorded by the census as migration.

6   One example of this situation involves the experience of the Abinotci Mino Ayawin program in Winnipeg, a child-and-family support program aimed at Aboriginal families with children at high risk. The program was designed and initially staffed on a neighbourhood basis to coordinate and focus the resources of several agencies on the needs of families. High levels of mobility among client families resulted in frequent loss of contact with parents and children and the need to abandon the neighbourhood-based staffing approach. In order to maintain service continuity, program staff were required to serve families throughout the city, resulting in increased service costs and difficulties with arranging and coordinating other agency involvement.

References

Beavon D. and M.J. Norris. 1999. *Dimensions of geographic mobility and churn in social cohesion: The case of Aboriginal Peoples*. Ottawa: Research and Analysis Directorate, Indian and Northern Affairs Canada.

Bostrom, H. 1984. Government policies and programs relating to people of Indian ancestry in Manitoba. In *Dynamics of government programs for urban Indians in Prairie provinces*, ed. R. Breton and G. Grant. Montreal: Institute for Research on Public Policy.

Canada. Department of Indian Affairs and Northern Development. 1997. *Gathering strength: Canada's Aboriginal action plan*. Ottawa: Indian and Northern Affairs Canada.

Clatworthy, S.J. 1980. *The demographic composition and economic circumstances of Winnipeg's Native population*. Winnipeg: Institute of Urban Studies.

-----. 1983. *Native housing conditions in Winnipeg*. Winnipeg: Institute of Urban Studies.

-----. 1995. *The migration and mobility patterns of Canada's Aboriginal population*. Ottawa: Royal Commission on Aboriginal Peoples.

-----. 2002. *Patterns of residential mobility among Aboriginal Peoples in Canada*. Regina: Urban Aboriginal Strategy Federal Workshop.

Clatworthy S.J. and H. Stevens. 1987. *An overview of the housing conditions of registered Indians in Canada*. Ottawa: Indian and Northern Affairs Canada.

Clatworthy, S.J., J. Hull, and N. Loughren. 1997. *Implications of First Nations demography*. Ottawa: Research and Analysis Directorate, Indian and Northern Affairs Canada.

Clatworthy, S.J. and M. Cooke. 2001. *Patterns of registered Indian migration between on- and off-reserve locations*. Ottawa: Research and Analysis Directorate, Indian and Northern Affairs Canada.

Cooke, M.J. 1999. On leaving home: Return and circular migration between First Nations and Prairie cities. MA thesis, University of Western Ontario.

Cooke, M.J. and D. Belanger. 2006. Migration theories and First Nations mobility: Towards a systems perspective. *Canadian Review of Sociology and Anthropology* 24(2): 141–64.

Guimond, E. 1999. Ethnic mobility and the demographic growth of Canada's Aboriginal population from 1986–1996. Report on the demographic situation in Canada, 1998–1999. Ottawa: Statistics Canada.

Hanselmann, C. 2001. Urban Aboriginal People in Western Canada: Realities and policies. Report by the Canada West Foundation. Calgary: Canada West Foundation.

Norris, D.A. and E. T. Pryor. 1984. Demographic change in Canada's North. In *Proceedings—International Workshop on Population Issues in Arctic Societies*. Gilbjerghoved, Gilleleje, Denmark, May 2–5.

Norris, M.J. 1985. Migration Patterns of Status Indians in Canada, 1976–1981. Paper prepared for the Demography of Northern and Native Peoples in Canada, Canadian Population Society session, Statistics Canada, June.

-----. 1990. The demography of Aboriginal People in Canada. In *Ethnic demography: Canadian immigrant, racial and cultural variations*, ed. S. S. Halli, F. Trovato, and L. Driedger. Ottawa: Carleton Univ. Press.

-----. 2000. Aboriginal Peoples in Canada: Demographic and linguistic perspectives. In *Visions of the heart: Canadian Aboriginal issues*, 2nd ed., ed. D.A. Long and O.P. Dickason. Toronto: Harcourt Brace.

-----. 2002. *Registered Indian mobility and migration: An analysis of 1996 Census data*. Ottawa: Indian and Northern Affairs Canada.

Norris, M.J., D. Beavon, E. Guimond, and M.J. Cooke. 2000. Migration and residential mobility of Canada's Aboriginal groups: An analysis of census data. Poster prepared for the Annual Meeting of the Population Association of America, Los Angeles. Indian and Northern Affairs Canada, Ottawa, March.

Norris, M.J. and S.J. Clatworthy. 2003. Aboriginal mobility and migration within urban Canada: Outcomes, factors and implications. In *Not strangers in these parts: Urban Aboriginal Peoples*, ed. David Newhouse and Evelyn Peters. Ottawa: Policy Research Initiative.

Norris, M.J., Marty Cooke, and Stewart Clatworthy. 2003. Aboriginal mobility and migration patterns and the policy implications. In *Aboriginal conditions: Research as a foundation for public policy*, ed. J. White, P. Maxim, and D. Beavon. Vancouver: UBC Press. 108–129.

Norris, M.J., M. Cooke, E. Guimond, D. Beavon, and S. Clatworthy. 2004. Registered Indian mobility and migration in Canada: Patterns and implications. In *Population mobility and Indigenous Peoples in Australasia and North America*, ed. J. Taylor and M. Bell. London: Routledge. 136–160

Reeves, W. and J. Frideres. 1981. Government policy and Indian urbanization: The Alberta case. *Canadian Public Policy* 7(4): 584–95.

Rossi, P H 1955. *Why families move. A study in the social psychology of urban residential mobility*. Glencoe, IL: Free Press.

Siggner, A.J. 1977. Preliminary results from a study of 1966–1971 migration patterns among Status Indians in Canada. Ottawa. Indian Affairs and Northern Development.

Spector, A. (Ark Research Associates). 1996. The housing conditions of Aboriginal Peoples in Canada. Ottawa: Canada Mortgage and Housing Corporation.

Trovato, F., A. Romaniuc, and I. Addai. 1994. *On- and off-reserve migration of Aboriginal Peoples in Canada: A review of the literature*. Ottawa: Department of Indian Affairs and Northern Development.

Tuzzo, Victoria. Homeless and highly mobile: Meeting the reading and special education needs for students experiencing homelessness and high mobility rates. Williamsburg, VA: The College of William and Mary,

U.S. General Accounting Office 1994. Elementary school children: Many change schools frequently, harming their education. Report to the Honorable Marcy Kaptur, House of Representatives, GAO/HEH-S94-95. Washington, DC: ED369 526. <**archive.gao.gov./t2pbat4/150724.pdf**>

14

A New Beginning: A National Non-Reserve Aboriginal Housing Strategy

Steve Pomeroy,
on behalf of The National Aboriginal Housing Association/
Association Nationale d'Habitation Autochtone (NAHA/ANHA)[1]

Introduction

Why do we need a national non-reserve housing strategy? In 1972, Ron Bassford, the federal minister responsible for housing, declared that access to adequate housing was a right of all Canadians, including Aboriginal People. He committed his government to ensuring the building or acquisition of 50,000 housing units for Aboriginal individuals residing off-reserve. To deliver on this commitment, in 1973, the rural and remote housing program was established and urban native housing targets were established within the private, non-profit housing program delivered by the Canada Mortgage and Housing Corporation (CMHC). An Urban Native Housing Program was created in 1985.

In the intervening 30 years, less than 20,000 units were delivered (9,000 in rural communities and 11,000 in cities and towns). It should be noted, however, that the urban program was specifically targeted to those of native ancestry, while a large percentage of the rural program served non-Aboriginal households. In 1993, the federal government, as part of its fiscal restraint policy, halted all new spending for social housing, including any new non-reserve Aboriginal housing. In 1996, the federal government moved to transfer administrative responsibility for existing social housing, including off-reserve Aboriginal housing, to provinces and territories. To date, no province has accepted responsibility for new non-reserve commitments, and non-reserve Aboriginal housing organizations have been caught in a jurisdictional bind.

With the exception of a few locally supported initiatives, no new housing has been constructed for non-reserve Aboriginal households since 1993. It is time to end the jurisdictional dispute and work collectively in Canada to ensure our growing non-reserve Aboriginal population has access to safe, affordable housing. As of the 2001 Census, 71% of the Aboriginal population lives off-reserve, with almost three-quarters of those people living in urban areas.

The National Aboriginal Housing Association/Association Nationale d'Habitation Autochone (NAHA/ANHA) was created in 1993–1994 with funding from the federal government. It is a membership-based organization representing non-reserve Aboriginal housing and shelter providers across Canada. There are over 110 existing urban housing providers, and many homelessness and supportive shelters serving Indian, Métis, and Inuit communities. NAHA/ANHA was created to link such organizations by providing support and guidance in strategic planning and national policy development and to advance the housing goals of all non-reserve Aboriginal housing interests. The Association's Board of Directors is made up of representatives from each of the provinces and territories. NAHA/ANHA has consulted widely with its members and partners on the guiding principles upon which to base a national housing strategy.

Guiding Principles for a New National Non-Reserve Housing Strategy

The national housing strategy of the NAHA/ANHA contains the following points:

1. Fiduciary responsibility, self-determination, and the need to consult
   - Federal government has responsibility to ensure an Aboriginal component in any federal unilateral or bilateral housing program;
   - Programs must provide for self-determination and self-governance by promoting community-based, non-profit ownership;
   - Consultation with the Aboriginal community a prerequisite
2. Cultural sensitivity and well-being
   - Housing program delivery guidelines must facilitate the integration of culturally appropriate and sensitive management styles, as well as promote sound, efficient property management regimes;
   - Programs must respect the differing needs of First Nations, Métis, and Inuit
3. Access to adequate resources
   - Any future housing initiative must provide adequate capital assistance to non-reserve Aboriginal communities to ensure delivery of appropriate, affordable housing;
   - Affordability must be based upon the principle of households paying less than 30% of minimum wage in each jurisdiction

Method for Determining Affordability

The data used in this report have been drawn primarily from a special request to Statistics Canada to generate a series of tables specifically from data on non-reserve Aboriginal households[2] (i.e., living off-reserve). These tables are augmented with data from the 2001 Aboriginal Peoples Survey. There is a major constraint in using census data to undertake a housing analysis, or any analysis that seeks specifically to examine shelter costs as a percentage of income (i.e., affordability). The Canadian Census collects data for income in the year prior to the census year (i.e., 2000) and shelter expenses (like rent) at the time of the census (i.e., May 2001). As a result, there is a time lag between the two data sources used to determine affordability. By the time rent data are collected, the household may have experienced a change in income that was reported the previous year. In a number of cases, this generates shelter costs in excess of 100% of reported income. The method used to minimize this distortion is to exclude any household for which reported shelter costs exceed 100% of reported income. For Aboriginal households, the 10% of households that are non-reserve are excluded from the analysis for this reason. The households that have higher shelter-to-income ratios, which are the focus of this needs assessment, will be undercounted since these tend to be mobile households with fluctuating or unreported income and shelter costs. In the extreme, if all the excluded Aboriginal households are paying more than 50% of household income on housing, the incidence of severe rent burden would increase from 15% to 23% of Aboriginal households. For this reason, use of absolute values is deliberately limited. Estimates in this research rely more heavily on comparative statistics: Aboriginal versus Non-Aboriginal households.

Three key indicators are used in these analyses:

1. The incidence of households that are in core housing need (paying 30% of household income or more on rent)[3]

2. The incidence of households that are severely rent burdened (paying greater than 50% of household income to cover rental costs)

3. Dwellings in need of major repair [4]

Key Findings: Non-Reserve Housing Need

In the 2001 Census, the total Aboriginal population in Canada is reported as being just under one million persons, living in 320,000 households. In total, 71% of the Aboriginal population lives off-reserve, with almost three-quarters living in urban areas. Just over half of off-reserve Aboriginal households own their home, and 48% are renters. Prior analysis by CMHC has revealed that housing needs are significantly higher among renters than owners, so the focus of NAHA/ANHA's assessment is exclusively on Aboriginal renter households living off-reserve.

Among non-Aboriginal households, there is an even split between family and non-family households (predominantly single persons). By comparison, there is a much larger representation of family households (71%) in the non-reserve Aboriginal population. The comparatively higher proportion of family versus non-family households among Aboriginal peoples has important implications for program responses. This population has a greater need for bigger unit sizes suitable for larger families, which are more typical in the Aboriginal population.

Aboriginal households have a higher incidence of affordability problems than do non-Aboriginal. For example, 37% of Aboriginal households spend more than 30% of their household income on rent, while 15% (1 in every 6) experience severe rent burden. Although non-family households make up a smaller proportion of Aboriginal households (30%), these primarily single-person households experience a greater incidence of serious rent burden. Among non-family Aboriginal households, 20% spend more than 50% of their household income on housing, versus 13% of Aboriginal family households. Overall, members of the Aboriginal population have a lower average income than non-Aboriginals; at a national level, the average household income of Aboriginal households is 87% of that of non-Aboriginal households. So, on average, Aboriginal households have less money to spend on rent than the rest of the Canadian population.

Aboriginal renter households also tend to live in lower quality dwellings. For example, 16.5% of dwellings rented by Aboriginals are in need of major repair, as compared to 9% of non-Aboriginal households.

Method for Determining Cost of Affordable Housing Construction

The 2000 and 2003 federal budgets contained a total budgetary commitment of $1 billion to address the need for affordable housing. The commitment was comprised of an initial $600 million for urban and $80 million for rural and remote areas. Subsequently, a further $320 million was identified in the 2003 federal budget and was allocated across provinces on a per capita basis (the same basis as the original $680) and extended the ongoing provincial/territorial programs created in the initial round. The current federal/provincial/territorial framework for the affordable rental program identifies average market rent as the basis for grant eligibility. It further specifies a maximum federal grant level of $25,000 per unit to be equally matched by provincial and/or local sources.

NAHA/ANHA examined the typical cost of new affordable housing construction for a cross-section of 14 metropolitan and non-metropolitan cities (Calgary, Edmonton, Fredcricton, Halifax, Ottawa, Prince George, Quebec City, Regina, Saskatoon, Sudbury, Thunder Bay, Toronto, Vancouver, and Winnipeg) with either a higher absolute number or a high proportion of Aboriginal renter households. For illustrative purposes, these costs estimates are presented on a per unit basis for two unit types: a 450-square-foot bachelor/studio unit intended for low-income singles, and a 900-square-foot, three-bedroom apartment for families. These units are at the smaller end of the scale for a family type unit, especially for Aboriginal households, where a larger-than-average family size is typical.

For each city, two levels of affordability were examined:

1. Rents set at the average market rent level, as specified in the annual CMHC survey of market rents (October 2003) for the specific location and unit size (bachelor/studio unit and three-bedroom)

2. Rents set at 30% of annualized minimum wage, assuming either a single

earner (for bachelor/studio units) or 1.5 earners at minimum wage for family units, which reflects a blend of single and dual earner families

For each level, the amount of capital grant funding required to allow rents to be set at the respective target benchmarks was determined.

Key Findings: Capital Grant Funding Requirements

The resulting capital grant requirements for illustrative bachelor/studio units (single persons) and three-bedroom units (families) are presented in this section.

At the average market rent benchmark, bachelor/studio units can be developed with grant levels ranging from $18,000 (Quebec City) to $47,000 (Regina). At this rent benchmark, it is possible to build bachelor/studio units within the maximum grant level of $50,000 in all communities.

The situation for three-bedroom units is directly affected by the higher cost of these units. At the average market rent target, the maximum grant level of $50,000 is insufficient in 8 of the 14 cities (Calgary, Edmonton, Fredericton, Prince George, Quebec City, Regina, Saskatoon, and Sudbury) profiled. When a lower rent target is set, based on 30% of minimum wage, the grant requirements increase and exceed the maximum of $50,000 for the bachelor/studio units in 10 of 14 the cities (Calgary, Edmonton, Fredericton, Halifax, Ottawa, Quebec City, Regina, Saskatoon, Toronto, and Vancouver). At the 30% of minimum wage affordability target, the $50,000 maximum is not sufficient for three-bedroom units in all 14 cities. Grant equity in excess of $80,000 per unit is required for these family-sized units to ensure that rents are affordable to families earning minimum wage.

Since small bachelor/studio units require less grant money to build, there may be a systematic program bias against funding the larger family units typically required by non-reserve Aboriginal households in the current federal, provincial, and territorial framework process. There needs to be an explicit policy to address this potential bias and to prescribe a level of funding for family units. Overall, it is concluded that the current federal, provincial, and territorial program criteria (average market rent and a maximum $50,000 cost-shared grant) are insufficient to support the production of rental units affordable to low-income, working Aboriginal households. A more realistic average amount is in the order of $70,000–$75,000.

Discussion

Affirmative Budget Allocation for Non-Reserve Aboriginal Housing

We believe that, in the short term, the current federal budget commitment, with co-operation from the provinces and territories, is sufficient to eliminate severe rent burden (>50%) among the off-reserve Aboriginal population over the coming decade. An estimated 71% of the Aboriginal population lives off-reserve, which comprises 2.4% of the Canadian population. Based on the non-reserve population share alone, a minimum 2.4% of the total housing budget should be allocated to Aboriginals living in urban and rural areas. NAHA/ANHA believes that, as part of the federal government's broader initiative to stimulate construction of new rental units, it would be effective to include a specific allocation in the budget to recognize the higher incidence of need among the non-reserve Aboriginal population, as well as the higher subsidy requirements necessary to meet the housing demands of this population. An allocation of 7.5% of the current federal capital budget ($1 billion) would provide $75 million (with matched cost sharing from provincial and territorial governments) that could facilitate the construction of 2,200 units annually. NAHA/ANHA believes this reflects a realistic goal to eliminate fully the problem of severe rent burden (spending more than 50% of household income) among non-reserve Aboriginal households (total 22,000) over the next decade.

Enhancing the National Strategy

The proposed affirmative budget allocation approach to create new affordable rental housing allocations is only the first phase of a national non-reserve housing strategy. The persistently high rates of homelessness and housing in need of major repair are unacceptable. While a target of the action plan is the elimination of severe rent burdens in excess of 50%, NAHA/ANHA has also emphasized that a rent burden of 30% or more of household income is problematic since it exceeds Canadian norms. NAHA/ANHA is requesting the federal government, as part of its review of Aboriginal programming in cities and towns, to agree to convene a national roundtable that would bring together federal, provincial, and territorial officials, NAHA/ANHA, First Nations, Métis, and Inuit national representatives, and the Federation of Canadian Municipalities. The roundtable process should examine specific initiatives to reduce rent burdens in excess of 30% through increased budget allocations for new housing and acceptable forms of rental assistance.

The federal government should also look at targeted rental repair assistance to bring the housing conditions of Aboriginal-occupied rental units in line with the standards of the non-Aboriginal rental population. NAHA/ANHA is also calling upon the federal government to ensure that future homelessness funding is based upon acceptable, Aboriginal, community-based plans and delivery networks, and that specific targets be mandated within the existing spending envelopes under both the Urban Aboriginal Strategy and the Supporting Community Partnerships Initiative.

Recommendations

NAHA/ANHA is recommending a six-point agenda for action to address the poor housing conditions in which a significant proportion of Canada's non-reserve Aboriginal population live. It is an agenda that will require the co-operation of all levels of government and the Aboriginal community.

1. **Setting the framework**: NAHA/ANHA's overview of housing need and cost of remedies, along with its guiding principles, provide the basis for developing an affordable rental housing development framework.

2. **Fixing existing programs**: All levels of government must work together to fix the flawed federal/provincial/territorial affordable rental housing framework agreement.

3. **Developing a consultative framework**: NAHA/ANHA is calling upon the federal government to take the lead in the development of a consultative framework on future housing policy with NAHA/ANHA, First Nations, Métis, and Inuit representatives. We will urge the federal government to invite provincial and territorial participation, as well as representation from cities and towns.

4. **Protecting the existing portfolio**: Canada's 11,000 existing Aboriginal housing units and nearly 9,000 rural and native housing units must be protected for future generations. The federal government has the responsibility of communicating standards and expectations to its provincial and territorial partners on the future management and operation funding to ensure that the small but significant portfolio continues to meet the needs of Aboriginal households.

5. **Recognizing aboriginal housing as a cornerstone to sustainable communities**: Increasingly, the future of our people is tied to the future of Canada's cities and towns. All levels of government must recognize that sustainable Aboriginal communities are built on a foundation of safe, affordable, and culturally appropriate housing.

6. **Measuring success**: There must be an accountability framework to measure success in achieving a national non-reserve Aboriginal housing strategy. NAHA/ANHA, working with its partners, will seek public participation in this process.

Endnotes

1   The Board of Directors gratefully acknowledges the financial support of the Queen's Privy Council Office and the Office of the Interlocutor for Metis and Non-Status Indians.

2   In this chapter the CMHC definition of Aboriginal households has been used. An Aboriginal household is defined as: 1) any single-family household where at least one spouse, common-law partner, or lone parent is considered part of the Aboriginal identity population; 2) at least 50% of the household members are considered to be part of the Aboriginal identity population; 3) any multiple-family household where at least one of the families in the household is an Aboriginal household (as defined above); or 4) any non-family household where at least 50% of the household members are considered to be part of the Aboriginal identity population.

3   The measure of 30% is a threshold that is widely used to define affordability. It is the basis for the CMHC affordability measure in its core need model and subsidy payments in most social housing programs across Canada.

4   This is self-reported data based on a set of criteria described in the census questionnaire. Dwellings are identified by the occupant to be either not in need of repair, in need of minor repair, or in need of major repair (major repair relates to defined structural, electrical, and plumbing deficiencies).

15

A New Open Model Approach to Projecting Aboriginal Populations

Stewart Clatworthy, Mary Jane Norris, and Éric Guimond

Introduction

Changes in the size, composition, and geographic distribution of populations can have a substantial impact on the demand for a wide range of goods and services. Ways of understanding and projecting demographic changes among Canada's Aboriginal populations are critical to the development of sound social and economic policies, as well as to the design, financing, and delivery of many programs and services to Aboriginal populations and communities. Population projections not only provide critical inputs to budgeting and to policy and program development, but may also provide important information for negotiations concerning Aboriginal self-government, land claims, and treaty entitlements.

Methods used to project numbers for Canada's Aboriginal populations have evolved considerably over the course of the past 30 years. This evolution has resulted, in large part, from the recognition that factors other than the traditional demographic components of fertility, mortality, and migration also play significant (and, in some contexts, the most important) roles in shaping Aboriginal population growth and change. These other factors, which include legislation, parenting patterns, the transfer of legal entitlement and/or Aboriginal identity from one generation to the next, and ethnic mobility, present considerable challenges to the development of Aboriginal population projections. This paper discusses the nature of these factors and their implications for the development of Aboriginal population projections.

This paper is structured into four sections. Section 2 provides a brief discussion of the traditional or "closed" population projection model, its implied assumptions, and its limitations within the context of projecting Aboriginal populations. Section 3 identifies the structure and components of an alternative projection model, which incorporates the main features of an "open" population and illustrates how this type of model has be applied within the context of projecting the Registered Indian population. Section 4 extends the discussion to include additional issues and challenges which arise within the context of projecting other Aboriginal population groups. A final section looks at some of the existing gaps in demographic research, which need to be addressed in order to advance the development of more appropriate Aboriginal population projection methodologies.

The Traditional "Closed" Population Projection Model

Until recently, population projections of Canada's Aboriginal Peoples have been constructed within the context of the traditional "closed" population model. The basic form of this model explicitly incorporates five factors depicted in equation 1:

$$P_{l,t+i} = P_{l,t} + B_{l,i} - D_{l,i} + NMI_{l,i}, \quad [1]$$

where $P_{l,t+i}$ refers to the population in area l at time $t+i$, Pl,t refers to the baseline population in location l at time t, Bl,i refers to the number of births to females in location l during the time interval i, Dl,i refers to the number of deaths in location l during the time interval i, and NMl,i refers to the number of net migrants to/ from location l during the time interval i. The baseline population, deaths, and net migration parameters included in the model are configured for both age and gender groups.

The traditional closed population model implicitly assumes that:

- All survivors remain members of the population
- All descendants born to females become members of the population
- No one from outside the population can become a member of the population

Canada's Aboriginal populations display many attributes that are inconsistent with the implied assumptions of the closed population model. First and foremost is the fact that Canada's Aboriginal populations are defined not only on the basis of descent (i.e., ethnic origins) but according to other factors, such as legislation and self-identification (or ethnic affiliation).

Clatworthy (2003) has discussed how legislative amendments introduced by the 1985 *Indian Act* (Bill C-31) created the opportunity for many individuals and their children to reacquire Indian registration. The provisions in Bill C-31 have resulted in the transfer of large numbers of individuals into the registered Indian population from other Aboriginal subgroups, most notably from the non-registered Indian population. As Clatworthy (2001) has also noted, the process of reinstatement and registration under Bill C-31 is far from complete, and further additions to the population are expected to occur over the course of the next two decades. The assumptions of the traditional model that no one can enter the population except through birth to a female member of the population, or leave the population except through death, are clearly inconsistent with recent evidence.

The 1985 *Indian Act* also introduced a new set of inheritance rules governing entitlement to Indian registration for all children born to a registered Indian after April 16, 1985. The new rules, which are contained in Section 6 of the 1985 *Indian Act*, provide for registration under one of two sub-sections:

- ***Section 6(1)***, where both of the individual's parents are (or are entitled to be) registered

- *Section 6(2)*, where one of the individual's parents is (or is entitled to be) registered under Section 6(1) and the other parent is not registered

As discussed more fully later in this paper, one of the implications of these rules is that parenting patterns are now a central factor in determining whether descendant children qualify for Indian registration. Exogamous parenting, by either males or females, will result in children who qualify for registration in situations where the Indian parent is registered under Section 6(1). In cases where an Indian parent is registered under Section 6(2), exogamous parenting will result in children who lack entitlement to Indian registration. Given this situation, the contribution of fertility to the growth of the registered Indian population cannot be captured without addressing the parenting patterns and fertility attributes of both males and females.

It is clear from the above discussion that the traditional model is inappropriate for projecting the registered Indian population. For many of the same reasons, the traditional model is also severely limited in its ability to project accurately the populations of other Aboriginal subgroups. This is the case especially with respect to Aboriginal populations that are defined on the basis of identity or self-declared affiliation.

Recent research by Guimond (1999) on the subject of ethnic mobility addresses some of the main issues in this regard. Guimond distinguishes between two types of ethnic mobility: inter-generational and intra-generational. With respect to the former, he notes: "Ethnic mobility can occur when children's identity is first identified. Parents and children do not necessarily have the same ethnic affiliation, more especially if the mother and father do not belong to the same ethnic group." Guimond's research has also identified exogamous parenting to be common among all Aboriginal groups. As such, the interplay of parenting patterns, male and female fertility, and the transfer of identity to descendant children constitutes a critical dimension of population changes among all Aboriginal groups. With respect to the latter type of ethnic mobility, Guimond notes, "Ethnic mobility may also result from a change in individuals' ethnic affiliation between two points in time." In his analysis of the demographic growth of Aboriginal populations from 1986 to 1996, Guimond clearly demonstrates that a substantial portion of Aboriginal population growth can only be accounted for by changes in how individuals reported their identity. His work also suggests that intra-generational ethnic mobility during this period involved both individuals who shifted identity from one Aboriginal group to another and individuals who shifted identity from non-Aboriginal to Aboriginal. Guimond concludes that this latter dimension of intra-generational mobility (i.e., non-Aboriginal to Aboriginal) has been responsible for much of the pronounced growth in the Aboriginal identity population as reported by the Census of Canada over the course of the period from 1986 to 1996.

An "Open" Population Projection Model

In light of the above discussion, the traditional closed population model can no longer be viewed as applicable when projecting the populations of any of the Aboriginal subgroups. For more than a decade, research has been underway to recast Aboriginal population projections using an "open" population model. The shift to an open population model involves the explicit recognition of additional factors that affect population and change. The general model of interest within the context of Canada's Aboriginal populations is depicted in equation 2:

$$P_{j,t+i} = P_{j,t} + \alpha B_{j,i} - D_{j,i} + NM_{j,i} + EIM_{j,i} + EOM_{j,i} \cdot \quad [2]$$

The open model contains three new factors in addition to those shown in the closed population model:

- α, which refers to a set of rules or assumptions that govern how population membership (e.g., identity or registration entitlement) is transferred to or inherited by descendant children, $B_{j,i}$, born in location j during the time interval i
- $EIM_{j,i}$, which refers to the number of individuals who transfer into the population (i.e., ethnic in-migrants) of location j during the time interval i
- $EOM_{j,i}$, which refers to the number of individuals who transfer out of the population (i.e., ethnic out-migrants) of location j during the time interval i

The conceptual shift to an open population perspective introduces many new complexities and challenges to the development of Aboriginal population projections.

An Open Model for the Registered Indian Population

Some additional features of the open population model depicted above can be illustrated within the context of a specific variant of the model configured for the registered Indian population. As in the discussion in section 2, the registered Indian population can be viewed as an open population that is circumscribed or defined by legislation. Individuals can enter or be added to the population over time through the registration and reinstatement provisions of the 1985 *Indian Act* (Bill C-31). This process can be viewed as the equivalent of ethnic in-migration, or the $EIM_{j,i}$ term of the general model. The set of rules contained in Section 6 of the 1985 *Indian Act* determines which descendants are entitled to registration based on the registration attributes of their parents. In concert with the parenting patterns and fertility attributes of males and females, this set of rules constitutes the $\alpha B_{j,i}$ term of the general model. Unlike previous versions of the *Indian Act*, where individuals could lose registration through exogamous marriage or other events, registration under the 1985 *Indian Act* is permanent and cannot be lost. As such, there is no requirement for the ethnic out-migration ($EOM_{j,i}$) term to be included in the registered Indian model.

Table 15.1: Parenting Combinations and Consequences for Indian Registration Entitlement Under Section 6 of the 1985 Indian Act

Parent's Entitlement	Parent's Entitlement	Child's Entitlement
Section 6(1)	Section 6(1)	Section 6(1)
Section 6(1)	Section 6(2)	Section 6(1)
Section 6(1)	Not Entitled	Section 6(2)
Section 6(2)	Section 6(2)	Section 6(1)
Section 6(2)	Not Entitled	Not Entitled
Not Entitled	Not Entitled	Not Entitled

The applicable projection model within the context of the registered Indian population is summarized in equation 3:

$$P_{j,t+i} = P_{j,t} + \alpha\, B_{j,i} - D_{j,i} + NM_{j,i} + EIM_{j,i} . \quad [3]$$

Several prior projections of the registered Indian population contained procedures developed for estimating and incorporating future additions to the population associated with the registration and reinstatement provisions of the 1985 *Indian Act* (Nault et al. 1993; Loh 1995; Norris et al. 1996; Clatworthy 2001). These projections reveal that new Bill C-31 registrations and reinstatements are declining, and that this component of registered Indian population growth is expected to continue declining in importance over the course of the next two decades. As this aspect of the registered Indian model has been discussed at length elsewhere, the primary focus of this study will now shift to the more complex issue of configuring the registered Indian model to incorporate the interplay of parenting patterns, fertility, and the inheritance rules governing entitlement to Indian registration (i.e., the $\alpha B_{j,i}$ term of the projection model).

Parenting Patterns and Entitlement to Indian Registration

As discussed above, Section 6 of the 1985 *Indian Act* distinguishes between two classes of registered Indians: Section 6(1) and Section 6(2). As noted by Clatworthy and Smith (1992), these two classes differ in their ability to pass an entitlement to Indian registration to their children. The range of parenting combinations, and their consequences for descendants in terms of Section 6 registration entitlement, are summarized in **Table 15.1**. As the table shows, those registered under Section 6(1) have the ability to pass entitlement to Indian registration to all of their offspring, regardless of the registration status of their parenting partner. Those registered under Section 6(2) have the ability to pass entitlement to Indian registration to offspring only if their parenting partner is also entitled to Indian registration. Exogamous parenting by those registered under Section 6(2) results in descendant children who lack entitlement to Indian registration. Children of this third population group, non-registered descendants, will qualify for registration only if their other parent is registered under Section 6(1).

The differential consequences of exogamous parenting among the population subgroups discussed above implies the need for registered Indian population projection models to distinguish the population not only on the basis of age and gender, but by Section 6 registry entitlement (i.e., Section 6(1), Section 6(2), and not entitled).

Measuring Parenting Patterns and Rates of Exogamous Parenting

The rules governing the transfer of Indian registration entitlement to descendants are gender neutral, meaning that they apply in the same fashion to both male and female parents. This aspect of the rules is important, as it means that the model must also explicitly incorporate the parenting and fertility patterns of both gender groups.

Measures of the parenting patterns of registered Indian males and females can be obtained from data contained on the Indian Register, which links parents and their children. The register, however, does not contain a complete record of all children born to registered Indian parents: specifically, children born to a parent registered under Section 6(2) and whose other parent is not registered do not qualify for Indian registration and are not contained in the register. At the present time, estimates of the parenting patterns of the registered Indian population rely upon data for children who have at least one parent registered under Section 6(1). Apart from any late reporting of births, the Indian Register contains a complete record of these children and the registry status of both of their parents.

Within the context of developing registered Indian population projections, the critical aspect of parenting patterns relates to exogamous parenting. Clatworthy (2001) has recently estimated gender-specific rates of exogamous parenting in the form of conditional probabilities. For example, in the case of females, the exogamous parenting rate is expressed as the likelihood that a child born to a registered Indian female has a non-registered father. For purposes of calculating the rates, he distinguishes among three groups of births:

- Female exogamous births (x), or children born to a registered Indian female and non-registered male
- Male exogamous births (y), or children born to a registered Indian male and non-registered female
- Endogamous births (z), or children born to two registered Indian parents

Given these groups, exogamous parenting rates are calculated as follows:

- For females $\qquad x / (x + z)$
- For males $\qquad y / (y + z)$
- For both gender groups combined $\qquad (x + y) / (x + y + z)$

Figure 15.1: Estimated Rate of Exogamous Parenting by Gender and Location, Registered Indian Population, Canada, 1985-1999

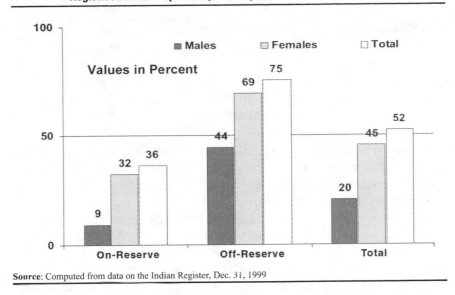

Source: Computed from data on the Indian Register, Dec. 31, 1999

Using this procedure, Clatworthy estimates the combined rate of exogamous parenting among registered Indians during the 1985 to 1999 time period, at the national level, to be about 52%. As illustrated in **Figure 15.1**, rates of exogamous parenting among registered Indians vary between gender groups and by on-off-reserve residence and are substantially higher among females than males and among both gender groups living off-reserve, as opposed to on-reserve. In light of the inheritance rules contained in the 1985 *Indian Act*, the high rates of exogamous parenting have substantial implications for any future population entitled to Indian registration. Over time, persistent exogamous parenting will result in the loss of registration entitlement for a growing proportion of the descendants of the registered Indian population.

Implications for Measuring Fertility

The *gender neutral* aspect of the inheritance rules also has implications for fertility measurements, and the manner in which this factor is included in the model. The general problem arises in situations involving exogamous parenting. Some aspects of the problem may be highlighted by focusing more closely on the consequences for registration entitlement among descendants of various parenting patterns associated with males and females registered under Section 6(1) and 6(2) of the 1985 *Indian Act*. **Table 15.2** (page 250) isolates the pertinent parenting patterns.

Table 15.2: Parenting Combinations by Gender and Registration Entitlement Group and Consequences for Indian Registration Entitlement Under Section 6 of the 1985 Indian Act

Father's Entitlement	Mother's Entitlement	Child's Entitlement
Section 6(1)	Not registered (A)	Section 6 (2) (1)
Section 6 (2)	Not registered (B)	Not Entitled (2)
Not registered	Section 6 (1) (C)	Section 6 (2) (3)
Not registered	Section 6 (2) (D)	Not Entitled (4)
Section 6 (1) or 6 (2)	Section 6 (1) or 6 (2) (E)	Section 6 (1) (5)

Within the context of the registered Indian population, conventional measures of female fertility, such as the total fertility rate (TFR), are normally derived from data collected by the Canadian census concerning the number of children ever born to registered Indian females, or data in the Indian Register concerning child/woman ratios. Within the content of the parenting patterns displayed in **Table 15.2**, the "children ever born" method captures only the fertility attributes of a portion of the mothers who produce children entitled to Indian registration (i.e., mothers in groups C, D, and E). All children born through the exogamous parenting of Indian males and non-registered females (i.e., children in groups 1 and 2) are excluded in spite of the fact that some of these children (i.e., group 1) are entitled to Indian registration. More detailed research on registered Indian fertility by Clatworthy (1994), and on the fertility of other Aboriginal groups by Robitaille and Guimond (2003), demonstrate that the conventional measures of female-only fertility underestimate the true fertility of the population by failing to capture the male contribution to the group's fertility, which arises through exogamous parenting.

Estimating conventional measures of registered Indian fertility using Indian Register data on child/woman ratios is more problematic. Using this method, three groups of children would be included in the numerator of the ratio (groups 1, 3, and 5). The denominator of the ratio would include all registered women (i.e., mothers in groups C, D, and E, as well as all other registered Indian women who have not had children during the reference period). In light of the information provided in **Table 15.2**, the child/woman ratio based on the register data contains several sources of error, as summarized below:

- The numerator of the ratio includes some children who are not born to registered females (i.e., children in group 1) and excludes some children who are born to registered females (i.e., children in group 4).

- The denominator of the ratio excludes some mothers who have given birth to children who are entitled to registration (i.e., mothers in group A).

- Mothers (group B) and children (group 2) associated with exogamous

Figure 15.2: Estimated Births Per 1,000 Population by Age, Gender, and Location, Registered Indians, 1999

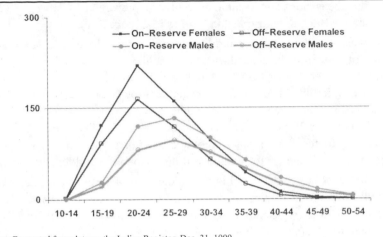

Source: Computed from data on the Indian Register, Dec. 31, 1999

parenting by males registered under Section 6(2) are excluded entirely from the ratio.

These inconsistencies between the numerator (i.e., the population of children) and denominator (i.e., the population of women) of the child/woman ratio imply that this method cannot provide unbiased measures either of the fertility of Indian females or the fertility attributes of the total registered Indian population.

Problems associated with conventional measures of fertility flow largely from the exogamous parenting of registered Indian males and non-registered females, which has the effect of producing an independent male component to the total fertility of the population group. Recent research by Clatworthy (2001) provides some estimates of the scale of the male dimension of registered Indian fertility. Based on data for the time period 1985–1999, Clatworthy estimates that roughly 24,000 (or more than 10%) of the 228,000 children added to the register have resulted from exogamous parenting between Indian males and non-Indian females. Among the population residing off-reserve in some provinces/regions, children with registered Indian fathers and non-registered mothers account for up to 36% of all children registered during the period. Clearly, the scale of the independent contribution of males to total fertility implies the need for registered Indian projections to address this dimension of fertility explicitly.

Estimating Gender-specific Fertility Rates

Estimates of age- and gender-specific fertility rates for registered Indians can be calculated from the data on the Indian Register that links children to parents. As in the case of estimating exogamous parenting rates, the register data support direct fertility estimates only for the population registered under Section 6(1). Lacking complete data for those registered under Section 6(2), rates for this group are assumed (for purposes of the projections) to be the same as those registered under Section 6(1), who are living in the same location. Estimates of registered Indian fertility by age, gender, and location of residence, prepared by Clatworthy (2001) using data for 1999, are illustrated in **Figure 15.2** (page 251).

As revealed in the figure, the fertility rates of both males and females vary by location of residence. In general, rates among the population living on-reserve are about 30–40% higher than those of the population off-reserve. Pronounced differences in fertility also exist between gender groups, both on- and off-reserve. Female fertility rates are significantly higher compared to those of males for all age cohorts under 30 years. For older cohorts, male fertility rates exceed those of females. The fertility estimates presented in **Figure 15.2** can be employed in projections to estimate the total number of births to males and females annually.

The Indian Register data used in the calculation of fertility rates can also be manipulated to provide estimates of the total fertility rate of females and males. In 1999, the TFR for registered Indian females was estimated to be about 3.2 births per woman on-reserve, and about 2.1 births per woman off-reserve. Comparable rates estimated for registered Indian males were 2.5 births per man on-reserve, and 1.7 births per man off-reserve.

Creating an Operational Projection Model

Having identified and, where applicable, provided measures of the key components of the model's $\alpha \mathbf{B}_{j,i}$ term (i.e., the inheritance rules, male and female rates of exogamous parenting, and male and female rates of fertility), how can these components be made operational in the projection model?

The Three-parameter Approach

A recent model developed for projecting the registered Indian population by Clatworthy (2001) incorporates these three sets of factors into the projection model using a two-stage process. In addition to location of residence, the model distinguishes members of the population by age (five-year age cohorts), gender and Section 6 registration status (i.e., Section 6(1), Section 6(2), and non-entitled descendants). In the initial stage, three sets of parameters—male and female fertility rates and the rate of exogamous parenting by females—are used to generate the total number of births to males and females and the number of exogamous births generated by females. Given these estimates, the number of endogamous births to males and females, and the number of exogamous births to males, can be calculated as a residual. In a second stage, births associated with endogamous and exogamous parenting are assigned to registration subgroups by applying the logic of inheritance rules contained in Section 6 of the 1985 *Indian Act*. The specific steps involved in the process are described in **Figure 15.3** (pages 253–254) using, as an example, actual projection data for the on-reserve population in the province of Ontario for the year 2030.

Figure 15.3: Sequence of Steps Involved in Computing and Allocating Births in the Projection Model

Step 1: Compute Total Births by Gender and Registration Group

Apply the male and female fertility rates to the child-bearing population of each registration group to yield the number of births to male and female parents. For the on-reserve population of Ontario in the year 2030, this results in:

	7,384 births to females registered under Section 6(1)
	3,082 births to females registered under Section 6(2)
	243 births to female descendants who are not entitled to registration
	5,915 births to males registered under Section 6(1)
	2,414 births to males registered under Section 6(2)
	157 births to male descendants who are not entitled to registration

Total female births = 10,709
Total male births   = 8,486

Step 2: Apply Rate of Exogamous Parenting for Females to Calculate Exogamous Female Births by Registration Group and Compute Endogamous Births as Residual

Exogamous parenting rate for on-reserve females in Ontario = 25.48

Exogamous births for	Section 6(1) females = 7,384 * .2548 = 1,881
	Section 6(2) females = 3,082 * .2548 = 785
	Non-entitled females = 243 * .2548 = 62

Total exogamous female births = 2,728

Endogamous births for	Section 6(1) females = 7,384 - 1,881 = 5,503
	Section 6(2) females = 3,082 - 785 = 2,297
	Non-entitled females = 243 - 62 = 181

Total endogamous female births = 7,981

Step 3: Set Male Endogamous Births = Female Endogamous Births and Distribute Across Registration Groups According to Proportional Distribution of Total Male Births

Male endogamous births = female endogamous births = 7,981

Registration distribution of male parents:	Section 6(1) = 5,915 / 8,486 = .6970
	Section 6(2) = 2,414 / 8,486 = .2845
	Non-entitled = 157 / 8,486 = .0185

Endogamous births for	Section 6(1) males = 7,981 * .6970 = 5,563
	Section 6(2) males = 7,981 * .2845 = 2,270
	Non-entitled males = 7,981 * .0185 = 148

Step 4: Calculate Exogamous Male Births by Residual

Exogamous births for	Section 6(1) males = 5,915 - 5,563 = 352
	Section 6(2) males = 2,414 - 2,270 = 144
	Non-entitled males = 157 - 148 = 9

Total exogamous male births = 352 + 143 + 9 = 505

Total births =   endogamous births (7,981) +

exogamous female births (2,728) +

exogamous male births (505)   = 11,214

Step 5: Apply Proportions of Endogamous Male Births by Registration Group to Distribution of Endogamous Female Births to Estimate Endogamous Parenting Combinations

Proportion of endogamous male births	Section 6(1) = .6970
	Section 6(2) = .2845
	Non-Entitled = .0185

Distribution of endogamous female births	Section 6(1) = 5,503
	Section 6(2) = 2,297
	Non-Entitled = 181

Endogamous parenting patterns

Male Registration Group	Female Registration Group		
Section 6(1)	Section 6(1)	Section 6(2)	Non-Entitled Descendant
Section 6(2)	5,503 * .6970 = 3,836	2,297 * .6970 = 1,601	181 * .6970 = 126
Non-Entitled Descendant	5,503 * .2845 = 1,566	2,297 * .2845 = 653	181 * .2845 = 51
	5,503 * .0185 = 102	2,297 * .0185 = 42	181 * .0185 = 3

Totals may not sum due to rounding error.

Step 6: Add Endogamous to Exogamous Births to Construct Total Parenting Pattern

Males	Females				
	Section 6(1)	Section 6(2)	Non Entitled Descendant	Exogamous	Total
Section 6(1)	3,836	1,601	126	352	5,915
Section 6(2)	1,566	653	51	144	2,414
Non-Entitled Descendant	102	42	3	9	156
Exogamous	1,881	785	62	—	2,728
Total	7,385	3,081	242	505	11,213

Step 6: Add Endogamous to Exogamous Births to Construct Total Parenting Pattern

Section 6(1) = Births involving two registered parents = 3,836 + 1,601 + 1,566 + 653 = 7,656

Section 6(2) = Births involving Section 6(1) parent and non-registered descendant or exogamous partner = 102 + 1,881 + 126 + 352 = 2,461

Non-Entitled Descendants = Births involving Section 6(2) and non-registered descendants or exogamous partner = 42 + 785 + 51 + 144 + 3 + 9 + 62 = 1,096

Allocate births (i.e. Pop. 0-4 Years) to gender groups, assuming 105 males per 100 females

Section 6(1)		Section 6(2)		Non-Entitled Descendant		Total	
Male	Female	Male	Female	Male	Female	Male	Female
3,921	3,735	1,261	1,200	561	535	5,743	5,470
						Total	11,213

Figure 15.4: Projected Population of Survivors and Descendants by Indian Registration Entitlement, Canada, 1999-2099

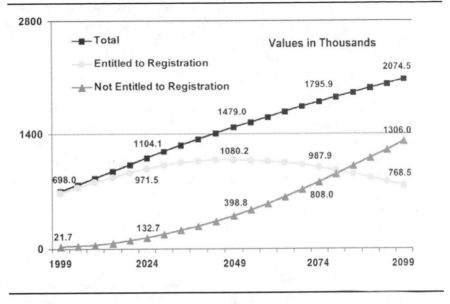

One important feature of the projection model relates to the manner in which exogamous parenting is conceptualized. In this regard, the model views exogamous parenting as parenting between registered Indians or their descendants (regardless of registration status) and individuals who are not registered and are not descended from the registered Indian population. This concept is consistent with the measured rate of exogamous parenting that is currently being captured in the Indian Register data.[1] One of the consequences of exogamous parenting is that it will, over time, generate a growing group of individuals that is not registered but is descended from the registered Indian population. The existence of a growing population of non-registered descendants within First Nations communities, especially reserves, will alter the registration mix of potential partners (mates), and serve to increase the likelihood of parenting between a registered and non-registered descendant. The projection model incorporates the compounding effect of exogamous parenting by viewing all parenting between descendants (regardless of their registration attributes) as endogamous. As the registration mix of the descendant population changes over time to include larger numbers of non-registered individuals, endogamous parenting among descendants will also result in a growing number of offspring who are not entitled to Indian registration.

The model's use of the three parameters (male and female fertility rates and the rate of exogamous parenting by females) for the purpose of generating births also allows it to capture the impact on births that is the result of changes in the assumed rates of exogamous parenting. Clatworthy (1994) and, more recently, Guimond (forthcoming), have examined the relationship between the rate of exogamous parenting and fertility, and concluded that in situations where fertility is the same, populations with higher rates of exogamous parenting will produce larger numbers of children. This can be most simply explained by considering a population group comprised of 100 males and 100 females. For this population, the maximum number of endogamous unions would be 100. This same population, however, could produce 200 exogamous unions. If these unions have the same fertility characteristics, then twice as many children would be expected to result from the population group under conditions of exogamous, as opposed to endogamous, partnering.

The total number of births generated using the three-parameter model is automatically adjusted if the assumed rate of female exogamous parenting is altered. This can be illustrated by changing the assumed rate of exogamous female parenting in the Ontario example provided in **Figure 15.3**. In this example, the assumed rate of exogamous female parenting of 25.48% resulted in 11,214 total births, including 2,728 exogamous female births, 7,981 endogamous births, and 505 exogamous male births. If one repeats the calculations in **Figure 15.3** using an assumed rate of exogamous female parenting of 40%, the total number of births projected by the model increases to 12,770, including 4,284 exogamous female births, 6,425 endogamous births, and 2,061 exogamous male births.[2]

Selected Results from Recent National Level Projections

Recent projections of the registered Indian population at the provincial/regional and national levels have been undertaken using Clatworthy's three-parameter approach. The projections were designed to explore the longer term implications of the 1985 *Indian Act* amendments for the registered Indian population. The projection time frame spans 100 years, or roughly four generations into the future. The projection scenario highlighted in this section is based on assumptions of declining fertility and mortality, modest net migration to reserves declining to zero after 20 years, and declining inflows of new registrants/reinstatements under Bill C-31, reaching zero after 40 years. The projections also explore four scenarios concerning future rates of exogamous parenting, including a stable rate scenario and three scenarios involving increases of 10, 20, and 30%, respectively, in the rate of exogamous parenting. Results presented here derive from the scenario that assumes a gradual rise in the rate of exogamous parenting of 20% over 40 years, and remaining stable thereafter.

Figure 15.4 (page 255) illustrates the projected population of survivors and descendants by entitlement to Indian registration. The total population is expected to continue to increase at a gradually declining rate throughout the entire period, reaching about 2.07 million after 100 years. The population entitled to Indian registration, however, is projected to grow for only about 50 years, reaching about 1.08 million. Over the remaining 50 years of the projection period, the population entitled to Indian registration is projected to fall to about 768,500, a level slightly higher than that estimated in 1999. Significant growth in the population of survivors and descendants who do not qualify for Indian registration is expected to occur throughout the projection period. The non-entitled component of the population is expected to grow from the 1999 level of about 21,700 to nearly 399,000 individuals within 50 years. Within 100 years, non-entitled descendants are projected to number about 1.31 million, and will form a sizable majority of the descendant population.

The projection results also reveal that, within 45 years, children who are entitled to Indian registration will form a minority of all children born to the population. While the impact of the interplay between the inheritance rules and exogamous parenting are clearly substantial in the longer term, a significant impact is also expected in the short term. Clatworthy's results suggest that, during the 1999–2004 period, about 1,780 children annually will be born into the population who lack entitlement to Indian registration. Within 25 years, this number is expected to increase fourfold, to about 7,340 children annually. Roughly 111,500 children born to the population over the next 25 years are projected to lack entitlement to Indian registration.

Implications for Projecting Other Aboriginal Populations

In the discussion earlier, it was noted that the 1985 *Indian Act* amendments influenced not only the growth and composition of the registered Indian population but of other Aboriginal populations as well, as many of those who acquired or reacquired Indian registration are believed to have been members of other Aboriginal subgroups (Norris, Kerr, and Nault 1996).

The projection results presented in the previous section imply the possibility that non-registered descendants of the registered Indian population may flow back into the populations of other Aboriginal subgroups. At this point, research has not been undertaken to establish how non-registered descendants of the registered Indian population identify themselves. There is some evidence from census data concerning child-woman ratios to suggest that the non-registered (i.e., non-status) Indian population may have experienced a significant inflow of non-registered descendants of the registered Indian population since the 1985 *Indian Act* revisions. Estimates of total fertility rates and children ever born (constructed from the Indian Register and the census) rank the fertility of registered Indians significantly higher than that of non-registered Indians. Child/woman ratios from the census suggest the opposite. For example, registered Indian and non-registered Indian TFR estimates for 1991 are 2.8 and 2.0, respectively, while the corresponding child/woman ratios are 445 and 615 children per 1,000 women (Norris, 1997). The higher child/woman ratios calculated for the non-registered Indian population would appear to result from the outflow of non-entitled descendants of registered Indians into the non-registered Indian population. If it is the case that the majority of the non-entitled descendants of the registered Indian population maintain their North American Indian identity, then the non-registered Indian population can be expected to experience a substantial increase in growth—growth that originates within the registered Indian population. It remains uncertain as to what the future identity patterns of non-entitled descendants will be, since flows to other groups including Métis, Inuit, and non-Aboriginal groups, are also possible.

The possibility of flows of descendants from the registered Indian population to other Aboriginal population groups raises a number of difficult questions. If non-entitled descendants identify as non-registered Indians, how can one project the non-registered Indian population without also projecting the registered Indian population at the same time? If some of the non-entitled descendants have a non-registered parent who is Métis or Inuit, are they more likely to identify as Métis or Inuit? If so, is there not also a need to project these population subgroups at the same time? Although specific answers to these questions remain unclear at his point, what is becoming clear is the need to consider the development of concurrent projection approaches.

Summary and Implications for Policy and Further Research

This study has examined a number of issues and challenges related to the projection of future numbers for Canada's Aboriginal populations. The projection model illustrated for the registered Indian population addresses many of these issues and, in doing so, may provide a useful framework for future development. Evidence presented in the study suggests a need for Aboriginal projections to be conducted concurrently and to be constructed in a fashion that recognizes and incorporates population flows among Aboriginal subgroups. A major constraint in this regard relates to our limited knowledge about several key factors affecting Aboriginal population growth. These factors include exogamous parenting, the contribution of males to group fertility and births, parenting patterns between members of different Aboriginal groups, and the consequences of both exogamous and endogamous parenting for the transfer of identity to descendants.

Although a considerable body of research concerning Aboriginal demography has been developed over the past two decades, little of this research has focused on the topics of Aboriginal family composition, marriage, and parenting patterns. Analysis of census data on families may provide some useful information concerning Aboriginal marriage and parenting patterns, the fertility of various marriage arrangements, and on the links between parent and child identity. In the short term, this type of research may provide valuable contributions to the development of more appropriate and accurate Aboriginal population projections. In the longer term, such research may support the construction of a concurrent projection model, which appears to be required.

The research issues raised above, however, relate to only part of the gap in our understanding and knowledge of factors influencing Aboriginal population growth and change. The construction of accurate Aboriginal projections is also dependent upon our ability to gain a better understanding of intra-generational ethnic mobility. While Guimond's (1999, forthcoming) pioneering work has provided some insights into the nature and scale of Aboriginal ethnic mobility, current knowledge of this issue falls far short of that required to support its inclusion in projection models. Clearly, a more concerted research effort is also called for on this important dimension of Aboriginal demographic change.

This is not simply a matter of science or technique. There are serious policy implications. Population projections are used in most planning processes, whether it is forecasting health care needs, educational requirements, housing, community infra-structure, or the many other supports needed by populations. It is safe to say that accurate projections allow for more accurate forecasts of these requirements. This means better utilization of scarce resources, and fewer situations of inadequate provision for social and economic needs.

Governments and non-governmental agencies request population projections more than any other single piece of demographic information (Kerr, Guimond, and Norris 2003). This is particularly true for populations, such as Aboriginal Peoples, where government has expanded responsibilities. Aboriginal population projections have been assessed as being quite limited for sometime (Kerr, Guimond, and Norris 2003), owing to knowledge gaps that this paper has identified concerning several key factors affecting Aboriginal population growth and ethnic mobility. The work presented in this paper goes some way towards improving our ability to develop more appropriate and accurate project populations and, consequently, is more conducive to policy making that is evidence based, relevant, and effective.

Endnotes

1   As the rules contained in Section 6 apply to children born after April 16, 1985, the population of non-entitled descendants that has reached child-bearing age is currently quite small. As such, exogamous parenting rates calculated from the register are capturing parenting between registered Indians and non-registered individuals who have not descended from the registered Indian population.

2   Assumptions concerning lower rates of female exogamous parenting will yield lower numbers of total births. The model illustrated in Figure 15.3, however, is limited in this regard, as it is possible to lower the female exogamous parenting rate to a level that results in a number of endogamous births greater than the total number of births to males. As such, the fertility and exogamous parenting parameters included in the model displayed must satisfy the condition that the total number of births to males is equal to or greater than the number of endogamous births. This condition would not be required if the male exogamous parenting rate (which is lower than the female rate) were used instead of the female rate. In projection situations where the rate of exogamous parenting is assumed to decline over time, the model should be configured using the exogamous parenting rate for whichever gender group has lower rates. Based on Clatworthy's (2001) estimates for 1999, rates of exogamous parenting are lower for males than females both on- and off-reserve in all provinces/regions.

References

Clatworthy, S. 1994. Revised projection scenarios concerning the population implications of Section 6 of the *Indian Act*. Indian and Northern Affairs Canada, Ottawa.

Clatworthy, S. 2001. Re-assessing the population impacts of Bill C-31. Research and Analysis Directorate, Indian and Northern Affairs Canada, Ottawa.

Clatworthy, S. 2003. Impacts of the 1985 amendments to the *Indian Act* on First Nations populations. In *Aboriginal conditions: Research as a foundation for public policy*, ed. Jerry White et al. Vancouver: UBC Press. 63–90.

Clatworthy, S. and A. H. Smith. 1992. Population implications of the 1985 amendments to the *Indian Act*. Assembly of First Nations, Ottawa.

Guimond, É. 1999. Ethnic mobility and the demographic growth of Canada's Aboriginal populations from 1986 to 1996, Statistics Canada, Cat. #91-209-XPE.

Guimond, É. Forthcoming. Mobilité ethnique et fécondité des groupes autochtones du Canada : aspects théoriques et évolution récente (1981–1996). PhD thesis, Université de Montréal.

Kerr, D., Éric Guimond, and Mary Jane Norris. 2003. Perils and pitfalls in Aboriginal demography: Lessons learned from the RCAP projections. In *Aboriginal conditions: Research as a foundation for public policy*, ed. Jerry White et al. Vancouver: UBC Press. 39–62.

Loh, S. 1990. Population projections of registered Indians, 1986–2011. Report prepared by Population Projections Section, Demography Division, Statistics Canada for Indian and Northern Affairs Canada (DIAND).

Loh, S. 1995. Projections of Canada's population with Aboriginal ancestry, 1991–2016. Revised version of report prepared earlier by F. Nault and E. Jenkins. Prepared by Population Projections Section, Demography Division for Employment Equity Data Program, Housing, Family and Social Statistics Division, Statistics Canada.

Loh, S., R.B.P. Verma, E. Ng, M. J. Norris, M.V. George, and J. Perreault. 1998. Population projections of registered Indians, 1996–2021. Report prepared by Population Projections Section, Demography Division, Statistics Canada for Indian and Northern Affairs Canada (DIAND).

Nault, F., J. Chen, M.V. George, and M.J. Norris. 1993. Population projections of registered Indians, 1991–2016. Report prepared by the Population Projections Section, Demography Division, Statistics Canada for Indian and Northern Affairs Canada (DIAND).

Norris, M.J., D. Kerr, and F. Nault. 1996. Summary report on projections of the population with Aboriginal identity, Canada, 1991–2016. Prepared by Population Projections Section, Demography Division, Statistics Canada, for the Royal Commission on Aboriginal Peoples, Canada Mortgage and Housing Corporation.

Norris, M.J. 1997. Impacts of legislative and demographic components in projecting the size, structure and composition of Aboriginal populations in Canada. Paper prepared for the Session on Population Estimates and Projections, Canadian Population Society Annual Meeting, 1997 Congress of the Social Sciences.

Norris, M.J. 2000. Aboriginal peoples in Canada: Demographic and linguistic perspectives. In *Visions of the heart: Canadian Aboriginal Issues*, ed. D. Long and O. P. Dickason. 2nd ed. Toronto: Harcourt Brace.

Norris, M.J, É. Guimond, and P. Saunders. 100 years of demography: An analysis within the Canadian context. Paper prepared for the Session on Aboriginal Demography, Canadian Population Society Annual Meeting, 2000 Congress of the Social Sciences, University of Alberta, Edmonton.

Norris, M.J., É. Guimond, and D. Beavon. 2001. Growth of aboriginal population in urban areas: Components and implications. Presentation, Research and Analysis Directorate, Indian and Northern Affairs, Canada.

Perreault, J., L. Paquette, and M.V. George. 1985. Population projections of registered Indians, 1982–1996. Report prepared by the Population Projections Section, Demography Division, Statistics Canada for Indian and Northern Affairs Canada.

Robitaille, N. and E. Guimond. 2003. "La reproduction des populations autochtones du Canada: exogamie, fécondité et mobilité ethnique," *Cahiers québécois de démographie*, 32(2): 295-314.

16

Spatial Residential Patterns of Aboriginals and their Socio-economic Integration in Selected Canadian Cities

T.R. Balakrishnan and Rozzet Jurdi

Introduction

In recent years, the Aboriginal population of Canada has been increasing at a faster rate than the non-Aboriginal population. Between 1996 and 2001, the non-Aboriginal population of Canada increased by 8.58%, while the Aboriginal population increased by 19.98%. About 35.9% of the Aboriginal population lives in the 23 census metropolitan areas (CMAs) of Canada, a proportion that has not changed since 1996 (Statistics Canada 2003). Though this is lower than the 62.5% of non-Aboriginal Canadians who live in metropolitan areas, it is clear that Aboriginal people have a large presence in Canadian urban areas. This situation is likely to continue, and, in fact, the urban Aboriginal population can even be expected to increase (Peters 2000).

A notable feature of the growth of the metropolitan Aboriginal population is its unevenness across the country. Some smaller metropolitan areas in Quebec, such as Sherbrooke, Chicoutimi, and Trois-Rivières, experienced negative growth, and even Montreal experienced lower-than-average population growth of Aboriginals (**Table 16.1** – page 264). The two largest CMAs (Toronto and Vancouver) also exhibited below-average growth at around 11% during the last decade. In comparison, some metropolitan areas in southwestern Ontario and in the western provinces showed greater than average Aboriginal population growth. Kitchener, Windsor, and Calgary each showed increases of more than 40% over the last ten years. The three metropolitan areas with the highest proportional populations of Aboriginal origin (about 10%) are Winnipeg, Regina, and Saskatoon. They did not show greater-than-average growth in their Aboriginal populations. Evidently, the Aboriginal population of Canada is redistributing according to changing migration patterns. The causes for this redistribution could be many, such as local economic conditions, the proximity of reserves to metropolitan areas, and the dynamics of on-reserve/off-reserve living conditions in the different provinces.

Our primary interest in this study is not so much the broader spatial patterns of the Aboriginal population, but rather their patterns within metropolitan areas at the small area level. Aboriginals in Canada have their distinct cultures and

Table 16.1. Aboriginal population in Canada's major metropolitan areas, 1996-2001

Census Metropolitan Areas	1996	2001	Percent change
Canada (total)	27296859	29639035	8.58
Aboriginal (total)	1101955	1319890	19.78
Calgary	23850	33735	41.45
Chicoutimi	2535	2110	-16.77
Edmonton	44130	55040	24.72
Halifax	7795	10870	39.45
Hamilton	10450	12865	23.11
Kitchener	5785	8310	43.65
London	7710	9865	27.95
Montreal	43675	49315	12.91
Oshawa	5705	7630	33.74
Ottawa	29415	33535	14.01
Québec	8100	10045	24.01
Regina	14570	16750	14.96
Saint John	2320	3155	35.99
Saskatoon	18160	21975	21.01
Sherbrooke	2255	2105	-6.65
St. Catherines	8245	8845	7.28
St. John	2530	3170	25.30
Toronto	39380	44205	12.25
Trois Riveres	2350	1910	-18.72
Vancouver	46805	52330	11.80
Victoria	10860	13150	21.09
Windsor	6435	9495	47.55
Winnipeg	52525	62875	19.70

Source: 2001 Census of Canada

languages. They have also been disadvantaged in their socio-economic development. New immigrants, especially those who are visible minorities, are to some
extent similar to the Aboriginals in that they also have their own culture and
language and are usually disadvantaged in their socio-economic resources. These
differences in culture and language from the societies of Canadians with western
European origins give rise to ethnic neighbourhoods and distinctive settlement
patterns observable among some ethnic groups. One can expect to see residential segregation of the Aboriginal populations in Canadian cities for a number of
reasons. Most of the Aboriginal population—because of lower incomes—may be
forced to settle in the poorer areas of the city, where the real estate prices and rents
are relatively low. Since the poorer areas are often found in the centre of cities, we
find a greater concentration of Aboriginals in the city core areas.

Apart from Aboriginals often being in the lower socio-economic classes, their greater social distance from the white European groups may also increase residential segregation of the Aboriginal population. Social distance is a measure of cultural affinity with another group. Greater social distance is often reflected in higher levels of residential segregation. In fact, many studies have found a parallel between social distance and residential segregation (Balakrishnan 1982; Lieberson and Waters 1988; Kalbach 1990). Aboriginal populations may also be concentrated for voluntary reasons. They may want to reside in close proximity to other Aboriginals so that social interaction can be maximized and they can better maintain their culture and values. The greater their self-identity, the more they can be expected to be residentially segregated from other groups.

The case of Aboriginal peoples in Canada is unique; they are different from recent immigrant groups. Minority groups such as the Chinese, South Asians, or members of the Caribbean or black community often have to go through various stages of acculturation (e.g., language acquisition, learning of new occupational skills, etc.) after immigrating to a new country. Living in a neighbourhood with a high number of people with a similar ethnic background may give them certain advantages in their integration, though it may also be argued that it may increase their isolation from the wider society, and thus have negative effects as far as integration is concerned (Hou and Picot 2004). In contrast, Aboriginal peoples have never been newcomers as they are the original people of Canada, and are well aware of mainstream Canadian culture, though they may often choose not to engage with it. They do not face the same culture shock as immigrants to Canada. They do, however, share the effects of discrimination and prejudice experienced by visible minorities in general.

In the case of immigrant groups, the degree of residential segregation decreases with the duration of stay in Canada, and in later generations, as they increase their social mobility (Balakrishnan 2003). For these groups, segregation levels are high due to the high rate of immigration but can be expected to decrease with time. Studies have shown that segregation for visible minority groups, such as the Chinese and South Asian communities, is much less in the areas of the cities where the socio-economic status of the residents is relatively high as measured by their income, education, and occupation, implying that with social mobility, segregation decreases (Balakrishnan and Hou 1999). This is not the case with the Aboriginal populations to date. The levels of segregation for Aboriginal peoples show no sign of decreasing over time (Maxim et al 2003). This may be because certain visible minorities are able to overcome segregation by increasing their socio-economic achievement, a process that has not been evident for Aboriginal peoples. One should also not expect that the situation of Aboriginals parallels that of the black community in the US. Aboriginals did not go through the experience of slavery which had profound implications for the black community in their ability to choose a place of residence (Massey and Denton 1993).

Objectives

The objective of this study is to examine the spatial residential patterns of Aboriginal peoples in the 23 census metropolitan areas of Canada in 2001 to see the validity of the following hypotheses.

- Hypothesis 1: The index of segregation will be positively correlated with the size of the CMA, as well as the size of the Aboriginal population.

Larger cities and a larger Aboriginal population will enable the Aboriginal community to benefit from advantages of size. A minimum threshold size is often necessary to maintain certain specialized institutions, such as ethnic community centres, places of worship, welfare organizations, and speciality stores. From a different perspective, where there is discrimination, large numbers can accentuate the situation as the minority becomes more visible and can be seen as a threat by the majority ethnic group(s).

- Hypothesis 2: The indices of segregation between Aboriginal peoples and the charter groups of British and French will be lower than between Aboriginals and the various visible minority groups, such as the Chinese, South Asians, and the black community, as well as from other European groups.

Aboriginal peoples have lived in Canada since well before the colonization by Europeans, and many generations of Aboriginal people have become quite familiar with the cultures of the major charter groups of the British and French. Though they may be disadvantaged economically and though many live on-reserve, more than half of Aboriginals live in the urban areas of Canada. Many are fluent in one or both of Canada's official languages. Urban Aboriginal people may in fact share a more similar lifestyle with Canadians of French and British origin than with recently arrived visible minorities, such as members of the Chinese, South Asian, or black communities. Therefore, we expect that, in spite of their common experience of facing discrimination and prejudice along with the other visible minorities, they will exhibit less segregation from British and French. Furthermore, because the Aboriginal culture and lifestyle are so different from those of other visible minority groups we might expect that their segregation from these groups will be greater.

- Hypothesis 3: Aboriginals will be concentrated in the poorer areas of cities.

Given the lower socio-economic achievement of Aboriginals, we expect to find this situation.

Data and Methods

The data come from the 2001 census data for the 23 census metropolitan areas of Canada. Census tract data are used to calculate the concentration, segregation, and dissimilarity indices. The Gini index of concentration used here is derived from concentration curves. The vertical axis shows the cumulative percentage of the Aboriginal population while the horizontal axis shows the cumulative percentage of the census tracts arranged in decreasing order of the Aboriginal population. A curve that coincides with the diagonal line indicates that the Aboriginal population is equally distributed among the census tracts, implying no spatial concentration. The farther the curve is from the diagonal, the greater the concentration. The Gini index is the ratio of the area between the curve and the diagonal, to the area of the triangle above the diagonal. Thus the range for the index is from 0 to 1, indicating no concentration or complete concentration.

The index of dissimilarity measures the differential distribution of two groups over a number of areas. It is the sum of either the positive or negative differences between the proportional distributions of two populations. The index ranges from 0 to 1, indicating complete similarity or dissimilarity in the distributions of two groups. The segregation index refers to the index of dissimilarity between an ethnic group and all other ethnic groups.

A socio-economic status index (SES) for each census tract was constructed combining measures for three variables: education, income, and occupation. It was assumed that a combination of three variables indicates SES better than any one taken separately. The three variables were operationalized as follows.

- *Education*: percentage of adults over 25 years of age with a university degree residing in the census tract
- *Income*: median family income in 2000 in the census tract
- *Occupation*: percentage employed in higher-status occupations (namely managerial, professional, and technical occupations) in 2001 in the census tract

The three variables were first standardized to the same overall mean of 50 and standard deviation of 10 in each CMA.

Findings

Population Size and Segregation

Total and Aboriginal populations for the various CMAs are shown in Table 16.2 (page 268) along with the segregation and concentration indices. Correlations between size and segregation indices are modest at best. In cities where there are relatively large numbers (about 9%) of Aboriginal people, such as Winnipeg, Regina, and Saskatoon, the indices are also high, over .300. Smaller CMAs with small Aboriginal populations such as Chicoutimi, Sherbrooke, St John, and Trois-Rivières have lower segregation indices. The three largest metropolitan areas of Canada—Toronto, Montreal, and Vancouver—have large Aboriginal populations of about 50,000. But, as a proportion of the city's population, they are low, for example only 1.0% in Toronto and 1.5% in Montreal. However, the segregation indices in these cities are fairly high, .345 in Toronto, .271 in Montreal,

Table 16.2. Total and Aboriginal population in Canada's major metropolitan areas and indices of segregation and concentration, 2001

Census Metropolitan Area	Total population in CMA	Aboriginal population	Percentage Aboriginal	Segregation index	Concentration index
Calgary	943310	33735	3.6	0.252	0.374
Chicoutimi	153020	2110	1.4	0.163	0.277
Edmonton	927020	55040	5.9	0.263	0.369
Halifax	355945	10870	3.1	0.196	0.349
Hamilton	655060	12865	2.0	0.287	0.412
Kitchener	409765	8310	2.0	0.236	0.368
London	427215	9865	2.3	0.259	0.389
Montreal	3380640	49315	1.5	0.271	0.410
Oshawa	293550	7630	2.6	0.232	0.346
Ottawa	1050755	33535	3.2	0.215	0.354
Québec	673105	10045	1.5	0.276	0.436
Regina	190020	16750	8.8	0.351	0.452
Saint John	121340	3155	2.6	0.251	0.370
Saskatoon	222635	21975	9.9	0.318	0.393
Sherbrooke	150390	2105	1.4	0.257	0.399
St. Catherines	371405	8845	2.4	0.235	0.382
St. John	171105	3170	1.9	0.197	0.392
Toronto	4647955	44205	1.0	0.345	0.497
Trois Riveres	134645	1910	1.4	0.231	0.349
Vancouver	1967480	52330	2.7	0.289	0.428
Victoria	306970	13150	4.3	0.268	0.407
Windsor	304955	9495	3.1	0.189	0.308
Winnipeg	661725	62875	9.5	0.306	0.392

Source: Special tabulations

Correlations between		Pearson
Index of segregation and total population in CMA	....	0.426
Index of segregation and Aboriginal population	....	0.483
Index of concentration and total population in CMA	....	0.562
Index of concentration and Aboriginal population	....	0.363
Indices of segregation and concentration	....	0.854

Table 16.3. Indices of dissimilarity between Aboriginals and other ethnic groups for Canada's major census metropolitan areas, 2001

	British	French	Other Western	Central & East European	Italian	Jewish	South Asian	Chinese	African	Caribbean
Calgary	0.275	0.238	0.271	0.287	0.366	0.562	0.486	0.461	0.339	0.334
Chicoutimi	0.203	0.179	0.257	0.339	0.473	0.974	0.851	0.553	0.666	0.782
Edmonton	0.292	0.248	0.297	0.263	0.344	0.627	0.574	0.459	0.406	0.445
Halifax	0.209	0.193	0.209	0.301	0.306	0.574	0.500	0.508	0.352	0.405
Hamilton	0.226	0.271	0.374	0.304	0.385	0.548	0.496	0.493	0.434	0.351
Kitchener	0.250	0.212	0.284	0.237	0.319	0.480	0.416	0.393	0.344	0.321
London	0.274	0.247	0.296	0.28	0.358	0.499	0.499	0.471	0.377	0.400
Montreal	0.560	0.240	0.378	0.505	0.518	0.832	0.725	0.608	0.546	0.564
Oshawa	0.233	0.183	0.261	0.275	0.326	0.483	0.426	0.445	0.354	0.343
Ottawa	0.350	0.184	0.356	0.368	0.424	0.607	0.521	0.534	0.486	0.421
Québec	0.299	0.281	0.342	0.352	0.405	0.861	0.851	0.639	0.568	0.591
Regina	0.368	0.345	0.356	0.362	0.482	0.526	0.597	0.474	0.499	0.550
Saint John	0.269	0.208	0.288	0.356	0.354	0.552	0.643	0.597	0.400	0.609
Saskatoon	0.331	0.304	0.338	0.298	0.328	0.599	0.656	0.437	0.499	0.487
Sherbrooke	0.326	0.251	0.274	0.286	0.313	0.675	0.697	0.717	0.585	0.434
St. Catherines	0.240	0.214	0.307	0.277	0.338	0.496	0.469	0.440	0.444	0.417
St. John	0.190	0.222	0.306	0.35	0.444	0.616	0.695	0.512	0.647	0.864
Toronto	0.283	0.267	0.301	0.421	0.529	0.749	0.576	0.618	0.505	0.484
Trois Rivieres	0.240	0.207	0.266	0.343	0.417	0.890	0.958	0.783	0.600	0.547
Vancouver	0.284	0.254	0.275	0.268	0.348	0.535	0.544	0.573	0.363	0.392
Victoria	0.266	0.213	0.257	0.264	0.282	0.435	0.478	0.494	0.352	0.389
Windsor	0.211	0.219	0.252	0.267	0.350	0.518	0.466	0.477	0.321	0.412
Winnipeg	0.352	0.321	0.354	0.342	0.418	0.660	0.553	0.468	0.393	0.433

Source: Special tabulations

Less than 100   Less than 500   Less than 1000

and .289 in Vancouver. It appears that the size of the Aboriginal population is more important than the size of the city itself for the magnitude of segregation. The correlation between Aboriginal population and index of segregation is .483. There is only modest support for the hypothesis that city size is positively associated with segregation.

Intergroup Segregation

Indices of dissimilarity between Aboriginals and other ethnic groups are presented in **Table 16.3** (page 269). With almost no exception, the lowest indices are found between Aboriginals and the charter groups of British and French, mostly between .200 and .300. This pattern is evident in every metropolitan area. Even in cities where there are a large proportion of Aboriginals—such as Winnipeg, Saskatoon, and Regina—the indices of dissimilarity from the British and French are lower in comparison to the other ethnic groups. The indices are somewhat higher for the other European groups, and much higher for the visible minority groups. In Toronto and Vancouver, where most of the Canadian Chinese population live, the indices of dissimilarity between Chinese and Aboriginal peoples are quite high, .618 in Toronto and .573 in Vancouver. They are high in the other CMAs as well, around .500. Similar patterns can be observed with members of the South Asian community as well. Most of the Canadian South Asian population lives in Toronto and Vancouver, where the indices of dissimilarity with Aboriginal peoples are .576 and .544 respectively. In Montreal the index is even higher at .725. The indices of dissimilarity between the Aboriginal community and the black community are slightly lower than with Chinese or South Asians but still higher than with the European groups. The highest segregation indices are found between Aboriginals and the Jewish population. Most of the Canadian Jewish population lives in Montreal and Toronto. The index of dissimilarity between Aboriginals and the Jewish population is very high both in Montreal at .832 and in Toronto at .749. These figures are comparable to the white–black segregation figures found in large American cities. These differences would be expected when we examine the socio-economic class of the Jewish population measured in terms of income and the same measures of the Aboriginal populations. Therefore, the residential segregation between these groups may be partly attributed to class segregation. At the same time, social distance and the need to live in close proximity to one's own group may also be factors.

Aboriginal Concentration and Social Status of Neighbourhoods

We have hypothesized that Aboriginal people are more likely to be concentrated in poorer neighbourhoods. They may not have the resources or disposable income and hence the option to choose among a variety of residential areas in the city. Discrimination in housing may also force them into the less desirable areas of the city. Without special tabulations for small areas by Aboriginal status and socio-economic characteristics, we cannot comment on the relative importance of class and Aboriginal status in selecting a place of residence. However, we can look at the overall status of neighbourhoods in which Aboriginals are found concentrated, and thus indirectly test the hypothesis. Census tracts in which the percentage of Aboriginals is found to be greater than the percentage in the metropolitan area as a whole were identified as areas of concentration.

Table 16.4 (page 272) presents the mean socio-economic status (SES) indices of those tracts so identified in the 13 largest CMAs. Because small numbers of census tracts may distort the values, we have excluded the other CMAs. The SES index for each census tract takes into account the proportion in the higher occupations, proportion of adults over 25 with a university degree, and median family income in the tract. This index was computed for each census tract in a metropolitan area and standardized to a distribution with a mean of 50 and a standard deviation of 10 for that CMA. With hardly any exception, the social status of the neighbourhoods where Aboriginals are over-represented have the lowest SES when compared to the other groups. In every city they are also below the city mean. The disparity is most evident in the cities where they form the largest proportion. For example, in Winnipeg, the average SES index of Aboriginal neighbourhoods is only 43.2 compared to the city average of 50.0 and 53.0 for the British. Other visible minority groups live in much better areas. The same is true in Regina and Saskatoon, the mean SES index being 42.7 and 42.8 respectively. Aboriginals seem to do best in the three largest CMAs of Montreal, Toronto, and Vancouver. The mean SES index of neighbourhoods where Aboriginals are over-represented was 48.6 in Toronto, 47.6 in Montreal, and 47.2 in Vancouver. Though still below the city average of 50.0, they are higher than in all the other CMAs.

Conclusions

A main reason to study residential segregation is that it is a measure of how well or how poorly a group has integrated into the society at large. We have postulated that segregation can be a result of social class, social distance, or cultural identity. In the case of the Aboriginal population, it is clear that social class is indeed the important factor. They are socio-economically disadvantaged in relation to other groups, especially the European ethnic groups. Their lower class status limits their choice of residential location. Social distance as a causal factor for Aboriginal segregation in the urban areas is less clear. They have been in Canada a long time and intermarriage with whites has been considerable, as evidenced in the increasing number of persons claiming mixed heritage. In comparison, interracial marriages between whites and visible minorities, such as those in the Chinese, South Asian, and black communities, are comparatively lower. In lifestyle choices (such as food, clothing, sports, etc.) Aboriginals are closer to the British or French than to the visible minorities.

We also venture to state that cultural identity plays a lesser role in the case of Aboriginal segregation than in the case of the Chinese, South Asian, or black

Table 16.4. Mean indices of socio-economic status for concentrated ethnic groups for Canada's major census metropolitan areas with Aboriginal population over 10,000, 2001

	Calgary		Edmonton		Halifax		Hamilton		Montreal		Ottawa		Québec	
British	52.0	119	52.7	102	52.7	44	52.8	92	53.2	270	53.4	129	52.4	72
French	49.6	93	49.5	91	50.4	40	50.0	74	50.8	461	47.5	105	53.7	79
Aboriginal	44.3	84	44.0	74	46.0	36	45.2	69	47.6	357	46.5	102	48.7	59
Other Western European	51.4	97	51.4	89	51.4	37	54.2	69	53.7	326	53.6	127	53.5	66
Central & Eastern European	53.1	101	49.6	93	53.5	39	48.7	67	52.2	296	53.3	120	51.0	67
Italian	52.6	80	50.7	71	54.0	31	49.6	65	50.0	203	53.4	92	52.0	65
Jewish	55.0	56	55.5	52	54.4	27	52.2	46	56.6	123	55.0	71	56.7	19
South Asian	48.3	45	52.6	57	53.7	30	51.0	58	51.2	188	52.8	86	55.8	20
Chinese	50.0	62	50.8	75	50.4	33	49.8	58	50.7	276	52.0	84	53.1	52
African	49.1	80	49.1	80	46.0	27	50.6	59	49.6	327	48.0	68	50.3	49
Caribbean	47.9	80	50.3	74	50.9	31	49.1	66	47.8	254	50.6	79	51.4	58
Total tracts	142		202		85		171		846		234		165	

	Regina		Saskatoon		Toronto		Vancouver		Victoria		Winnipeg	
British	54.6	22	55.2	25	51.9	450	52.6	204	52.3	36	53.0	88
French	49.9	20	50.3	21	51.7	448	51.1	194	47.3	33	49.6	60
Aboriginal	42.7	20	42.8	16	48.6	346	47.2	153	45.1	29	43.2	59
Other Western European	51.6	27	51.9	25	52.7	426	51.0	202	50.4	32	51.6	87
Central & Eastern European	53.1	27	52.9	23	50.9	371	51.5	220	49.9	40	51.7	65
Italian	51.8	21	50.7	23	49.4	253	50.9	135	48.8	30	53.3	65
Jewish	54.3	17	56.1	19	57.3	167	55.4	121	51.9	24	55.0	30
South Asian	55.6	13	58.2	19	47.4	281	45.0	101	50.4	22	53.4	43
Chinese	52.9	18	54.2	14	51.0	242	50.3	146	50.9	25	52.2	45
African	52.5	21	53.0	14	47.0	279	49.6	149	47.3	24	49.9	57
Caribbean	51.4	15	51.6	24	46.2	338	50.2	179	50.4	28	51.8	61
Total tracts	50		51		924		386		68		163	

Source: Special tabulations

*Note: The means of SES indices are 50 for each CMA

communities. Institutional completeness is found to be lower among Aboriginal peoples when compared to other visible minorities. For example, in urban areas, specialized stores, places of worship, and ethnic media are found to a much smaller extent among Aboriginals than among the other visible minorities. This is explained in part by the existence, for many, of home communities where they have family and other contacts, but the argument can still be made that the cities are not being created as ethnically complete and separate places for Aboriginal peoples. Our findings in Aboriginal residential segregation are in line with these observations. Though social class results in a certain level of segregation for the Aboriginals, it is less than that of the other visible minorities, for whom social distance and distinct cultural identity accentuates segregation from the European ethnic groups. We also feel that the greater cultural dissimilarity between Aboriginals and other visible minorities may be the cause of greater segregation between these groups.

The differences among the CMAs in Aboriginal segregation and the lack of a strong relationship between Aboriginal size and segregation raise interesting questions. Do the migration patterns of Aboriginals from the reserves to the cities and vice versa affect settlement patterns in the cities, and if so, is proximity a factor? Do local municipal policies for affordable housing development projects play a role in segregation? The fact that some cities attract Aboriginals while others do not seems to indicate that the push factors (factors that make people leave a community, such as high cost of living, poor transportation, high unemployment, high crime rates, etc.) and pull factors (attractive factors, such as lower cost of living, better schools and recreation, good climate, etc.) differ by CMA, and these may be relevant in understanding not only the growth of the Aboriginal populations in the different cities but their segregation patterns as well.

References

Balakrishnan, T.R. 1982. Changing patterns of ethnic residential segregation in the metropolitan areas of Canada. *Canadian Review of Sociology and Anthropology.* 19: 92–110.

Balakrishnan, T.R. and Feng Hou. 1999. Residential patterns in cities. In *Immigrant Canada*, eds. Shiva Halli and Leo Driedger. Toronto: University of Toronto Press. 116–147.

Hou, Feng and Garnett Picot. 2004. Visible minority neighbourhoods in Toronto, Montreal and Vancouver. *Canadian Social Trends.* 72: 8–13.

Kalbach,Warren E. 1990. Ethnic residential segregation and its significance for the individual in an urban setting. In *Ethnic Identity and Equality: Varieties of Experience in a Canadian City*, eds. Raymond Breton et al. Toronto: University of Toronto Press. 92–134.

Lieberson, Stanley and Mary C. Waters. 1988. From many strands: Ethnic and racial groups in contemporary America. *Journal of the American Statistical Association* 85(411): 903-904.

Massey, Douglas and Nancy Denton. 1993. *American Apartheid.* Cambridge: Harvard University Press.

Maxim Paul, et al. 2003. Urban Residential Patterns of Aboriginal People in Canada. In *Not Strangers in These Parts: Urban Aboriginal People*, eds. D. Newhouse and Evelyn Peters. Ottawa: Policy Research Secretariat. 79–91.

Peters, Evelyn. 2000. Aboriginal People in Urban Areas. In *Visions of the Heart: Canadian Aboriginal Issues*, 2nd ed. eds. David Long and Olive Patricia Dickason. Toronto: Harcourt Brace Canada. 237–270.

Statistics Canada. 2003. Census of Canada 2001 electronic files.

Notes on Contributors

Linda Archibald

Linda Archibald specializes in qualitative research and evaluation with a particular emphasis on Aboriginal health and social justice issues. Her recent work with the Aboriginal Healing Foundation (AHF) on promising healing practices was published as volume III of AHF's final report. Linda has been the Canadian Aboriginal AIDS Network's evaluator since 2004. Her approach to research and evaluation is participatory and community based. She works from her solar-powered log cabin near Killaloe, Ontario.

T.R. Balakrishnan

T.R. Balakrishnan is an adjunct research professor of sociology at the University of Western Ontario. His research areas are ethnic relations, immigration, urban spatial patterns, and family. He has published articles and books, the most recent being *Family and Childbearing in Canada* (University of Toronto Press 1993). He is past president of the Canadian Population Society.

Dan Beavon

Daniel Beavon is the director of the Research and Analysis Directorate, Indian and Northern Affairs Canada. He has worked in policy research for twenty years and has dozens of publications to his credit. He manages an Aboriginal research program on a variety of issues, increasing the amount and quality of strategic information available to the policy process. Much of his work involves complex horizontal and sensitive issues requiring partnerships with other federal departments, academics, and First Nations organizations.

Matt Berman

Matt Berman is a professor of economics at the University of Alaska Anchorage (UAA). He has been researching social science and public policy issues at the Institute of Social and Economic Research (ISER) since 1981. He first went to Alaska in 1978 as a Rockefeller Foundation post-doctoral fellow. ISER is part of the College of Business and Public Policy at UAA. For the 2006-07 academic year he is visiting at the Fisheries Centre at the University of British Columbia in Vancouver BC. His primary areas of interest include economic organization and non-market valuation. Research interests include sustainable communities (institutions and uncertainty, rural mixed economies), natural resources (social-ecological systems, spatial ecosystem services, political economy and institutions), and health and safety (alcohol policy, aviation safety).

Peter Bjerregaard

Peter Bjerregaard is a research professor at the Danish National Institute of Public Health in Copenhagen. He is currently working on a research program on public health in Greenland.

Julie Bernier

Julie Bernier has a MSc in statistics from Laval University. After having worked as a consultant in statistics and taught statistics at Laval University, Ms Bernier joined Statistics Canada in 1995. She joined the Health Analysis and Measurement Group in 2000 as the chief of the analysis section. Her research domains are generic measurement of population health, the definition of health, health-related quality of life, and the measurement of preferences toward health states. Ms Bernier is also part of the Statistics Canada training institute where she teaches data analysis and record linkage techniques. She is a member of the Canadian Statistical Society and the Internal Society for Quality of Life (ISOQOL) and part of the Budapest Initiative.

Marlene Brant Castellano

Marlene Brant Castellano, a Mohawk and Professor Emerita of Trent University, has served as a professor and chair of Native Studies at Trent University and co-director of research for the Royal Commission on Aboriginal Peoples. Her recent writing has focused on traditional knowledge, research ethics, and preparation of the final report of the Aboriginal Healing Foundation, volume I: *A Healing Journey*. She has been awarded LLD degrees from Queen's, St. Thomas and Carleton universities, a National Aboriginal Achievement Award and appointment to the Order of Ontario. In 2005 she was named an Officer of the Order of Canada.

Jennifer Brennan

Jennifer Brennan is a graduate of both Carleton University (BA Hons) and the University of Alberta (MA political science). Ms. Brennan has worked for First Nations throughout her career, assisting, developing, and advising on policy matters at the local, tribal council, regional, and national levels of First Nation governments. Since 2004, Ms Brennan has served as the Assembly of First Nations' director of strategic policy and planning. In this role, she has served as lead representative on the Canada-Aboriginal roundtable processes, the First Ministers meeting processes, and has facilitated national policy discussions and engagement with federal and provincial governments.

Carole Cancel

Carole Cancel is a French PhD candidate at both the INALCO Institute (Institut National des Langues et Civilisations Orientales) in Paris and Laval University in Quebec City, under the joint supervision of Michèle Therrien and Frédéric Laugrand. Her second year master's thesis dealt with Inuit women in politics and was supplemented by fieldwork in Ottawa and Montreal conducted in spring 2005. Her thesis in progress examines the structures of Inuit contemporary discourse in the Canadian Arctic with an anthropological perspective. This work is set up on a precise study of Inuktitut (Inuit language spoken in the Eastern Canadian Arctic), and more particularly on terminology development. The study is carried out through a morpho-semantic approach derived from ethnolinguistics. Ms Cancel started learning Inuktitut at Carleton University in 2003-04 (instructor Jeela Palluq), then at the INALCO since 2004 (instructors Michèle Therrien, Nicole Tersis, Vladimir Randa, and Philippe Le Goff), with regular interaction with Inuktitut speakers, mainly in Nunavut.

Geeta Cheema

Geeta Cheema completed her master's degree at the University of Victoria School of Public Administration. Her thesis research project—a case study of an Aboriginal health advisory committee—was motivated by her interest in understanding health inequity, cultural conflict, and public sector management. Her original research paper was selected to receive a graduate student award at the 2006 Aboriginal Policy Research Conference. She will continue to investigate her research interests through doctoral studies in public health.

Stewart J. Clatworthy

Stewart Clatworthy operates Four Directions Project Consultants, a Winnipeg-based management consulting firm specializing in socio-economic research, information systems development, and program evaluation. Since 1980, Mr. Clatworthy has completed numerous studies on Aboriginal demography and migration, population, membership and student enrolment projections, and socio-economic, housing and employment conditions. Through this research, he has gained a national reputation as a leading scholar of Canadian Aboriginal socio-economic and demographic circumstances.

Stephen Cornell

Stephen Cornell is a professor of sociology and of public administration and policy at the University of Arizona, where he also directs the Udall Center for Studies in

Public Policy. He co-founded the Harvard Project on American Indian Economic Development and is a faculty associate with the University of Arizona's Native Nations Institute for Leadership, Management, and Policy. He works closely with Indigenous communities in the US, Canada, and elsewhere on self-determination, governance, and development issues.

Janice Forsyth

Janice Forsyth is an Aboriginal scholar/assistant professor in the Faculty of Physical Education and Recreation Studies at the University of Manitoba. Her research interests include examinations of power relations in contemporary Aboriginal sport practices in Canada.

Éric Guimond

Éric Guimond is of Micmac and French descent and a specialist in Aboriginal demography. His educational background includes demography, community health, physical education, and Aboriginal studies. He also possesses university research and teaching experience with expertise in projection models of population and Aboriginal groups. He is completing PhD studies (University of Montreal) on the topic of ethnic mobility of Aboriginal populations in Canada. Currently, Éric is engaged in the projects relating to First Nation housing, Inuit social conditions, and the development of knowledge transfer mechanisms between research and policy. Éric is a senior research manager at the Strategic Research and Analysis Directorate at Indian and Northern Affairs Canada.

Joannie Halas

Joannie Halas is an associate professor in the Faculty of Physical Education and Recreation Studies and a research affiliate with the Health, Leisure and Human Performance Research Institute at the University of Manitoba. Her area of research includes access to quality physical education, cross-cultural pedagogy, and interpretive research methodologies.

Michael Heine

Michael Heine is an assistant professor (sport history) at the University of Manitoba. His research examines the traditional games practices of Alaskan and northern Canadian Aboriginal peoples. He collaborates with northern Aboriginal and government organizations in the development of coaching and instructional resources for Aboriginal traditional games.

Jack Hicks

Jack Hicks is a social research consultant living in Iqaluit, Nunavut and co-ordinator of the Qaujivallianiq inuusirijauvalauqtunik (learning from lives that have been lived) suicide follow-back study. He is involved in several other research initiatives including an evaluation of the implementation of the Greenland Home Rule Government's National Strategy for Suicide Prevention, the US National Science Foundation-funded research project "Migration in the Arctic," and the BOREAS collaborative research project "Understanding Migration in the Circumpolar North." He is also an external PhD student at Ilisimatusarfik (University of Greenland), writing a dissertation on "Internal colonialism and the social determinants of elevated rates of suicide among Inuit youth." From the creation of Nunavut in 1999 until the fall of 2004 he was the Government of Nunavut's Director of Evaluation and Statistics.

Rozzett Jurdi

Rozzet Jurdi is a doctoral student in the Department of Sociology at the University of Western Ontario. She specializes in social demography, ethnic relations, immigration, and the family. She has published articles on topics such as ethnic relations and demography of the Middle East.

André Légaré

André Légaré is a PhD candidate in the Department of Geography at the University of Saskatchewan. For the past 20 years, he has written extensively on governance in the Canadian north. Mr. Légaré is the author of a recently published book entitled *The Evolution of the Government of the Northwest Territories* (1998). He presently makes his home in Yellowknife where he works as a chief negotiator on Aboriginal land claims and self-government.

Marion Maar

Marion Maar is a medical anthropologist and an assistant professor at the Northern Ontario School of Medicine. She has worked in the area of Aboriginal health research and program development for 12 years. Prior to her academic appointment, she was the research and evaluation coordinator for an Aboriginal Health Access Centre on Manitoulin Island for eight years. She has collaborated with Aboriginal communities on many research projects, including Aboriginal research ethics, FASD, mental health and prescription drug use, oral health, diabetes, community violence prevention, and health services research. Ms Maar has also worked as an Aboriginal health services consultant and as a program evaluator collaborating with regional and provincial health research committees. She is a council member, treasurer, and research portfolio holder of the Aboriginal Telehealth Knowledge Circle. Her research continues to focus on Aboriginal community-based health research with an emphasis on the Ontario region. Ms Maar is involved in teaching and curriculum development at the Northern Ontario School of Medicine, focusing on e-health, northern health, culturally competent care, Aboriginal intergenerational health, and chronic issues.

Paul Maxim

Paul Maxim became Associate Vice President for Research at Wilfrid Laurier University in July 2006. Prior to that he was with the Department of Sociology at the University of Western Ontario. His primary research interests are in demographic processes and the socio-economic participation of Aboriginal people in Canadian society. He is the author of numerous articles and books including *Quantitative Research Methods in the Social Sciences* (1999) and his most recent book, released by UBC Press in September 2003, *Aboriginal Conditions: Research as a Foundation for Public Policy*, co-edited with Jerry White and Dan Beavon.

Lorrilee McGregor

Lorrilee McGregor, MA, is an Anishinaabe from Whitefish River First Nation, where she lives and works. Ms. McGregor earned an undergraduate degree from the University of Toronto, focusing her studies on environment and resource management issues. Her master of Arts degree is in environment and community from Antioch University in Seattle, Washington, where she focused on Indigenous knowledge. Ms McGregor has 17 years of experience working with Aboriginal communities and organizations at the local, regional, and national level. Since 2001, she has operated a research and consultation company called Community Based Research, which utilizes participatory action research methods in the health, education, and environment sectors. In the past she has served on her community's Band Council as well as a local health board. She has been a member of the Manitoulin First Nations Research Ethics Committee since 2004 and was recently appointed the chairperson.

Jean-Pierre Morin

Jean-Pierre Morin completed his master's degree in Canadian history at the University of Ottawa in 1999. Since 2000, he has been the staff historian for the Treaty Policy Directorate at Indian and Northern Affairs Canada in Ottawa.

Mary Jane Norris

Mary Jane Norris is a senior research manager with the Strategic Research and Analysis Directorate at Department of Indian and Northern Affairs Canada. She has specialized in Aboriginal studies and demography over the past 25 years and has held previous research positions with the Demography Division of Statistics Canada and the Aboriginal Affairs Branch of Canadian Heritage. As part of her specialization in Aboriginal demography and demo-linguistics, her areas of research and publication include Aboriginal languages, migration, and population projections. She is of Aboriginal ancestry, with family roots in the Algonquins of Pikwákanagán (Golden Lake), in the Ottawa Valley. She holds a master's in sociology and a BA (Hons.) in sociology and economics from Carleton University.

Evelyn Peters

Dr. Peters completed her BA (Hons.) at the University of Winnipeg, and her master's and PhD in geography at Queen's University in Kingston. Between 1990 and 1993, she held a post-doctoral Canada Research Fellowship. Upon completing her doctoral degree, she taught at Carleton University for one year before taking up a tenure stream appointment at Queen's University. In 1994–95, she worked as a policy analyst on urban Aboriginal issues with the Royal Commission on Aboriginal Peoples. In 2001, she moved to the Department of Geography at the University of Saskatchewan to take up a Canada Research Chair position. The focus of Dr. Peters' research has been First Nations and Métis people in cities.

Steve Pomeroy

Steve Pomeroy is the president of Focus Consulting Inc, based in Ottawa, and specializes in affordable housing policy and research. With over 23 years of experience he has authored of over 70 policy and research reports since establishing Focus Consulting in 1994. Mr Pomeroy is highly respected and widely acknowledged as one of the leading housing policy researchers in Canada and has developed housing strategies for a number of provinces and municipalities.

Chantelle A.M. Richmond

Chantelle Richmond is an Ojibway woman and a PhD candidate in the Department of Geography at McGill University. Her doctoral research explores the role of the social environment as a health determinant among Canadian Indigenous populations, in particular that of social support. Part of her dissertation will be published in a fall 2007 issue of the *American Journal of Public Health*. Ms Richmond seeks to continue her work on the social determinants of Indigenous health in Canada, and among Indigenous peoples globally. She looks forward to an academic career within a Canadian university, where she may work to initiate positive changes for the health of Indigenous peoples. She also looks forward to training many graduate students and to raising the public's consciousness around the determinants of Indigenous health through her capacity as a teacher, researcher, and advocate for health and social equality.

Vince Robillard

Vince Robillard (Black Lake Band Member) has worked with Prince Albert Grand Council since 1994 in a variety of capacities, most recently as acting director of operations. Previously he was the SIIT/Urban Services Executive Director, Indian Child and Family Services Coordinator, and Labour Force Coordinator. He was Director of the Athabasca Child and Family Services from 1999 to 2000. Prior to that Mr Robillard was employed with Cameco Corporation from 1991 to 1994 and was supervisor of employee relations at Rabbit Lake Mine Site, and the Northern Affairs Officer in La Ronge. He has a degree in social work and graduated from grade twelve at St. Mary's High School.

Nancy A. Ross

Nancy Ross is an assistant professor in the Department of Geography at McGill University. She has an ongoing research program investigating income inequality as a determinant of population health in North America. The program encompasses a broad range of studies, including the relationship between residential segregation, public goods in urban areas, and health outcomes. Ms Ross is continuing work at the health region level in Canada on the determinants of disability-free life expectancy as well as regional and neighbourhood scale work on the net social-contextual influences on health status. She currently holds research funding from the Canadian Population Health Initiative (CPHI), the Canadian Institute of Health Research (CIHR), Fonds de la recherche en santé du Quebec (FRSQ) and Fonds québécois de la recherche sur la société et la culture (FRSC).

Mariette Sutherland

Mariette Sutherland is from the Whitefish River First Nation in Northern Ontario. Her educational background includes a degree in chemical engineering from McMaster University, a certificate in international business strategy from the London School of Economics, as well as a certificate in economic development from the Univerisity of Waterloo. Her experience as former executive director of the Noojmowin Teg Health Centre, an Aboriginal health access centre based on Manitoulin Island gave her first-hand exposure to the health needs and priorities of rural Northern First Nations. A committed volunteer, Ms Sutherland has served on several regional and provincial health boards and committees. She currently devotes her time to a number of community-based health research and planning projects.

Jerry White

Jerry White was chair of the Department of Sociology at the University of Western Ontario until June of 2006. He is currently professor and senior adviser to the Vice President (Provost) at Western and the director of the Aboriginal Policy Research Consortium (International). Jerry is the co-chair of the Aboriginal Policy Research Conference (with Dan Beavon and Peter Dinsdale) and a member of the Board of Governors for Western. He has written and co-written 11 books and numerous articles on health care and Aboriginal policy, the most recent being *Aboriginal Conditions* (UBC Press 2003) and *Permission to Develop* (TEP 2004). He is co-editor of the six-volume series on Aboriginal policy research of which this is one volume.

Susan Wingert

Susan Wingert is a PhD candidate in the Department of Sociology at the University of Western Ontario. She is also a research associate with the Aboriginal Policy Research Consortium. Her research interests include social inequality, race/ethnicity, culture, and mental health. Currently, her research examines social determinants of mental health in the off-reserve population.